Nicholas O'Nion
92, King E
Little I

Gray
Essex.

Dec 25th 1959.

BRITISH NAVAL AIRCRAFT
1912–58

H.M.S. *Ark Royal* with Sea Hawks aboard. The angled deck can be clearly seen:
also the steam catapult installation. (*Official Admiralty Photo*.)

BRITISH
NAVAL AIRCRAFT
1912–58

OWEN THETFORD

PUTNAM
42 GREAT RUSSELL STREET
LONDON: MCMLVIII

Also by Owen Thetford

AIRCRAFT OF THE ROYAL AIR FORCE 1918–58

A companion work

BRITISH CIVIL AIRCRAFT

*is in preparation, in
two volumes, by*
A. J. Jackson

*Made and printed in Great Britain
by Richard Clay and Company, Ltd.,
for the publishers, Putnam & Co., Ltd.,
42 Great Russell Street, London, W.C.1.*

CONTENTS

6

PREFACE

British Naval Aircraft has been written as a companion volume to my earlier book *Aircraft of the Royal Air Force*, and the same format has been adopted: each main type of aircraft is illustrated with one or more photographs and a three-view general arrangement drawing, accompanied by general narrative on operational history and a technical specification. Once again the aircraft have been arranged aphabetically under manufacturers, and thence chronologically in the order of their appearance. An index to the manufacturers appears at the front of the book, a further index at the back of the book listing aircraft under their type names.

Over 100 main types are included, ranging from the Avro 504 to the Wight 'Converted' Seaplane. There are also appendices covering over 130 more types of aircraft, airships which came under the control of the Royal Navy between January 1914 and December 1919, and brief particulars of seaplane-carriers and aircraft-carriers which have embarked British naval aircraft.

Whereas the R.A.F. book began with the formation of that Service in April 1918, the present work has taken as its starting point the beginning of properly organised naval flying with the creation of the Royal Flying Corps, Naval Wing, constituted by Royal Warrant on 13 May 1912. Whilst not claiming to be utterly exhaustive (a few types presented to the Admiralty by enthusiastic private aviators prior to this date have not been included), it is nevertheless true that virtually every aircraft used since 1912 by the Naval Wing, the Royal Naval Air Service and the Fleet Air Arm has found a place, including those of foreign origin.

In addition to the technical data presented, every effort has been made to include all relevant information on the units equipped with the various types and the ships in which they were carried: the greater part of this data has never before been available in a single volume. Much new information will also be found in the pages dealing with the more famous aircraft of the 1914–18 and 1939–45 periods, which have been treated at the somewhat greater length warranted by their historical importance.

In preparing this book I have been privileged to enjoy the co-operation of many willing helpers, both organisations and individuals. I offer my thanks to Mr. L. E. Bradford, whose skill and care are once again evident in the three-view drawings; to the Naval Information Department of the Admiralty, and to Mr. A. J. Charge and his staff at the Imperial War Museum. I am also indebted to the public relations departments of many British aircraft firms: in particular to the Fairey Aviation Company, who responded most willingly and efficiently to my many demands on

9

their time and records. I would also like to acknowledge the assistance I have received from Messrs J. M. Bruce, F. Cheesman, D. B. Robertson, and H. H. Russell.

I must add, finally, that no information contained in this book concerning British aircraft and engines currently included in the official *Initial* and *Part Publication* Lists, other than that made publicly available, has been obtained from official sources.

O. G. T.

London,
  February, 1958

INTRODUCTORY NOTE

THE DEVELOPMENT OF BRITISH NAVAL AVIATION SINCE 1912

Although the very earliest beginnings of British naval aviation can be traced back to July 1908, when it was proposed that the new post of Naval Air Assistant be established at the Admiralty, it was not until 1912 that heavier-than-air aircraft began to be taken seriously for naval purposes. There are a number of reasons why this should be so. One of the contributory factors was the severe blow suffered by the original plans to foster lighter-than-air aircraft when No. 1 Rigid Naval Airship (otherwise known as the *Mayfly*) met with complete disaster in September 1911. As if to emphasise the superior potentialities of the aeroplane, this airship setback was followed soon afterwards by two great milestones in British sea-flying: the first successful ascent from water by a British seaplane on 18 November 1911 and the first take-off from the deck of a British warship on 10 January 1912. The first feat was achieved by Cdr. Oliver Schwann flying an Avro biplane (35-h.p. Green engine) at Barrow-in-Furness; the second by the celebrated Cdr. C. R. Samson (then a lieutenant) in a Short S.27, which, fitted with pontoons, took off from an improvised platform on the foredeck of H.M.S. *Africa* anchored in Sheerness Harbour. The first British flight from a ship under way was also made by a Short S.27 biplane: the date was 9 May 1912 and the pilot Lt. R. Gregory, R.N. The flight took place from H.M.S. *Hibernia* as she was steaming at about ten knots in Weymouth Bay. Both Samson and Gregory had been among the first four officers of the Royal Navy to be selected for flying instruction when, early in 1911, the Admiralty accepted an offer from Mr. (later Sir) Francis McClean, a member of the Royal Aero Club, to lend two of his privately-owned aeroplanes and the facilities of the Aero Club's aerodrome at Eastchurch, Isle of Sheppey, for this purpose. Their instructor was Mr. George

A modified Short S.27 pusher biplane on the launching ramp of H.M.S. *Hibernia* in May 1912. (*Imp. War Museum Photo.*)

Cockburn, who provided his services free of charge. Lts. Samson, Gregory, Longmore, and Gerrard (the last-named being a member of the Royal Marine Light Infantry) were not, however, the first British naval officers to fly: this honour goes to Lt. G. C. Colmore, R.N., who qualified at his own expense on 21 June 1910 with Aviator's Certificate No. 15.

As mentioned in the preface, properly organised naval aviation in Great Britain did not begin to get into its stride until after the formation of the Royal Flying Corps, with its separate Naval and Military Wings, on 13 May 1912. This arrangement, always unpopular with the Admiralty, lasted officially until the Royal Naval Air Service attained recognition as a separate Service on 1 July 1914: in reality the R.N.A.S. had been operating under this title since a few months after the Naval Wing was formed.

By the end of 1912 the Royal Navy had 16 aircraft in service, comprised of 13 landplanes (8 biplanes and 5 monoplanes) and 3 hydro-aeroplanes: the term seaplane was not introduced until 17 July 1913. The year 1912 had also witnessed the first experiments in bomb-dropping (Cdr. Samson had dropped a dummy 100-pounder from a Short biplane), the transmission of wireless signals from a Short seaplane, the inclusion of aircraft in the annual Naval Review and the establishment at the Isle of Grain of the first of a chain of coastal seaplane stations. By the summer of 1913 further stations had been established at Calshot, Cromarty, Felixstowe and Great Yarmouth, and in July aircraft participated for the first time in the annual naval manoeuvres. A notable event of this period was the operation of two seaplanes from the forward launching platform of the light cruiser H.M.S. *Hermes*. One of these aircraft was a Short Folder: this marked the beginning of the use of aircraft with folding wings aboard ship, a practice which persists to the present day.

At the beginning of 1914, the R.N.A.S. had over 100 trained pilots, and from 1 January it became responsible for the operation of all airships which remained under naval control until December 1919. A review of R.N.A.S. airships and their activities during this period will be found in the appendices. In the few months that remained before the outbreak of war, the R.N.A.S. pressed ahead with characteristic vigour in experiments with armament. Lt. Clark Hall did successful firing trials with a 1½-pounder gun mounted in the nose of a Short Gun-Carrier, and on 28 July Lt. A. M. Longmore (later Air Chief Marshal Sir Arthur Longmore) made the first successful torpedo drop from the air in a Short seaplane (160-h.p. Gnome engine) at Calshot. When war finally broke out a few days later, the R.N.A.S. had on strength a total of 78 aircraft, comprised of 40 landplanes, 31 seaplanes and 7 airships. Its strength in personnel amounted to 130 officers and about 700 petty officers and ratings.

By 1 April 1918 (when it was merged with the R.F.C. to form the Royal Air Force) the R.N.A.S. had grown to a force of 67,000 officers and men, with 126 air stations at home and abroad and 2,949 aeroplanes and 103 airships on its strength. It had fought not only at sea, from seaplane-carriers and coastal air stations, but in the Dardanelles and on the Western Front. Indeed, the R.N.A.S. squadrons based in Belgium and France established a most enviable record: their offensive spirit was demonstrated as early as 22 September 1914, when four aircraft from

Commander Samson's Eastchurch Squadron of the R.N.A.S. at Dunkirk in 1914. The aeroplanes are (left to right): Henri Farman F.20, Samson's B.E.2A (No. 50), Sopwith Tractor Biplane and Short No. 42. (*Photo: G. S. Leslie*)

Cdr. Samson's Eastchurch squadron (ordered overseas on 27 August) made the first British air raid on German territory. More details will be found in the following pages of the remarkable pioneering raids by the R.N.A.S. on Zeppelin sheds at Dusseldorf and Friedrichshafen and of the commendable foresight shown by the Admiralty in fostering the development of the long-range bomber: the R.N.A.S. was the first air service to give practical expression to the conception of strategic bombing. In air fighting, too, it proved more than a match for the enemy as the narrative on the Sopwith Pup, Triplane and Camel will go to show.

At home stations the task of the R.N.A.S. was twofold: it was responsible from 3 September 1914 for the air defence of Great Britain as well as for anti-submarine and anti-Zeppelin patrols over the sea. This somewhat surprising situation came about because the R.F.C. was wholly occupied in France from the outbreak of war and it was not until March 1916 that the R.F.C. established Home Defence squadrons. The exploits of the R.N.A.S. flying-boats over the North Sea form an especially exciting chapter of British naval aviation history: their historic achievements are recorded in the main text.

No. 2 Wing, R.N.A.S. at Imbros in 1915: the aeroplanes are Henri Farman F.27s and Nieuport two-seaters. (*Photo: G. S. Haigh*)

As will be evident from the foregoing remarks, by far the greater proportion of the R.N.A.S. effort in the First World War was by seaplanes or flying-boats at coastal air stations or landplanes at shore bases. Aircraft carried in ships played a subordinate rôle: the aircraft-carrier as it is known today did not make its appearance until the closing phases of the war. The aircraft-carrier was evolved by gradual stages from the early seaplane-carrier which originally had no take-off facilities, the aircraft being hoisted over the side to take off from the sea. Later a take-off platform was added, sloping down to the bows to provide a clear run. These platforms were at first used by seaplanes which had wheels (later wheeled trolleys) fitted beneath the floats: only later were landplanes flown from launching platforms. Among the first seaplane-carriers were the converted cross-Channel steamers *Empress*, *Engadine* and *Riviera*, which were commandeered by the Admiralty on 11 August 1914: these three ships launched the seven seaplanes used in the celebrated Cuxhaven raid of Christmas Day, 1914. Another early seaplane-carrier, the former Isle of Man steamer *Ben-My-Chree*, carried the Short seaplane which on 12 August 1915 made the first successful air-torpedo attack in history while operating in the Dardanelles. These early seaplane-carriers were, nevertheless, of limited value, as they were severely handicapped by their inability to keep station with the Fleet (they had to stop when hoisting their seaplanes overboard), and the seaplanes themselves could operate in only the calmest of seas because of the fragility of their floats. The launching platform (first fitted on the pre-war *Hermes*, sunk in October 1914) overcame this difficulty only when the ship was fast enough to provide enough air speed over the deck: some carriers so fitted (e.g. *Ark Royal*) were too slow and continued to launch their seaplanes the old

The non-rigid airship S.S.Z.59 landing aboard the carrier H.M.S. *Furious* in 1917. (*Imp. War Museum Photo.*)

14

Squadron Commander Dunning lands his Sopwith Pup aboard H.M.S. *Furious* on 2 August 1917. This was the first carrier landing ever made by an aeroplane. (*Imp. War Museum Photo.*)

way. More successful were the carriers *Campania* and *Vindex*, which proved capable of handling the faster single-seaters of the day. On 6 August 1915 a Sopwith Baby on wheeled floats took off from *Campania* for the first time: this was followed by the first normal landplane take-off by a Bristol Scout from *Vindex* on 3 November 1915. Still the problem remained of getting an aircraft back on to the ship, and it was not until 2 August 1917 that this feat was achieved by Sqn. Cdr. E. H. Dunning, who flew his Sopwith Pup round the funnel of H.M.S. *Furious* and contrived to alight on the 228-feet-long forward flying-deck. This experiment, and the disaster which overtook Dunning a few days later when he repeated it, led to the provision of a flying-on deck 284 feet long aft of the super-structure. This deck was provided with an early form of arrester gear comprised of longitudinal wires and transverse ropes weighted with sandbags and a rope crash-barrier to protect the superstructure. The wires were engaged by spring-clip hooks on the aeroplane's axle, and a further hook engaged the transverse ropes. Some aircraft flown from *Furious* at this period (mainly Pups and 1½ Strutters) had a skid under-carriage instead of wheels. The system was not a success owing to the eddies and hot-air current set up by the funnel and superstructure, and *Furious* was modified after the Armistice to have a flush deck extending from bow to stern. Although *Furious* was not wholly satisfactory until after this modification had been effected, she could claim to have been the only carrier of the First World War to have launched a major air action. This was the famous raid of 19 July 1918, when seven Sopwith Camels flown off *Furious* made a successful attack on the Zeppelin base at Tondern, destroying *L.54* and *L.60*.

The first carrier to enter service with a flush deck already fitted was

Sopwith 2F.1 Camels on the flying-off deck of H.M.S. *Furious* in 1918.
(*Imp. War Museum Photo.*)

Argus (converted from the Italian liner *Conte Rosso*), but as she did not begin her trials until October 1918, she was too late to play any active part in the war. If the war had been prolonged by a few months, *Argus* would have taken into action a squadron of 18 Sopwith Cuckoos, the first landplane torpedo-carrying aircraft to be embarked in an aircraft-carrier.

By 1917 the Admiralty had realised that landplanes, with their superior performance, offered much better prospects for air operations with the Fleet than the more cumbersome seaplane. Unfortunately there were

Sopwith F.1. Camels of No. 10 (Naval) Squadron seen on the Western Front
in 1918. (*Photo: G. S. Leslie*)

not enough ships with flying-off decks to enable an effective force to be deployed. Other means were sought, chief among them being the introduction of extemporised platforms on existing light cruisers and, later, the mounting of short take-off platforms above the gun-turrets of battleships. The first successful experiment of this kind took place in June 1917, when F./Cdr. F. J. Rutland flew a Sopwith Pup off the light cruiser *Yarmouth*. On 1 October 1917 the same officer repeated his success by flying a Pup off a platform superimposed on the 15-inch gun turret of the battleship *Repulse*: the platform could be turned into wind without the ship altering course and during the take-off was in fact at an angle of 45 degrees from the bow. The final stage in these experiments was achieved on 4 April 1918, when the practice was extended to two-seater aircraft: a Sopwith 1½ Strutter was flown off a turret platform aboard

A Camel seen at the moment of take-off from a lighter towed behind a destroyer in the North Sea. (*Imp. War Museum Photo.*)

H.M.A.S. *Australia*. By the end of the First World War over 100 aircraft were being carried in this way by ships of the Grand Fleet: 22 light cruisers had been fitted with flying-off platforms and all battleships and battle-cruisers carried a two-seat aircraft on the forward turret platform and a single-seat fighter on the rear turret platform.

One other method of using aircraft at sea remains to be mentioned: the towed lighter. These lighters were designed to be towed behind a destroyer, measured 58 feet long by 16 feet wide, and could reach 32 knots without throwing up sheets of spray. Their original purpose was to convey large flying-boats across the North Sea so as to increase their radius of action over the Heligoland Bight area, but in 1918 it was discovered that they could also be used with 30-feet-long take-off platforms for launching single-seat fighters. The first successful take-off, using a

A Beardmore W.B.III leaves the steep forward launching platform of H.M.S. *Pegasus* in 1918. (*Imp. War Museum Photo.*)

Sopwith Camel, was by Lt. S. D. Culley on 31 July 1918: a few days later he destroyed the Zeppelin *L.53* by using this technique.

In the years immediately after the Armistice, naval aviation, in common with the rest of the R.A.F. of which it formed a part, shrank to a tiny force; economy was the watchword, and by the end of 1919 it had been reduced to one spotter-reconnaissance squadron, one fighter flight and half a torpedo squadron. There was also a seaplane flight and a flying-boat flight. The next twenty years were to witness a determined campaign by the Admiralty to regain control of naval flying, a campaign which reached a successful conclusion in May 1939, when it could be announced that the take-over from the R.A.F. was complete. This victory was achieved by gradual stages, the first being in 1921, when the Admiralty obtained agreement that naval officers should be trained as air observers. In 1923 a Committee of Inquiry recommended that all observers in naval aircraft should be naval officers and that up to 70 per cent of the pilots should be naval officers with dual R.A.F. and naval rank. In April 1924 the carrier-borne branch of the R.A.F. was named the Fleet Air Arm, a title which is retained to the present day, though it was abandoned for a period between 1939 and 1953, when the term Air Branch of the Royal Navy, or Naval Aviation, was in vogue officially, though the old title persisted in popular usage. Finally, in 1937, it was announced in the House of Commons that control of the F.A.A. would be handed over entirely to the Royal Navy within two years; all personnel would be naval, and the Admiralty would have its own shore stations for the first time since the days of the old R.N.A.S. The first naval air stations so established were Donibristle, Eastleigh, Evanton, Ford, Hatston, Lee-on-Solent, St. Merryn and Worthy Down.

Strength in aircraft grew painfully slowly during the inter-war years. In January 1924 there were 78 naval aircraft in 13 flights: this had increased to 18 flights (128 aircraft) by October 1924, to 24 flights (144 aircraft) by September 1930 and to 26 flights (156 aircraft) in September 1932. On 3 April 1933 the squadron (with 9 or 12 aircraft) was introduced as the basic carrier flying unit and the existing flights (each of 6 aircraft) were merged except for a number which carried on as catapult aircraft in cruisers and capital ships. By May 1935 there were 175 aircraft in 15 squadrons: this had increased to 217 aircraft in March 1936. When war broke out in September 1939 the Royal Navy could muster only 20 squadrons with a total of 340 aircraft, 225 of which were in carriers and the rest in catapult flights.

The inter-war years saw the introduction of five new aircraft-carriers in addition to the two inherited from the war years (*Furious* and *Argus*). These were *Eagle* (1922), *Hermes* (1923), *Glorious* and *Courageous* (1928) and *Ark Royal* (1938). From 1919 until 1922 *Argus* was the only fleet carrier in commission: originally she had no arrester gear, but later a most unusual system was adopted which employed the longitudinal wires (as tried in *Furious*) in conjunction with the deck lift, which was lowered about 9 inches so that aircraft dropped into it and were then finally halted by a sloping ramp. This curious technique led, understandably enough, to a high proportion of accidents, and was shortly superseded by a combination of longitudinal wires and transverse wooden flaps. These flaps were knocked flat by the aircraft as it ran along the deck. This system was little better: it caused a great deal of damage to undercarriages. In 1926 the arrester-gear principle was abandoned and aircraft landed on a plain deck until 1931, when experiments began aboard *Courageous* with transverse arrester wires utilising friction brake-drums with an

This photograph of a Parnall Panther aboard H.M.S. *Argus* illustrates well the longitudinal arrester wires, the hinged wooden flaps mounted transversely, the hooks on the axle and the forward hydrovane. The period was 1919–20. (*Imp. War Museum Photo.*)

A Fairey IIID seaplane leaves its wheeled launching trolley after taking off from H.M.S. *Argus* in August 1922. (*Air Ministry Photo.*)

electrical resetting mechanism. This system was finally perfected in 1933, when hydraulic resetting gear superseded the electrical. This method of deck landing proved completely successful, and is still used today. The arrester wires were engaged by a retractable hook suspended below the rear fuselage, and there was no longer any danger of the aircraft tipping forward on its nose, as was common with the old axle hooks. Initial experiments were conducted with a Fairey IIIF, and the first standard installations of the rear hook were in the Osprey and Nimrod.

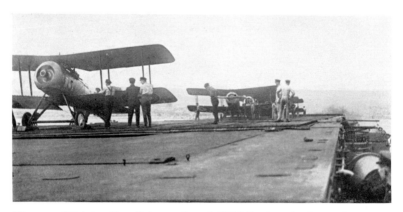

Nieuport Nightjar fleet fighters aboard H.M.S. *Argus* in September 1922. (*Air Ministry Photo.*)

Another innovation of the inter-war years was catapult launching of aircraft from ships. Early experiments with catapult launch had been conducted aboard the steam hopper *Slinger* with a Fairey N.9 seaplane in 1917–18, but it was not until October 1925 that a standard F.A.A. aircraft was so launched from a warship. This was by a Fairey IIID seaplane flown by Wg. Cdr. Burling from *Vindictive*. Thereafter, catapult aircraft were much used for reconnaissance purposes aboard cruisers and battleships, and continued to serve in this rôle until the Second World War. The classic example of the use of catapult aircraft in a naval battle was that of the Fairey Seafox of the cruiser *Ajax*, which spotted for the guns during the Battle of the River Plate in December 1939. During the early thirties an improved type of catapult (then known as accelerator)

A typical Fleet Air Arm scene of the inter-war period: Fairey IIIF spotter-reconnaissance aircraft of No. 824 Squadron fly over H.M.S. *Eagle*. (*Charles E. Brown Photo.*)

was introduced in aircraft-carriers. In this type the hydro-pneumatic mechanism was installed below the deck and the aircraft was pulled off by means of a towing-bridle which ran through a slot in the deck. This system remained in use until superseded by the steam catapult in 1954, by which time, with the increase in all-up weights and wing-loadings, catapult take-off had become the more usual instead of merely an optional technique from a carrier deck. The steam catapult was invented by Cdr. C. C. Mitchell, O.B.E., R.N.V.R., and enables the latest jet fighters and strike aircraft to be dispatched even when the carrier is at anchor. Before its introduction, carriers used their accelerators only when free take-off was impracticable due to insufficient wind across the carrier deck or when a large number of aircraft awaiting dispatch restricted the take-off run forward.

From the mid-twenties until the Second World War most cruisers and battleships of the Royal Navy carried catapult aircraft for reconnaissance purposes. This picture of a Hawker Osprey being catapulted off was taken about 1936.

Another take-off device, introduced during the Second World War with the advent of heavily-loaded strike aircraft and the faster monoplane fighters, was rocket assisted take-off gear, known as RATOG. Such equipment was, of course, rendered superfluous by the steam catapult.

Until the Spitfire and Hurricane were adopted for carrier duties in 1942, the performance of F.A.A. aircraft had always lagged behind that of their R.A.F. land-based counterparts. This was due to a number of

A Blackburn Shark, wings folded, on the deck lift of H.M.S. *Courageous*. Note the mixture of R.A.F. and naval personnel, an arrangement which lasted until 1939. (*Charles E. Brown Photo.*)

factors arising out of the peculiar nature of naval work. Firstly, more equipment had to be carried, such as arrester gear, flotation gear (until 1923 this took the form of external air bags with a hydrovane added for good measure), extra wireless, provision for wing folding and so forth: all this meant greater all-up weight, with consequent loss of performance. Secondly, owing to restricted space aboard carriers, there was a tendency to combine two or even three operational functions in one aeroplane: this technique precluded optimum performance in any of the rôles. Single-seat biplane fighters were less handicapped, and were only marginally slower than their land-based equivalents, but the disparity was marked

Famous aircraft: famous ship. Fairey Swordfish flying over H.M.S. *Ark Royal* in 1939. (*Charles E. Brown Photo.*)

from 1937 onwards, when the monoplane fighter came into general use in land-based squadrons: at the outbreak of war the F.A.A. still had nothing better than the 250-m.p.h. four-gun Sea Gladiator. In the reconnaissance rôle, performance had shown an upward trend with the abandonment of the cumbersome three-seat spotter and the introduction of the two-seat fighter-reconnaissance aircraft (typified by the Osprey) around 1932, but this 170-m.p.h. biplane was still in service in 1939. For strike purposes, the F.A.A. had from the days of the Cuckoo and Dart pinned its faith in the torpedo: this faith was amply rewarded by such outstanding successes as Taranto in 1940, but it cannot be denied that, technically, deck-landing torpedo aircraft showed little progress in the inter-war years, and it was not until as late as 1943 that all-metal mono-planes (Barracudas) began to replace the antiquated biplanes in the first-line squadrons. In all categories except one (the dive-bomber, represented by the Skua monoplane) the F.A.A. was a force equipped throughout with biplanes when it went to war in 1939, and there was much truth in the charge that it had been unjustly neglected by the powers-that-be. Although the position was largely retrieved by the skill

A Fairey Albacore takes off from H.M.S. *Formidable*, a typical fleet carrier of the Second World War. (*Imp. War Museum Photo.*)

Swordfish aboard H.M.S. *Striker* prepare for an anti-submarine patrol. This picture gives a good idea of the restricted deck area of a wartime escort carrier. (*Imp. War Museum Photo.*)

and daring of its aircrews, the F.A.A.'s plight received little attention until February 1942, when the public outcry aroused by the escape of the German battleships through the English Channel led to some measure of priority being given to the question of naval aircraft supplies. By the autumn of 1942 the carrier-borne squadrons had begun to receive Seafires (naval versions of the Spitfires), and for the first time possessed a single-seat fighter comparable with any land-based type. These saw action for the first time during the Allied invasion of North-West Africa in November 1942. In 1943–44 the situation was further improved by the large-scale deliveries of Lend–Lease aircraft such as the Corsair, Hellcat and Avenger, and it was these types which formed a large proportion of the British East Indies and Pacific Fleets in the operations leading to the final defeat of Japan.

The events of the Second World War brought full recognition of the value of air power at sea and effected such a revolution in naval thinking that by 1945 the carrier had already begun to assume its post-war rôle as the modern equivalent of the battleship, the backbone of the Fleet. Carriers had proved their ability not only in the classic rôle of providing fighter protection, reconnaissance facilities and strike forces for the Fleet itself, but also showed that there was a place for the smaller carrier as a close escort for convoys and for off-shore operations in support of the Army in beach-head fighting. From 1941 onwards the large Fleet Carrier was progressively supplemented by the Merchant Aircraft Carrier (flat-tops converted from cargo ships) and the Convoy Escort Vessel (about 50 of which were supplied by the U.S.A. for the duration of the war), which could be built more rapidly and economically than the full-size carrier. The smaller carriers proved especially valuable in countering the U-boat menace, particularly in those stretches of the ocean beyond the range of land-based aircraft of Coastal Command. Of all the U-boats sunk in the Second World War, about half were destroyed from the air.

In August 1945 the F.A.A. had grown to a first-line strength of 1,300 aircraft, with an additional 10,000 in training and second-line duties or in reserve. Strength in personnel amounted to 70,000. Nor was there any shortage of carriers. Apart from the smaller escort carriers obtained under Lend–Lease arrangements, there were six Fleet Carriers (*Implacable, Indefatigable, Indomitable, Illustrious, Formidable* and *Victorious*) and five of

Fleet Air Arm Corsair fighters prepare to take off from a carrier of the East Indies Fleet for a strike on Sourabaya in May 1944. (*Photo: W. E. Rolfe*)

25

the new class of Light Fleet Carriers completed or on the point of completion (*Glory, Ocean, Theseus, Triumph* and *Warrior*). With the exception of *Victorious*, withdrawn for complete modernisation in 1950 and recommissioned in January 1958, all the wartime Fleet Carriers had been scrapped or reduced to reserve by 1955 and had been superseded by

With the British Pacific Fleet in 1945. A flak-damaged Firefly of No. 1770 Squadron aboard H.M.S. *Indefatigable* is handled by a deck party. (*Imp. War Museum Photo.*)

The Vampire, modified for deck flying, which made the first landing by a pure jet aboard an aircraft-carrier in December 1945. The carrier is H.M.S. *Ocean*. (*Charles E. Brown Photo.*)

Supermarine Attackers, the first operational jet fighters ever used by the Fleet Air Arm, seen aboard H.M.S. *Eagle*. Attackers entered squadron service in August 1951. (*Official Admiralty Photo.*)

Eagle (commissioned March 1952) and the new *Ark Royal* (commissioned February 1955). These 46,000-ton carriers were supplemented by three of 27,000 tons: *Albion*, *Bulwark* and *Centaur*, laid down in 1944–45 and completed in 1953–54.

The years 1945–56 were to bring far-reaching changes in the technique of deck-flying; changes which marched in step with the spectacular increases in aircraft performance as a result of the changeover from piston engines to jets. The period also provided in the Korean War (1950–53) and the Suez operation (1956) further evidence, if evidence were needed, of the unique ability of the aircraft-carrier to provide effective mobile task forces in localised war situations.

The F.A.A. led the world in experiments with pure jets aboard aircraft-carriers. Within a few months of VJ-Day, on 4 December 1945, a specially modified Vampire had been successfully landed aboard the Light Fleet Carrier *Ocean*. It also led the world in introducing three inventions which enabled the aircraft-carrier to deal efficiently with the faster jets: these were the steam catapult (already mentioned), the angled deck and the mirror landing-sight. The angled deck and the steam catapult were to some extent complementary, in that they enabled flying-off and landing-on to take place simultaneously. With the greater speeds and higher wing-loadings of modern aircraft, it was becoming increasingly difficult to follow the old system, introduced about 1939, of using the first third of the deck for catapult take-off whilst aircraft landing-on used the remaining two-thirds, the two areas being separated by a crash barrier.

To increase the deck area was impossible without making the carrier itself much bigger. The problem was solved by the ingenious method (invented by Capt. D. R. F. Cambell, D.S.C., R.N.) of splitting the flight deck diagonally: this eliminated the need for a barrier, and meant that aircraft which failed to hook the arrester wires could take off again without encroaching on the space reserved for the forward catapult area. It also had the incidental advantage of leaving an aircraft parking area forward of the superstructure. The first aircraft-carrier of the Royal Navy with an angled deck was *Centaur*, completed in September 1953.

The mirror landing-sight, developed by Cdr. H. C. N. Goodhart, R.N., was introduced to overcome the deficiencies of manual control of deck landing by a signals officer, known as the batsman. With the steadily increasing approach speeds of modern aircraft (the Sea Fury piston-engined fighter introduced in 1947 raised approach speeds to 105 m.p.h.— they had been less than 60 m.p.h. in the days of the Flycatcher) the old type of steepish descending approach at a speed little above the stall, followed by a flare-out and engine-cut, was modified in 1948 to a more nearly level approach at higher speed. The batsman technique, already severely strained by the new approach methods, became finally impracticable when jet fighters lifted approach speeds still higher (not far short of 140 m.p.h.), and the introduction of the mirror-sight eliminated the time-lag between the batsman's signal and the pilot's reaction to it which could be disastrous at such speeds. With the mirror, the pilot received a direct visual guide to his angle of descent relative to the horizontal (indicated by means of lights), and had merely to fly straight on to the deck with no flare-out and no engine-cut until after touch-down. A further refinement of this system was the provision of an audio airspeed indicator (heard in the pilot's earphones), which eliminated the need to

Operations in Korean waters, 1950 to 1953. A Sea Fury with rocket-projectiles is manoeuvred into position on the flight deck of H.M.S. *Glory*. (*Official Admiralty Photo.*)

The Fleet Air Arm at Suez, November 1956. A flak damaged Sea Venom of No. 893 Squadron makes a belly landing aboard H.M.S. *Eagle*. (*Official Admiralty Photo.*)

watch his instrument panel, and thus deflect his eyes from the mirror-sight during final approach.

The F.A.A.'s first operational jet squadron was No. 800, which received its Attackers in August 1951. By 1955 the transition to jets in first-line fighter and strike squadrons had been completed: piston-engined aircraft remained only in second-line squadrons and for certain specialised duties such as airborne early warning—radar-equipped aircraft which extended the Fleet's radar range and helped to direct strike forces on to their targets as well as to vector interceptions. An interesting aspect of British naval aircraft equipment policy was the employment from 1953 onwards of turboprop aircraft in the strike rôle (Wyverns) and from 1955 in the anti-submarine rôle (Gannets). Another radical departure in the equipment field was the steadily increasing importance given to helicopters from 1950 onwards. Originally, the helicopter's place in naval aviation was that of ship-to-shore communications and 'plane-guard' duties aboard carriers, hovering in the vicinity of the ship during flying operations to rescue any crews unfortunate enough to crash into the sea. As more powerful types of helicopter became available, however, it soon became apparent that this class of aircraft had important potentialities for the anti-submarine rôle, and the F.A.A.'s first anti-submarine helicopter squadron (No. 845) began operations in March 1954. The helicopter's ability to operate from the deck of any ship, and not merely an aircraft-carrier, clearly extends its usefulness for submarine search and strike even further. An additional helicopter rôle, first demonstrated at Suez in 1956, is that of providing air lifts for assault troops between the decks of carriers and the territory to be invaded.

29

Swept wing transonic fighters join the Royal Navy. Supermarine Scimitars being flown off H.M.S. *Ark Royal* by means of the two steam catapults on the forward deck. (*Official Admiralty Photo.*)

Mention has already been made of the value of a carrier task force in providing air support in localised wars: the aircraft-carrier's ability to operate where land bases are not available and the fact that it presents a moving target has also been urged in its favour by advocates who see in it an alternative method of launching nuclear-armed strike aircraft against land targets. Whether for use against land targets or enemy fleets, it has now become Admiralty policy to equip the F.A.A. with aircraft capable of delivering atomic bombs: the Scimitar was the first F.A.A. aircraft capable of carrying a nuclear weapon and also the first swept-wing aircraft in the transonic class to enter F.A.A. service. The first experimental flight of Scimitars was formed at Ford in August 1957, marking the beginning of a new era in naval air warfare. Also under development for the F.A.A. is another nuclear strike aircraft, the Blackburn N.A.39, powered by two de Havilland Gyron Junior turbojets of immense power.

Entering service shortly after the Scimitar (which replaces the Sea Hawk as the standard single-seat interceptor as well as being equipped for strike duties) is the two-seat Sea Vixen, a transonic all-weather fighter which supersedes the subsonic Sea Venom. Both Scimitar and Sea Vixen can be armed with Firestreak air-to-air guided missiles. It remains an open question whether these aircraft will, like the R.A.F.'s P.1, prove to be the last manned fighters of the F.A.A., or whether a further manned fighter capable of Mach 2 plus will be taken into service before ship-to-air guided missiles take over the interception rôle. Certainly the Scimitar and Sea Vixen will remain with carriers for many years, and their ability to protect the Fleet has recently been further enhanced by the introduction of improved radar surveillance carried in specialised air direction frigates surrounding the carrier task force.

This brief outline of the development of British naval flying over nearly half a century must conclude with a few remarks on the Royal Navy's present strength in aircraft-carriers and the immediate future prospects. At the time the Naval Estimates were presented in 1958 there were five aircraft-carriers in commission: the three large fleet carriers *Ark Royal*, *Eagle* and *Victorious* and the two smaller carriers *Albion* and *Bulwark*. All these incorporate the angled deck, but only *Victorious* has the fully angled deck. Steam catapults, essential for the flying-off of Scimitars and Sea Vixens, are possessed only by *Ark Royal* and *Victorious*. Modernisation of other carriers is therefore essential. The carrier *Centaur* (sister ship of *Albion* and *Bulwark*) is already undergoing modernisation and one new Fleet Carrier (*Hermes*) is building. No more fleet carriers are in prospect, though *Eagle* will be withdrawn in 1959 for large-scale modernisation and will be commissioned again in 1962 or 1963.

The long-range plan for the disposition of the Royal Navy's carriers was, by the terms of the 1958 Estimates Memorandum, to station two carriers in the Atlantic and Mediterranean areas in support of N.A.T.O. (with a third carrier in immediate reserve) and one carrier east of Suez to support the South-East Asia Treaty Organization (with a second carrier available as necessary to provide commando support with helicopters).

The 1958 Naval Estimates also disclosed that a number of well-known naval air stations are to be closed. Ford, Bramcote, Eglinton, Brawdy

The Fleet Air Arm today. A Scimitar single-seat fighter approaches to land aboard H.M.S. *Ark Royal* with undercarriage and arrester hook extended.
(*Official Admiralty Photo.*)

and Worthy Down are all due to be axed by the end of 1961 but Yeovilton, Lossiemouth, Culdrose, Abbotsinch, Arbroath and Lee-on-Solent are to stay.

The question is bound to be asked as to whether carriers can survive in an age of nuclear weapons. Present thinking is that they can, for in addition to their inherent mobility they will be able to deploy more accurate and powerful defensive fire-power (using both air-to-air and ship-to-air missiles) than at any previous time in carrier history. Moreover, they are impracticable targets for the long-range ballistic missiles which threaten land bases. Such factors suggest that the power of the Fleet and its Air Arm will continue to play an important, perhaps even decisive rôle, in the future.

BRITISH
NAVAL AIRCRAFT
1912–58

Avro 504B (N 5273) built by Sunbeam. (*Imp. War Museum Photo.*)

Avro 504

For over 15 years the Avro 504 was the standard trainer of the British flying services, and on this fact alone its reputation stands secure in aviation history. It is less often appreciated that in the opening phases of the 1914–18 War it was used in first-line squadrons of the R.F.C. and the R.N.A.S. for reconnaissance and bombing and that, with the R.N.A.S., Avro 504s were responsible for one of the most audacious operations of the First World War.

The prototype of the immortal 504 series was tested at Brooklands in July 1913. In general appearance it resembled very closely the thousands of production aircraft that were to follow; the main differences were in the square-section cowling for the 80-h.p. Gnome engine, the straight top longeron of the fuselage and the fact that lateral control was dependent on wing-warping instead of conventional hinged ailerons. Very early in the 504's career the wing-warping was discarded in favour of normal ailerons and a better streamlined cowling fitted.

For 1913, the Avro 504 presented a thoroughly modern appearance, an appearance matched by a correspondingly good performance. Its sole rival in this respect was the Sopwith Tabloid, which turned out to have an even better performance, but in the event (chiefly due to its adoption as a trainer) the Avro outlived the Tabloid by many years.

The original military orders for the Avro 504 were complicated by the fact that the Admiralty specified a different wing spar from that agreed by the War Office, and until the emergence of the R.A.F. in 1918 this difference between the R.F.C. and R.N.A.S. versions remained.

At the outbreak of war in August 1914 the R.N.A.S. had only one Avro 504 on its strength, but by the middle of December 1914 No. 1 Squadron R.N.A.S. (Sqn. Cdr. A. M. Longmore) had five more among its equipment. This squadron was sent to France in February 1915 to relieve Wg. Cdr.

C. R. Samson's famous Eastchurch Squadron, which had been overseas since 27 August 1914 and which had taken delivery of its first Avro 504 on 27 November. The Eastchurch Squadron's Avro lost little time in getting into action, and on 14 December 1914, flown by F./Sub-Lt. R. H. Collet, dropped four 16-lb. bombs on the Ostend–Bruges railway.

Routine sorties of this kind, however, would have contributed little to the fame of the Avro 504 as a weapon of war; what focused attention on the type was the magnificent and now historic raid of 21 November 1914, when three Avro 504s of the R.N.A.S. bombed the Zeppelin sheds at Friedrichshafen, on Lake Constance. This raid provided a good example of the Admiralty's remarkable foresight in promoting the use of the bombing aeroplane, a policy which was later pursued with even more vigour in 1916 with the establishment of Nos. 3 and 5 Wings for bombing duties.

The R.N.A.S. unit which bombed Friedrichshafen formed at Manchester, under the command of Sqn. Cdr. P. Shepherd, in October 1914, and it was decided to launch the attack from Belfort, a few miles from the Franco-Swiss border and about 120 miles from the target. The four Avro 504s concerned were Nos. 179, 873, 874 and 875; No. 179 was the first of the type to be made for the Admiralty and hence, by the R.N.A.S. system of those days, sometimes used as a designation. The raid was at first delayed by bad weather, but when the aircraft eventually set off, each loaded with four 20-lb. bombs, No. 873 was flown by Sqn. Cdr. E. F. Briggs, No. 874 by F./Lt. S. V. Sippe and No. 875 by F./Cdr. J. T. Babington. No. 179, flown by F./Sub-Lt. R. P. Cannon, was forced to retire owing to a broken tailskid. The raiders flew north of Basle, followed the Rhine at a height of about 5,000 ft., came down to within 10 ft. of the water over Lake Constance to escape detection and then climbed to 1,200 ft. again about five miles from the target. The three Avros dived to about 700 ft. to release their bombs, and the effect was catastrophic. A gasworks exploded and sent gigantic flames into the sky and one of the

Avro 504A of the type used in the R.N.A.S. raid on the Zeppelin sheds, 1914. (*Imp. War Museum Photo.*)

Avro 504C (No. 1488) of the R.N.A.S. at St. Pol. (*Photo from H. H. Russell.*)

Zeppelins was gravely damaged. Sqn. Cdr. Briggs was shot down and taken prisoner, but the other aircraft returned safely. Perhaps the best summary of this truly remarkable achievement is that by Walter Raleigh, the official historian, who wrote in *The War in the Air*:

'The pilots deserve all praise for their admirable navigation, and the machines must not be forgotten. There have since been many longer and greater raids, but this flight of 250 miles, into gun-fire, across enemy country, in the frail little Avro with its humble horse-power, can compare as an achievement with the best of them.'

Although the Zeppelin sheds were not attacked again, Avros 504s took part in other notable bombing raids. One of these occurred on 24 March 1915, when five aircraft of No. 1 Squadron, R.N.A.S., flown by Sqn. Cdr. I. T. Courtney, F./Lts. B. C. Meates and H. L. Rosher and F./Sub-Lts. B. L. Huskisson and F. G. Andreae, raided the submarine depot at Hoboken near Antwerp and destroyed two U-boats, as well as setting the shipyard on fire.

Avros 504s were also employed as anti-Zeppelin fighters, and on the night of 16–17 May 1915 both the *L.Z. 38* and *L.Z. 39* were intercepted by Avros flown by F./Sub-Lt. R. H. Mulock (who later commanded No. 3 Squadron, R.N.A.S.) and F./Cdr. A. W. Bigsworth respectively. Both

Avro 504E (No. 9277) of the R.N.A.S. (*Imp. War Museum Photo.*)

Zeppelins escaped destruction, but *L.Z. 39* was badly damaged by the four 20-lb. bombs which were dropped on its envelope as Bigsworth climbed above it over Ostend. One variant of the Avro 504, the 504C, was specially developed for anti-Zeppelin patrols and about 80 were supplied to the R.N.A.S. It had an auxiliary fuel-tank in place of the front cockpit, which increased its endurance to eight hours, and frequently carried a Lewis machine-gun firing upwards at an angle of 45 degrees through the centre section.

The Avro 504C shared with the 504B, 504E and 504G (which were all variants built exclusively for the R.N.A.S.) a distinctive type of tail in which the familiar comma rudder of the 504 was replaced by vertical tail surfaces of elongated pattern. This tail assembly was used only on R.N.A.S. 504s; another distinctive feature of naval Avros were the long-span ailerons. The Avro 504B was employed chiefly for training purposes and about 190 were built. The Avro 504G, of which 30 were built,

Avro 504K with 100-h.p. Gnome Monosoupape. (*Imp. War Museum Photo.*)

was a gunnery-training development of the 504B and it was fitted with a single, fixed, synchronised Vickers machine-gun forward and a Lewis machine-gun on a Scarff ring aft.

The Avro 504E differed more markedly from the classic 504 configuration than the other R.N.A.S. variants. Whereas the 504B, C and G had all retained the 80-h.p. Gnome engine, the 504E had a 100-h.p. Gnome Monosoupape; it also reverted to the straight-top longeron of the original Avro 504. Another noticeable feature of the 504E was the heavy reduction of wing stagger; this resulted from the changed centre of gravity position due to the installation of the main fuel-tank between the two cockpits and the re-positioning of the rear cockpit further aft. The Avro 504Es served at R.N.A.S. flying schools at Chingford, Cranwell and Fairlop.

Mention must be made of two important experiments in naval flying which were carried out by the Avro 504B and C. The 504B was used in pioneering work on deck-arrester gear and the 504C (under the new designation 504H) became in 1917 one of the first aircraft to be launched by catapult gear: the pilot was F./Cdr R. E. Penny.

With the amalgamation of the R.F.C. and R.N.A.S. to form the R.A.F. in 1918, the Avro 504K was also used at former R.N.A.S. training schools, and this type remained in service for the training of F.A.A. pilots during the nineteen-twenties. In 1923, at Leuchars, pilots scheduled for Panther spotter-reconnaissance flights first completed a course on Avro 504Ks, or dual Snipes, so as to accustom themselves to the vagaries of rotary engines; there were no dual-control Panthers. At about the same period all naval officers trained as pilots did their *ab initio* instruction on Avro 504 Ks at Netheravon.

UNITS ALLOCATED

No. 1 Squadron, R.N.A.S. (Dover and Dunkirk); No. 2 Wing, R.N.A.S. (Imbros); No. 3 Squadron (formerly Eastchurch Squadron) R.N.A.S. (Dunkirk); No. 4 Squadron, R.N.A.S. (Dover and Eastchurch). R.N.A.S. training schools at Chingford, Cranwell, Fairlop, Frieston, Manston, Port Victoria and Redcar.

TECHNICAL DATA (AVRO 504, 504B & 504C)

Description: Avro 504: Single-seat bombing aircraft; Avro 504B: two-seat trainer; Avro 504C: single-seat anti-Zeppelin fighter.

Manufacturers (504): A. V. Roe & Co. Ltd., Miles Platting, Manchester. (504B): A. V. Roe & Co. Ltd., and sub-contracted by Parnall & Sons, Bristol; Regent Carriage Co. Ltd., Fulham; Sunbeam Motor

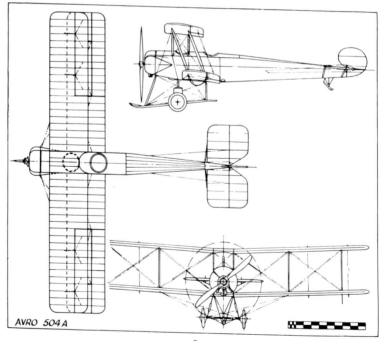

AVRO 504 A

Car Co. Ltd., Wolverhampton. (504C): A. V. Roe & Co. Ltd., and sub-contracted by Brush Electrical Engineering Co. Ltd., Loughborough.

Power Plant (504): One 80-h.p. Gnome; (504B): one 80-h.p. Gnome or 80-h.p. Le Rhone; (504C): one 80-h.p. Gnome.

Dimensions: Span, 36 ft. Length, 29 ft. 5 in. Height, 10 ft. 5 in. Wing area, 330 sq. ft.

Weights (504): Empty, 924 lb. Loaded, 1,574 lb.

Performance: (504): Maximum speed, 82 m.p.h. at sea level. Climb 7 mins. to 3,500 ft. Endurance, $4\frac{1}{2}$ hrs.

Armament: The Avro 504 equipped as a bomber carried four 20-lb. bombs in improvised racks below the bottom wings and four small incendiaries. For anti-Zeppelin patrols, the Avro 504C had a single Lewis gun firing incendiary ammunition.

Bison II on a flight from Hal Far, Malta.

Avro Bison

Speaking of the Avro Bison and the Blackburn Blackburn in his book *Flying and Soldiering*, R. R. Money recalled that, in both types, 'a 450 h.p. Napier Lion engine towed an unwieldy contraption about the sky'. There is no denying that the Bison, like other British naval aircraft of the early nineteen-twenties, was uncommonly ugly. The cumbersome lines of these early Fleet spotters resulted from the attention given to the needs of the naval observers and wireless operators, who were provided with an enormous cabin, with generous windows, in which to go about their duties with maps, plotting tables, wireless sets and other impedimenta. Welcome as this no doubt was to the naval observer, it resulted in a fuselage of ungainly proportions with an unusually large cross-section, paying little regard to the requirements of aerodynamics. The body of the Bison was set so high that the line from the pilot's cockpit to the airscrew boss ran at a downward angle of about 45 degrees. To assist the pilot when landing and taking off, it was found necessary to fit an aiming-rod parallel with the line of flight.

The prototype Bison I (N 153) first appeared in 1921, and a second prototype (N 154) was exhibited in the New Types Park at the R.A.F. Display at Hendon in 1923. The production aircraft followed the Mk. II pattern, in which the gap was increased and the top wing raised above the fuselage; on the Mk. I the wing was attached to the top of the fuselage. A long dorsal fin extension was also added, no doubt to counteract the huge keel surface presented by the fuselage. About 40 Bison (including N 9601 to N 9615 and N 9837 to N 9853) are believed to have been built for the F.A.A., and production of the type ceased in April 1927.

The first Bisons in service went to No. 3 Squadron, where they superseded the Westland Walrus shortly before the unit's disbandment in April 1923. This was a general reconnaissance squadron of the R.A.F.'s Coastal Area. The first purely naval unit to be equipped was No. 423 Fleet Spotter Flight, also at Gosport, in 1923. The Bison was retired from the F.A.A. in 1929, when it was finally superseded by the Fairey IIIF in Nos. 447 and 448 Flights.

No. 3 Squadron, R.A.F. (Fort Brockhurst, Gosport); No. 421 Flight (Gosport and H.M.S. *Furious*); No. 421A Flight (H.M.S. *Furious*, Home Fleet); No. 421B. Flight (H.M.S. *Eagle*, Mediterranean Fleet); No. 423 Flight (Gosport and H.M.S. *Eagle*, Mediterranean Fleet); No. 447 Flight (H.M.S. *Furious*, Home Fleet) and No. 448 Flight (Hal Far, Malta and H.M.S. *Eagle*, Mediterranean Fleet).

TECHNICAL DATA (BISON II)

Description: Carrier-borne fleet spotter-reconnaissance aircraft with a crew of three or four. Available both as landplane and amphibian. Wooden structure, fabric covered.

Manufacturers: A. V. Roe & Co. Ltd., Manchester.

Power Plant: One 450-h.p. Napier Lion II.

Dimensions: Span, 46 ft. Length, 37 ft. Height, 14 ft. 2 ins. Wing area, 620 sq. ft.

Weights: Empty, 4,163 lb. Loaded, 6,336 lb.

Performance: Maximum speed, 110 m.p.h. Cruising, 90 m.p.h. Climb, 24 mins. to 10,000 ft. Range, 360 miles. Service ceiling, 12,000 ft.

Armament: One free-mounted Lewis machine-gun on Scarff ring amidships.

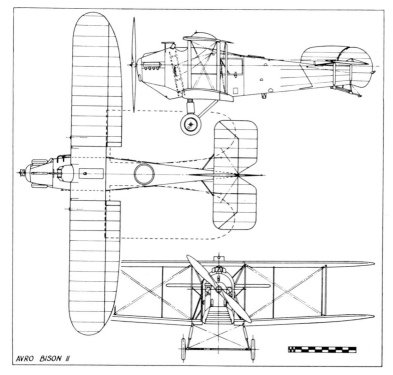

AVRO BISON II

B.E.2C (No. 8300) of the R.N.A.S. (*Imp. War Museum Photo.*)

B.E.2C

The B.E.2C is more often associated with the R.F.C., yet over 300 aircraft were delivered to the R.N.A.S., where they were employed for bombing duties, for anti-submarine patrols and for training purposes.

Much has been written about the B.E.2C's dismal failure as a fighting machine with the R.F.C. on the Western Front, its heavy losses in 1915–16 and the 'Fokker fodder' scandal. With the R.N.A.S., however, it earned a somewhat happier reputation, perhaps because it was employed chiefly in theatres of war where the opposition was less vigorous. The R.N.A.S. was, in fact, the first service to use the B.E.2C in overseas zones other than France when, in April 1915, two B.E.2Cs accompanied the Farmans, Voisins and a Breguet of No. 3 Wing to Tenedos to take part in the Dardanelles campaign. In August 1915 they were joined by six more belonging to No. 2 Wing, R.N.A.S. All these naval B.E.2Cs had 70-h.p. Renault engines, as fitted in the prototype which first flew in June 1914.

On 13 November 1915 a B.E.2C of No. 2 Wing flown by F./Cdr. J. R. W. Smyth-Pigott made a daring night-bombing attack on a bridge at Kuleli Burgas spanning the Maritza river, a vulnerable point on the Berlin–Constantinople railway. Smyth-Pigott bombed from 300 ft. and was awarded the D.S.O. for his gallantry, though the target was not destroyed.

Many of the B.E.2Cs used as bombers by the R.N.A.S. had a small bomb-rack beneath the cowling, as illustrated, and some were flown as single-seaters with the front cockpit faired over.

In the United Kingdom the R.N.A.S. used B.E.2Cs for anti-submarine and Zeppelin patrols from coastal air stations until as late as 1918. On 28 November 1916, off Lowestoft, three B.E.2Cs flown by F./Lt. Cadbury and F./Sub-Lts. Pulling and Fane brought down the Zeppelin *L 21*.

The R.N.A.S. received 337 B.E.2C's altogether; 161 with Renault engines, 153 with the R.A.F.1A and 23 with the Curtiss OX-5. The last B.E.2C (No. 10,000) left the Blackburn factory on 3 July 1917.

No. 1 Wing, R.N.A.S. (Dunkirk), No. 2 Wing, R.N.A.S. (Imbros and Mudros), No. 3 Wing, R.N.A.S. (Imbros and Tenedos), No. 7 (Naval) squadron (East Africa). Also coastal air stations at Eastbourne, Hornsea, Great Yarmouth, Port Victoria, Redcar, Scarborough and training schools at Chingford and Cranwell.

TECHNICAL DATA (B.E.2C)

Description: Two-seat bomber and anti-submarine patrol aircraft. Wooden structure, fabric covered.

Manufacturers: Admiralty contracts to Beardmore; Blackburn; Eastbourne; Grahame-White; Hewlett and Blondeau; Martinsyde; Ruston, Proctor; Vickers; Vulcan and G. & J. Weir.

Power Plant: 70-h.p. Renault, 90-h.p. R.A.F. 1A or 90-h.p. Curtiss OX-5.

Dimensions: Span, 37 ft. Length, 27 ft. 3 in. Height, 11 ft. 1½ in. Wing area, 371 sq. ft.

Weights: Empty, 1,370 lb. Loaded, 2,142 lb.

Performance: Maximum speed, 72 m.p.h. at 6,500 ft. Climb, 6½ mins. to 3,500 ft.; 45 mins. to 10,000 ft. Endurance, 3¼ hrs. Service ceiling, 10,000 ft.

Armament: Renault-engined bombers carried up to four 25-lb. bombs under engine nacelle. R.A.F.-engined single-seaters carried two 112-lb. bombs or ten 20-lb. bombs below the wings.

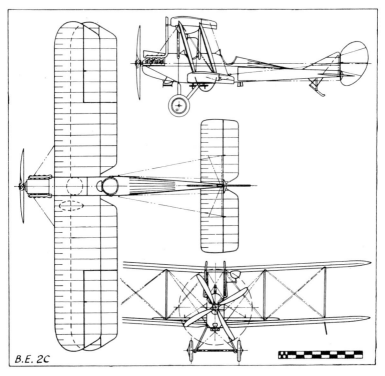

B.E. 2C

Beardmore W.B. III (N 6101). (*Imp. War Museum Photo.*)

Beardmore W.B. III

The Beardmore W.B. III was introduced towards the end of the First World War and, although it can lay claim to no memorable engagements with the enemy, it is nevertheless interesting historically as an early attempt to produce an aircraft exclusively for carrier-borne flying. It was not an original design, being a derivative of the Sopwith Pup, but the ingenuity that went into its modification for aircraft-carrier work was quite remarkable. The adaptation was the work of Mr. G. Tilghman Richards, and the manufacturers were no strangers to the Pup, as they had been the first company to build Pups under licence for the R.N.A.S.

The prototype W.B. III (No. 9950) was in fact converted from the last of a batch of Sopwith Pups built at Dalmuir. It differed from the Pup in having folding wings to conserve hangar space aboard ship. Unlike the Pup, the wings had no stagger and the dihedral angle was reduced. The normal centre-section struts were replaced by full-length interplane struts adjacent to the fuselage and the ailerons were operated by control rods, the upper and lower ailerons being rigidly connected by a light strut. This latter feature was abandoned in later production aircraft, which reverted to cable controls. Other modifications included wingtip skids and a lengthened fuselage, which was adapted to carry emergency flotation gear, and a remarkable system whereby the undercarriage was retracted to further economise in space when stored.

Two official designations were applied to the W.B. IIIs in service, S.B.3D and S.B.3F. The former indicated an aircraft with an undercarriage which could be jettisoned in the event of 'ditching', the latter of a folding undercarriage. Production orders for 100 W.B. IIIs reached Beardmores (N 6100 to N 6129 and N 6680 to N 6749), but it is possible that not all were built. On 31 October 1918, 55 W.B. 111s were in service, including 18 with the Grand Fleet.

44

Aircraft-carriers *Furious*, *Nairana* and *Pegasus*.

TECHNICAL DATA (W.B. III)

Description: Single-seat carrier-borne scout. Wooden structure, fabric covered.

Manufacturers: William Beardmore & Co. Ltd., Dalmuir, Dumbarton-shire.

Power Plant: One 80-h.p. Le Rhone or 80-h.p. Clerget.

Dimensions: Span, 25 ft. (10 ft. 4 in. folded). Length, 20 ft. 2½ in. Height, 8 ft. 1¼ in. Wing area, 243 sq. ft.

Weights: Empty, 890 lb. Loaded, 1,289 lb.

Performance: Maximum speed, 103 m.p.h. at sea level; 91 m.p.h. at 10,000 ft. Climb, 9 mins. to 5,000 ft.; 24 mins. to 10,000 ft. Endurance, 2¾ hrs. Service ceiling, 12,400 ft.

Armament: One Lewis gun mounted above centre-section firing over airscrew.

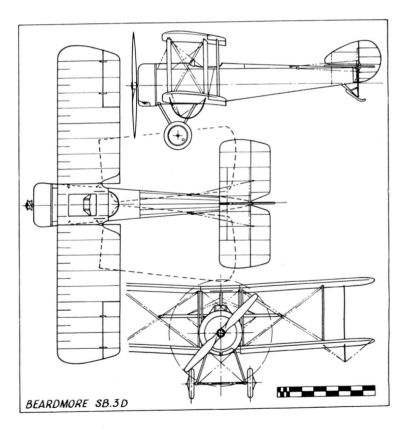

BEARDMORE SB.3D

Dart II (N 9997) with smoke-screen apparatus. (*Air Ministry Photo.*)

Blackburn Dart

The Blackburn Company's association with torpedo aircraft began with the twin-engined G.P. seaplane of 1916 and was continued with the building of 80 Sopwith Cuckoos and the three Blackburn Blackburd prototypes (N 113–115), the first Blackburn aircraft specially designed for torpedo-dropping. Next, in 1919, came the Swift. The Swift was the immediate predecessor of the Dart, which it closely resembled, and was exhibited at Olympia in 1920. The prototype (N 139) was followed by overseas orders, but none were built for the F.A.A.

The Dart (prototypes N 140, N 141 and N 142) appeared in 1920 and, unlike the Swift and Blackburd, which had to drop their wheels to release the torpedo, featured a split-leg under-carriage, one of the first of its kind. Darts entered service with Nos. 460 and 461 Flights in 1923 (a prototype having been shown at Hendon in 1922), and the type remained with the F.A.A. until 1933, though in diminishing numbers from 1929.

The Dart lent itself well to carrier operation, being easy to land on a deck, and on 1 July 1926 F/Lt. Boyce made the first night landing aboard an aircraft-carrier (H.M.S. *Furious*) whilst flying a Dart, N 9804. Although it did not have a high performance, the Dart did its job well and enabled the F.A.A., during its formative period, to develop its theories of torpedo attack. Darts were occasionally used in air-defence exercises, notably in 1931, when aircraft of No. 463 Flight operated in night camouflage.

No accurate records have survived of Dart production totals, but the type continued to be built until 1928, and it is estimated that about 70 were supplied to the F.A.A. A twin-float seaplane version of the Dart was also built, fitted with a second cockpit and dual control, and a number of these were operated for several years by one of the four R.A.F. Reserve Training Schools of the late nineteen-twenties. The Dart was finally declared obsolete in April 1935.

UNITS ALLOCATED

No. 460 Flight (*Eagle*, Mediterranean Fleet, 1923–31); No. 461 Flight (Gosport and *Furious*, Home Fleet, 1923–29); No. 462 Flight (Gosport and *Furious*, Home Fleet, 1924–29); No. 463 Flight (*Courageous*, Mediterranean Fleet, 1928–33); No. 464 Flight (*Courageous*, Mediterranean Fleet, 1928–33). Also served briefly with No. 810 Squadron before converting to Ripons after its formation out of Nos. 463 and 464 Flights in April 1933.

TECHNICAL DATA (DART II)

Description: Single-seat carrier-borne torpedo-carrier. Composite wood and metal structure, fabric covered.
Manufacturers: Blackburn Aeroplane & Motor Co. Ltd., Leeds, Yorks.
Power Plant: One 450-h.p. Napier Lion IIB or V.
Dimensions: Span, 45 ft. 6 in. Length, 35 ft. 6 in. Height, 12 ft. 3 in. Wing area, 651 sq. ft.
Weights: Empty, 3,843 lb. Loaded, 6,400 lb.
Performance: Maximum speed, 110 m.p.h. at sea level. Climb, 750 ft./min. Range, 256 miles. Service ceiling, 15,000 ft.
Armament: Provision for one 18-in. torpedo beneath the fuselage.

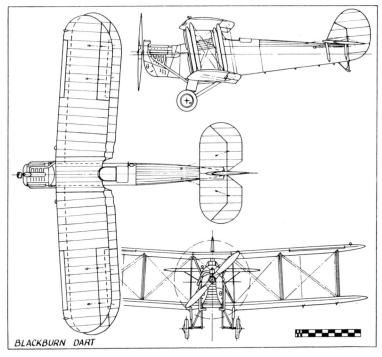

BLACKBURN DART

Blackburn II (N 9828). (*Air Ministry Photo.*)

Blackburn Blackburn

The Blackburn Blackburn was a contemporary of the Avro Bison, and when it came to ugliness there was little to choose between the two. Both types were designed for spotting and reconnaissance duties, working in close co-operation with Fleet gunnery, and the bulky, ungainly fuselage resulted from the need to provide a cabin for the navigator/observer and wireless operator. Possibly because the performance suffered so badly, subsequent spotter-reconnaissance aircraft showed less thought for the comfort of the observer.

The Blackburn bore a close relationship to the Dart, and the first prototype (N 150) appeared the same year. In this original version the fuselage connected directly with both upper and lower wings; subsequently the gap between the wings was increased by raising the top wing on struts above the fuselage, and the wing petrol-tanks were eliminated. In this form the Blackburn entered service in 1923 as the Mk. II. The first unit to be equipped was No. 422 Fleet Spotter Flight, which served first in H.M.S. *Eagle* with the Mediterranean Fleet and afterwards in H.M.S. *Argus* on the China Station.

In 1926, the Blackburn Blackburn also entered service with No. 420 Fleet Spotter Flight, where it superseded the ageing Westland Walrus, and operated for a time at Gosport before embarking in H.M.S. *Furious* for duties with the Home Fleet.

In May 1929 the Blackburn flights were redesignated Nos. 450 and 449 Fleet Spotter Reconnaissance Flights respectively: this was part of a general re-organisation of spotter flights involving the disbandment of the original Nos. 420, 421, 422 and 423 Flights and the creation of Nos. 440 to 450 Flights inclusive.

Blackburns finally disappeared from the Fleet Air Arm in 1931, when both Nos. 449 and 450 Flights re-equipped with Fairey IIIFs. Although no detailed records have survived, it is estimated by the manufacturers that between 50 and 70 were built. At least one Blackburn (N 9833) was fitted with twin floats and, due to specially strengthened keels, could be landed on a carrier. Another variant was a two-seat trainer with side-by-side cockpits. This was known as the Blackburn Bull, and is described and illustrated in the Appendix. The Blackburn was finally declared obsolete in March 1933.

UNITS ALLOCATED

No. 420 Flight (Gosport and *Furious*, Home Fleet, 1926–8); No. 422 Flight (*Eagle*, Mediterranean Fleet and *Argus*, China Station, 1923–8); No. 449 Flight (*Furious*, Home Fleet and *Courageous*, Mediterranean Fleet, 1929–31); No. 450 Flight (*Argus*, China Station and *Courageous*, Mediterranean Fleet, 1929–31).

TECHNICAL DATA (BLACKBURN II)

Description: Fleet spotter-reconnaissance aircraft with a crew of three or four. Composite wood and metal structure, fabric covered.
Manufacturers: Blackburn Aeroplane & Motor Co. Ltd., Leeds, Yorks.
Power Plant: One 450-h.p. Napier Lion IIB or V.
Dimensions: Span, 45 ft. 10 in. Length, 39 ft. Height, 16 ft. Wing area, 662 sq. ft.
Weights: Empty, 4,034 lb. Loaded, 6,112 lb.
Performance: Maximum speed, 100 m.p.h. Climb, 650 ft./min. Range, 210 miles. Service ceiling, 11,750 ft.
Armament: One Lewis machine-gun on Scarff ring in rear cockpit.

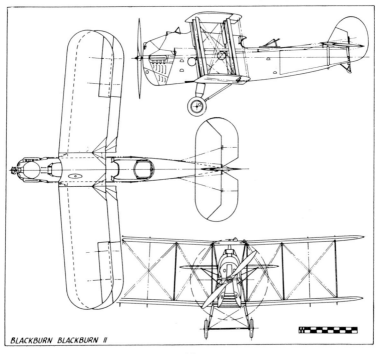

BLACKBURN BLACKBURN II

Ripon II (S 1564). (*Air Ministry Photo.*)

Blackburn Ripon

The Ripon succeeded the Dart as the F.A.A.'s standard torpedo aircraft, first entering service with No. 462 Flight in August 1929. Its increased radius of action, roughly twice that of the Dart, meant that an observer had to be carried to do the navigation. For this reason its rate of climb was not so good as the Dart, though it was faster.

The prototype Ripon Mk. I (N 203) appeared in 1928 and was followed by a Mk. II prototype (N 231). The production version was designated Ripon IIA and was of composite wood and metal construction; later an all-metal version appeared under the designation Ripon III. A total of 92 Ripons was built for the F.A.A., and the last aircraft (K 3559) was flown in December 1933.

Known production batches of Ripons included aircraft in and around S 1265 to S 1271, S 1358 to S 1368, S 1426 to S 1432, S 1468 to S 1473, S 1553 to S 1572, S 1652 to S 1674, K 2884 to K 2887 and K 3546 to K 3559. Of these aircraft, S 1268 and S 1468 were both fitted with twin floats at one period. The all-metal Ripon III was S 1272.

The Ripon was a multi-purpose aircraft; it was fitted with spools for catapulting and could be used for long-range reconnaissance with armament removed and extra fuel-tanks installed to give a total endurance of 14 hrs. For precision bombing, the observer was provided with an aiming window in the floor of the fuselage.

In addition to succeeding Darts in Nos. 460, 461 and 462 Flights, Ripons provided the initial equipment of No. 465 Flight formed on 20 March 1931, and of No. 466 Flight formed on 31 March 1931. From January 1934 Ripons began to be superseded by Baffins, and the last in service were those of No. 811 Squadron aboard H.M.S. *Furious*.

No. 460 Flight (*Glorious*, Mediterranean Fleet); No. 461 Flight (*Glorious*, Mediterranean Fleet); No. 462 Flight (*Furious*, Home Fleet and *Glorious*, Mediterranean Fleet); No. 465 Flight (Gosport and *Furious*, Home Fleet); No. 466 Flight (Gosport and *Furious*, Home Fleet); No. 810 Squadron (*Courageous*); No. 811 Squadron (*Furious*) and No. 812 Squadron (*Glorious*).

TECHNICAL DATA (RIPON IIA)

Description: Two-seat carrier-borne torpedo-bomber. Composite wood and metal structure, fabric covered.

Manufacturers: Blackburn Aeroplane & Motor Co. Ltd., Brough, E. Yorks.

Power Plant: One 570 h.p. Napier Lion XIA.

Dimensions: Span, 44 ft. 10 in. (19 ft. folded). Length, 36 ft. 9 in. Height, 12 ft. 10 in. Wing area, 649 sq. ft.

Weights: Empty, 4,255 lb. Loaded, 7,405 lb.

Performance: Maximum speed, 126 m.p.h. at sea level; 118 m.p.h. at 15,000 ft. Cruising, 109 m.p.h. Climb, 610 ft./min. Endurance (normal), 3 hrs. Service ceiling, 13,000 ft.

Armament: One fixed Vickers machine-gun forward and one free-mounted Lewis machine-gun aft. Provision for one Mk. VIII or Mk. X torpedo; alternatively one 1,100-lb. smoke-container or a bomb-load comprised of three 230/250-lb. or three 520/550-lb. bombs on universal carriers under wings and fuselage and light series carrier for 20-lb. practice bombs below starboard wing.

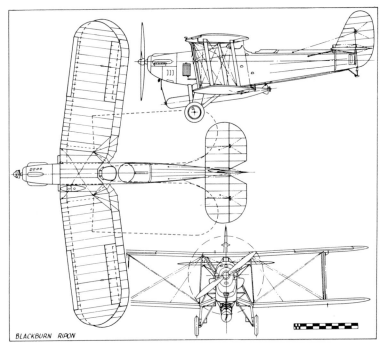

BLACKBURN RIPON

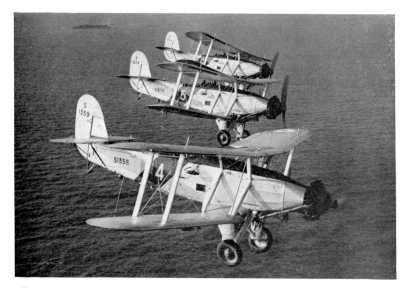

Baffins (S 1359 (nearest camera)) converted from Ripons. (*Chas. E Brown Photo.*)

Blackburn Baffin

The Baffin succeeded the Ripon as the F.A.A.'s standard torpedo-bomber, and it was the first of the many Blackburn aircraft supplied for service in carriers to introduce an air-cooled radial engine, all its predecessors having had the Napier Lion. Indeed, the Lion had been used in every F.A.A. aircraft from 1925 to 1932, with the exception of the Flycatcher. The Baffin's use of a radial had a precedent among Blackburn torpedo-bombers in the Beagle (N 236) of 1928, which mounted a Bristol Jupiter, but this type never went beyond the prototype stage.

The prototype Baffin differed from production aircraft in having its Pegasus engine in a Townend ring; all Baffins in service had an un-cowled engine. Originally designated B-5, it was named Baffin in September 1933 after a production order had been placed. Fifteen Baffins were built as such, with the numbers K 3589, K 3590, K 4071 to K 4080 inclusive and K 4776 to K 4778 inclusive. There were in addition some 62 Ripons converted into Baffins; these retained their original serial numbers. The last of the true-built Baffins (K 4778) was delivered in June 1935.

The first F.A.A. squadron to receive the Baffin was No. 812, which relinquished its Ripons in January 1934. Next came No. 810 Squadron, in August 1934, and No. 811 Squadron in May 1935. In 1935 Baffins of No. 810 Squadron had the honour of leading the formation of F.A.A. aircraft taking part in the Jubilee Naval Review.

The Baffin offered only a marginally better performance than the Ripon and was in service for only a few years. No. 812 Squadron was the last to retain the type, until December 1936. In Nos. 812 and 811

Squadrons the Baffin was supplanted by the Fairey Swordfish, and in No. 810 Squadron by the Blackburn Shark. It was finally declared obsolete in September 1937.

No. 810 Squadron (*Courageous*); No. 811 Squadron (*Furious*); No. 812 Squadron (*Glorious*).

TECHNICAL DATA (BAFFIN)

Description: Two-seat carrier-borne torpedo-bomber. Composite wood and metal structure, fabric covered.

Manufacturers: Blackburn Aircraft & Motor Co. Ltd., Brough, E. Yorks.

Power Plant: One 565-h.p. Bristol Pegasus I.M.3.

Dimensions: Span, 45 ft. 6½ in. (17 ft. 10 in. folded). Length, 38 ft. 3¾ in. Height, 13 ft. 5½ in. Wing area, 649 sq. ft.

Weights: Empty, 4,180 lb. Loaded, 7,610 lb.

Performance: Maximum speed, 136 m.p.h. at 5,000 ft.; 125 m.p.h. at sea level. Climb, 480 ft./min. at sea level; 600 ft./min. at 5,000 ft. Range, 450 miles at 100 m.p.h. Service ceiling, 15,000 ft.

Armament: One fixed Vickers machine-gun forward and one free-mounted Lewis machine-gun on Fairey high-speed mounting aft. Provision for one 1,576-lb. Mk. VIII or Mk. X torpedo or one 2,000-lb. bomb. Alternatively, six 230/250-lb. or three 530-lb. bombs could be carried, plus four 20-lb. practice bombs.

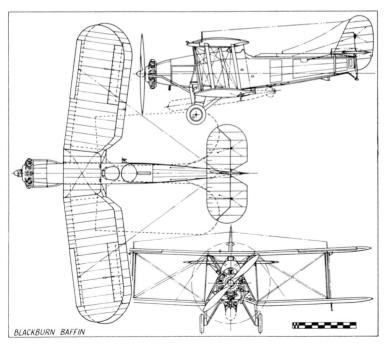

BLACKBURN BAFFIN

Shark II (K 8454) with deck hook extended. (*Chas. E. Brown Photo.*)

Blackburn Shark

The Shark was the last of the series of Blackburn torpedo biplanes for the F.A.A., and it embodied the experience gained with such stalwarts as the Dart, Ripon and Baffin. It had its genesis in the private venture Blackburn B-6 of May 1934. This became prototype (K 4295) that made its first public appearance at the R.A.F. Display at Hendon in 1934. It was designed to operate either as a landplane or as a seaplane (see Appendix), and the F.A.A. used both, though the landplane predominated.

Blackburns received their first production contract for 16 Shark Is (K 4349 to K 4364) in August 1934, and in May 1935 the type entered service with No. 820 Squadron, formerly equipped with Fairey Seals.

The Shark II was the next version, for which K 4295 again served as the prototype. A small order for three (K 4880 to K 4882) in June 1935 was followed by further contracts for 53 Mks. IIs (K 5607 to K 5659) in September 1935 and for 70 (K 8450 to K 8519) in January 1936. The year 1936 saw two more first-line squadrons equipped with the Shark, Nos. 810 and 821, formerly Baffins and Seals respectively. First-line service of the Shark was to be relatively brief, for in 1938 all three squadrons went over to the Fairey Swordfish, and the type was used thereafter chiefly in the training rôle. The Shark I became obsolete in May 1938.

The final production version of the Shark was the Mk. III (see three-view), which introduced the added refinement of a glazed canopy for the crew. Ninety-five Shark IIIs (K 8891 to K 8935 and L 2337 to L 2386) were built to a contract received in January 1937. This variant, which was still widely used for the training of observers and telegraphists at the outbreak of war in 1939, was built to Spec. S. 19/36. Final production of the Shark for the F.A.A. totalled 238. From July 1938 a number of Sharks

54

were reconditioned at Blackburn's new Dumbarton factory and test-flown from Abbotsinch.

No. 810 (*Courageous*), No. 820 (*Courageous*) and No. 821 (*Furious*). Also Nos. 753 and 754 Training Squadrons at Lee-on-Solent.

TECHNICAL DATA (SHARK II)

Description: Two–three-seat torpedo-spotter-reconnaissance landplane or seaplane. Metal structure, with Alclad monocoque fuselage and fabric-covered wings.

Manufacturers: Blackburn Aircraft Co. Ltd., Brough, E. Yorks., and Dumbarton, Scotland.

Power Plant: One 700-h.p. Armstrong Siddeley Tiger VIc.

Dimensions: Span, 46 ft. (15 ft. folded). Length, 35 ft. 2¼ in. (38 ft. 5 in. as seaplane). Height, 12 ft. 1 in. Wing area, 489 sq. ft.

Weights: Empty, 4,333 lb. Loaded, 8,050 lb.

Performance: Maximum speed: 152 m.p.h. at 6,500 ft. Cruising, 118 m.p.h. Initial climb, 895 ft./min. Range, 625 miles with bombs or 792 miles without bombs. Maximum range, 1,130 miles. Endurance, 4·9 hrs. Service ceiling (with bombs), 16,400 ft.

Armament: One fixed 0·303 Vickers machine-gun forward and one flexible 0·303 Vickers-Berthier gun aft. One 1,500-lb. torpedo or equivalent load of bombs.

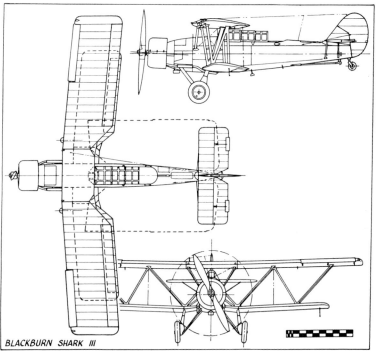

BLACKBURN SHARK III

Skuas of No. 803 Squadron. (*Chas. E. Brown Photo.*)

Blackburn Skua

The Skua will go down in F.A.A. history as its first operational mono-plane and also the first British aircraft specifically designed for dive-bombing to enter squadrons. There had been earlier examples of monoplanes for the F.A.A. such as the Blackburn Airedale, a parasol monoplane designed for Fleet spotting in 1926, but none of them had entered service.

Designed to Spec. O. 27/34, the first prototype Skua (K 5178) flew in 1937 and was followed by a second prototype (K 5179), both aircraft having been ordered by the Air Ministry in April 1935. The designer was Mr. G. E. Petty. The first prototype was exhibited in the New Types Park at the R.A.F.'s final Hendon Display in 1937, where it was seen in public for the first time. Both prototypes, unlike the production aircraft, were powered by Bristol Mercury poppet-valve engines.

In July 1936 the Air Ministry placed a production contract for 190 aircraft, and these Skuas (L 2867 to L 3056 inclusive) were fitted with the Bristol Perseus sleeve-valve engine.

The first F.A.A. unit to be equipped with Skuas aboard an aircraft carrier was No. 800 Squadron. This was in November 1938, when six Skuas superseded Nimrod and Osprey biplanes aboard *H.M.S. Ark Royal*, the Royal Navy's latest carrier at that time. With the outbreak of war, Skuas were also equipping Nos. 801 and 803 Squadrons in *Ark Royal*. The first notable action by a Skua was by one of No. 803's aircraft which on 25 September 1939 shot down a Dornier Do 18 flying-boat off Norway, the first enemy aircraft claimed by Britain in the Second World War. On 10 April 1940 Skuas of Nos. 800 and 803 Squadrons based at Hatston dive-bombed and sank the German cruiser *Königsberg* in Bergen Fjord. In the Dunkirk evacuation, Skuas of No. 801 Squadron operated with Coastal Command from R.A.F. Detling, as dive-bombers and fighters. Skuas were also active off Dakar in September 1940 when aircraft of No. 800 Squadron from *Ark Royal* bombed the battleship *Richelieu*.

Skuas remained operational until 1941, being replaced by Fulmars during March in No. 800 Squadron and by Sea Hurricanes in No. 801 (during August) and No. 803 (during May). They continued for several years as trainers and target-tugs.

Nos. 800 (*Ark Royal*), 801 (*Ark Royal* and *Furious*), 803 (*Ark Royal*) and 806 (R.N.A.S. Eastleigh).

TECHNICAL DATA (SKUA II)

Description: Two-seat deck-landing fighter and dive-bomber. All-metal stressed-skin construction.

Manufacturers: Blackburn Aircraft Co. Ltd., Brough, E. Yorks.

Power Plant: One 905-h.p. Bristol Perseus XII.

Dimensions: Span, 46 ft. 2 in. (15 ft. 6 in. folded). Length, 35 ft. 7 in. Height, 12 ft. 6 in. Wing area, 312 sq. ft.

Weights: Empty, 5,490 lb. Loaded, 8,228 lb.

Performance: Maximum speed: 225 m.p.h. at 6,500 ft. or 204 m.p.h. at sea level. Cruising, 144 to 165 m.p.h. at 15,000 ft. Initial climb, 1,580 ft./min. Range, 760 miles. Endurance, 4½ hours. Service ceiling, 20,200 ft.

Armament: Four Browning machine-guns in the wings and one manually-operated Lewis gun in rear cockpit. One 500-lb. bomb on ejector arm in recess below fuselage and eight 30-lb. practice bombs on light series carriers below wings.

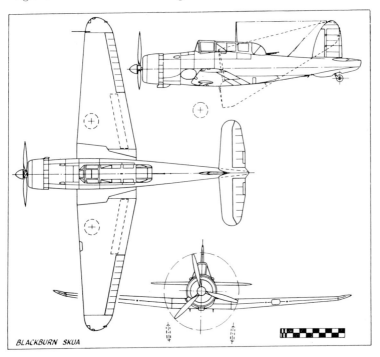

BLACKBURN SKUA

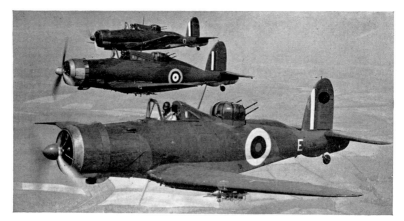

Roc Is (L 3114 nearest camera). ('*The Aeroplane*' Photo.)

Blackburn Roc

The Roc was the first aircraft ever used in the F.A.A. to be equipped with a power-driven gun-turret. It was designed to meet the requirements of Spec. O.30/35 and was intended as a F.A.A. equivalent of the R.A.F.'s Boulton Paul Defiant. The tactical concept of a turret fighter, which brought its four guns to bear in broadside attacks on enemy bombers, was subsequently proved to be unsound, and the Roc saw only very restricted first-line service.

The design of the Roc was based closely on that of the Skua dive-bomber; the main points of difference were the slightly widened fuselage to accommodate the Boulton Paul turret and the use of increased dihedral on the wings from the centre-section outwards, with no turned-up wing-tips.

Manufacture of the Rocs was entrusted to the Boulton Paul factory, where the production order was received on 28 April 1937. The contract was for 136 aircraft (L 3057 to L 3192 inclusive) and the first Roc flew on 23 December 1938. Production of Rocs finally ceased in August 1940.

Although originally intended for the purpose, Rocs never actually operated from aircraft-carriers, being confined to shore stations. They first entered service with No. 806 Squadron at Eastleigh in February 1940; this unit had eight Skuas and four Rocs on strength. After only a few months' service these aircraft were superseded by 12 Fairey Fulmars in July 1940, before embarkation in H.M.S. *Illustrious*.

In No. 801 Squadron Rocs came into service in June 1940, the unit's equipment consisting of six Rocs and six Skuas. The squadron was re-armed in August 1941 with 12 Sea Hurricanes and subsequently served in *Argus* and *Eagle*.

The Roc ended its days on training and target-towing duties and few remained in service after 1942.

Nos. 801 and 806 Squadrons, both shore-based.

TECHNICAL DATA (ROC)

Description: Two-seat Fleet fighter. All-metal stressed-skin construction.
Manufacturers: Boulton Paul Aircraft, Ltd., Wolverhampton.
Power Plant: One 905-h.p. Bristol Perseus XII.
Dimensions: Span 46 ft. Length, 35 ft. 7 in. Height, 12 ft. 1 in. Wing area, 310 sq. ft.
Weights: Empty, 6,121 lb. Loaded, 8,800 lb.
Performance: Maximum speed, 194 m.p.h. Cruising, 135 m.p.h. Climb, 1,130 ft./min. Endurance, $4\frac{1}{2}$ hrs. Service ceiling, 14,600 ft.
Armament: Four Browning machine-guns in electrically-operated Boulton Paul turret amidships. Light series bomb carriers below the wings.

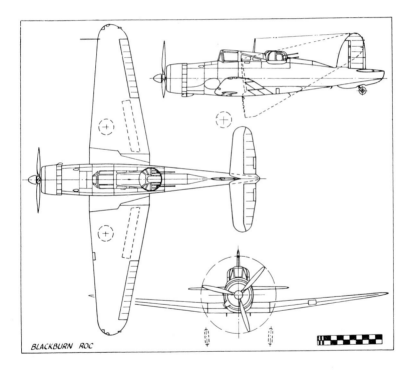

BLACKBURN ROC

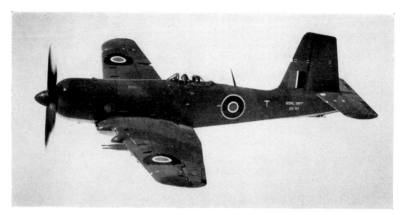

Firebrand T.F. 5 (EK 747). (*Crown Copyright Photo.*)

Blackburn Firebrand

Although first conceived as early as 1940, the Firebrand did not reach a first-line squadron until 1945, and it saw no action in the Second World War. During these five years it altered its rôle from that of a short-range interceptor to a torpedo-carrying strike fighter.

The prototype (DD 804) was designed to Spec. N. 11/40 and, fitted with a Napier Sabre III, first flew on 27 February 1942. It carried no armament, but the second prototype (DD 810), which flew in July 1942, had four 20-mm. guns. By this time, however, it was clear that the Seafire enjoyed a lead in performance and it was decided to utilise the Firebrand's undoubted load-carrying capacity for torpedo work. Accordingly, the Firebrand II prototype (NV 636, actually DD 810 rebuilt) first flew on 31 March 1943, equipped to carry an 18-in. torpedo between the wheel bays in a widened centre-section. Production of the Firebrands I and II (see Appendix) was limited to 21, and with the Mk. III a change was made to the Centaurus radial due to the shortage of Sabre engines which were going into Typhoons for the R.A.F. The prototype Firebrand III (DK 372) met the requirements of Spec. S. 8/43, and first flew on 21 December 1943. It was followed by a second prototype (DK 373) and 24 production aircraft (DK 386 to DK 412), but suffered from inadequate directional control at take-off. This was rectified in the Mk. IV by an enlarged fin and rudder, and this variant also introduced a two-position torpedo mounting and wing dive-brakes. Firebrand IV production totalled 140 (EK 601 to EK 740), the first flying on 17 May 1945.

In September 1945 No. 813 Squadron at Ford re-formed with 15 Firebrand IVs and became the first F.A.A. squadron to fly single-seater torpedo aircraft since the Dart had been retired in 1933. No. 813's Firebrands participated in the Victory Flypast over London in June 1946.

The final Firebrand variants were the Mks. V and VA, production of which ceased at the end of 1947. Detail improvements included horn

60

balanced elevators and longer-span aileron tabs, and the Mark VA also
had powered ailerons. Production totalled 150 (EK 741 to EK 850) and
there were also about 40 Mk. IV conversions. The Firebrand was
superseded in the F.A.A. during 1953 by the Westland Wyvern.

UNITS ALLOCATED

No. 813 (R.N.A.S. Ford) and No. 827 (*Eagle*, 1952–53).

TECHNICAL DATA (FIREBRAND T.F. 5)

Description: Single-seat deck-landing torpedo-strike fighter.   Maker's
    designation: B-45.
Manufacturers: Blackburn Aircraft Co. Ltd., Brough, E. Yorks.
Power Plant: One 2,500-h.p. Bristol Centaurus IX.
Dimensions: Span, 51 ft. 3½ in. Length, 38 ft. 11 in. Height, 14 ft. 11 in.
    Wing area, 381½ sq. ft.
Weights: Empty, 11,835 lb. Loaded, 17,500 lb. (maximum).
Performance: Maximum speed, 350 m.p.h. at 13,000 ft., or 342 m.p.h. with
    torpedo. Cruising, 256 m.p.h. Initial climb, 2,600 ft./min., or 2,200
    ft./min. with torpedo. Range, 740 miles at 256 m.p.h., or 627 miles
    at 289 m.p.h. Service ceiling, 28,500 ft.
Armament: Four 20-mm. Hispano guns in wings and provision for one
    1,850-lb. torpedo, or two 1,000-lb. bombs or rocket-projectiles.

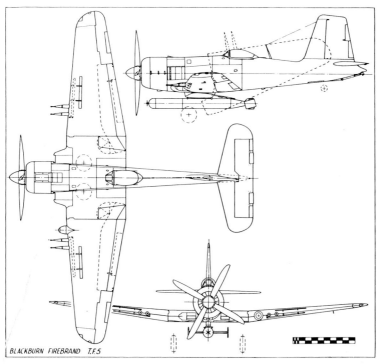

BLACKBURN FIREBRAND T.F.5

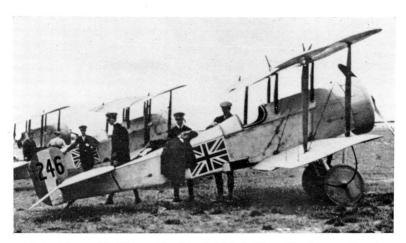

Bristol Scout 'C' (No. 1246) of the R.N.A.S. (*Imp. War Museum Photo.*)

Bristol Scout C and D

The Bristol Scout occupies a unique position in British naval flying by being the first landplane with a wheeled undercarriage to take off from the deck of an aircraft-carrier. This feat was achieved on 3 November 1915 when F./Sub-Lt. H. F. Towler flew his Scout C from the short flying-deck of the seaplane carrier *Vindex*. Two Bristol Scouts were accommodated, and for stowage they were dismantled. As there were no facilities for landing-on, flotation bags were fitted so that the aircraft could 'ditch' alongside.

The R.N.A.S. used both the Bristol Scout C and D, both of which were developments of the original Bristol Scout flown in February 1914. The R.F.C. was the first Service to adopt the type (on 5 November 1914), but the R.N.A.S. followed soon afterwards with an order for 24 (Nos. 1243 to 1266) on 7 December 1914. Some of these early Scout Cs served with the R.N.A.S. on the Western Front in 1915. They were followed by a second batch of 50 Scout Cs (Nos. 3013 to 3062).

Later Admiralty orders were for the Scout D, which differed from the C in having shorter ailerons, increased dihedral and wingtip skids further outboard. Of the 80 Scout Ds delivered to the R.N.A.S., the first 60 had 100-h.p. Gnome Monosoupape engines (Nos. 8591 to 9000 and N 5390 to 5399), and the final 20 (N 5400 to N 5419) the 80-h.p. Gnome, as on the Scout Cs.

Despite its fine design, the Bristol Scout was handicapped by lack of effective armament. It was used extensively for anti-Zeppelin patrols, both from carriers in the North Sea and from land bases such as Redcar and Great Yarmouth, but with no real success. One method of attack was to climb above the Zeppelin and drop Ranken darts.

The R.N.A.S. also employed Bristol Scouts in the Dardanelles campaign, sometimes to escort bombing raids.

No. 2 Wing, R.N.A.S. (Belgium, Imbros and Mudros); 'A' Flight, R.N.A.S. (Thasos). Coastal air stations at Eastchurch, East Fortune, Great Yarmouth, Port Victoria and Redcar. Training schools at Chingford and Cranwell. Seaplane carrier *Vindex*.

TECHNICAL DATA (SCOUT C)

Description: Single-seat scout, land-based or carrier-borne. Wooden structure, fabric covered.

Manufacturers: British & Colonial Aeroplane Co. Ltd., Filton and Brislington, Bristol.

Power Plant: One 80-h.p. Gnome.

Dimensions: Span, 24 ft. 7 in. Length, 20 ft. 8 in. Height, 8 ft. 6 in. Wing area, 198 sq. ft.

Weights: Empty, 750 lb. Loaded, 1,190 lb.

Performance: Maximum speed, 93 m.p.h. at sea level. Climb, $9\frac{1}{2}$ mins. to 6,000 ft. Endurance, $2\frac{1}{2}$ hrs. Service ceiling, 15,000 ft.

Armament: Anti-Zeppelin aircraft carried 48 Ranken darts. Some Scout Ds had one Lewis gun above centre-section.

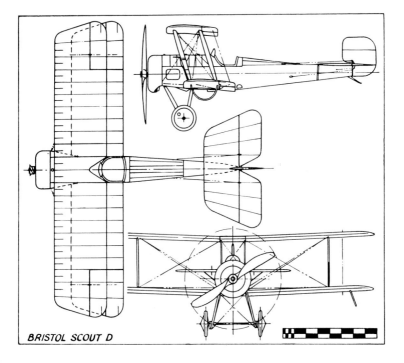

BRISTOL SCOUT D

Caudron G. IV of the R.N.A.S. (*Imp. War Museum Photo.*)

Caudron G. IV

This curious-looking aircraft was a twin-engined derivative of the earlier Caudron G. III (see Appendix), which had served with the R.N.A.S. from its very early days. One Caudron G. III (90-h.p. Gnome engine) was on the strength of the R.N.A.S. on 4 August 1914, when the total muster was 40 landplanes and 31 seaplanes. Subsequently, the type was widely used by the R.N.A.S. for pilot training both in Great Britain and in France.

Although used chiefly by the French Air Force over the Western Front and, to a more limited extent, by the R.F.C., the Caudron G. IV has a definite place in the history of the R.N.A.S. As has been recorded elsewhere, the R.N.A.S. was quick to appreciate the value of the bomber in air operations, and as early as March 1916 the Fifth Wing, specially trained for long-range bombing duties, had taken up its station at Coudekerque under the command of Sqn. Cdr. Spenser Grey. In the absence of more suitable British types, the initial equipment of this Wing was comprised of French Breguets and Caudron G. IVs. Later, the Sopwith 1½ Strutter was added. Caudron G. IVs also formed part of the equipment of No. 4 Wing, which arrived at Petite Synthe from Eastchurch under the command of Sqn. Cdr. C. L. Courtney on 11 April 1916.

The Caudrons of Nos. 4 and 5 Wings, R.N.A.S., were busily engaged during 1916 in day and night raids on German seaplane, submarine and Zeppelin bases in Belgium. On 2 August 1916 they took part in a daylight raid on the enemy aerodrome at St. Denis Westrem, near Ghent, at the request of General Trenchard. The 10 Caudrons (plus one Farman) attacked in line astern, directed by Very signals from one of the five escorting Sopwith 1½ Strutters, an early example of 'master-bomber' tactics.

The cumbersome Caudrons remained with the R.N.A.S. until the spring of 1917, when the Handley-Page O/100 made its appearance. One of their last major operations was against Bruges docks in February 1917 with No. 7 Naval Squadron.

Altogether, the R.N.A.S. took delivery of 55 Caudron G. IVs, the parent firm supplying 43, starting with No. 3289, and the British Caudron Company 12, beginning at No. 3333.

Nos. 4 and 5 Wings, R.N.A.S. (Belgium); No. 7 (Naval) Squadron.

TECHNICAL DATA (CAUDRON G. IV)

Description: Two-seat long-range day or night bomber. Wooden structure, fabric covered.

Manufacturers: Caudron Freres, Rue (Somme), Le Crotoy.

Manufacturers: Caudron Freres, Rue (Somme), Le Crotoy. Sub-contracted by the British Caudron Co.

Power Plant: Two 80-h.p. Le Rhone or two 100-h.p. Anzani.

Dimension: Span, 55 ft. 5 in. Length, 23 ft. 6 in. Height, 8 ft. 5 in. Wing area, 427½ sq. ft.

Weights: Empty, 1,870 lb. Loaded, 2,970 lb.

Performance: Maximum speed, 82 m.p.h. at 6,500 ft.; 80 m.p.h. at 10,000 ft. Climb, 33 mins. to 10,000 ft. Endurance, 4 hrs. Service ceiling, 14,000 ft.

Armament: One machine-gun mounted in front cockpit and bombs on racks beneath wings.

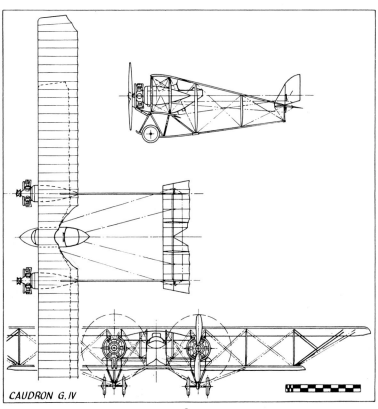

CAUDRON G. IV

Corsair II (JT 228). (*Chas. E. Brown Photo.*)

Chance Vought Corsair

The shortest possible list of truly outstanding Allied single-seat fighter aircraft in the Second World War would have to include the name of the Corsair. It ranks with such classic aircraft as the Spitfire, the Hurricane, the Mustang and the Thunderbolt. Nor is that all: the Corsair can claim one of the longest unbroken records of first-line service of any piston-engined fighter ever built. First in action early in 1943, the Corsair was progressively improved and was still giving a good account of itself during the Korean War and, even as late as 1954, in the fighting in Indo-China. With the F.A.A., the Corsair had a much briefer history, but no account of this remarkable fighter could ignore its outstanding record in wider service.

The Corsair was first conceived as early as June 1938, when design work began on the XF4U–1 for the U.S. Navy. At the time of its first flight, on 29 May 1940, it was the most powerful naval fighter ever built, with a Pratt and Whitney XR-2800-4 engine of 1,850 h.p. The choice of this engine, combined with the need to economise in stowage space for carrier operations, led to the adoption of the characteristic 'inverted-gull' wing. This feature enabled a large-diameter airscrew to be used to absorb the immense thrust, reduced the length of the undercarriage leg and allowed the outer wing panels to be folded upwards whilst still clearing the roof of the hangar below deck. Another technical innovation was the use of spot-welding in the skin covering, reducing surface friction to a minimum. Reduction in drag was further effected by the way in which the inner sections of the wing joined the cylindrical fuselage at right angles, eliminating the need for fillets.

By the time that the first production Corsair emerged in June 1942, extensive changes had been effected. The fuselage was lengthened to accommodate additional fuel, and the cockpit was moved aft to a point

level with the trailing-edge. The twin guns in the fuselage were abandoned, and instead six guns were mounted in the wings, which had previously carried only two. Finally, the new 2,100-h.p. R-2800-8 engine was
installed.

Following deck-landing trials with the U.S. Navy, it was decided to
allocate the Corsair for shore duties with the U.S. Marine Corps. Though
subsequently used aboard carriers by both the U.S. Navy and the F.A.A.,
the Corsair called for skilful handling due to the restricted forward
visibility and, for this reason, later models had the pilot's seat raised about
7 in. and a large, single-piece canopy fitted.

In U.S. service the F4U-1 Corsair made its first operation on 15
February 1943 at Guadalcanal where it equipped the Marine Corps
Squadron VMF 124. Its superiority over Japanese fighters was quickly
apparent, and by the end of 1943 the U.S.M.C. Corsairs had destroyed
the impressive total of 584 enemy aircraft.

Meanwhile, delivery of the first batch of Corsairs supplied to the F.A.A.
under Lend–Lease arrangements had begun. These were the Corsair
Mk. Is (JT 100 to JT 194), the equivalent of the F4U-4, and the Corsair
Mk. IIs (JT 195 to JT 704), the British version of the F4U-5. The first
Corsair squadron of the F.A.A. was No. 1830, which formed at Quonset,
the U.S. Navy base, on 1 June 1943. By the end of 1943 seven more
squadrons had been equipped. Based either at Quonset or Brunswick,
they worked up in the U.S.A. before being shipped to the United Kingdom in escort carriers. Corsair squadrons went on forming in this way
right through 1944 and early 1945. No less than 19 F.A.A. squadrons
received Corsairs, the last unit being No. 1853 Squadron, which formed
at Brunswick as late as 1 April 1945.

In home waters F.A.A. Corsairs first went into action when aircraft of
No. 1834 Squadron embarked in *Victorious* joined Hellcats of No. 800
Squadron (*Emperor*), Wildcats of No. 898 Squadron (*Searcher*) and Seafires
of No. 801 Squadron (*Furious*) in providing fighter cover for the memorable
attack by Fairey Barracudas on the German battleship *Tirpitz* on 3 April
1944. As related in the narrative on the Barracuda, this attack was a
resounding success, and further strikes from carriers off the Norwegian
coast took place on 17 July and on 22, 24 and 25 August 1944. In the
July attack Corsairs of No. 1841 Squadron (*Formidable*) provided the
fighter cover, and in the final strikes of August 1944 No. 1841's Corsairs
were joined by those of its sister squadron in *Formidable*, No. 1842.

These operations were the work of Corsair IIs, which differed from
the Corsair I in having certain modifications to make them suitable for
operations aboard British carriers. The improved-visibility cockpit
canopy has already been mentioned; additionally the Corsair II introduced clipped wings (of 16 in. less span) to accommodate British below-
deck hangars and undercarriages with a long-stroke oleo leg. Another
point of difference was that the Corsair I had no provision for carrying
bombs, whereas the Corsair II could mount 2,000 lb. of bombs, or additional fuel in long-range tanks up to a total of 471 gallons.

The Corsair I and II were followed in the F.A.A. by the Corsair III
(JS 469 to JS 888 and JT 963 to JT 972) and the Corsair IV (KD 161 to
KD 999, KE 100 to KE 117 and KE 310 to KE 429), making a grand
total of 2,012 Corsairs manufactured for the Royal Navy and the

R.N.Z.A.F. The Corsair III was the equivalent of the F3A-1 (Brewster-built Corsair) and, like the Corsair I, carried no bombs. The Corsair IV corresponded to the F4U-6 and carried the same bomb-load or fuel-tanks as the Corsair II.

The most important contributions of the F.A.A. Corsairs to British naval operations were against the Japanese with the East Indies and Pacific Fleets during 1944–45. On 19 April 1944, in an attack on Sabang by two Barracuda squadrons from *Illustrious*, Corsairs of Nos. 1830 and 1833 Squadrons from the same carrier provided fleet-defence patrols, and repeated these operations on 6 May 1944, when two Avenger squadrons hit Sourabaya, and, on 21 June 1944, when 15 Barracudas struck the Andaman Islands.

In the historic attack on the oil refineries at Palembang on 24 January 1945, 16 Corsairs of Nos. 1830 and 1833 Squadrons joined in the destruction of 13 Tojo fighters, and in the period 26 March to 14 April 1954 these units made nearly 400 of the 2,000 sorties flown from the four large carriers of the British Pacific Fleet. During this period of intensive flying the Corsairs carried out daily sweeps in the all-out effort to neutralise the Japanese airfields in the Sakishima Islands.

Between 17 July and 10 August 1945, Corsairs of Nos. 1834 and 1836 Squadrons (*Victorious*) and Nos. 1841 and 1842 Squadrons (*Formidable*) carried out a series of strikes in the Tokyo area, and it was during one of these operations that a Corsair pilot earned for the F.A.A. its second V.C. of the Second World War. The pilot in question was Lt. R. H. Gray, of the Royal Canadian Naval Volunteer Reserve, who on 9 August 1945 was leading a formation of No. 1841 Squadron's Corsairs in a strike on Shiogama. Lt. Gray, in spite of intense opposition from shore batteries and ships, pressed home his attack on an enemy destroyer lying in the harbour

Corsairs with long-range tanks aboard a carrier of the British East Indies Fleet in 1944. (*Imp. War Museum Photo.*)

68

Corsair II fighters of the F.A.A. in echelon formation. (*Imp. War Museum Photo.*)

of Onagawa Wan and succeeded in sinking it with a direct hit even although his own aircraft was in flames. Immediately after this gallant attack Lt. Gray lost his life as his Corsair plunged into the sea.

With the end of the war against Japan, the Corsair squadrons disbanded fairly rapidly, and by the end of 1945 only four remained. These squadrons (Nos. 1831, 1846, 1850 and 1851) stayed with the post-war F.A.A. until the following summer, the last to go being Nos. 1831 and 1851, which disbanded on 13 August 1946.

So disappeared the Corsair from the F.A.A., but, as related above, it continued in production for the U.S. Navy and Marines until 24 December 1952, by which time a grand total of 12,571 had been built. The later versions were the F4U-4B (with R-2800-18W engine and four 20-mm. guns), the F4U-5NL all-weather fighter with a radome below the starboard wing, the F4U-5N night-fighter and other specialised variants such as the AU-1 (originally F4U-6), all of which saw extensive service in Korea. The final version, the F4U-7, was exported to France and fought in Indo-China.

UNITS ALLOCATED

No. 1830 (June 1943 to July 1945; embarked *Illustrious*); No. 1831 (July 1943 to December 1943 and November 1944 to August 1946; embarked *Slinger, Pursuer, Glory* and *Vengeance*); No. 1833 (July 1943 to July 1945; embarked *Illustrious*); No. 1834 (July 1943 to October 1945; embarked *Khedive* and *Victorious*); No. 1835 (August 1943 to November 1943 and December 1944 to August 1945; embarked *Premier*); No. 1836 (August 1943 to October 1945; embarked *Atheling* and *Victorious*); No. 1837 (September 1943 to August 1945; embarked *Begum, Atheling* and *Illustrious*); No. 1838 (October 1943 to September 1944; embarked *Begum* and *Atheling*); No. 1841 (March 1944 to October 1945; embarked *Smiter, Formidable* and *Illustrious*); No. 1842 (April 1944 to October 1945; embarked *Rajah, Formidable* and *Illustrious*); No. 1843 (May 1944 to December 1945; embarked *Trouncer* and *Arbiter*); No. 1845 (June 1944 to October 1945; embarked *Puncher, Slinger, Formidable* and *Victorious*); No. 1846 (July 1944 to July 1946; embarked *Ranee* and *Colossus*); No. 1848 (July 1944 to November 1944; embarked *Ranee*); No. 1849 (August 1944 to December 1944; embarked *Reaper*); No. 1850 (August 1944 to August 1946; embarked *Reaper* and *Vengeance*); No. 1851 (September 1944 to August 1946; embarked *Thane, Venerable* and *Vengeance*); No. 1852 (February to August 1945; embarked *Patroller*) and No. 1853 (April to August 1945; embarked *Rajah*).

TECHNICAL DATA (CORSAIR I AND IV)

Description: Single-seat carrier-borne or shore-based fighter and fighter-bomber. All-metal stressed-skin construction.

Manufacturers: Chance Vought Aircraft Division, United Aircraft Corporation, Stratford, Connecticut. Other variants sub-contracted by Brewster Aeronautical Corporation and Goodyear Aircraft Corporation.

Power Plant: One Pratt & Whitney Double Wasp R-2800-8 developing 2,000 h.p. at 1,500 ft. in Mk. I and 2,250 h.p. at sea level in Mk. IV.

Dimensions: Span, 41 ft. (Mk. I): 39 ft. 8 in. (Mk. IV). Length, 33 ft. 4 in. Height, 15 ft. 1 in. Wing area, 314 sq. ft. (Mk. I): 305 sq. ft. (Mk. IV).

Weights (Mk. I): Empty, 8,800 lb. Loaded, 11,800 lb. (maximum). (Mk. IV): Empty, 9,100 lb. Loaded, 12,100 lb. (maximum).

Performance (Mk. I): Maximum speed, 374 m.p.h. at 23,000 ft. Cruising, 251 m.p.h. at 20,000 ft. Climb, 10·8 mins. to 20,000 ft. Range, 673 miles (normal) or 1,125 miles (with extra tanks). Service ceiling, 34,500 ft. (Mk. IV): Maximum speed, 415 m.p.h. at 19,500 ft. Cruising, 261 m.p.h. at 20,000 ft. Climb, 10·1 mins. to 20,000 ft. Range, 500 miles (with 2,000 lb. of bombs) or 1,562 miles (with no bombs and maximum fuel). Service ceiling, 34,000 ft.

Armament: (Mk. I): Four fixed 0·50-calibre guns in the wings. (Mk. IV): Four fixed 0·50-calibre guns in the wings and provision for two 1,000-lb. bombs beneath the centre-section.

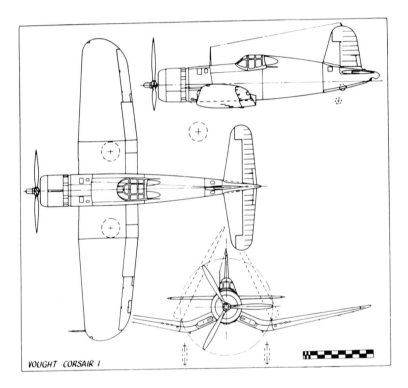

VOUGHT CORSAIR I

Curtiss H. 4 Small America (No. 3592). (*Imp. War Museum Photo.*)

Curtiss H. 4 Small America

The H. 4 was the first of the Curtiss flying-boats acquired from the U.S.A. to enter service with the R.N.A.S. The firm of Curtiss had been the first to produce a successful flying-boat, which flew on 12 January 1912, and in the following year a British agency for Curtiss boats was acquired by the White and Thompson Company of Bognor, Sussex. It was in this way that John Porte, whose name is synonymous with the development of flying-boats for the R.N.A.S. during the First World War, first came into contact with Curtiss types and soon afterwards joined the parent company in the U.S.A., for in 1913 he was the White and Thompson Companys' test pilot.

If the World War had not intervened, John Porte was to have flown the Atlantic in a flying-boat named *America*. In the event, he re-joined the R.N.A.S. as a squadron commander in August 1914 and persuaded the Admiralty to purchase two Curtiss flying-boats (Nos. 950 and 951), which were delivered in November 1914. These boats were tried out at Felixstowe air station and were followed by 62 production aircraft, eight of which (Nos. 1228 to 1235) were built in Britain. Curtiss supplied an initial batch of four (Nos. 1236 to 1239) and a second of 50 (Nos. 3545 to 3594). The entire series was given the official designation H. 4 and acquired the name Small America, retrospectively, after the introduction later of the larger H. 12, or Large America.

Despite numerous deficiencies such as poor seaworthiness, the H. 4 boats saw operational service. More important, however, was the contrition they made to the evolution of flying-boats generally as a result of the experiments they underwent at the hands of John Porte, a designer and innovator of genius. The H. 4s so employed were Nos. 950, 1230, 1231, 3545, 3546 (the 'Incidence Boat'), 3569 and 3580. Various hulls and planing bottoms were tried to improve take-off and alighting characteristics. This knowledge was put to good use in the later Curtiss and Felixstowe flying-boats.

A few H. 4 flying-boats were still in service as late as June 1918 when, it is recorded, Nos. 1232, 1233 and 1235 were at Killingholme coastal air station.

Description: Reconnaissance flying-boat with a crew of four. Wooden structure with wood and fabric covering.

Manufacturers: Curtiss Aeroplanes and Motors Corporation, Buffalo, Hammondsport, N.Y. Sub-contracted by Aircraft Manufacturing Co. in Great Britain.

Power Plant: Variously, two 90-h.p. Curtiss OX-5, two 100-h.p. Anzani or two 110-h.p. Clerget. One H. 4 (No. 1258) with two 150-h.p. Sunbeam.

Dimensions: Span, 72 ft. 0 in. Length, 36 ft. 0 in. Height, 16 ft. 0 in.

Weights: Empty, 2,992 lb. Loaded, 4,983 lb.

Performance: Not available.

Armament: Flexibly-mounted machine-gun in bows and light bombs below the wings.

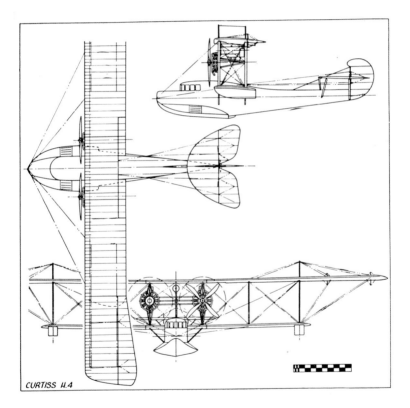

CURTISS H.4

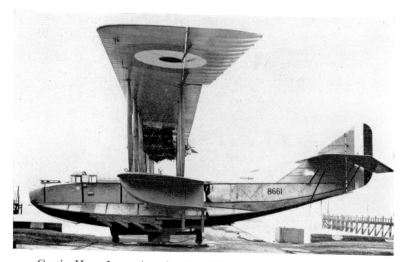

Curtiss H. 12 Large America (No. 8661). (*Imp. War Museum Photo.*)

Curtiss H. 12 Large America

The H. 12, known as the Large America, was by far the most famous of the series of Curtiss flying-boats used by the R.N.A.S. It was developed from the H. 4 Small America and was both larger and more powerful. Despite a distinguished operational record, related in detail in C. F. Snowden-Gamble's classic *The Story of a North Sea Air Station*, the H. 12 was handicapped by weakness of the hull planing bottom which made take-off hazardous in all but the calmest of seas.

The original power plant of two 160-h.p. Curtiss engines proved inadequate and was superseded by two Rolls-Royce engines. A total of 71 H. 12s reached the R.N.A.S., the first batch being Nos. 8650 to 8699 and the second N 4330 to N 4350. Great Yarmouth air station made its first H. 12 patrol with No. 8660 on 1 May 1917 and Felixstowe air station with No. 8661 on 13 April 1917, initiating the famous 'Spider-web' patrols.

In both its rôles, as an anti-submarine reconnaissance aircraft and as an anti-Zeppelin fighter, the H. 12 enjoyed outstanding successes. The first of these was on 14 May 1917, when No. 8666 from Great Yarmouth, flown by F./Lt. Galpin, shot down the airship *L. 22* about 18 miles N.N.W. of Texal Island. This was the first Zeppelin claimed by a flying-boat. The second Zeppelin to be shot down by an H. 12 was *L. 43*, which fell to Felixstowe's No. 8677, flown by F./Sub-Lt. Hobbs, on 14 June 1917.

Against U-boats the first success went to F./Sub-Lts. Morrish and Boswell, who destroyed *UC-36* on 20 May 1917, and the second to H. 12s 8662 and 8676, *UB-20* on 29 July 1917. Another victory was scored on 22 September 1917, when No. 8695 was instrumental in sinking *UC-72*. Another submarine, the *UC-6*, was claimed by F./Sub-Lts. Hobbs and Dickey on 28 September 1917.

Some of the H. 12s were modified later in their careers, and were almost indistinguishable from the F. 2A. These H. 12s were styled 'Converted Large Americas'. On 31 October 1918, when there were 18 H. 12 boats still in service, six were of the converted type.

'War Flight' of R.N.A.S., Felixstowe and 'Boat Flight' of R.N.A.S., Great Yarmouth (later No. 228 Squadron, R.A.F.). Also at R.N.A.S., Killingholme.

TECHNICAL DATA (CURTISS H. 12)

Description: Anti-submarine and anti-Zeppelin patrol flying-boat with crew of four. Wooden structure with wood and fabric covering.

Manufacturers: Curtiss Aeroplanes and Motors Corporation, Buffalo, Hammondsport, N.Y.

Power Plant: Originally two 275-h.p. Rolls-Royce Eagle I. Later two 345-h.p. Eagle VII or 375-h.p. Eagle VIII.

Dimensions: Span, 92 ft. 8½ in. Length, 46 ft. 6 in. Height, 16 ft. 6 in. Wing area, 1,216 sq. ft.

Weights: Empty, 7,293 lb. Loaded, 10,650 lb.

Performance: Maximum speed, 85 m.p.h. at 2,000 ft. Climb, 3·3 mins. to 2,000 ft.; 29·8 mins. to 10,000 ft. Endurance, 6 hrs. Service ceiling, 10,800 ft.

Armament: Up to four Lewis guns on flexible mountings and four 100-lb. or two 230 lb. bombs below the wings.

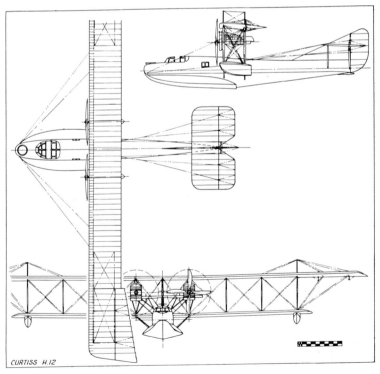

CURTISS H.12

Curtiss H. 16 Large America (No. 4060). (*Imp. War Museum Photo.*)

Curtiss H. 16 Large America

The H. 16 was an improved and enlarged version of the more famous H. 12 and was delivered to Britain in 1918. It represented a notable advance on the H. 12, in that it incorporated the stronger and more seaworthy Porte-type hull, thus bringing the American boats into line with their British counterparts, the Felixstowe series, whose design they had originally helped to inspire. The wheel had turned full circle.

The initial Admiralty contract for H. 16 flying-boats covered 15 aircraft, N 4060 to N 4074, fitted with twin 250-h.p. Rolls-Royce Eagle engines. This was followed by an additional contract for 110 aircraft, N 4890 to N 4999, but the end of the war saw the last 50 cancelled. The second batch of H. 16s mounted twin 320-h.p. Rolls-Royce Eagle engines.

H. 16 Large Americas rivalled the Felixstowe boats in performance, but they figured less in records of the period and no particularly outstanding operations are associated with the type. On 31 October 1918 there were some 69 on charge with the R.A.F., but 39 of these were in store or with contractors. At about the same time another 50 or so H. 16s were operated round British shores by the U.S. Navy. The U.S. Navy versions had twin 330-h.p. Liberty engines and were based at Killingholme. It is alleged that one of the American H. 16s at Killingholme was actually looped by an over-exuberant pilot!

UNITS ALLOCATED

H.16s served with No. 228 Squadron at Great Yarmouth, which moved to Killingholme on 1 January 1919 and disbanded on 30 June 1919.

TECHNICAL DATA (CURTISS H. 16)

Description: Anti-submarine patrol flying-boat with a crew of four. Wooden structure with wood and fabric covering.

Manufacturers: Curtiss Aeroplanes and Motors Corporation, Buffalo, Hammondsport, N.Y.

Power Plant: Two 320/345-h.p. Rolls-Royce Eagle VIII.

Dimensions: Span, 95 ft. Length, 46 ft. 1½ in. Height, 17 ft. 8 in. Wing area, 1,200 sq. ft.

Weights: Empty, 7,363 lb. Loaded, 10,670 lb.

Performance: Maximum speed, 98 m.p.h. at 2,000 ft.; 95 m.p.h. at 6,500 ft.; 92 m.p.h. at 10,000 ft. Climb, 512 ft./min.; 3·7 mins. to 2,000 ft.; 14·6 mins. to 6,500 ft.; 28 mins. to 10,000 ft. Endurance, 6 hrs. Service ceiling, 12,500 ft.

Armament: Twin Lewis machine-guns on ring mounting in bows and amidships. Provision for two further Lewis guns to fire through the side of the hull and for bombs mounted on racks beneath the wings.

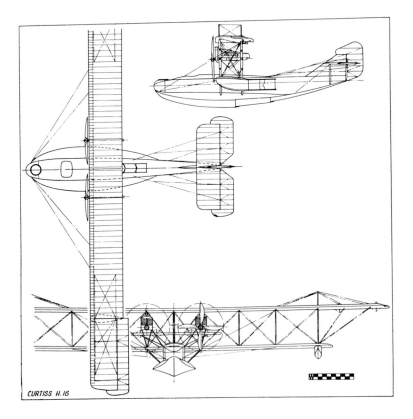

CURTISS H.16

Seamew I (FN 475) with landplane undercarriage. (*Crown Copyright Photo.*)

Curtiss Seamew

The Curtiss Seamew, as used by the F.A.A., was the British version of the SO3C-2 Seamew (originally known as the Seagull) of the U.S. Navy. The prototype (XSO3C-1) made its first flight in 1940. It was designed by Don. R. Berlin in the tradition of the U.S. Navy's medium-powered scout-observation class, convertible for land or seaplane duties, and followed the Curtiss SOC-1 Seagull biplane of 1935. In the event, the earlier biplane, like Britain's Swordfish, outlived its intended replacement, and at the end of 1944 about 70 Seagull biplanes remained with the U.S. Navy. The Seamews, on the other hand, had been withdrawn from the U.S. Navy in early 1944, apart from a few converted as target drones.

About 800 Seamews were built in 1941–2 and 250 were scheduled for delivery to Great Britain under Lend–Lease arrangements. Of these aircraft, the first 100 (FN 450 to FN 499 and FN 600 to FN 649) were certainly delivered, but it is doubtful if the remaining 150 (JW 550 to JW 699) ever reached the Royal Navy. To these Seamew Is were added a further 30 aircraft known as Queen Seamews. These were numbered JX 663 to JX 669, JZ 771 to JZ 774 and KE 286 to KE 304, and were converted for use as radio-controlled target drone aircraft to supplement the Queen Bees already in service.

Although intended chiefly for catapult launching from warships, the Seamews with the F.A.A. in fact saw no operational service, and from 1943 onwards were relegated to the training rôle. Some of them served with F.A.A. establishments in Canada and at Worthy Down in Hampshire, where they trained wireless-telegraphist/air gunners.

The narrow-track spatted undercarriage of the landplane Seamew was fitted to the float attachment, and was so far aft that a steep ground angle resulted. This, by all reports, made for difficult ground handling and landing characteristics, and did not improve the Seamew's popularity.

Nos. 744 and 745 Training Squadrons at Yarmouth, Canada and Worthy Down, Hampshire.

TECHNICAL DATA (SEAMEW I)

Description: Two-seat reconnaissance aircraft suitable for catapult launch and equipped with either land or seaplane undercarriage. All-metal stressed-skin construction.

Manufacturers: Curtiss Airplane Division of the Curtiss-Wright Corporation, Buffalo, N.Y.

Power Plant: One 520-h.p. Ranger SGV-770-6.

Dimensions: Span, 38 ft. Length (seaplane), 36 ft. 10 in.; (landplane), 34 ft. 2 in. Height, 11 ft. 5 in. Wing area, 290 sq. ft.

Weights (seaplane): Empty, 4,284 lb. Loaded, 5,729 lb. (Landplane); Empty, 4,113 lb. Loaded, 5,588 lb.

Performance (seaplane): Maximum speed, 190 m.p.h. at 7,500 ft. Cruising, 126 m.p.h. Endurance, 8 hrs.

Armament: One fixed machine-gun forward and one free-mounted machine-gun aft.

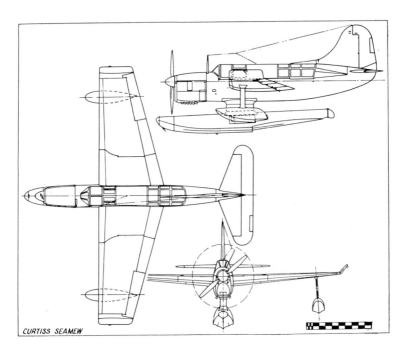

CURTISS SEAMEW

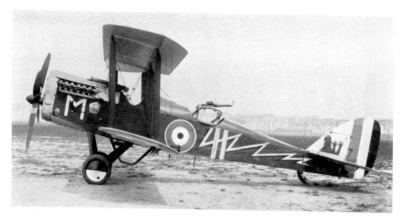

D.H. 4 (N 5997) of No. 2 (Naval) Squadron. (*Air Ministry Photo.*)

de Havilland 4

The D.H. 4 was the first British aeroplane ever designed specifically for day-bombing duties. In this rôle it excelled, and it remained to the end of the First World War one of the truly outstanding aircraft of its day.

The prototype (No. 3696) of 1916 had a B.H.P. engine, but the first production aircraft, which went to the R.F.C., were powered by the Rolls-Royce Eagle. In the R.N.A.S., D.H. 4s first saw service with squadrons in 1917, going to No. 2 (Naval) Squadron at St. Pol in March and to No. 5 (Naval) Squadron at Coudekerque at the end of April. No. 2 Squadron specialised in reconnaissance, and spotted for the guns of naval monitors. On 1 April 1918, No. 2 became No. 202 Squadron, and its D.H. 4s photographed the entire defensive system of Zeebrugge and Ostend before the Royal Navy's blocking operations of 22/23 April. Meanwhile, No. 5 Squadron's D.H. 4s had from July 1917 operated exclusively on day bombing raids, attacking naval targets as well as German Air Force bases at Ghistelles, Houtave and elsewhere.

D.H. 4s also served with distinction at R.N.A.S. coastal air stations. Great Yarmouth received its first D.H. 4 in August 1917 and a year later, on 5 August 1918, a D.H. 4 from this station, A 8032 flown by Major E. Cadbury and Capt. R. Leckie, shot down the Zeppelin *L. 70* in flames. A few days later, on 12 August 1918, four D.H. 4s of No. 217 (formerly No. 17 (Naval) Squadron) sank the submarine *U.B.-12.* In the Aegean, Naval D.H. 4s bombed the Sofia–Constantinople railway and the cruiser *Goeben.*

UNITS ALLOCATED

Nos. 2, 5, 6, 11 and 17 (Naval) Squadrons (later Nos. 202, 205, 206, 211 and 217 R.A.F.) in Belgium and Nos. 212 and 273 at R.N.A.S. coastal air stations at Port Victoria, Redcar and Great Yarmouth. 'C' Squadron at Imbros and 'D' Squadron at Stavros, No. 220 (Mudros), No. 221 (Stavros), No. 222 (Thasos), No. 223 (Mitylene, Stavros and Mudros), No. 224 (Andrano).

Description: Two-seat day bomber, reconnaissance or anti-Zeppelin patrol aircraft. Wooden structure, fabric covered.

Manufacturers: Aircraft Manufacturing Co. Ltd., Hendon, London. Subcontracted by F. W. Berwick & Co. Ltd., Westland Aircraft and Vulcan Motor & Engineering Co. Ltd.

Power Plant: Variously one 200-h.p. R.A.F. 3a; 230-h.p. B.H.P.; 250-h.p. Rolls-Royce Eagle III, 322-h.p. Eagle VI, 325-h.p. Eagle VII or 375-h.p. Eagle VIII.

Dimensions: Span, 42 ft. 4¾ in. Length, 30 ft. 8 in. Height, 10 ft. 5 in. Wing area, 434 sq. ft.

Weights (with 250-h.p. Eagle): Empty, 2,303 lb. Loaded, 3,313 lb.

Performance (with 250-h.p. Eagle): Maximum speed, 119 m.p.h. at 3,000 ft. Climb, 1 min. 5 secs. to 1,000 ft.; 46 mins. to 16,500 ft. Endurance, 3½ hrs. Service ceiling, 16,000 ft.

Armament: Twin, synchronised Vickers forward and one Lewis aft. Bomb-load: two 230-lb. or four 112-lb., or depth-charges.

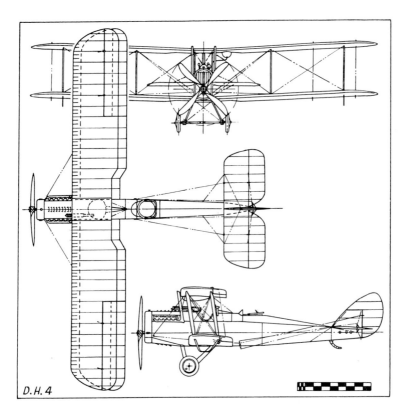

D.H.4

D.H. 6 with Curtiss OX-5 engine. (*Imp. War Museum Photo.*)

de Havilland 6

The stark, utilitarian lines of the D.H. 6 can be ascribed to the fact that it was designed for rapid and simple production in 1916 at a time when the R.F.C. was expanding and needed many more training aircraft in a hurry. Captain (now Sir Geoffrey) de Havilland achieved this purpose admirably, and over 2,200 D.H. 6s were built by the parent company and seven sub-contracting firms.

Few aeroplanes can have had so many nicknames, for the D.H. 6 was variously known as 'The Sky Hook', 'The Crab', 'The Clutching Hand', 'The Flying Coffin', The Dung-hunter' and 'The Sixty'. As a trainer, the D.H. 6 saw widespread service at home and overseas during 1917, but was gradually withdrawn with the subsequent standardisation of the Avro 504K.

By a curious turn of events, the D.H. 6's decline as a trainer witnessed its introduction in a first-line operational rôle as an anti-submarine hunter with the R.N.A.S. Early in 1918 the Admiralty asked for additional aircraft to patrol off the coast between the Tyne and the Tees, an area where U-boats were doing great damage, and the first two Flights of D.H. 6s formed at Cramlington in March. In June 1918 a further 192 D.H. 6s were made available for anti-submarine work, and 32 more Flights were established at coastal air stations, five of them operated by the U.S. Navy.

Little success was achieved by the D.H. 6s, nor could it be expected with a performance so inferior that, in order to lift a mere 100 lb. of bombs, the observer had to be discarded. Modifications such as the introduction of back-stagger and a new aerofoil section did little to improve the lack of speed, and D.H. 6s fitted with the far from reliable Curtiss OX-5 engine suffered frequent descents in the sea. Fortunately, the type floated for long periods and thus improved the chance of rescue.

On only one occasion did a D.H. 6 come near to destroying a U-boat. This was on 30 May 1918, when *UC-49* was attacked, but it crash-dived and made its escape.

Thirty-four flights allocated as follows: two flights (Cramlington); five flights (Humber to Tees); four flights (Tees to St. Abbs Head); four flights (Portsmouth Group); eight flights (South Western Group); six flights (Irish Sea) and five flights with U.S. Navy (N.E. Ireland).

TECHNICAL DATA (D.H. 6)

Description: Two-seat elementary trainer, later used for anti-submarine patrol. Wooden structure, fabric covered.

Manufacturers: Aircraft Manufacturing Co., Ltd., Hendon. Sub-contracted by Grahame-White Aviation Co.; Gloucestershire Aircraft Co.; Harland & Wolff; Kingsbury Aviation Co.; Morgan & Co.; Ransome, Sims & Jeffries and Savages Ltd.

Power Plant: One 90-h.p. R.A.F. 1a, 90-h.p. Curtiss OX-5 or 80-h.p. Renault.

Dimensions: Span, 35 ft. 11 in. Length, 27 ft. $3\frac{1}{2}$ in. Height, 10 ft. $9\frac{1}{2}$ in. Wing area, 436 sq. ft.

Weights: Empty, 1,460 lb. Loaded, 2,027 lb.

Performance: Maximum speed, 75 m.p.h. at 2,000 ft. Climb, 35 mins. to 6,500 ft. Service ceiling, 6,100 ft.

Armament: Up to 100 lb. of bombs below wings.

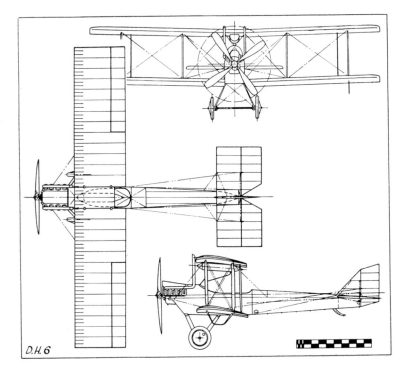

D.H.6

D.H. 9. (*Imp. War Museum Photo.*)

de Havilland 9

With the exception of the B.E. 2c, the D.H. 9 was the most severely criticised British aeroplane of the First World War. It was designed as a replacement for the D.H. 4 in day bomber squadrons, where it was intended to offer a much wider radius of action. In the event its performance fell far short of expectations, and it was actually inferior to the type it superseded. Although this fact was known before it entered service, it was decided (fantastic as it sounds) to proceed with large-scale production despite protests from commanders in the field. The inevitable results followed. Losses were high, one of the worst incidents being on 31 July 1918, when only two out of 12 D.H. 9s returned from a raid over Germany.

The fault lay not in the aeroplane but in the engine, the B.H.P., which failed to deliver its designed power of 300 h.p. and remained unreliable to the end. As a result, forced landings were common, and with full bomb-load the D.H. 9 could rarely exceed 13,000 ft., leaving it at the mercy of enemy fighters.

The prototype (A 7559) flew in July 1917 and production aircraft entered squadrons early in 1918. Although chiefly identified with the Independent Force, R.A.F., and the raids on Germany, the D.H. 9 in fact saw a good deal of service on naval work of various kinds; with R.N.A.S. bombing squadrons in Belgium before they became R.A.F. squadrons, on naval co-operation work in the Mediterranean and for anti-Zeppelin and anti-submarine patrols from coastal air stations in the United Kingdom. Some of these latter squadrons (technically R.A.F., but employed exclusively on maritime duties) retained D.H. 9s as late as July 1919, when they disbanded.

During raids on Bruges Docks with the 5th Wing, R.N.A.S., in March 1918, D.H. 9s of No. 6 Naval Squadron destroyed three cement barges, a submarine, two torpedo boats and a cargo vessel. This unit operated from Petite Snythe until transferred to the R.A.F. on 1 April 1918.

Nos. 2, 6 and 11 Naval Squadrons (later Nos. 202, 206 and 211 Squadrons, R.A.F.) in Belgium. Sea patrol: No. 212 (Great Yarmouth); No. 236 (Mullion); No. 250 (Padstow); No. 273 (Durgh Castle). Aegean: Nos. 220, 221, 222 and 223. Mediterranean: Nos, 224, 225, 226 and 227. Also No. 269 (Port Said).

TECHNICAL DATA (D.H. 9)

Description: Two-seat day bomber, also used for anti-submarine patrol. Wooden structure, fabric covered.

Manufacturers: Aircraft Manufacturing Co., Ltd., Hendon, London and fifteen sub-contractors.

Power Plant: One 230-h.p. B.H.P. or Siddeley Puma.

Dimensions: Span, 42 ft. 4$\frac{5}{8}$ in. Length, 30 ft. 6 in. Height, 11 ft. 2 in. Wing area, 434 sq. ft.

Weights: Empty, 2,203 lb. Loaded, 3,669 lb.

Performance: Maximum speed, 111$\frac{1}{2}$ m.p.h. at 10,000 ft.; 104$\frac{1}{2}$ m.p.h. at 13,000 ft. Climb, 1 min. 25 secs. to 1,000 ft.; 31 mins. 55 secs. to 13,000 ft. Endurance, 4$\frac{1}{2}$ hrs. Service ceiling, 15,500 ft.

Armament: One fixed, synchronised Vickers machine-gun forward and either single or double free-mounted Lewis aft. Bomb-load of two 230-lb. or four 112-lb. bombs.

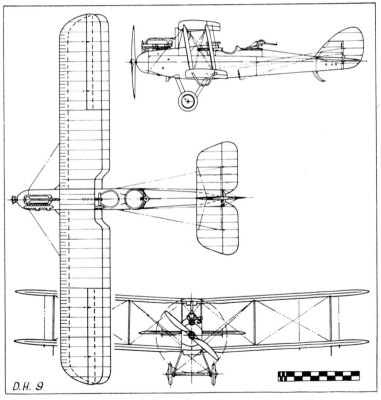

D.H. 9

Sea Mosquito T.R. 33 (TW 256) from Lee-on-Solent. (*Chas. E. Brown Photo.*)

de Havilland Sea Mosquito T.R. 33

The Sea Mosquito was evolved to meet the requirements of the Admiralty's Specification N 15/44, the first to be issued for a twin-engined aircraft capable of carrier-borne operations. The pre-prototype of the Sea Mosquito was a converted Mosquito VI (LR 359), which, fitted with an improvised arrester gear, became the first British twin-engined aircraft ever to land on the deck of an aircraft-carrier. This notable event took place aboard H.M.S. *Indefatigable* on 25 March 1944, the pilot being Lt.-Cdr. E. M. Brown, M.B.E., D.S.C. This 'navalised' Mosquito had special large-diameter (12 ft. 6 in.) four-blade airscrews which gave the Merlin 25 engines a thrust improvement of 5 to 10 per cent: folding wings were not introduced until the second conversion was made on Mosquito VI LR 387. This aircraft also had the nose radome.

Production of the Sea Mosquito, designated T. R. Mk. 33, started at de Havilland's Leavesden factory late in 1945 and the first aircraft (TW 227) flew on 10 November. The first 13 production aircraft had the original type of rubber-block suspension on the undercarriage and fixed wings. The first Sea Mosquito brought up to full Naval requirements (TW 241) incorporated folding wings and a Lockheed oleo landing leg which offered a better rebound ratio for deck flying. Two special prototypes (TS 444 and TS 449) were also built at Leavesden for handling trials at Boscombe Down. Original Admiralty contracts for 97 Sea Mosquitos were later reduced and final deliveries totalled 50.

All production Sea Mosquitos had provision for an 18-in. torpedo and for maximum range carried two 50-gallon fuel-tanks beneath the wings; alternatively two 30-gallon tanks combined with two rocket-projectiles.

Sea Mosquito T.R. 33s first entered service with No. 811 Squadron at Ford, where they superseded Mosquito VIs in August 1946. They remained with the Royal Navy for just under a year, being disbanded at Brawdy in July 1947.

The Sea Mosquito T.R. 33 was followed by the T.R. 37, small numbers of which were delivered. This type is dealt with in the Appendix.

No. 811 (R.N.A.S. Ford and Brawdy). Also No. 772 Training Squadron.

TECHNICAL DATA (SEA MOSQUITO T.R. 33)

Description: Two-seat carrier-borne, or shore-based, long-range strike aircraft. All-wooden construction.

Manufacturers: Watford Division of de Havilland Aircraft Co. Ltd., Leavesden, Herts.

Power Plant: Two 1,640-h.p. Rolls-Royce Merlin 25.

Dimensions: Span, 54 ft. 2 in. (27 ft. 3 in. folded). Length, 42 ft. 3 in. Height, 13 ft. 6 in. Wing area, 454 sq. ft.

Weights: Empty, 17,165 lb. Loaded, 22,500 lb.

Performance: Maximum speed, 385 m.p.h. at 13,500 ft. Climb, 3,000 ft./min. Range, 1,260 miles. Service ceiling, 30,000 ft.

Armament: Four British Hispano 20-mm. guns forward and provision for eight 60-lb. rocket-projectiles, four beneath each wing. One 18-in. torpedo below fuselage or 2,000 lb. of bombs comprised of two 500-lb. bombs internally in the rear bomb-bay and two 500-lb. bombs externally beneath the wings.

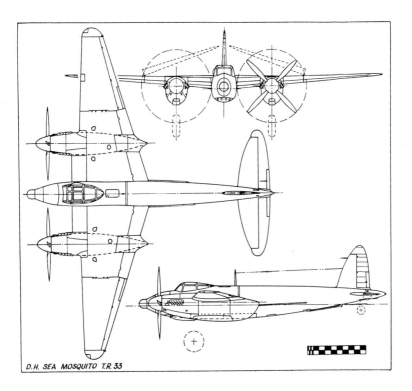

D.H. SEA MOSQUITO T.R. 33

Sea Hornet F. 20s from Hal Far, Malta. (*Official Admiralty Photo.*)

de Havilland Sea Hornet F. 20

The Sea Hornet was the F.A.A.'s version of the R.A.F.'s Hornet long-range fighter, and it became the first twin-engined single-seat fighter to be operated from aircraft-carriers of the Royal Navy. It was evolved to meet Spec. N. 5/44, and the first prototype (PX 212) made its maiden flight on 19 April 1945. This was a converted Hornet I and, like the second prototype (PX 214), did not have folding wings. The first fully navalised conversion (PX 219) was produced by Heston Aircraft Ltd. and was equipped with folding wings, arrester gear, tail-down accelerator gear and special naval radio equipments.

The first production Sea Hornet F. 20 (TT 186) flew on 13 August 1946 and early production aircraft carried out their Service trials with No. 703 Squadron at Lee-on-Solent. The first front-line unit of the F.A.A. to be equipped with Sea Hornet F. 20s was No. 801 Squadron, which had flown Seafires when disbanded after the war and which re-formed on 1 June 1947 at Ford. After a spell at Arbroath, No. 801's Sea Hornets embarked in H.M.S. *Implacable* in 1949, and the unit retained these aircraft until re-equipped with Sea Furies in 1951.

Although No. 801 Squadron was the only first-line unit equipped throughout with Sea Hornet F. 20s, the type formed the partial equipment of other units. In 1948, two Sea Hornet F. 20s joined two Sea Furies and a Vampire of No. 806 Squadron to form the composite aerobatic team which toured Canada and the U.S.A. with great success.

Total production of the Sea Hornet F. 20 amounted to 77 aircraft, the last (WE 242) being delivered on 12 June 1951. A variant of the type was the Sea Hornet P.R. 22, details of which will be found in the Appendix.

Sea Hornet F. 20s continued in service with second-line units for many years after they had left the first-line of the F.A.A., and No. 728 Fleet Requirements Unit was still using them at Hal Far, Malta, as late as 1955.

No. 801 Squadron (Ford, Arbroath, Lee-on-Solent, *Implacable* and *Indomitable*); No. 806 Squadron (two aircraft only); No. 809 Squadron (four aircraft only); No. 703 Trials Squadron; No. 728 Fleet Requirements Unit and No. 771 Fleet Requirements Unit.

TECHNICAL DATA (SEA HORNET F. 20)

Description: Single-seat medium-range carrier-borne strike fighter. Wooden fuselage and composite plywood and light alloy wing.

Manufacturers: de Havilland Aircraft Co. Ltd., Hatfield, Herts.

Power Plant: Two 2,030-h.p. Rolls-Royce Merlin 133/134.

Dimensions: Span, 45 ft. Length, 36 ft. 8 in. Height, 14 ft. 2 in. Wing area, 361 sq. ft.

Weights: Loaded, 18,250 lb.

Performance: Maximum speed, 431 m.p.h. at 10,000 ft.; 467 m.p.h. at 22,000 ft. Climb, 4,000 ft./min. Range, 1,500 miles with auxiliary tanks. Service ceiling, 35,000 ft.

Armament: Four fixed 20-mm. guns forward and provision below wings for eight 60-lb. rocket-projectiles or 2,000 lb. of bombs or two mines.

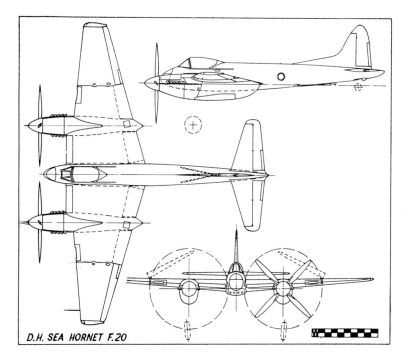

D.H. SEA HORNET F.20

Sea Hornet N.F. 21 (VW 849) of No. 809 Squadron. (*'Flight' Photo.*)

de Havilland Sea Hornet N.F. 21

The Sea Hornet N.F. 21, the only two-seat version of the Hornet, was produced to Spec. N. 21/45 and from 1949 to 1954 was the F.A.A.'s standard carrier-borne night-fighter. Its comprehensive radar equipment and the presence of a navigator also made it useful as a lead aircraft in a strike formation.

As with the single-seat Sea Hornet, the night-fighter was first produced as a conversion of a Hornet I (PX 230), the modifications being carried out by Heston Aircraft Ltd. This aircraft first flew on 9 July 1946; it had the A.S.H. scanner in the nose and flame-damping exhausts, but the folding wings and long dorsal fin fillet did not appear until the second prototype conversion (PX 239) was introduced.

Production of the Sea Hornet N.F. 21 began with VV 430 and total output reached 78, the last aircraft (VZ 699) being completed on 3 November 1950. After prolonged tests with the Naval Air Fighting Development Unit and the Service Trials Unit at Ford, the Sea Hornet N.F. 21 entered first-line service with No. 809 Squadron at Culdrose on 20 January 1949. No. 809 Squadron was re-formed specially for the Sea Hornet night-fighter and, until re-equipped with Sea Venoms in 1954, was the only first-line squadron to use the type.

Sea Hornet N.F. 21s first embarked with No. 809 Squadron in H.M.S. *Vengeance* in 1950 and formed part of the F.A.A.'s first All-Weather Air Group. The range of the N.F. 21 was well demonstrated in November 1950, when an aircraft of No. 809 Squadron flew from Gibraltar to Lee-on-Solent non-stop at an average speed of 330 m.p.h.

After their retirement from first-line duties, Sea Hornet N.F. 21s continued to serve on radar training duties with second-line squadrons for a number of years, one of the longest-lived examples being the first produc-

tion aircraft (VV 430), which remained with No. 771 Fleet Requirements
Unit at Hurn until October 1955.

No. 809 Squadron (Culdrose, Malta and Leuchars; embarked *Vengeance, Indomitable* and *Eagle*); No. 728 Squadron; No. 762 Squadron; No. 771 Squadron; No.
787 Squadron.

TECHNICAL DATA (SEA HORNET N.F. 21)

Description: Two-seat carrier-borne night-fighter and all-weather strike-
fighter. Wooden fuselage and composite plywood and light alloy
wing.
Manufacturers: de Havilland Aircraft Co. Ltd., Hatfield and Chester.
Power Plant: Two 2,030-h.p. Rolls-Royce Merlin 134/135.
Dimensions: Span, 45 ft. Length, 37 ft. Height, 14 ft. Wing area, 361
sq. ft.
Weights: Empty, 14,230 lb. Loaded, 19,530 lb.
Performance: Maximum speed, 430 m.p.h. at 22,000 ft.; 365 m.p.h. at
sea level. Climb, 4,400 ft./min. Range, 1,500 miles. Service ceiling,
36,500 ft.
Armament: Four fixed 20-mm. guns forward and provision for eight 60-lb.
rocket-projectiles or two 500-lb. or two 1,000-lb. bombs.

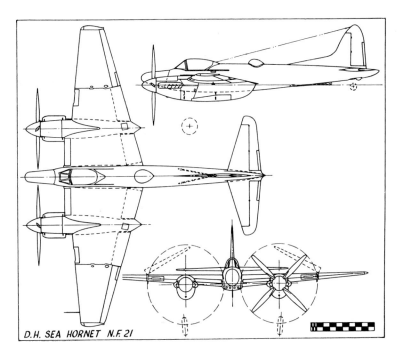

D.H. SEA HORNET N.F. 21

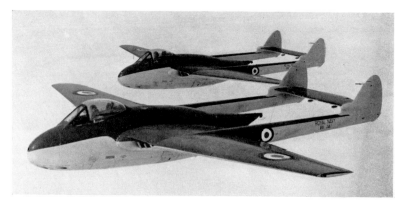

Sea Vampire F. 20s (VV 141 nearest camera). (*'Flight' Photo.*)

de Havilland Sea Vampire F. 20

The Sea Vampire has the distinction of being the first pure jet aircraft ever to operate from the deck of an aircraft-carrier. This event took place on 3 December 1945 aboard H.M.S. *Ocean*, one of the 14,000-ton light fleet carriers of the *Colossus* class. The aircraft was the converted Vampire I third prototype (LZ 551) and the pilot Lt.-Cdr. E. M. Brown, R.N.V.R. The first deck landing was followed by trials in which fifteen take-offs and landings were completed in only two days.

The production version of the Sea Vampire, the F. 20, was a navalised version of the Vampire F.B. 5, with the same clipped wings, but strengthened to take increased acceleration and landing loads, and with dive-brakes and landing-flaps enlarged. An 'A' type arrester hook was also fitted in a fairing in the tail of the nacelle, just above the jet outlet. The first production Sea Vampire F. 20 (VV 136) made its first flight in October 1948 and 18 aircraft were built, the last machine (VV 165) being delivered in June 1949. They were employed by the Royal Navy for jet familiarisation duties in second-line squadrons and first operated during 'Exercise Sunrise', when Lts. G. Baldwin, D.S.C., and K. Shepherd, of the Carrier Trials Unit, made over 200 deck landings with their Sea Vampires. A solitary Sea Vampire F. 20 participated in the Coronation Naval Review in 1953, piloted by Rear Admiral W. T. Couchman, Flag Officer, Flying Training. An experimental development of the Sea Vampire, designated F. 21, was used in the early part of 1949 aboard H.M.S. *Warrior* for deck-landing trials with undercarriage-less aircraft. For this experiment, *Warrior* had rubberised deck surfaces and the aircraft had strengthened undersides to the fuselage to permit landing with the undercarriage retracted.

The Sea Vampire single-seaters made an important contribution to the training of the F.A.A.'s first generation of jet pilots, and were followed in service by the two-seat Sea Vampire T. 22, which is described and illustrated in the Appendix.

No. 700 Squadron (Ford), No. 702 Squadron (Culdrose) and No. 787 Squadron.

TECHNICAL DATA (SEA VAMPIRE F. 20)

Description: Single-seat carrier-borne fighter-trainer. All-metal stressed-skin construction.

Manufacturers: de Havilland Aircraft Co. Ltd., Hatfield, Herts.

Power Plant: One 3,000-lb. thrust de Havilland Goblin 2.

Dimensions: Span, 38 ft. Length, 30 ft. 9 in. Height, 8 ft. 10 in. Wing area, 266 sq. ft.

Weights: Loaded, 12,660 lb.

Performance: Maximum speed, 526 m.p.h. Climb, 10 min. to 25,000 ft. Range, 590 miles at 350 m.p.h. at sea level; 1,145 miles at 350 m.p.h. at 30,000 ft. Endurance, 2 hrs. at 220 m.p.h. at sea level; 2·35 hrs. at 350 m.p.h. at 30,000 ft.

Armament: Four 20-mm. guns.

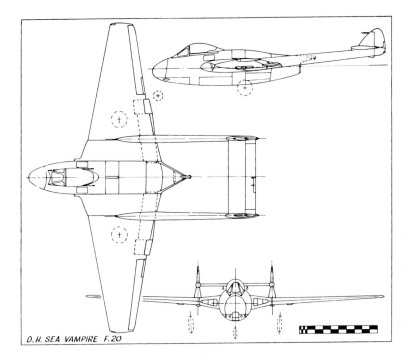

D.H. SEA VAMPIRE F.20

Sea Venom F.A.W. 21s of No. 890 Squadron. (*'Flight' Photo*.)

de Havilland Sea Venom

The Sea Venom was the Royal Navy's first jet all-weather fighter, and it succeeded the Sea Hornet N.F. 21 in carriers during 1954. It was developed initially from the R.A.F.'s Venom N.F. 2 night-fighter, the prototype of which (G-5-3) was taken over for trials by the Royal Navy as WP 227. The first true prototype (WK 376) was designated Sea Venom N.F. 20, and did its first carrier take-off during trials in *Illustrious* on 9 July 1951. Folding wings were not fitted until the third prototype (WK 385) was introduced.

With production, the designation changed to F.A.W. 20 the first of which (WM 500) flew on 27 March 1953. Fifty were built, the last aircraft (WM 567) being delivered on 6 June 1955. The F.A.W. 20 was followed in production by the F.A.W. 21, which introduced the up-rated Ghost 104, power-operated ailerons, American radar, clear-view frameless canopy and, eventually, Martin–Baker Mk. 4 ejector seats. The Mk. 21 also differed in having no tailplane extensions outboard of the tail booms. The first F.A.W. 21 (WM 568) flew on 22 April 1954 and the last (XG 680) on 6 June 1957. The final production version (beginning with XG 681) was the F.A.W. 22, which had the Ghost 104 replaced by the Ghost 105. With the delivery of the last F.A.W. 22 (XG 737), a total of 256 Sea Venoms had been built.

Sea Venom F.A.W. 20s first entered service with No. 890 Squadron, re-formed at Yeovilton on 20 March 1954; the unit converted to F.A.W. 21s before embarking in a carrier. The second Sea Venom squadron was No. 809, which from 1949 had been the F.A.A.'s only all-weather squadron with Sea Hornets. From 1955 onwards the all-weather force of Sea Venoms expanded, and by the time of the Anglo-French intervention in Egypt in October and November 1956, five squadrons were available for operations in the Eastern Mediterranean. Flying from *Albion* and *Eagle*, Sea Venoms of Nos. 809, 891, 893, 894 and 895 Squadrons co-operated

94

with R.A.F. Venoms from Cyprus in large-scale ground-attack sorties and made a notable contribution to the accurate army support operations.

UNITS ALLOCATED

Nos. 808, 809, 890, 891, 893, 894 and 895 Squadrons and No. 766 Training Squadron. Embarked in *Albion*, *Ark Royal* and *Eagle*. Also with No. 831 Squadron for airborne early warning duties.

TECHNICAL DATA (SEA VENOM F.A.W. 21)

Description: Two-seat carrier-borne all-weather fighter and strike fighter. All-metal stressed-skin construction.

Manufacturers: de Havilland Aircraft Co. Ltd., Hatfield and Chester.

Power Plant: One 4,850-lb. thrust de Havilland Ghost 104.

Dimensions: Span, 42 ft. 10 in. Length, 36 ft. 7¼ in. Height, 8 ft. 6¼ in. Wing area, 279·8 sq. ft.

Weights: Not released.

Performance: Not released.

Armament: Four fixed 20-mm. guns and provision for bombs or eight 60-lb. rocket-projectiles below the wings.

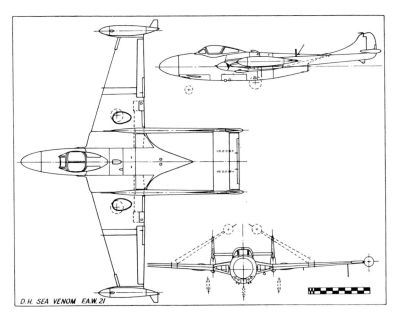

D.H. SEA VENOM F.A.W. 21

Sea Vixen F.A.W. 20 (XJ 474). (*de Havilland Photo.*)

de Havilland Sea Vixen

With the Sea Vixen, which began quantity production in 1957 to replace the Sea Venom, the F.A.A. acquired its first swept-wing two-seat all-weather fighter. The Sea Vixen was developed from the D.H. 110, which grew out of the requirements of the Naval Specifications N. 40/46 and N. 14/49, and the R.A.F.'s Specifications F. 44/46 and F. 4/48. The original two prototypes were ordered as potential R.A.F. all-weather fighters but, in the event, the rival Javelin was standardised and, thereafter, the D.H. 110 was extensively re-engineered to suit it for deck-landing use. The Royal Navy's official adoption was announced early in 1955.

The first prototype D.H. 110 (WG 236) flew on 26 September 1951 and first exceeded the speed of sound in a dive on 9 April 1952. The second prototype (WG 240) flew on 25 July 1952, and it was with this aircraft that flight trials resumed on 11 June 1954, following the grounding of the D.H. 110 after the accident in which the first prototype was destroyed at the Farnborough Air Display in 1952. Modifications included the incorporation of an 'all-flying' tailplane, a reduction in ventral fin area and an increase of wing chord outboard of the boundary layer fences.

Although not equipped with an arrester hook, WG 240 did 'touch-and-go' carrier trials from H.M.S. *Albion* in the autumn of 1954. The first fully-arrested landing-on was aboard H.M.S. *Ark Royal* on 5 April 1956, the aircraft being the semi-navalised intermediate prototype (XF 828), which was built at Christchurch and first flown on 20 June 1955. This aircraft became known as the Sea Vixen Mk. 20X, to distinguish it from the fully-navalised production Sea Vixen F.A.W. 20, the first example of which (XJ 474) flew on 20 March 1957. The Mk. 20 introduced a hydraulically steerable nosewheel, power-folding wings and a pointed nose radome, the latter hinged to starboard to go down the deck-lift. The second production Sea Vixen (XJ 475) was exhibited at the Farnborough Air Display in 1957, with four D.H. Firestreak guided missiles on pylons below the wings.

Description: Two-seat carrier-borne all-weather interceptor fighter. Naval
  Spec. N. 139. All-metal stressed-skin construction.
Manufacturers: de Havilland Aircraft Co. Ltd. (Airspeed Division), Christ-
  church, Hants., and Broughton, near Chester.
Power Plant: Two Rolls-Royce Avon Series 200.
Dimensions: Span, 50 ft. (22 ft. 3 in. folded). Length, 53 ft. 6½ in. (50 ft.
  2½ in. with nose folded). Height, 11 ft.
Weights: Not released.
Performance: Details restricted, but an unofficial maximum speed has been
  quoted of 720 m.p.h.
Armament: Four fixed 30-mm. Aden guns in fuselage and provision for four
  D.H. Firestreak guided missiles on underwing pylons, plus bombs or
  long-range tanks on two outer pylons.

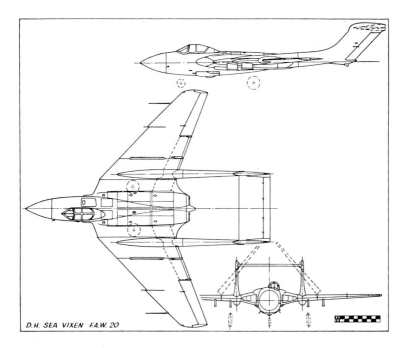

D.H. SEA VIXEN F.A.W. 20

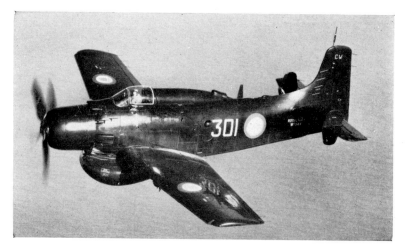

Skyraider A.E.W. 1 (WT 944) from Culdrose. (*Crown Copyright Photo.*)

Douglas Skyraider

The Skyraider, about forty of which were supplied to the Royal Navy under the Mutual Defence Assistance Programme, first reached Great Britain in November 1951, and it at once filled an important gap in British naval aviation. Its great virtue was its ability to carry nearly a ton of powerful radar equipment, complete with pilot and two radar operators, and to act as an early warning airborne radar picket. No British aircraft capable of doing this job was then available to the Royal Navy and the Skyraider thus occupied a unique position.

The technique of using early warning radar aircraft from carriers was pioneered by the U.S. Navy in the Second World War, initially in the Grumman Avenger. It extends the range of radar well beyond that of the aircraft-carrier's own installations and can protect a fleet at sea from low-flying surprise attacks, as well as providing direction for air strikes and aiding the anti-submarine force.

Characterised by its huge ventral radome, the 'Guppy' version of the Skyraider is designated AD-4W in the U.S. Navy and A.E.W. 1 in the F.A.A. It is one of many variants of the original AD-1 (initially XBT2D-1) single-seat attack aircraft which first flew in April 1945. It was originally conceived in July 1944 as a replacement for the celebrated Dauntless dive-bomber.

The Skyraiders were pioneered in British service by No. 778 Squadron at Culdrose, Cornwall, and after intensive operational training, including carrier trials in *Eagle*, were grouped into a first-line unit, No. 849 Squadron, in 1953. No. 849's Skyraiders operate with a Headquarters Flight, permanently based at Culdrose, and four operational Flights (A, B, C and D), each of four aircraft for detachment as separate units with carriers at sea.

An interesting sidelight on the Skyraider is that, pending its replacement by the Gannet A.E.W. 3, it was the last example of a piston-engined aircraft (excluding helicopters) in first-line service with the F.A.A.

UNITS ALLOCATED

No. 778 Training Squadron and No. 849 Squadron (R.N.A.S. Culdrose).

TECHNICAL DATA (SKYRAIDER A.E.W. I)

Description: Three-seat radar-equipped carrier-borne radar picket. All-metal, stressed-skin construction.
Manufacturers: Douglas Aircraft Co., Inc., El Segundo, California.
Power Plant: One 2,700-h.p. Wright Cyclone R-3350-26WA.
Dimensions: Span, 50 ft. $0\frac{1}{4}$ in. Length, 39 ft. $3\frac{3}{4}$ in. Height, 15 ft. 8 in. Wing area, 400 sq. ft.
Weights: Empty, 10,550 lb. Loaded, 25,000 lb.
Performance: Cruising speed, 250 m.p.h. Maximum range, 3,000 miles.
Armament: None carried.

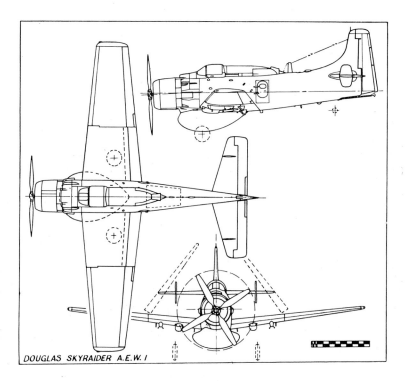

DOUGLAS SKYRAIDER A.E.W. I

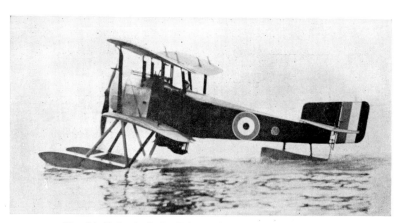

Hamble Baby built by Fairey. (*Imp. War Museum Photo.*)

Fairey Hamble Baby

Although in the first place a derivative of the Sopwith Baby, the Hamble Baby was so extensively re-designed by the Fairey Company in 1916 that it must be considered as a separate type, more particularly in view of the incorporation of the Fairey Patent Camber Gear. The introduction of this latter device was a landmark in aircraft development, for it was the first time that trailing-edge flaps, to increase wing lift, made their appearance. These flaps extended along the entire trailing-edge of each wing and were also used for normal aileron control. They remained a standard feature of Fairey naval aircraft right down to the Seal of 1932.

The original Hamble Baby was converted from a Sopwith Baby (No. 8134) and emerged with new wings, incorporating the camber gear, a new set of floats and a re-designed tail reminiscent of the Campania. This square-cut tail became something of a Fairey trademark and was to be seen for many years after the war on such types as the IIID and Flycatcher.

Fifty Hamble Baby seaplanes were built by the Fairey factory, airframes N 1320 to N 1339 having a 110-h.p., and N 1450 to N 1479 a 130-h.p., Clerget engine. By far the majority of Hamble Babies, however, were made under sub-contract by the Bristol firm of Parnall and Sons, who built 130. The Parnall aircraft could be readily distinguished by their retention of the original Sopwith-type floats and tail assembly. The first 56 Parnall-built Hamble Babies were seaplanes, N 1190 to N 1219 with 110-h.p. Clerget engines, and N 1960 to N 1985 with the 130-h.p. version, but the remainder (ending N 2059) were landplanes as illustrated in the Appendix on page 377. These were known as Hamble Baby Converts, and were extensively used for training by the R.N.A.S. school at Cranwell.

Hamble Babies gave good service with the R.N.A.S. during 1917–18 on anti-submarine patrols from coastal stations at home and overseas, as well as with seaplane carriers, and their ability to carry two 65-lb. bombs was a direct outcome of their camber-gear innovation. By the end of the war, however, they were giving way to later types and only 18 remained in service on 31 October 1918.

R.N.A.S. Stations at Calshot, Cattewater and Fishguard. Overseas with seaplane carrier *Empress* and at seaplane stations in the Aegean and in Egypt.

TECHNICAL DATA (HAMBLE BABY SEAPLANE)

Description: Single-seat anti-submarine patrol seaplane. Wooden structure, fabric covered.

Manufacturers: Fairey Aviation Co. Ltd., Hayes, Middlesex. Sub-contracted by Parnall & Sons, Bristol.

Power Plant: One 110-h.p. or 130-h.p. Clerget.

Dimensions: Span, 27 ft. 9¼ in. Length, 23 ft. 4 in. Height, 9 ft. 6 in. Wing area, 246 sq. ft.

Weights: Empty, 1,386 lb. Loaded, 1,946 lb.

Performance: Maximum speed, 90 m.p.h. at 2,000 ft. Climb, 5½ mins. to 2,000 ft.; 25 mins. to 6,500 ft. Endurance, 2 hrs. Service ceiling, 7,600 ft.

Armament: One fixed, synchronised Lewis gun forward and two 65-lb. bombs on racks below fuselage.

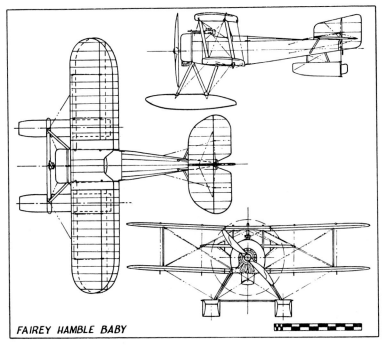

FAIREY HAMBLE BABY

F. 22 Campania seaplane. (*Photo from J. M. Bruce.*)

Fairey Campania

The Campania is important in the history of British naval aviation as the first aircraft specifically designed for operation from a carrier vessel. It was designed in 1916, when the Fairey Company was only a year old, and was that famous concern's second type of aircraft. It took its name from the fact that the carrier for which it was designed was *Campania*, a former Cunard passenger liner purchased by the Admiralty in October 1914. *Campania* was commissioned in April 1915, after being converted to carry 10 seaplanes and fitted with a 120-ft. flying-off deck above the forecastle. By the time that Fairey Campanias first operated from *Campania* in 1917, the flying-off deck had been lengthened to 200 ft. The Campanias took off with the aid of a wheeled trolley, which was left behind as the aircraft became airborne.

The prototype Campania (N 1000) had the Fairey works designation F. 16 and mounted a 250-h.p. Rolls-Royce Mk. IV engine, later named Eagle IV. With the second prototype (N 1001) a number of changes were introduced, including an improved wing section, larger fin and rudder and the more powerful 275-h.p. Rolls-Royce Mk I (later Eagle V) engine. This version had the Fairey works number F. 17 and was the first to be ordered in quantity. With Campania N 1006 a change of power-plant was necessitated by the temporary shortage of Eagles, and the Sunbeam Maori II was substituted. The Fairey works number changed to F. 22 with this modification, but in later production aircraft the Eagle was re-introduced.

Production contracts for Campanias included airframes N 2360 to N 2399 from the parent company and N 1840 to N 1889 from sub-contractors, but not all were completed. On 31 October 1918 some 42 Campanias were serving at coastal air stations and with seaplane carriers. Campanias continued to serve for a period after the Armistice, and in 1919 five were aboard the seaplane carrier *Nairana* (together with two Camels) during operations against the Bolsheviks from Archangel.

R.N.A.S. Stations at Calshot, Dundee and Portland. H.M. Seaplane Carriers *Campania*, *Nairana* and *Pegasus*.

TECHNICAL DATA (F. 22 CAMPANIA)

Description: Two-seat coastal patrol or carrier-borne reconnaissance seaplane. Wooden structure, fabric covered.

Manufacturers: Fairey Aviation Co. Ltd., Hayes, Middlesex. Sub-contracted by Barclay, Curle & Co. Ltd., of Glasgow.

Power Plant: One 250-h.p. Sunbeam Maori II or 345-h.p. Rolls-Royce Eagle VIII.

Dimensions: Span, 61 ft. 7½ in. Length, 43 ft. 0⅝ in. Height, 15 ft. 1 in. Wing area, 627 sq. ft.

Weights: Empty, 3,672 lb. (Maori) or 3,874 lb. (Eagle). Loaded, 5,329 lb. (Maori) or 5,657 lb. (Eagle).

Performance (Maori II): Maximum speed, 85 m.p.h. at sea level. Climb, 7 mins. to 2,000 ft.; 38 mins. to 6,500 ft. Endurance, 4½ hrs. Service ceiling, 6,000 ft. (Eagle VIII): Maximum speed, 80 m.p.h. at 2,000 ft. Climb, 41½ mins. to 6,500 ft. Endurance, 3 hrs. Service ceiling, 5,500 ft.

Armament: Lewis gun on Scarff ring and bombs on racks below fuselage.

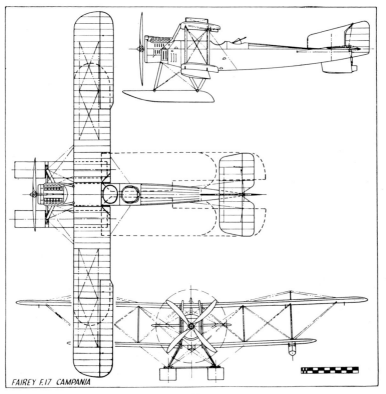

FAIREY F.17 CAMPANIA

Fairey IIIC (N 9236). (*Imp. War Museum Photo.*)

Fairey IIIC

The Fairey IIIC was a development of the IIIA and IIIB (described and illustrated in the Appendix), and was the last of the Series III to be delivered from the Fairey works before the Armistice of November 1918. In that month the first IIIC was received by Great Yarmouth air station, but it was too late to see any action in the First World War.

Generally considered to be the first general-purpose seaplane for British naval aviation, the IIIC combined the scouting rôle of the IIIA landplane with the bombing duties of the IIIB seaplane. In configuration, too, it merged the features of the two earlier types, having the equal span wings of the IIIA and the float undercarriage of the IIIB. Its advantage over both its predecessors was in the installation of the powerful Rolls-Royce Eagle VIII engine which improved the power/weight ratio by as much as 26 per cent.

The first Fairey IIIC (N 2246) left the factory in September 1918 and a total of 35 was delivered. Fairey IIICs served both at home and overseas until the autumn of 1921, when they were finally supplanted by the more famous IIID.

Despite a relatively brief Service career, the IIICs did see active service, for they equipped part of the North Russian Expeditionary Force in 1919, based at Archangel. They were taken to the scene of action in H.M.S. *Pegasus* and on 8 June 1919 made a bombing attack on four Bolshevik naval vessels, though without much effect. Later, they attacked enemy rail communications. At least seven IIICs served in Russia and it is possible that they worked with No. 266 Squadron, which is recorded as having seaplanes in action with British Forces in North Russia in 1919.

UNITS ALLOCATED

No. 229 (formerly R.N.A.S. Great Yarmouth) and No. 267 (Malta). Also with North Russian Expeditionary Force in H.M.S. *Pegasus*.

Description: Two-seat general purposes seaplane. Wooden structure, fabric covered.

Manufacturers: Fairey Aviation Co. Ltd., Hayes, Middlesex.

Power Plant: One 375-h.p. Rolls-Royce Eagle VIII.

Dimensions: Span, 46 ft. $1\frac{1}{4}$ in. Length, 36 ft. Height, 12 ft. $1\frac{3}{4}$ in. Wing area, 476 sq. ft.

Weights: Empty, 3,392 lb. Loaded, 4,800 lb.

Performance: Maximum speed, $110\frac{1}{2}$ m.p.h. at 2,000 ft., or $102\frac{1}{2}$ m.p.h. at 10,000 ft. Climb: 2 mins. 20 secs. to 2,000 ft. and 18 mins. to 10,000 ft. Endurance, $5\frac{1}{2}$ hrs. Service ceiling, 15,000 ft.

Armament: One fixed Vickers gun forward and one manually-operated Lewis gun on Scarff ring aft. Provision for light bomb-load on external racks beneath the wings.

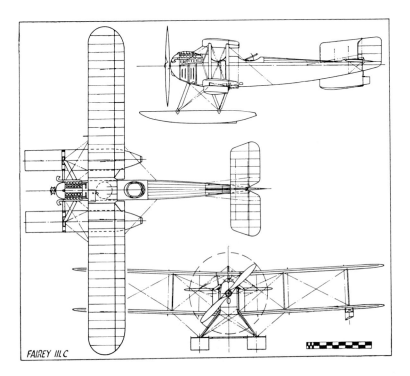

FAIREY IIIC

IIID (N 9479) with dual control at Hal Far, Malta.

Fairey IIID

From 1924 until 1930 the Fairey IIID was one of the leading types used by the F.A.A. It was developed from a proven design, the IIIC of 1918, and in due course was succeeded by the classic IIIF. It was the first of the III Series to enter service in large numbers, was strongly built and immensely reliable, and it could be flown either as a landplane from carriers or shore stations, or as a seaplane catapulted from warships.

The first IIID (N 9450) appeared as a seaplane and was powered by an Eagle VIII engine. It was flown for the first time by Col. Vincent Nicholl, at Hamble in August 1920. Production was ordered to Spec. 38/22, and all the first aircraft (N 9451 to N 9499) had Eagle engines. The second batch (N 9567 to N 9578) had Lion engines, but the Eagle was installed again in IIIDs N 9630 to N 9635. Thereafter the Lion engine was standardised, the Lion II being used in the IIIDs N 9636 to N 9641 and N 9730 to N 9791; the Lion V in S 1000 to S 1035 and S 1074 to S 1108. The last of 207 IIIDs reached the F.A.A. in 1926.

The first units equipped with the IIID were Nos. 441 and 444 Flights in 1924. No. 441 Flight used landplanes (equipped with arrester hooks on their axles) aboard H.M.S. *Argus*, which had fore-and-aft arrester wires; this technique led to accidents, and, from 1926, IIIDs were flown without arrester hooks from carrier decks. The IIIDs of No. 444 Flight aboard H.M.S. *Vindictive* were seaplanes: a IIID flown by Wg. Cdr. Burling became, on 30 October 1925, the first standard seaplane of the F.A.A. to be catapulted from a ship at sea.

No. 441 Flight had relinquished Parnall Panthers to receive IIIDs; in 1926 another Panther Flight, No. 442, followed suit. In No. 440 Flight, the Fairey IIID supplanted Seagull III amphibians in 1925.

Fairey IIIDs were particularly active in the Far East: those of H.M.S. *Pegasus* carried out an aerial survey of Malaya from Singapore, and in 1927 a special force shipped to Hong Kong in H.M.S. *Argus* went to the aid of the Shanghai Defence Force to protect British interests against rebel Chinese forces. The IIIDs flew both as landplanes from the Shanghai racecourse and as seaplanes from the Whangpoo River.

No. 440 Flight (1925–8, Calafrana, Malta and *Hermes*, China Station); No. 441 Flight (1924–9, Leuchars, Calafrana and *Argus*, China Station); No. 442 Flight (1926–30), Leuchars, *Tamar* and *Hermes*, China Station); No. 443A Flight (1925–8, Leuchars and *Furious*, Home Fleet); No. 443B Flight (Leuchars); No. 444 Flight (1924–30, Lee-on-Solent and *Vindictive*, China Station); Seaplane Training Flight, Lee-on-Solent; Spotter-Reconnaissance Training Flight, Leuchars. Also No. 481 Flight (Malta), later No. 202 Squadron, R.A.F.

TECHNICAL DATA (FAIREY IIID)

Description: Three-seat spotter-reconnaissance landplane or seaplane. Wooden structure, fabric covered.

Manufacturers: Fairey Aviation Co. Ltd., Hayes, Middlesex.

Power Plant: One 375-h.p. Rolls-Royce Eagle VIII or 450-h.p. Napier Lion IIB, V or VA.

Dimensions: Span, 46 ft. $1\frac{1}{4}$ in. Length (seaplane), 37 ft. Height (seaplane), 11 ft. 4 ins. Wing area, 474 sq. ft.

Weights (Eagle engine): Empty, 3,248 lb. Loaded, 4,918 lb.

Performance (Eagle engine): Maximum speed, 106 m.p.h. Climb, 6 mins. 40 secs. to 5,000 ft. Range, 550 miles at 100 m.p.h. Service ceiling, 17,000 ft.

Armament: One Vickers gun forward and one Lewis gun aft.

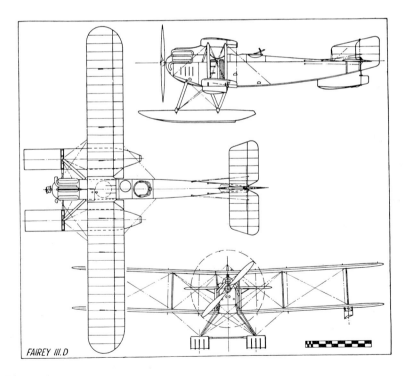

FAIREY III.D

Flycatcher I (N 9928). (*Chas. E. Brown Photo.*)

Fairey Flycatcher

No pilot who flew with the F.A.A. during the early days will ever forget the Flycatcher. This rugged little biplane made an enduring impression on all who flew it: for aerobatics it was superb, it was comfortable to fly, easy to land aboard a carrier and possessed a delightful full-throttle roar that never failed to impress spectators. Its appearance, too, was of a strongly individual character, with marked dihedral on the top wings but none on the bottom wings, a somewhat ungainly undercarriage and a fuselage which, combined with the characteristic fin and rudder, gave the impression of being 'cocked-up' at the rear end. Another feature of the Flycatcher, first seen on the Fairey Hamble Baby and shared with the Flycatcher's contemporaries, the IIID and the IIIF, was the Fairey patent camber-changing mechanism on the wings. Flaps which ran along the entire trailing-edges of both wings (the outer sections serving also as ailerons) could be lowered for landing and taking off. These flaps steepened the glide path and shortened both take-off and landing runs, both invaluable aids to deck-flying operations.

For over a decade, from 1923 to 1934, the Flycatcher was a standard first-line fighter of the F.A.A. and, indeed, from 1924 until 1932 (when the first Hawker Nimrods came into service) was the only type of Fleet fighter. Like its stable-mate, the IIIF, the Flycatcher served in all the aircraft-carriers of its day and was also used (like its forebears in the First World War) as a landplane fighter from short take-off platforms mounted on the gun-turrets of capital ships. It was the last Fleet fighter to employ this technique. The land undercarriage was readily interchangeable with twin floats, and in some Flycatchers the floats incorporated wheels which permitted amphibious operations.

The prototype Flycatcher (N 163) appeared in 1922 and was first flown by Lt.-Col. Vincent Nicholl, D.S.O., D.F.C. Following Service trials at Martlesham Heath, this aircraft went aboard H.M.S. *Argus* in February 1923 for deck trials. For this purpose two steel jaws were fitted on the undercarriage spreader bar to engage the fore and aft arrester wires then in use. This type of arrester gear remained standard on Flycatchers until the fore-and-aft wire system was abandoned about 1926. In this connection it is interesting to note that the Flycatcher was the first F.A.A. aircraft to be fitted with hydraulic wheel-brakes, which reduced the landing run to a mere 50 yds.

The Flycatcher was built to Spec. 6/22, and the first prototype, fitted with a Jaguar engine, was followed by a second (N 164) fitted as a seaplane, and a third (N 165), also with Jaguars. The first prototype was later re-engined with a Jupiter, but the Jaguar was adopted as standard in production aircraft. The third prototype (N 165) was used for trials with the amphibian type undercarriage. Although no Flycatchers had folding wings, they were built in such a way that the airframe could be dismantled so that no section exceeded 13 ft. 6 in. in length, thus aiding stowage aboard ship.

Production Flycatchers began to leave the Fairey factory in 1923, and repeated contracts kept the works busy until 1930. A total of 192 Flycatchers was delivered to the F.A.A., the last aircraft (S 1418) being flown to Gosport on 20 June 1930. The serial numbers allocated to Flycatchers were N 9611 to N 9619, N 9655 to N 9680, N 9854 to N 9895, N 9902 to N 9965, S 1060 to S 1073, S 1273 to S 1297 and S 1409 to S 1418. A number of these aircraft call for special mention. Flycatcher N 9678 was the first production amphibian, flown at Northolt on 19 February 1924 by Capt. Norman Macmillan. The second amphibian (N 9953) was flown at Hamble in October 1925. The Flycatcher seaplane N 9913 was used for catapult trials aboard H.M.S. *Vindictive* in 1925.

Flycatchers first entered service with No. 402 Flight in 1923: other standard Fleet fighters at this time were Nieuport Nightjars of No. 401

Flycatchers practise formation flying. (*Air Ministry Photo.*)

109

Flight and Parnall Plovers of Nos. 403 and 404 Flights. The rotary-engined Nightjars belonged to an essentially 1914–18 conception of the fighter, but the Plovers were radial-engined aircraft not unlike the Flycatcher in general appearance. The Plover, however, could not stand up to the competition of the Flycatcher and was soon eclipsed. In 1924 both Nightjars and Plovers gave way to the Flycatcher in Nos. 401, 403 and 404 Flights and two new units, Nos. 405 and 406 Flights, received Flycatchers as initial equipment. Other new Flycatcher flights were No. 407 in 1928, No. 408 in 1929 and No. 409 in 1932. In 1933, with the formation for the first time of squadrons in the F.A.A., No. 801 Squadron (formerly No. 401 Flight) retained Flycatchers for a time until superseded by Nimrods and Ospreys.

By 1934 Flycatchers were entirely superseded by Nimrods and Ospreys in first-line Fleet fighter squadrons, and in that year they also disappeared from catapult flights aboard warships, which received Osprey seaplanes. The last units equipped with Flycatchers were No. 403 Flight (with five aircraft), which served on the China Station with the 5th Cruiser Squadron, and No. 406 Flight (with two aircraft), operating with the East Indies Squadron. Both Flights exchanged their Flycatchers for Ospreys in June 1934.

The exploits of Flycatchers during their many years of service with the F.A.A. are well described in a most engaging book entitled *Aviation Memoirs*, by Owen Cathcart-Jones. In this book the author recalls incidents in No. 403 Flight, serving in H.M.S. *Hermes* around 1926–27, and with No. 404 Flight in H.M.S. *Courageous* during 1928. No. 403 Flight's Flycatchers were flown as seaplanes from Hong Kong harbour during operations against Chinese pirates raiding coastal shipping. Also to be found in the pages of *Aviation Memoirs* is an account of how the celebrated 'blue note' of the Flycatcher originated. Such was the strength of the Flycatcher's airframe that it could be dived vertically with engine full on until it reached its terminal velocity; in fact it was the first aircraft to be required to undertake such a test by the Air Ministry. If during the course of such a dive the engine was suddenly throttled back, the most curious sound was heard on the ground. It is alleged that a F.A.A. pilot named Aldridge became so proficient at this trick that he could control the sound effects and almost play a tune with his engine. Another explanation of the tremendous noise generated by the Flycatcher in dive-bombing attacks is that the airscrew blades fluttered when pulling out of the dive. Be that as it may, the Flycatcher was always a star turn at air displays where it gave such demonstrations, and it delighted the crowds. The Flycatcher enabled the F.A.A. to develop a tactic known as converging bombing, whereby three fighters attacked the same target from different directions simultaneously, diving steeply from an altitude of about 2,000 ft. straight at the objective. Memorable exhibitions of converging bombing were given by Flycatchers at a number of R.A.F. Hendon Displays. Nos. 405 and 443 Flights participated in 1928 and No. 405 Flight in 1929. For this type of work the Flycatcher was armed with four 20-lb. bombs with which, it was somewhat optimistically predicted by the Admiralty, they would be able to attack enemy surface units that came within range, in addition to their normal duties of repelling air attack by close patrol above the carrier or fleet.

Flycatcher amphibian. The wheels can just be seen projecting below the floats. (*Air Ministry Photo.*)

Aboard aircraft-carriers Flycatchers proved extremely amenable, and and it is recorded that on 26 November 1929 a Flycatcher from Hal Far, Malta, landed aboard H.M.S. *Courageous* at night, this being the first night-landing on a carrier deck by a Fleet fighter. Flycatcher flights prided themselves on their skilful handling aboard ship, and the record strike-down and stowage was when six aircraft were landed aboard and stowed in their hangars within 4 mins. 20 secs. Flying-off operations were no less spectacular. Aboard the carriers *Furious*, *Courageous* and *Glorious*, the fighter flights, known as 'slip-flights', were housed in a forward hangar, and the Flycatchers took off from a 60-ft. tapered runway (below the main flying-deck) straight out of their hangar and over the bows. They returned, of course, to the main deck above. Some records claim that a favourite party-piece of the Flycatchers (no doubt unauthorised) was to do a slow roll immediately after leaving the carrier, presumably in this case from the main flying-deck, as 'slip-flight' invariably dropped out of sight below the bows and almost touched the water before gaining height.

Perhaps the oddest sight the Flycatcher presented was when it operated from a land aerodrome as an amphibian. The wheels of this aircraft projected only a little way below the floats and were scarcely visible at some distance as Flycatcher amphibians taxied across the grass. This form of undercarriage was immensely strong, and the amphibians could land and take off from a ploughed field. They were less successful, however, in operating from the water, where they were allegedly reluctant to 'unstick', and the book *Aviation Memoirs* refers to training aircraft 'charging up and down the River Tay near Tayport in a vain attempt to get off the water'.

The Flycatcher was finally declared obsolete in April 1935, and with its passing an era in British deck-flying came to an end.

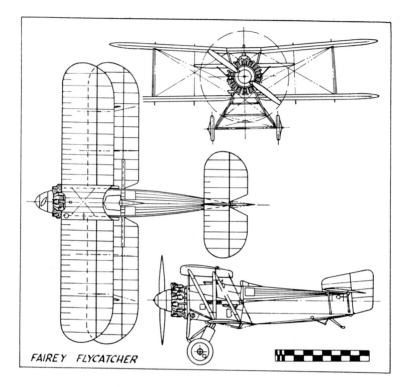

FAIREY FLYCATCHER

No. 401 Flight (1924–33; Leuchars, Hong Kong, *Argus, Courageous* and *Furious*); No. 402 Flight (1923–32; Malta, *Eagle* and *Courageous*): No. 403 Flight (1924–34; Leuchars, *Hermes* and Catapult Flight, 5th Cruiser Squadron, China); No. 404 Flight (1924–33; Leuchars, Donibristle, *Argus* and *Courageous*); No. 405 Flight (1924–33); Leuchars, *Furious* and *Glorious*); No. 406 Flight (1924–34; Leuchars, Donibristle, *Glorious* and East Indies Catapult Squadron); No. 407 Flight (1928–32; *Courageous* and *Furious*); No. 408 Flight (1929–32; Donibristle, *Glorious* and *Courageous*); No. 409 Flight (1932); No. 801 Squadron (1933–34; *Furious*); Base Training Squadrons at Leuchars and Gosport until March 1932. Also from capital ships as turret-platform fighter.

TECHNICAL DATA (FLYCATCHER I)

Description: Single-seat carrier-borne, seaplane or amphibian fighter. Wooden wings with fabric covering and composite wood and metal fuselage, metal and fabric covered.

Manufacturers: Fairey Aviation Co. Ltd., Hayes, Middlesex.

Power Plant: One 400-h.p. Armstrong Siddeley Jaguar IV.

Dimensions: Span, 29 ft. Length, 23 ft. (29 ft. as an amphibian). Height, 12 ft. (13 ft. 4 in. as an amphibian). Wing area, 288 sq. ft.

Weights: Empty, 2,039 lb. Loaded, 2,979 lb. (3,579 lb. with floats).

Performance: Maximum speed, 133 m.p.h. at 5,000 ft. (126 m.p.h. as a seaplane); 129½ m.p.h. at 10,000 ft.; 117½ m.p.h. at 15,000 ft.; 110 m.p.h. at 17,000 ft. Initial climb, 1,090 ft./min. 3 mins. 55 secs. to 5,000 ft.; 9 mins. 29 secs. to 10,000 ft.; 18 mins. 50 secs. to 15,000 ft.; 25 mins. 23 secs. to 17,000 ft. Range, 263 miles at maximum speed at 10,000 ft. (1·82 hrs); 311 miles at 110 m.p.h. at 10,000 ft. Service ceiling, 19,000 ft. (14,000 ft. as seaplane).

Armament: Twin synchronised Vickers guns. Provision for four 20-lb. bombs below wings.

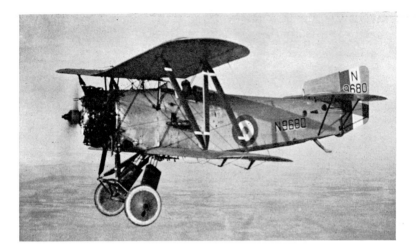

Flycatcher (N 9680) fitted with bomb-racks. (*Air Ministry Photo.*)

IIIF Mk. I (S 1189) on a flight from Leuchars. (*Air Ministry Photo*.)

Fairey IIIF

The Fairey IIIF is one of the best-remembered types of the F.A.A.'s biplane era and, indeed, a classic design in the history of British aviation. It was the last of the renowned Fairey III Series, which began in 1917, and was introduced as a successor to the Fairey IIID. Fairey IIIFs were supplied to the F.A.A. and the R.A.F. proper, and a grand total of 622 was built. Over 340 of these went to the F.A.A., making the IIIF the most widely-used aeroplane in the F.A.A. between the wars. Between 1928 and 1936, IIIFs served in every aircraft-carrier of the Royal Navy and were a familiar sight at naval air stations from Leuchars to Hong Kong. They were also widely employed as twin-float seaplanes in catapult reconnaissance flights aboard capital ships and cruisers.

The prototype IIIF (N 198) was first flown by Capt. Norman Macmillan at Northolt on 19 March 1926. It bore a strong family resemblance to the earlier IIID, but was of improved aerodynamic form with a smooth, pointed nose and a streamlined instead of slab-sided fuselage. A Fairey-Reed metal airscrew was fitted and a neat undercarriage replaced the somewhat cumbersome assembly on the IIID. It was fitted out as a three-seater, carrying a wireless-telegraphist/airgunner as well as the pilot and naval observer. All subsequent IIIFs for the F.A.A. were three-seaters, the two-seater going to the R.A.F. Composite construction was used, with metal tubular fuselage and wooden wings. One feature in which the IIIF differed from its predecessors in the III Series was its tail assembly. The traditional rectangular fin and rudder with a straight sloping line along the top was replaced by a 'stepped' outline resulting from a taller, balanced rudder. This was retained in the early production IIIFs, but was later superseded by an elongated curved fin and rudder with inset balance. The first prototype IIIF was followed by a second (N 225) and was built to Spec. 19/24.

Production of the IIIF Mk. I for the F.A.A. was preceded by an interim non-standard batch of aircraft from the end of the IIID contract, numbered S 1139 to S 1148. Of these aircraft, S 1147 became the first two-seat general-purpose type and S 1148 was allocated for deck-landing trials aboard H.M.S. *Furious* in 1927. Standard production IIIF Mk. Is (S 1168 to S 1182) were of composite construction and installed the Lion VA engine. The first production Mk. I (S 1168) was first flown at Northolt by Capt. Norman Macmillan on 18 February 1927.

On 18 August 1927, again at Northolt, Capt. Macmillan flew the first IIIF Mk. II (S 1208), fitted with the Lion XI engine. Thirty-two of these aircraft were built (S 1208 to S 1227 and S 1250 to S 1261), and they were all of composite construction.

Meanwhile, on 2 March 1927, the second IIIF (N 225) was flown as the prototype for the Mk. III. The IIIF Mk. III saw the change from composite to all-metal construction, the mainplanes having corrugated drawn-tube spars with pressed ribs clipped on. Production of the IIIF Mk. III began with S 1303, which flew on 26 March 1929. The Lion XIA was fitted, and this engine remained standard in the rest of the IIIFs built for the F.A.A. Serial numbers allocated to IIIF Mk. IIIs were S 1303 to S 1356, S 1370 to S 1408 and S 1454 to S 1463. The final batch of 10 aircraft listed were built as dual-control trainers.

The IIIF Mk. IIIM was followed by the IIIF Mk. IIIB, another all-metal variant, which had a strengthened fuselage for catapulting and a number of detail changes. The first IIIF Mk. IIIB (S 1474) was flown at Northolt by C. S. Staniland on 6 June 1930. This was the last IIIF variant for the F.A.A. which took delivery of 166. The Mk. IIIBs were allocated the serial numbers S 1474 to S 1552, S 1779 to S 1844 and S 1845 to S 1865. The final IIIF for the F.A.A. was delivered on 10 September 1932.

The Fairey IIIF first entered service with the F.A.A. in 1928, when it

IIIF Mk. II (S 1210). (*Air Ministry Photo.*)

superseded the Fairey IIID in No. 440 Flight and formed the initial equipment of Nos. 445 and 446 Flights. In 1929 IIIFs followed Avro Bisons in Nos. 447 and 448 Flights and IIIDs in No. 441 Flight. Re-equipment continued in 1931 with IIIFs in place of Blackburn Blackburns in Nos. 449 and 450 Flights, and the last remaining IIIDs were also replaced in Nos. 442 and 444 Flights. Finally, in 1932, the IIIF was issued to No. 460 Flight in place of Blackburn Ripons.

From April 1933, when F.A.A. Flights were merged, IIIFs equipped five spotter-reconnaissance squadrons. No. 820 Squadron was formed from No. 450 Flight; No. 822 Squadron from Nos. 442 and 449 Flights; No. 823 Squadron from Nos. 441 and 448 Flights; No. 824 Squadron from Nos. 440 and 460 Flights and No. 825 Squadron from Nos. 440 and 460 Flights. In 1934 the IIIF was largely supplanted by the Seal, but IIIFs remained with No. 822 Squadron in *Furious* until 1936. The IIIF Mk. III was not finally declared obsolete until January 1940.

As the IIIF was used in aircraft-carriers at a period when the arrester wire technique was out of favour it did not carry any form of arrester hook as standard, but one aircraft was used for early experiments with the rear fuselage type of deck hook later standardised on Seals, Ospreys and other biplanes of the 'thirties. This was a swinging triangular steel frame with a spring-loaded hook at the apex. This hook could be lowered by the pilot when required, and raised flush with the fuselage for normal flight. First ship trials with this IIIF took place aboard *Courageous* in 1931, the arrester wires being of the transverse type, instead of the longitudinal system used in the 'twenties when hooks on the axle were in vogue.

Earlier mention has been made of the IIIF's use as a seaplane. In this form it departed from the traditional three-float undercarriage familiar on the earlier III Series seaplanes: instead it used long twin floats providing stability both laterally and fore and aft, thus dispensing with the tail float. The IIIF Mk. IIIB, being stressed for catapult work, was issued in seaplane form for use aboard warships, and it served for several

IIIF Mk. IIIM (S 1307).

IIIF Mk. IIIB (S 1821) of No. 824 Squadron. (*'The Aeroplane' Photo.*)

IIIF Mk. IIIB (S 1502) on floats. (*Air Ministry Photo.*)

years in this rôle until superseded by the Hawker Osprey. Eight IIIF sea-planes were allocated to H.M.S. *York*, five to H.M.S. *Exeter*, two to H.M.S. *Hood* and one each to H.M.S. *Norfolk*, *Valiant* and *Dorsetshire*. IIIF seaplanes were also used from catapults on aircraft-carriers, including *Hermes* and *Glorious*. Another IIIF Mk. III (S 1317) was used for catapult launch experiments at the Royal Aircraft Establishment at Farnborough, whilst three more (including S 1536) were modified for radio-controlled pilotless aircraft experiments. These special IIIFs, known as Fairie Queens, had increased dihedral on the wings to aid stability, and had a fully automatic pilot. One of them was shipped out to Gibraltar, where it acted as a target for ships of the Home Fleet. Later it was sent to Malta and was eventually shot down by the guns of the Mediterranean Fleet.

IIIF Mk. IIIB (S 1781) with deck-arrester hook. (*Photo: A. J. Jackson.*)

Other IIIFs at Hal Far, Malta, were equipped with a windmill-driven winch and towed aerial drogues to provide the Royal Navy with gunnery practice. A similar duty for the Home Fleet was performed by target-towing IIIFs of the Base Training Squadron at Gosport. Other IIIFs at Gosport were used for the training of wireless-telegraphist/airgunners, and at Lee-on-Solent (the School of Naval Co-operation) naval observers were trained.

Although it could also be used for precision high-bombing attacks on enemy fleets (a tactic never taken very seriously by the Admiralty), the IIIF was first and foremost a spotter-reconnaissance aircraft and, with the closely-related Seal, was the last representative of this class in the F.A.A. Thereafter reconnaissance duties were combined with other work, producing the fighter-reconnaissance aircraft (such as the Osprey) and the torpedo-spotter-reconnaissance aircraft (such as the Shark and Swordfish).

UNITS ALLOCATED

No. 440 Flight (*Hermes*, China Station); No. 441 Flight (*Argus*, China Station; *Glorious*, Mediterranean Fleet); No. 442 Flight (Gosport and *Furious*, Home Fleet); No. 443 Flight (Lee-on-Solent; *Furious*, Home Fleet; Catapult Flight, West Indies and South Africa); No. 444 Flight (Lee-on-Solent and Catapult Flight, Home Fleet Capital Ships); No. 445 Flight (*Courageous*, Mediterranean and Home Fleets); No. 446 Flight (*Courageous*, Mediterranean and Home Fleets); No. 447 Flight (*Furious*, Home Fleet; *Glorious*, Mediterranean Fleet; 1st Cruiser Squadron and Capital Ships, Mediterranean Fleet); No. 448 Flight (*Eagle* and *Glorious*, Mediterranean Fleet); No. 449 Flight (*Courageous* and *Furious*, Home Fleet); No. 450 Flight (*Courageous*, Home Fleet); No. 460 Flight (*Glorious*, Mediterranean Fleet); No. 820 Squadron (*Courageous*, Home Fleet); No. 822 Squadron (*Furious*, Home Fleet); No. 823 Squadron (*Glorious*, Mediterranean Fleet); No. 824 Squadron (*Eagle*, Mediterranean Fleet); No. 825 Squadron (*Glorious*, Mediterranean Fleet).

Description: Three-seat carrier-borne or catapulted seaplane for spotter-reconnaissance duties. All-metal structure, fabric covered.
Manufacturers: Fairey Aviation Co. Ltd., Hayes, Middlesex.
Power Plant: One 570-h.p. Napier Lion XIA.
Dimensions: Span, 45 ft. 9½ in. Length, 34 ft. 4 in. (36 ft. 4 in. as seaplane).
    Height, 14 ft. 2¾ in. Wing area, 443½ sq. ft.
Weights: Empty, 3,923 lb. Loaded, 6,301 lb.
Performance: Maximum speed, 120 m.p.h. at 10,000 ft. Climb, 6·4 mins. to
    5,000 ft. Endurance, 3 to 4 hrs. Service ceiling, 20,000 ft.
Armament: One fixed Vickers gun forward and one manually-operated
    Lewis gun on Scarff ring or Fairey high-speed mounting in rear
    cockpit. Provision for up to 500 lb. of bombs below the wings.

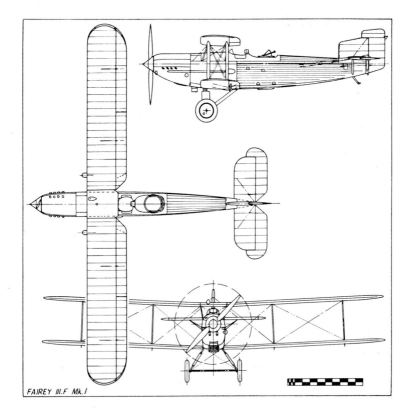

FAIREY III.F Mk.I

Seal (K 3481) of No. 820 Squadron. (*Chas. E. Brown Photo.*)

Fairey Seal

The Seal was the F.A.A. equivalent of the R.A.F.'s Gordon; both types superseded the IIIF in their respective Services. As with the prototype Gordon, the first Seal was a converted IIIF and was in fact originally known as the IIIF Mk. VI. The conversion was made to Spec. 12/29 from a IIIF Mk. IIIB (S 1325), and the first flight took place on 11 September 1930. The seaplane version (still S 1325) flew for the first time at Hamble on 29 September 1932.

Delivery of the production Seal began in 1933 and continued until March 1935. One aircraft (K 3485), from the initial batch of eleven (K 3477 to K 3487), was taken off the line for modification as the dual-control trainer prototype. Air Ministry contracts totalled 91, the remaining aircraft being K 3514 to K 3545, K 3575 to K 3579, K 4201 to K 4225 and K 4779 to K 4796.

The first F.A.A. Units to be equipped with the Seal were Nos. 820 and 821 Squadrons, both of which embarked in H.M.S. *Courageous* in 1933. No. 821 Squadron was formed from Nos. 445 and 446 Flights in April 1933, and it is possible that a few Seals may have been used before the merger took place. The next Seal squadron was No. 824, which converted from IIIFs in December 1934, followed by No. 823 Squadron in August 1935. The last to receive Seals, No. 822 Squadron, took over No. 821 Squadron's aircraft when it re-equipped with Sharks in 1936. No. 820 Squadron retained its Seals only to 1935, when it became the first Shark squadron. All other Seal squadrons had by 1938 converted to the Fairey Swordfish, but the type stayed until the outbreak of war.

As well as serving in aircraft-carriers, the Seal was also employed in catapult flights in warships as a twin-float seaplane. A notable fact about the Seal is that it was the first Fairey type to be fitted as standard with the swinging, triangular steel frame arrester hook beneath the rear fuselage, engaging transverse arrester wires. This was an improved version of the experimental type tried out on the IIIF.

No. 820 Squadron (*Courageous*); No. 821 Squadron (*Courageous*); No. 822 Squadron (*Furious*); No. 823 Squadron (*Glorious*); No. 824 Squadron (*Hermes* and *Eagle*); No. 825 Squadron; No. 702 Catapult Flight. Base Training Squadron, Gosport.

TECHNICAL DATA (SEAL)

Description: Three-seat spotter-reconnaissance carrier-borne landplane or twin-float seaplane. All-metal structure, fabric covered.

Manufacturers: Fairey Aviation Co. Ltd., Hayes, Middlesex.

Power Plant: One 525-h.p. Armstrong Siddeley Panther IIA.

Dimensions: Span, 45 ft. 9 in. Length, 33 ft. 8 in. as landplane or 35 ft. 4 in. as seaplane. Height, 12 ft. 9 in. as landplane or 14 ft. 4 in. as seaplane. Wing area, $443\frac{1}{2}$ sq. ft.

Weights: Loaded, 6,000 lb.

Performance: Maximum speed, 138 m.p.h. as landplane or 129 m.p.h. as seaplane. Climb, 5·34 mins. to 5,000 ft. Endurance, $4\frac{1}{2}$ hrs. Service ceiling, 17,000 ft. (or 13,900 ft. as seaplane).

Armament: One fixed Vickers gun forward and one Lewis gun aft.

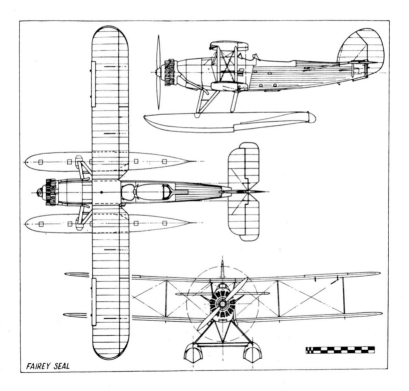

FAIREY SEAL

Swordfish I (L 9781) flies over *Ark Royal*, 1939. (*Chas. E. Brown Photo.*)

Fairey Swordfish

The name of the Swordfish will remain imperishable in the annals of the F.A.A. Few aeroplanes, with the exception of the Spitfire, ever received and deserved such universal acclaim. It was known to everybody as the 'Stringbag'; its achievements became a legend, and it earned the affection and respect of thousands of F.A.A. pilots during its decade of active service with the Royal Navy.

Perhaps the most remarkable thing about this very remarkable aeroplane was its longevity. Although by all normal standards it was already obsolescent at the outbreak of war in 1939, it confounded the prophets by remaining operationally effective until after VE-Day. Indeed, it outlasted its intended replacement, the Albacore, which disappeared from first-line naval squadrons long before the Swordfish, in November 1943. The reason for this unprecedented feat was not immediately apparent, for the Swordfish was slow and altogether antiquated in appearance. The secret lay in its magnificent handling qualities—qualities that made it uniquely suitable for deck-flying and the problems of torpedo or dive-bombing attacks. Perhaps the finest tribute to the Swordfish's flying characteristics has been paid by Terence Horsley in his book *Find, Fix and Strike*.

'You could pull a Swordfish off the deck and put her in a climbing turn at 55 knots. It would manœuvre in a vertical plane as easily as it would straight and level and even when diving from 10,000 feet the A.S.I. never rose much beyond 200 knots. The controls were not frozen rigid by the force of the slipstream and it was possible to hold the dive within 200 feet of the water. The Swordfish could be ditched safely and even its lack of speed could be turned to advantage against fighters. A steep turn at sea level towards the attacker just before he came within range and the difference in speed and small turning circle made it impossible for the fighter to bring its guns to bear for more than a few seconds. The approach to the carrier deck could be made at staggeringly slow speed, yet response to the controls remained firm and insistent. Consider what such qualities meant on a dark night when the carrier's deck was pitching the height of a house.'

Time and again the Swordfish proved its worth and fully justified the F.A.A.'s belief in the torpedo-bomber as a weapon against enemy navies. The tradition of torpedo aircraft had been kept alive since the early successes of the First World War, but it was not until the Norwegian campaign of 1940 that Swordfish, of Nos. 816 and 818 Squadrons in H.M.S. *Furious*, carried out the first, co-ordinated, torpedo attack launched from a carrier in the history of naval warfare. A few months later, at Taranto, other Swordfish brought to fruition a plan first worked out at the Admiralty in 1938, resulting in one of the most brilliant naval victories of the war.

The origins of the Swordfish dated back to 1933, when its forerunner, the Fairey T.S.R. I (S 1533), took the air for the first time at Fairey's Great West Aerodrome on 21 March. This biplane, produced as a private venture by Fairey, differed from its famous descendant in a number of details, but it already possessed what were to be the essentials of the Swordfish. It had a shorter fuselage, a fin and rudder of higher aspect ratio and, originally, a spatted undercarriage. It was flown both with a Siddeley Tiger and a Bristol Pegasus engine, driving a two-blade airscrew. After promising initial tests, the T.S.R. I was lost in an accident on 11 September 1933, the pilot escaping by parachute. It was followed by the T.S.R. II, which became the Swordfish prototype (K 4190). In this aircraft an extra bay was incorporated in the fuselage and the tail assembly was re-designed. It flew for the first time on 17 April 1934. On 10 November 1934 the twin-float seaplane conversion made its first flight at Hamble. Catapult-launching trials later took place aboard H.M.S. *Repulse*.

Following successful tests at Martlesham, the T.S.R. II was adopted by the Air Ministry and named the Swordfish. The first contract for 86 aircraft was placed in April 1935 and three more (a development batch) added in May. Successive contracts followed, and by early 1940, when Faireys handed over Swordfish production to Blackburn, to make way for Albacores at Hayes, the parent company had delivered 692 Swordfish. Peak output from Hayes was in 1937, when 201 were delivered. The first pre-production Swordfish (K 5660) was flown on 31 December 1935, and the first delivered to the Service (K 5661) reached Gosport on 19 February 1936. Serial numbers allocated to Fairey-built Swordfish were K 5660 to K 5662, K 5926 to K 6011, K 8346 to K 8449, K 8860 to K 8886, L 2717 to L 2866, L 7632 to L 7661, L 7670 to L 7701, L 9714 to L 9785 and P 3991 to P 4279.

The production Swordfish, designated Mk. I, was built to Spec. S. 38/34 (the prototype K 4190 was to Spec. S. 15/33) and mounted the 690-h.p. Pegasus IIIM. 3 engine driving a three-bladed Fairey-Reed fixed-pitch metal airscrew. Twin metal floats were readily interchangeable with the land undercarriage.

The Swordfish I was followed in production by the Mk. II, which first appeared in 1943. This variant was distinguished by a strengthened lower mainplane stressed for carrying and launching rocket-projectiles which eventually became an important part of the Swordfish's armament. Initial batches of Swordfish IIs retained the Pegasus IIIM. 3 engine, but later the Pegasus XXX was substituted. The final production version, which also appeared in 1943, was the Swordfish III, which mounted a radome containing an A.S.V. Mk. X radar scanner below the fuselage between the undercarriage legs. Also produced in small quantities, as a conversion of earlier marks, was the Swordfish IV, which had enclosed cockpits for use in Canada.

From December 1940 all Swordfish aircraft came from the Blackburn factory, which produced one in 1940, 415 in 1941, 271 in 1942, 592 in 1943 and 420 in 1944. The last of 2,391 Swordfish to be built (including the 692 by Fairey) was the Mk. III (NS 204), which was completed at Brough in December 1944.

The first F.A.A. squadron to be equipped with the Swordfish was No. 825, which received its aircraft in July 1936 in exchange for Fairey Seals. No. 825's Swordfish were embarked in H.M.S. *Glorious*, where they were still serving at the outbreak of war, protecting merchant shipping in the Indian Ocean. By the close of 1936 Swordfish had also replaced the Baffins of Nos. 811 and 812 Squadrons and the Seals of No. 823 Squadron. By 1938, when the Blackburn Sharks of Nos. 810, 820 and 821 Squadrons were superseded, the Swordfish had become the only torpedo-bomber in F.A.A. service. When the F.A.A. went to war in September 1939 it had 13 squadrons of Swordfish, forming the spearhead of its offensive force. During the war years a further 12 squadrons of Swordfish were formed, so that, from first to last, the F.A.A. had the astonishing total of 25 squadrons equipped with this veteran biplane. This figure excludes second-line squadrons and the various seaplane units for catapult operations. The last squadron to be formed with Swordfish was No. 860, which received six at Donibristle as late as 15 June 1943 for use aboard merchant aircraft carriers.

At the outbreak of war in 1939 Swordfish squadrons were embarked in five aircraft-carriers. These were: *Ark Royal* (Nos. 810, 814, 820 and 821 Squadrons), *Courageous* (Nos. 811 and 822 Squadrons), *Eagle* (Nos. 813 and 824 Squadrons), *Glorious* (Nos. 823 and 825 Squadrons) and the recently re-fitted *Furious* (Nos. 816 and 818 Squadrons). Also at sea were Swordfish spotter-reconnaissance seaplanes of Nos. 701 and 702 Catapult Flights, serving in battleships and cruisers.

The opening months of the war saw the Swordfish engaged on convoy escort and Fleet protection duties, and they saw no actual fighting until the Norwegian campaign opened in April 1940. It was during the Second Battle of Narvik, on 13 April 1940, that a catapult Swordfish in H.M.S. *Warspite* covered itself with glory during a naval battle in Ofot Fiord. This Swordfish not only spotted for the guns of *Warspite* and other vessels,

Swordfish I seaplane (L 2742) over Gibraltar. (*Chas. E. Brown Photo.*)

This Swordfish (L 7673) was still flying with the F.A.A. in 1944, six years after it first entered service in April, 1938. (*Imp. War Museum Photo.*)

A Swordfish in wartime camouflage sets off on a torpedo strike. (*Imp. War Museum Photo.*)

Swordfish II, carrying rocket-projectiles, aboard the escort-carrier *Tracker*.
(*Imp. War Museum Photo.*)

leading to the destruction of seven enemy destroyers, but itself bombed and sank an enemy submarine and finished off one of the destroyers in another bombing attack. It was piloted by P./O. F. C. Rice, and the submarine it sank, *U-64*, was the first to be destroyed by a F.A.A. aircraft in the Second World War.

The Norwegian campaign gave the F.A.A. its first chance to show its paces, and on 11 April torpedo-carrying Swordfish went into action for the first time, flying from *Furious*; later they joined Sea Gladiators in providing air cover for the military landings at Namsos, Aandalsnes and Narvik.

In May 1940 Swordfish began another type of operation for which they became famous: mine-laying and bombing of enemy-held Channel ports under the direction of R.A.F. Coastal Command. For this hazardous task they carried auxiliary fuel-tanks in the rear cockpit and operated with a crew of two. The pioneer squadron in this field was No. 812, which operated in turn from North Coates, Thorney Island, Detling and St. Eval during the period May 1940 to March 1941; targets attacked included oil-tanks at Calais and invasion barges at Rotterdam. From May to July 1940 Swordfish of No. 825 Squadron were also detached to Coastal Command, and these aircraft, flying from Detling, spotted for the bombardment of Calais by H.M.S. *Arethusa*.

With the entry of Italy into the war, Swordfish based in the Mediterranean area came into prominence. Swordfish of No. 767 Training Squadron, based in the south of France, attacked Genoa on 14 June 1940, using French bombs borrowed for the occasion. This was the first British air raid on Italy. Shortly afterwards this intrepid squadron divided up, one half going to Malta, where it became No. 830 Squadron, on 22 June 1940. On the night of 30 June/1 July it made its first operation from Malta, bombing oil-tanks at Augusta. From then onwards Malta-based Swordfish never ceased to be a thorn in the side of the enemy. Although the force never at any time exceeded 27 aircraft, it sank an average of 50,000 tons of shipping every month for nine months, the peak being 98,000 tons in one month. In 1942, joined by Albacores, the F.A.A.

torpedo force at Malta sank 30 ships in 36 night attacks, expending 67 torpedoes and losing only three aircraft.

In July 1940, after the defeat of France, Swordfish played an important part in the destruction of the French Fleet to prevent its use by the enemy. It was during these operations that Swordfish mounted the first successful air-torpedo attack against a capital ship in naval history. This was at Oran on 6 July 1940, when 12 Swordfish from Nos. 810 and 820 Squadrons aboard *Ark Royal* immobilised the battle-cruiser *Dunkerque*.

A few weeks later Swordfish were also to aid General Wavell in his first offensive against the Italians in the Western Desert: on 22 August Swordfish of No. 813 Squadron led by Captain Patch, D.S.O., D.S.C., of the Royal Marines, sank four enemy ships (including a submarine) in Bomba harbour, Libya, for the expenditure of only three torpedoes.

In November 1940 came the crowning achievement of the Swordfish's career: the epic attack on Taranto. This magnificent victory is a landmark in the history of naval air warfare, for it was the first time that aircraft had shown themselves capable of knocking out an entire enemy fleet and, unaided, altering the balance of power at sea. Taranto was indeed a suitable reward for all those whose years of work and faith in the F.A.A. had made such a triumph possible.

The attack took place on the night of 11 November 1940, when the moon was three-quarters full. Preliminary reconnaissance of Taranto harbour showed that the Italians had six battleships at anchor, as well as several cruisers and destroyers. The Swordfish, each specially fitted with long-range tanks in the rear cockpit displacing the third crew member, took off from *Illustrious*, 180 miles from the target. The first strike force, of 12 aircraft, was airborne at 8.30 p.m., and was followed by a second force of eight (later joined by a ninth aircraft) after an hour's interval. Eleven of the Swordfish carried torpedoes, six carried bombs and four were equipped with flares to illuminate the target. The first flare-droppers arrived over the target about 11 p.m. and the strike force (led by Lt.-Cdr. K. Williamson) dived to the attack through the middle of a balloon barrage. Despite intense anti-aircraft fire, they all hit the target and only one aircraft was lost. The second wave, which arrived at midnight, was equally successful and again only one Swordfish was lost. Next day, when the smoke cleared, air reconnaissance showed that the Italians had suffered a crippling blow: the three battleships *Cavour*, *Duilio* and *Italia* had all been severely damaged and two of them were under water. As well as this, the cruiser *Trento* and the destroyers *Libeccio* and *Pessango* had been hit, two auxiliary vessels sunk and seaplane hangers and oil-storage tanks knocked out. The Swordfish responsible for this holocaust had been drawn from Nos. 815 and 819 Squadrons (embarked in *Illustrious*), and Nos. 813 and 824 Squadrons from *Eagle*, temporarily embarked in *Illustrious* for the operation.

One of the Taranto squadrons, No. 815, struck again in the Battle of Cape Matapan, disabling the Italian cruiser *Pola* on 28 March 1941, and the same squadron fought gallantly in the Greek campaign until 23 April 1941. In May, flying from Cyprus, No. 815's Swordfish struck Vichy shipping and shore targets in Syria. The same month Swordfish of No. 814 Squadron assisted the R.A.F. in quelling the Iraqi rebellion, dive-bombing barracks at Samawa Nasariya. Before this they had wrought much execution among Italian shipping, whilst based at Port Sudan, in the East African campaign.

Meanwhile, out in the Atlantic, another great drama was being enacted: the hunting and destruction of the German battleship *Bismarck*. Swordfish participating in this historic engagement were from Nos. 810 and 818 Squadrons in *Ark Royal*, and Nos. 820 and 825 Squadrons in *Victorious*. The first attack on *Bismarck* was made by No. 825 Squadron, led by Lt.-Cdr. Eugene Esmonde, on 25 May, but it was not until the next day that No. 818 Squadron, led by Lt.-Cdr. T. P. Coode, succeeded in making the two torpedo hits on *Bismarck* which crippled her steering and finally enabled the Fleet to intercept and sink her with gunfire and surface torpedoes.

The name of the Swordfish will always be linked with that of the celebrated carrier *Ark Royal*, and it was one of her squadrons, No. 825, that figured in the tragic but heroic attack on the German battleships *Scharnhorst*, *Gneisenau* and *Prinz Eugen* as they escaped through the English Channel in February 1942. No. 825 Squadron had been aboard *Ark Royal* when she was sunk on 13 November 1941: all its Swordfish had been lost, but the crews survived, and it was six aircraft of the re-formed squadron, commanded by Lt.-Cdr. Esmonde, which made the disastrous sortie of 12 February 1942. Flying from Manston, Kent, the gallant little Swordfish force sighted the enemy about 10 miles off Ramsgate. From the moment they spotted the enemy's enormous fighter screen above the battleships the Swordfish crews knew that they had little chance of survival, but they never faltered in their mission. The Swordfish attacked in line astern, through devastating anti-aircraft fire. As they made their torpedo runs the enemy fighters attacked from astern. The outcome was utter disaster: every Swordfish was shot down and only five out of 18 members of the aircrews survived. All the survivors were decorated and a posthumous V.C. was awarded to Lt.-Cdr. Esmonde, then first to be won by a member of the F.A.A.

The English Channel episode was the last of the classic torpedo attacks by the Swordfish: henceforth it was to be used primarily in the anti-submarine rôle using depth-charges and later rocket-projectiles. The introduction of A.S.V. radar and the rocket-projectile—inventions

The last Swordfish to be built, the Mk. III (NS 204), leaves the Blackburn factory. (*Blackburn Photo.*)

Swordfish IV (HS 553) as used in Canada with enclosed cockpits. (*Crown Copyright Photo.*)

which sealed the fate of many a U-boat—was pioneered by Swordfish, and the new devices gave the old biplane a new lease of life for operations from the new 'flat-tops' converted from merchant-ships. The first air trials of A.S.V. radar in a Swordfish from St. Athan were a failure, but shortly afterwards, on 26 December 1939, a second experiment from Lee-on-Solent proved successful. By the end of 1941 Swordfish were taking A.S.V. radar on operations, and on the night of 21 December 1941 a Swordfish so equipped from No. 812 Squadron, based at Gibraltar, sank the first U-boat ever destroyed by an aircraft at night.

About two months previously, on 25 October 1941, the first experimental rocket-projectile (then a very secret weapon) had been fired from a Hurricane, and it fell to the lot of the Swordfish to test the suitability of this new armament for F.A.A. work. The first air test from a Swordfish took place at Thorney Island on 12 October 1942: just over seven months later, on 23 May 1943, a Swordfish of No. 819 Squadron from H.M.S. *Archer*, flown by Sub-Lt. H. Horrocks, scored the first operational success with the new weapon by sinking the submarine *U-752* about 750 miles west of Ireland. Five days later the feat was repeated by a Hudson of the R.A.F.

Swordfish had also been singularly successful against submarines during the Allied invasion of Madagascar. Using depth-charges, Swordfish of No. 829 Squadron from *Illustrious* sank the submarine *Bevezieres* on 5 May 1942 and another, *Le Heros*, on 8 May.

During the last three years of the war the Swordfish (succeeded in the big carriers by Albacores, Avengers and Barracudas) operated mainly from the smaller escort carriers, which carried both fighter and strike aircraft. They made a valuable contribution to the winning of the Battle of the Atlantic, and from August 1942 did valiant service in the escort of the North Russian convoys. In one of the Russian convoys, Swordfish embarked in the escort carriers *Vindex* and *Striker* flew 1,000 hours on

E

Swordfish with D-Day invasion stripes peel off to make a rocket strike.

anti-submarine patrol in the space of 10 days. In September 1944, *Vindex's* Swordfish sank four U-boats in a single voyage. Such feats were accomplished in the face of the most appalling weather conditions, frequently at night, and with all the arctic rigours of snow and ice on the decks. Yet, just as in earlier days, the Swordfish never failed its crews, and it is on record that an aircraft of No. 768 Training Squadron, in the escort carrier *Speaker*, completed 324 deck landings in four days without once becoming unserviceable. On another occasion Swordfish aboard the escort carrier *Nabob*, torpedoed and sinking, succeeded in flying ashore to safety even although the carrier's deck was sloping upwards towards the bows at about 20 degrees.

At the beginning of 1945, nine years after the first Swordfish had been delivered to the F.A.A., nine squadrons were still equipped with the type for first-line duties. Swordfish also served with No. 119 Squadron of the R.A.F. from bases in Belgium until VE-Day: one of them attacked a midget submarine only $3\frac{1}{2}$ hrs. before Germany's surrender! At long last, on 21 May 1945, the only remaining squadron to use the Swordfish officially in the F.A.A. was disbanded. This was No. 836 Squadron, the operational pool for all merchant aircraft carriers which, with No. 860 Squadron, had kept 19 'flat-tops' supplied with Swordfish. Another noteworthy date was 28 June 1945, when the last operational flight of a biplane in the F.A.A. was that of a Swordfish from the merchant aircraft carrier *Empire Mackay*.

So ended the fighting career of one of the greatest aircraft in the history of air warfare. A few examples of this grand old warrior remained at Royal Naval air stations for odd duties after the war and on 24 March 1953 the Swordfish NF 389 was transferred from the Torpedo Development Unit at Gosport to the Headquarters of the F.A.A. at Lee-on-Solent, where it has since been kept in flying trim and retained as a permanent exhibit. The only other Swordfish known to have survived in Great Britain are LS 326, retained by the Fairey Company under the civil registration G-AJVH, and NF 370 which is preserved in the Imperial War Museum at Lambeth.

UNITS ALLOCATED

No. 810 Squadron (equipped 1938; embarked in *Courageous, Ark Royal, Furious* and *Illustrious*); No. 811 Squadron (equipped 1936; embarked in *Furious* and then *Courageous* until latter was sunk 17 September 1939. Re-equipped with Swordfish from Chesapeakes November 1941; embarked in *Biter* and *Vindex*. Also shore-based with Coastal Command); No. 812 Squadron (equipped December 1936; embarked in *Argus, Furious* and *Ark Royal*. Also shore-based with Coastal Command); No. 813 Squadron (Formed January 1937; embarked in *Eagle, Illustrious, Campania* and *Vindex*); No. 814 Squadron (formed November 1938; embarked in *Ark Royal* and *Hermes*); No. 815 Squadron (formed October 1939; embarked in *Illustrious*); No. 816 Squadron (formed September 1939; embarked in *Furious* and *Ark Royal* until latter sunk 13 November 1941. Re-formed February 1942; embarked in *Avenger* and *Dasher* until latter blown up 27 March 1943. Re-formed again July 1943; embarked in *Tracker, Chaser* and *Activity*); No. 818 Squadron (formed September 1939; embarked in *Furious* and *Ark Royal*); No. 819 Squadron (formed January 1940; embarked in *Illustrious*. Re-formed October 1941; embarked in *Avenger, Archer* and *Activity*. Also shore-based with Coastal Command); No. 820 Squadron (equipped 1938; embarked in *Courageous, Ark Royal* and

Victorious); No. 821 Squadron (equipped 1938; embarked in *Courageous* and *Ark Royal*. No. 821X Flight embarked in *Argus*; shore-based in Malta from January 1941); No. 822 Squadron (equipped 1938; embarked in *Courageous* until latter sunk 17 September 1939. Re-formed October 1941); No. 823 Squadron (equipped 1936; embarked in *Glorious* until latter sunk 8 June 1940); No. 824 Squadron (equipped 1938; embarked in *Eagle* and *Illustrious*, then *Eagle* again until latter sunk August 1942. Re-formed March 1943; embarked in *Unicorn* and *Striker*); No. 825 Squadron (equipped July 1936; embarked in *Glorious*, *Furious*, *Victorious* and *Ark Royal* until latter sunk 13 November 1941. Re-formed early 1942; embarked in *Avenger*, *Furious*, *Vindex* and *Campania*); No. 830 Squadron (formed June 1940; shore-based in Malta); No. 833 Squadron (formed December 1941; embarked in *Biter*, *Avenger*, *Argus*, *Stalker* and *Activity*); No. 824 Squadron (formed December 1941; embarked in *Archer*, *Hunter* and *Battler*); No. 835 Squadron (formed March 1942; embarked in *Furious*, *Activity*, *Battler*, *Chaser* and *Nairana*); No. 836 Squadron (formed March 1942; embarked in *Biter*. Later became operational pool for MAC ships); No. 837 Squadron (formed May 1942; embarked in *Dasher* and *Argus*); No. 838 Squadron (formed May 1942; embarked in *Attacker*, *Rapana* and *Nairana*); No. 840 Squadron (formed June 1942; embarked in *Battler*, *Attacker* and *Empire MacAlpine*); No. 842 Squadron (formed February 1943; embarked in *Fencer*, *Indefatigable*, *Furious*, *Hunter*, *Fencer* and *Campania*); No. 860 Squadron (formed June 1943; became pool for MAC ships). Also Nos. 701, 702 and 705 Catapult Flights and No. 700 Squadron (pool for catapult aircraft from January 1940). Nos. 767 and 768 Training Squadrons; Nos. 733 and 789 Fleet Requirements Units; used in the R.A.F. by No. 119 Squadron (October 1944 to May 1945) and No. 202 Squadron (October 1940 to January 1942), the latter as floatplanes from Gibraltar. Some Swordfish were also employed pre-war

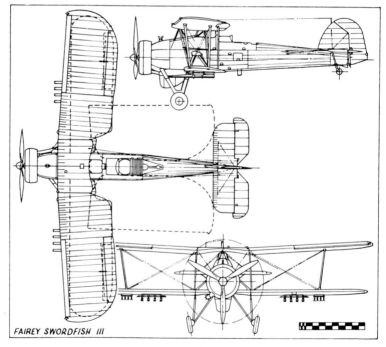

FAIREY SWORDFISH III

by the Torpedo Development Squadron at Gosport for the training of R.A.F. torpedo-bomber pilots.

Description: Carrier-based torpedo-spotter-reconnaissance aircraft, or twin-float seaplane for catapult operations aboard warships. Crew of three for reconnaissance or two for torpedo strikes. Metal structure, fabric covered.

Manufacturers: Fairey Aviation Co. Ltd., Hayes, Middlesex. Sub-contracted by Blackburn Aircraft Co. Ltd., Brough.

Power Plant: One 690-h.p. Bristol Pegasus IIIM. 3 or 750-h.p. Pegasus XXX.

Dimensions: Span, 45 ft. 6 in. (17 ft. 3 in. folded). Length, 36 ft. 4 in. (40 ft. 11 in. with floats). Height, 12 ft. 10 in. (14 ft. 7 in. on floats). Wing area, 607 sq. ft.

Weights (landplane): Empty, 5,200 lb. Loaded, 9,250 lb.

Performance: Maximum speed, 139 m.p.h. at 4,750 ft. Cruising, 104–129 m.p.h. at 5,000 ft. Climb, 10 mins. to 5,000 ft. Range, 546 miles with normal fuel and one 1,610-lb. torpedo. Maximum range for reconnaissance with no bomb-load and extra fuel (236 gal.), 1,030 miles. Service ceiling, 10,700 ft.

Armament: One fixed, synchronised Vickers gun forward and one Lewis or Vickers 'K' gun aft. Provision for one 18-in. 1,610-lb. torpedo or one 1,500-lb. mine below the fuselage or 1,500-lb. of bombs comprised of (*a*) two 500-lb. bombs below the fuselage and two 250-lb. bombs below the wings or (*b*) one 500-lb. bomb below the fuselage and two 500-lb. bombs below the wings. The Swordfish II could carry eight 60-lb. rocket-projectiles below the wings instead of torpedo or bombs.

Seafox (K 4305). (*Chas. E. Brown Photo.*)

Fairey Seafox

The Seafox was built to Spec. 11/32 as a light reconnaissance seaplane suitable for catapulting from cruisers of the Royal Navy. Though orthodox in configuration, it was unusual in providing an enclosed canopy for the observer whilst leaving the pilot in an open cockpit (this latter being necessary to facilitate catapult operations), and in combining a metal monocoque fuselage with fabric-covered wings. The prototype (K 4304) first flew at Hamble on 27 May 1936; it was followed by a second prototype (K 4305) with a land undercarriage, which flew on 5 November 1936.

Fairey's first contract for Seafoxes was received in January 1936; it was for 49 aircraft. These Seafoxes (K 8569 to K 8617) were followed by a second batch of 15 (L 4519 to L 4533), which were ordered in September 1936. All production Seafoxes, with the exception of L 4523 from the second contract, were delivered as seaplanes. The first production Seafox (K 8569) was delivered on 23 April 1937, and production did not cease until 1938.

At the outbreak of war in 1939, Seafox seaplanes were serving in a number of cruisers and formed the equipment of catapult reconnaissance flights; these flights were pooled on 21 January 1940 to form No. 700 Squadron, which had 11 Seafoxes on strength, as well as 12 Swordfish seaplanes and 42 Walrus amphibians.

The Seafox will always be associated with the Battle of the River Plate, on 13 December 1939, when the three cruisers *Ajax*, *Achilles* and *Exeter* engaged and defeated the German battleship *Admiral Graf Spee*. This was the first occasion in the Second World War in which a British naval aircraft had been employed to spot for the ships' guns in a sea battle. *Exeter's* two Walruses were both put out of action by gunfire and only one of the two Seafoxes (K 8581 and K 8582) in *Ajax* was able to get away. Flown by Lt. E. D. G. Lewin, with Lt. R. E. N. Kearney as observer, the Seafox spotted throughout the action and did reconnaissances every day until it was able to signal, at 8.54 p.m. on 17 December, that the *Graf Spee* had blown herself up. The pilot of the Seafox received the D.S.C. for his part in this action, being the first F.A.A. officer to be decorated in the Second World War.

No. 700 Squadron; Nos. 702, 713, 714, 716 and 718 Catapult Flights; Nos. 753 and 754 Training Squadrons.

TECHNICAL DATA (SEAFOX)

Description: Two-seat spotter-reconnaissance seaplane. All-metal structure with monocoque fuselage and fabric-covered wings.
Manufacturers: Fairey Aviation Co. Ltd., Hamble, Hants.
Power Plant: One 395-h.p. Napier Rapier VI.
Dimensions: Span, 40 ft. Length, 35 ft. $5\frac{1}{2}$ in. Height, 12 ft. 1 in. Wing area, 434 sq. ft.
Weights: Empty, 3,805 lb. Loaded, 5,420 lb.
Performance: Maximum speed, 124 m.p.h. at 5,860 ft. Cruising, 106 m.p.h. Climb, 10·4 mins. to 5,000 ft. Range, 440 miles. Endurance, $4\frac{1}{4}$ hrs. Service ceiling, 11,000 ft.
Armament: One Lewis gun in rear cockpit and provision for light bombs below the wings.

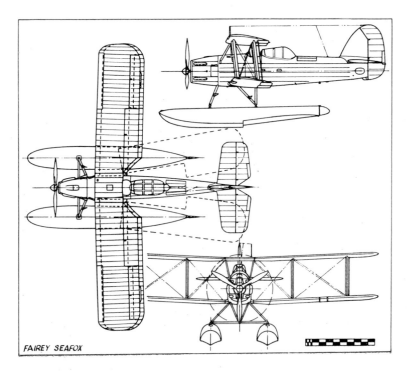

FAIREY SEAFOX

Albacore I (X 9053) of No. 820 Squadron. (*Imp. War Museum Photo.*)

Fairey Albacore

The Albacore was designed to Spec. S.41/36, which sought a replacement type for the Swordfish, but such were the qualities of the Swordfish that it outlived its intended successor. As events turned out, the Albacore merely supplemented the Swordfish and there were some F.A.A. pilots who preferred the older biplane. There is no denying, however, that the Albacore possessed many advantages, particularly in terms of crew comfort. In place of the Swordfish's draughty cockpits was a comfortable, enclosed cabin with heating circuits and such added refinements as a windscreen wiper and an automatic device to launch the dinghy without the intervention of the crew if the aircraft were to ditch. Also new was the all-metal monocoque fuselage (something of an innovation in British biplanes of the period) and the smooth-running sleeve-valve engine with its variable-pitch airscrew, which bestowed a very rapid take-off and ensured the greatest economy of fuel when cruising. Yet another advance was the introduction of hydraulic flaps to be used as air-brakes during dive-bombing.

The prototype Albacore (L 7074) was flown for the first time by C. S. Staniland at Fairey's Great West Aerodrome (now London Airport) on 12 December 1938. It was followed by a second prototype (L 7075) and production began in 1939 with L 7076, which was later flown experimentally as a floatplane. The two prototypes and 98 production aircraft had all been ordered from Faireys under an Air Ministry contract placed in May 1937. All the Albacores were built at the Hayes factory, and afterwards test-flown at Heathrow. When production finally ceased in 1943 a total of 800 had been delivered. The serial numbers allocated to production Albacores were L 7076 to L 7173, N 4152 to N 4200, N 4219 to N 4268, N 4281 to N 4330, N 4347 to N 4391, N 4420 to N 4425, T 9131 to T 9175, T 9191 to T 9215, T 9231 to T 9260, X 8940 to X 8984, X 9010 to X 9059, X 9073 to X 9117, X 9137 to X 9186, X 9214 to X 9233, X 9251 to X 9290, BF 584 to BF 618, BF 631 to BF 680, BF 695 to BF 739, and BF

758 to BF 777. Modifications to the Albacore in the course of production were remarkably few; the most notable was a change from the 1,065-h.p. Taurus II originally fitted to the 1,130-h.p. Taurus XII.

The first F.A.A. unit to be equipped with Albacores was No. 826 Squadron, which was formed specially for the new type. It received 12 Albacores at Ford, Sussex, on 15 March 1940. Albacores made their first operation with No. 826 Squadron on 31 May 1940, when they bombed road and rail communications at Westende and attacked E-boats off Zeebrugge. In June 1940 No. 826's Albacores moved to Bircham Newton, Norfolk, and they remained under Coastal Command's direction (with periods at Jersey and Detling) until November 1940. During this period they made repeated night attacks on targets from Borkum to Boulogne, laying mines and bombing shipping and harbour installations. Altogether, they made 22 night raids and dropped seven tons of mines and 56 tons of bombs. During the month of September they also escorted 57 convoys.

These shore-based operations were typical of the Albacore's operational life during 1940, and it was not until 1941 that it figured in carrier-borne actions. By the end of 1940 No. 826 had been joined by three more squadrons, all formed for Albacores: No. 829 formed in June at Lee-on-Solent, No. 828 in September at Ford and No. 827 in October at Yeovilton. No. 827's Albacores did anti-submarine patrols from Stornoway in the Hebrides; those of No. 829 Squadron carried out night attacks on Brest from bases at St. Eval and St. Merryn under the direction of Coastal Command. On 26 November 1940, Nos. 826 and 829 Squadrons became the first Albacore units aboard a carrier, embarking in H.M.S. *Formidable* to escort a convoy to Cape Town.

The first big naval action in which Albacores took part was the Battle of Cape Matapan in March 1941. During this engagement Albacore strikes by Nos. 826 and 829 Squadrons from *Formidable*, led by Lt.-Cdr. W. G. H. Saunt, D.S.C., succeeded in severely damaging the Italian battleship *Vittorio Veneto*. The Albacore pressed home their attacks with great gallantry, despite intense anti-aircraft fire and a splash barrage from the battleship's 15-in. shells. This was the first occasion on which Albacores had used their torpedoes in action, and the operation confirmed the effectiveness of this weapon, which had already been used with such striking success by Swordfish the previous November at Taranto.

In July 1941 Albacores were prominent again in the F.A.A. attack on Kirkenes and Petsamo. The object of this operation was to attack German shipping in the two harbours and to damage oil-tanks and dock installations. Albacores of Nos. 817, 822, 827 and 828 Squadrons from *Furious* and *Victorious* took part in this raid, but the element of surprise it had been hoped to achieve was lost, and casualties were very heavy.

Another phase of the Albacore's operational career was spent in Malta. From October 1941 until July 1943 No. 828 Squadron flew its Albacores from Hal Far, using mines and bombs against targets in Italy, Sicily and North Africa. On one occasion it attacked an enemy convoy, sinking one ship and damaging two others.

In March 1942 Albacores of No. 817 Squadron in *Victorious* joined in the hunt for the German battleship *Tirpitz* and made one attack with torpedoes, but without success.

By the middle of 1942 the Albacore had reached the peak of its operational career, and at this period no fewer than 15 squadrons of the F.A.A. were equipped with the type. They were engaged in a wide range of activities, both ashore and afloat. Those embarked in carriers were joining in the gruelling convoys to North Russia as well as flying anti-submarine patrols in the Mediterranean and the Indian Ocean. Ashore they were continuing their work with Coastal Command on mine-laying and anti-shipping strikes and, in the Western Desert, had adopted a new rôle of flare-dropping. Each Albacore carried 28 flares, and they did invaluable work illuminating targets for R.A.F. night bombers, as well as joining in the bombing themselves. During the two months prior to the Battle of El Alamein, Albacores dropped about 12,000 flares and laid bare most of Rommel's troop dispositions. The first Albacore squadron to join in the Western Desert fighting was No. 826, which began operations from Dekheila in July 1941. On 9 July 1942 nine Albacores of this squadron flew 250 miles behind the enemy lines, were refuelled at a secret rendezvous by Bombay transports, and flew on to deliver a night attack on an enemy convoy off Tobruk. Another Albacore squadron on Western Desert flare-dropping was No. 821, which operated during May and June 1942 and again during the Tunisian fighting from March to May 1943.

From February to March 1943 a special flight of Albacores from No. 815 Squadron was based at Dekheila to spot for the guns during Naval bombardments of ports along the North African coast. The same squadron was also active on anti-submarine patrols in the Eastern Mediterranean from bases at Nicosia and Haifa, no fewer than 17 U-boats being attacked.

During the allied invasion of North Africa in November 1942 Albacores of Nos. 817, 820, 822 and 832 Squadrons were in action. Their share of the operation was to fly anti-submarine patrols over the approaches to the landing beaches, and they also took part in bombing raids on land targets,

Albacores of Nos. 817 and 832 Squadrons aboard *Victorious*. (*Imp. War Museum Photo.*)

An Albacore lands aboard its carrier. (*Imp. War Museum Photo.*)

silencing the guns of enemy naval forts which were holding up the advance of the Commandos. One striking force of Albacores, led by Lt. J. G. A. McI. Nares, bombed La Senia airfield, destroying 47 aircraft in their hangars and at dispersals. One of the Vichy-French Dewoitine fighters that attacked them was shot down by one of the Albacore's air-gunners.

During 1943 Albacore squadrons progressively re-equipped with the Fairey Barracuda (except for No. 832, which received Grumman Avengers), and by November only two squadrons—Nos. 820 and 841—remained. No. 820 Squadron's Albacores were the last to serve in an aircraft-carrier (*Formidable*) and had taken part in the invasion of Sicily and the landing at Salerno, providing air cover at the beach-heads. No. 841 Squadron was unique in that its Albacores had spent their entire service, since July 1942, in shore-based operations under the direction of R.A.F. Fighter Command, flying chiefly from Manston. Its rôle was to attack enemy shipping in the English Channel and North Sea at night. Between 23 August 1942 and 21 November 1943 a total of 99 such attacks was made. With its disbandment in November 1943, No. 841 Squadron handed over its Albacores to No. 415 Squadron of the R.C.A.F., which continued to fly from Manston. So it came about that the Albacore, though no longer serving the F.A.A., nevertheless played a useful rôle in the D-Day operations of June 1944, preventing enemy shipping from interfering with the invasion fleets and spotting for Naval bombardments of the enemy coast.

UNITS ALLOCATED

No. 815 Squadron (August 1941 to July 1943; shore-based at Dekheila, Haifa and Nicosia); No. 817 Squadron (March 1941 to August 1943; shore-based at Crail, Hatston; embarked in *Victorious*); No. 818 Squadron (November 1941 to June 1942; embarked in *Formidable*, aircraft handed over to No. 796 Pool Squadron, E. Africa, after a brief period in Ceylon); No. 820 Squadron (June 1941 to November 1943; shore-based at Hatston and Crail; embarked in *Victorious* and *Formidable*; detachments to Algeria, Malta, Gibraltar and Alexandria); No. 821 Squadron (March 1942 to October 1943; shore-based at Dekheila, Nicosia, Hal Far, Castel Benito and Monaster); No. 822 Squadron (March 1942 to August 1943; shore-based at Crail, Donibristle, Macrihanish, Twatt, Gibraltar and Lee-on-Solent; embarked in *Furious*); No. 823 Squadron (April 1942 to June 1943; shore-based at Tangmere and Manston; embarked in *Furious*); No. 826 Squadron (March 1940 to August 1943; shore-based at Ford, Bircham Newton, Jersey, Detling, St. Merryn, Nicosia, Dekeila, Haifa, Benghazi, Blida and Hal Far; embarked in *Formidable*); No. 827 Squadron (October 1940 to August 1942; shore-based at Yeovilton, Stornoway, Thorney Island, St. Eval, Macrihanish, Hatston and Aden; embarked in *Victorious* and *Indomitable*); No. 828 Squadron (September 1940 to September 1943; shore-based at Ford, St. Merryn, Campbeltown, Hatston, Crail, Hal Far and Monaster; embarked in *Victorious*, *Argus* and *Ark Royal*); No. 829 Squadron (June 1940 to June 1941; shore-based at Lee-on-Solent, St. Eval, St. Merryn, Dekheila and Lydda; embarked in *Formidable* and *Illustrious*); No. 831 Squadron (April 1941 to May 1943; shore-based at Norfolk, U.S.A., Wingfield, Aden, Crail and Lee-on-Solent; embarked in *Indomitable*); No. 832 Squadron (April 1941 to November 1942; shore-based at Lee-on-Solent, Campbeltown, Hatston and Crail; embarked in *Victorious*); No. 841 Squadron (July 1942 to November 1943; shore-based at Lee-on-Solent, Macrihanish, Middle Wallop and Manston); No. 415 Squadron, R.C.A.F. (Manston); No. 119 Squadron, R.A.F.

TECHNICAL DATA (ALBACORE)

Description: Carrier-borne or shore-based torpedo-bomber with a crew of three. Metal monocoque fuselage and metal wings, fabric covered.

Manufacturers: Fairey Aviation Co. Ltd., Hayes, Middlesex.

Power Plant: One 1,065-h.p. Bristol Taurus II or 1,130-h.p. Bristol Taurus XII.

Dimensions: Span, 50 ft. Length, 39 ft. 9½ in. Height, 15 ft. 3 in. Wing area, 623 sq. ft.

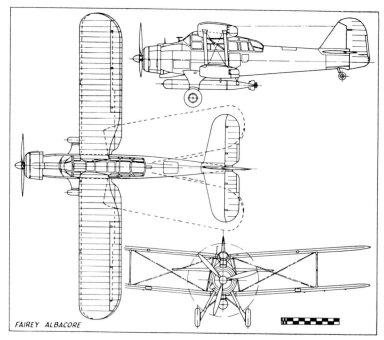

FAIREY ALBACORE

Weights: Empty, 7,200 lb. Loaded, 10,600 lb. (normal) or 12,600 lb. (maximum).

Performance: Maximum speed, 161 m.p.h. at 4,000 ft. Maximum cruising, 140 m.p.h. at 6,000 ft. Economical cruising, 116 m.p.h. at 6,000 ft. Climb, 8 mins. to 6,000 ft. Range, 930 miles with 1,610-lb. war-load or 710 miles with 2,000-lb. war-load. Service ceiling, 20,700 ft. (normal weight) or 15,000 ft. (maximum weight).

Armament: One fixed Vickers gun in starboard wing firing forward and twin Vickers 'K' guns in rear cockpit. Provision for one 18-in. 1,610-lb. torpedo beneath the fuselage or six 250-lb or four 500-lb. bombs in external racks below the wings.

Albacore I (N 4257) of the third production batch, N 4219 to N 4268.

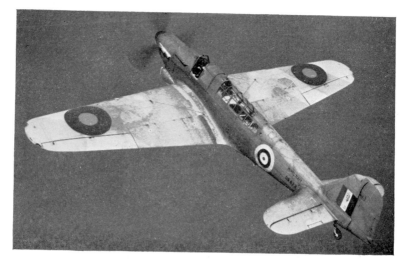

Fulmar II (DR 673). (*Crown Copyright Photo.*)

Fairey Fulmar

The Fulmar was a welcome arrival in the F.A.A., for until it entered squadron service in the summer of 1940 there were no carrier-borne fighters with the same weight of fire-power as the Hurricane and Spitfire of the R.A.F. It was the first Fairey fighter to be used by the F.A.A. since the Flycatcher had been retired in 1934, and the first with eight-gun armament. The existence of the Fulmar was kept a closely-guarded secret by the Admiralty for nine months after the prototype had flown and it was not until September 1940 that its name was first made known to the public.

The Fulmar was designed to Spec. O. 8/38 and was developed from the two P. 4/34 light bomber prototypes. The first P. 4/34 (K 5099) flew on 13 January 1937 and the second (K 7555) on 19 April 1937. The Fairey P. 4/34 was designed, like the Fulmar, by M. Lobelle and was of exceptionally clean aerodynamic form. It attained a maximum speed of 284 m.p.h. with a 1,030-h.p. Rolls-Royce Merlin II engine. The Fulmar bore a close resemblance to its forerunner, but had the 1,080-h.p. Merlin VIII engine, a non-continuous canopy, deck-arrester gear, the eight-gun armament previously mentioned, folding wings, catapult points and a dinghy. A notable point of exterior difference between the two types was that the Fulmar had a longer and more prominent radiator beneath the nose.

The prototype Fulmar (N 1854) made its first flight at Ringway on 4 January 1940, the pilot being Duncan Menzies. Production of 250 Fulmar Is followed at the Stockport factory, the serial numbers allocated to these aircraft being N 1855 to N 1893, N 1910 to N 1959, N 1980 to N 2016, N 3994 to N 4043, N 4060 to N 4100 and N 4116 to N 4147.

The second version of the Fulmar to be built was the Mk. II, which differed from its predecessor in having the 1,300-h.p. Merlin XXX engine and tropical equipment. The prototype Fulmar II was a converted Mk. I (N 4021), and it flew for the first time at Ringway on 20 January 1941. Production of 350 Fulmar II fighters ensued, the serial numbers being X 8525 to X 8574, X 8611 to X 8655, X 8680 to X 8714, X 8729 to X 8778, X 8798 to X 8817, BP 775 to BP 796, BP 812 to BP 839, DR 633 to DR 682 and DR 700 to DR 749. The last of 602 Fulmars (DR 749) was delivered to the F.A.A. in February 1943.

Fulmars first entered service with the F.A.A. in June 1940, going to No. 808 Squadron, stationed at Worthy Down. This squadron later embarked in *Ark Royal* and took part in some of the Mediterranean convoys taking supplies to Malta. In July 1940 No. 806 Squadron at Eastleigh took delivery of 12 Fulmars in place of its eight Skuas and four Rocs, and a third squadron (No. 807) formed at Worthy Down in September 1940. The year 1941 saw five more Fulmar squadrons formed. No. 809 Squadron took delivery at St. Merryn in January; No. 804 Squadron exchanged its Martlets for Fulmars and Sea Hurricanes in February; No. 800 Squadron converted from Skuas in April and No. 884 Squadron formed at Donibristle in November. No. 805 Squadron, formed on 1 January 1941 at Dekheila, Egypt, was the first Fulmar squadron to serve from a F.A.A. shore station overseas.

In 1942 the Fulmar went to six more squadrons (Nos. 803, 879, 886, 887, 889 and 893) and had reached the peak of its operational career. By 1943 it was being steadily superseded by the much faster Seafire, though a few remained with squadrons after this date. The last operational squadron with Fulmars was No. 813, which used a night-fighter version until its disbandment at Macrihanish on 1 March 1945. No. 813 Squadron received its first Fulmar night fighters in April 1944: they were taken over from No. 784 Training Squadron at Drem, which had pioneered F.A.A. night-fighter tactics with Fulmars.

Operationally, the Fulmar first saw action against the Italian Air Force during its defence of Malta convoys with Nos. 806, 807 and 808 Squadrons in the period September–October 1940. Fulmars of No. 806 Squadron, embarked in *Illustrious*, shot down 10 Italian bombers between 2 September and 14 October 1940, and in November, whilst giving fighter cover to

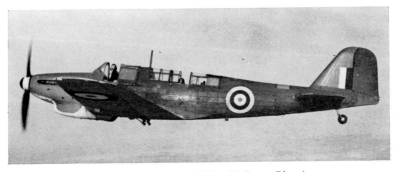

Fulmar I (N 1952). (*Chas. E. Brown Photo.*)

143

the Swordfish action at Taranto, shot down a further six enemy aircraft. In March 1941 Fulmars of No. 805 Squadron fought in the defence of Crete, alongside Brewster Buffaloes and R.A.F. Gladiators and Hurricanes.

Little publicity has ever been given to the fact that Fulmars played an important rôle in the shadowing of the German battleship *Bismarck* in May 1941. Six Fulmars of No. 800Z Squadron were aboard *Victorious* on 22 May when it was reported that *Bismarck* had put to sea from Bergen. *Victorious*, with other units of the Home Fleet, went in pursuit. Largely due to excellent night reconnaissance work by the Fulmars, Swordfish were able to attack with torpedoes shortly before midnight on 25 May.

Fulmars were next in action during the F.A.A. attack on Petsamo, up on the North Cape, in July 1941. Fulmars of No. 800 Squadron, in *Furious*, and No. 809 Squadron, in *Victorious*, provided fighter cover for four squadrons of Albacores. The raid met with stiff enemy fighter opposition, but Fulmars of No. 809 Squadron succeeded in shooting down four Messerschmitt Me 109s.

Another rôle in which Fulmars were active during 1941 was night-intrusion operations from shore-bases. From May to November, Fulmars of No. 800X Squadron carried out night-intruder raids without break from their base in Malta.

Early in 1942, when the threat of invasion by a Japanese fleet hung over Ceylon, Fulmars of No. 803 Squadron were active in the air defence of the island. They were just too late, however, to protect the carrier *Hermes* from enemy attack when she was sunk by the Japanese on 9 April 1942.

As previously mentioned, Fulmars provided fighter cover for most of the Malta reinforcement convoys during the island's prolonged siege. One of the most fiercely contested of these perilous voyages through the Mediterranean was that of August 1942. In this action, Fulmars of Nos. 804, 809 and 884 Squadrons took part and were aided by Sea Hurricanes and Grumman Martlets. During the desperate air battles which raged above the convoy, Lt.-Cdr. Parker, the C.O. of No. 884 Squadron, shot down two Cant Z 1007 bombers in his Fulmar.

From February 1942 twelve Fulmars of No. 889 Squadron provided fighter defence for the Suez Canal zone and in November, with the Allied invasion of North Africa, those of No. 809 Squadron operated from *Victorious* on tactical reconnaissance sorties over the landing beaches. Also present during the North African invasion were the Fulmars of No. 893 Squadron (which also had Martlets), embarked in *Formidable*. This squadron later took part in the invasion of Sicily in July 1943 and on convoys to North Russia from October to November 1943.

North Russian convoys also fell to the lot of No. 813 Squadron, embarked in *Campania* and *Vindex*. Equipped with 12 Swordfish and four Wildcats, No. 813 Squadron also had a flight of Fulmar night-fighters which took part in several of the Russian convoys, between September 1944 and March 1945.

The Fulmar fought well with the F.A.A. and, if it lacked the speed of a single-seat fighter, it could nevertheless use its heavy fire-power to great advantage by diving on an enemy aircraft from above. It wrought much execution among the slower Italian fighters, bombers and reconnaissance seaplanes, but was less effective against the faster German aircraft. This lack of speed was, of course, entirely due to the presence of the second

A Fulmar I lands aboard an aircraft-carrier. (*Imp. War Museum Photo.*)

'A Fulmar I (N 2005) of the third production batch, N 1980 to N 2016.

seat for the navigator, but it must be remembered that at the time the Fulmar was designed navigational aids were not sufficiently developed to ensure a single-seat fighter's return to its carrier in bad weather. Perhaps the best summary of the Fulmar's qualities appears in Terence Horsley's book *Find, Fix and Strike*:

'There was never anything wrong with the eight-gun Fulmar. It was a fine aeroplane, manœuvrable, with a good take-off, moderate climb, and plenty of endurance. It satisfied the demands for a navigator's seat and several wireless sets considered essential for Fleet work. It merely lacked the fighter's first essential quality—speed. Unless the pilot's first burst made a kill, he rarely got a second chance.'

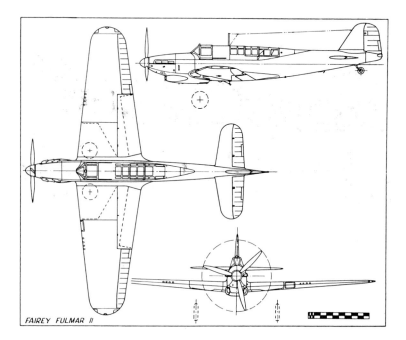

FAIREY FULMAR II

The first prototype Fulmar survives to the present day and is operated for communications work by its makers under the civil registration G-AIBE. It is converted to Mk. II standard, with a Merlin XXX, and is equipped to carry the pilot and two passengers.

UNITS ALLOCATED

No. 800X Squadron (*Furious*); No. 800Y Squadron (*Argus*); No. 800Z Squadron (*Victorious* and *Indomitable*); No. 803 Squadron (India and Ceylon); No. 804 Squadron (*Pegasus, Eagle, Argus* and *Furious*); No. 805 Squadron (with Buffaloes, Egypt and Crete); No. 806 Squadron (*Illustrious, Formidable* and *Indomitable*); No. 806B Squadron (with Wildcats, *Illustrious*); No. 807 Squadron (*Pegasus, Furious, Ark Royal, Argus, Eagle, Indomitable, Hunter* and *Battler*); No. 808 Squadron (*Ark Royal* and *Biter*); No. 809 Squadron (*Victorious*); No. 813 Squadron (with Swordfish and Wildcat, night-fighters in *Campania* and *Vindex*); No. 879 Squadron (St. Merryn); No. 884 Squadron (*Victorious*); No. 886 Squadron (Donibristle); No. 887 Squadron (Lee-on-Solent); No. 889 Squadron (Egypt); No. 893 Squadron (with Martlets, *Formidable*); No. 784 Night-fighter Training Squadron (Drem).

TECHNICAL DATA (FULMAR I)

Description: Two-seat carrier-borne fighter. All-metal stressed skin construction.
Manufacturers: Fairey Aviation Co. Ltd., Stockport, Cheshire.
Power Plant: One 1,080-h.p. Rolls-Royce Merlin VIII.
Dimensions: Span, 46 ft. 4½ in. Length, 40 ft. 3 in. Height, 14 ft. Wing area, 342 sq. ft.

Weight: Loaded, 9,800 lb.

Performance: Maximum speed, 280 m.p.h. Cruising, 235 m.p.h. Climb, 1,200 ft./min. Range, 800 miles. Service ceiling, 26,000 ft.

Armament: Eight fixed Browning guns mounted in the wings. Some aircraft with single Vickers 'K' gun in rear cockpit.

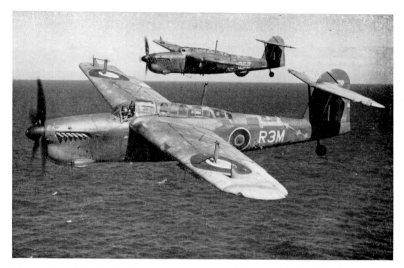

Barracuda II (MD 892) nearest camera, with Barracuda III behind. (*Chas. E. Brown Photo.*)

Fairey Barracuda (Mks. I to III)

The Barracuda was a beast of burden if ever there was one: few aeroplanes in the course of their career can have been cluttered up with such a remarkable variety of extraneous equipment. Radomes, radar masts, rockets, bombs, mines, torpedoes, lifeboats, even containers below the wings for dropping secret agents in France; all were to be seen festooned about the Barracuda at one time or another. Add to this propensity such intrinsic features as the shoulder wing with its Fairey–Youngman flaps below the trailing-edge, the curious undercarriage design and the high-mounted tailplane, and it will be evident why the sight of a Barracuda caused many a raised eyebrow among spectators new to the experience. Perhaps the most amazing sight of all was that of a Barracuda using rocket-assisted take-off gear being shot off the deck of a carrier amidst a cloud of smoke.

Yet, though it might not have been handsome, the Barracuda acquitted itself well in its exacting range of duties and it proved a valuable addition to the F.A.A.'s strike force in the later years of the war. Its high power loading, fully laden, was apt to cause difficulty for the inexperienced pilot, but it retained its excellent manœuvrability even when carrying a torpedo or bombs, and it proved especially useful as a dive-bomber, for which purpose the Fairey–Youngman flaps were inclined 30 degrees to act as dive-brakes. It was, in fact, as a dive-bomber that the Barracuda figured most prominently: it used the torpedo only rarely.

Design work on the Barracuda, then known as the Fairey Type 100, began in 1937. It was to meet the requirements of Spec. S. 24/37 and was intended as a replacement for the Albacore biplane. At the outset the

Rolls-Royce Exe engine was chosen as the power plant, but when this engine was abandoned the design was modified to take the Rolls-Royce Merlin. When the prototype (P 1767) made its maiden flight on 7 December 1940 it was the first all-metal monoplane torpedo-bomber for carrier-borne duties ever built in Great Britain.

It was due to no intrinsic fault that the Barracuda got off to a bad start. It made its appearance at a critical period of the war, when the resources of the aircraft industry were being concentrated on achieving maximum output of a few selected aircraft and, as a result, series production of the new monoplane was delayed for almost two years. A second prototype (P 1770) was flown on 29 June 1941, but it was until 18 May 1942 that the first production Barracuda Mk. I (P 9642) took the air. The initial production batch consisted of 25 aircraft, P 9642 to P 9666 inclusive. These were the only Mk. Is to be built, and all were fitted with the 1,260-h.p. Merlin 30 engine.

Production Barracudas differed from the original version of the prototype in having the characteristic high-mounted tailplane. On its first appearance the prototype P 1767 had an orthodox low-set tailplane, but it was found that this suffered from buffeting caused by turbulence when the large Fairey–Youngman flaps were lowered, so it was raised. The prototype Barracuda made its first deck-landing on 18 May 1941.

With the Barracuda Mk. II, the 1,640-h.p. Merlin 32 engine was installed, driving a four-blade airscrew instead of the three-blade type used on the Barracuda I. This increased the all-up weight from 13,500 lb. to 14,100 lb. The prototype for the Barracuda II (P 1767) flew for the first time on 17 August 1942, and by 1943 production of this major variant was in full swing, not only at Fairey's Stockport factory, but also by Blackburn at Brough and Boulton Paul at Wolverhampton. Later, the Westland Company at Yeovil also joined the Barracuda production group.

The last variant of the Barracuda produced during the war years was the Mk. III. The Barracuda III was generally similar to the Mk. II, but was intended chiefly for anti-submarine reconnaissance duties, and for this purpose mounted an A.S.V. Mk. X scanner in a radome under the rear fuselage. The prototype for the Barracuda III was a converted Mk. II, DP 855, which first flew in 1943.

Barracuda II (MD 717) built by Blackburn. (*Blackburn Photo.*)

The Barracuda III followed the Mk. II through the shops, and the grand total of Mks. I, II and III built amounted to 2,572. Of this total, 1,162 were built by the parent company at Heaton Chapel, 700 by Blackburn, 692 by Boulton Paul and 18 by Westland. Serial numbers allocated to Fairey-built aircraft were P 9667 to P 9691, P 9709 to P 9748, P 9787 to P 9836, P 9847 to P 9891, P 9909 to P 9943, P 9957 to P 9986, DT 813 to DT 831, DT 845 to DT 865, DT 878 to DT 887, LS 464 to LS 506, LS 519 to LS 556, LS 568 to LS 595, LS 618 to LS 653, LS 668 to LS 713, LS 726 to LS 763, LS 778 to LS 820, LS 833 to LS 878, LS 891 to LS 936, LS 949 to LS 974, PM 682 to PM 723, PM 738 to PM 780, PM 796 to PM 938, PM 852 to PM 897, PM 913 to PM 958, PM 970 to PM 999, PN 115 to PN 164, RK 328 to RK 369, RK 382 to RK 428, RK 441 to RK 485, RK 498 to RK 523 and TW 745 to TW 754.

The Barracuda first entered an operational unit on 10 January 1943, when No. 827 Squadron re-formed with 12 Mk. IIs at Stretton, Cheshire. No. 827 Squadron had until the previous August flown Albacores. During 1943 the Barracuda force was steadily built up. No. 810 Squadron, also at Stretton, became the second Barracuda unit in February 1943, and thereafter Albacore and Swordfish squadrons were re-equipped one by one, until in January 1944 the F.A.A. had 12 squadrons of Barracudas in the front line.

Barracudas were first in action in September 1943, when they served with No. 810 Squadron in *Illustrious* during the Allied landings at Salerno, but they did not spring into prominence until the following year, when they made their memorable attack on *Tirpitz*. *Tirpitz* was lying in Kaafiord, in the northern tip of Norway, where she had undergone

Barracuda II (P 9926), a Fairey-built aircraft, with torpedo. (*Imp. War Museum Photo.*)

repairs after the attack by British midget submarines in September 1943. The objective of the F.A.A. attack was to render the great battleship incapable of interfering with the convoys to North Russia.

Under the command of Admiral Sir Michael Denny, six aircraft-carriers gathered for the strike: they were *Furious, Victorious, Emperor, Fencer, Pursuer* and *Searcher*. Just before dawn on 3 April 1944, the force reached its flying-off position, and the aircraft took off whilst it was still dark. Forty-two Barracudas were flown off, in two groups of 21 each, and they had a strong escort of 80 fighters. The enemy was taken completely by surprise. Before anybody aboard *Tirpitz* realised what was happening, the Barracudas had dived between the high, steep sides of the fiord, shattering its customary silence, and delivered their heavy armour-piercing bombs with deadly accuracy. The second wave of Barracudas bombed blind through the smoke a minute later. The ship's anti-aircraft guns were manned too late to be fully effective, and only three Barracudas and a single fighter were lost. *Tirpitz* had received 15 direct hits from the 500-lb. and 1,000-lb. bombs of the Barracudas, 300 of her crew had been

Barracuda II built by Westland. (*Westland Photo.*)

killed and a great fire started amidships. This brilliantly successful operation was carried out by Barracudas of Nos. 827, 829 and 830 Squadrons from *Victorious* and No. 831 Squadron from *Furious*. The fighter cover was provided by Hellcats of No. 800 Squadron, Seafires of No. 801 Squadron, Wildcats of No. 898 Squadron and Corsairs of No. 1834 Squadron.

After this initial success, further Barracuda strikes were made on *Tirpitz* from May to August 1944. These took place on 15 May, 14 July, 22 August, 24 August and 25 August. By using smoke-screens, *Tirpitz* escaped further serious damage, though a direct hit by a 1,000-lb. bomb was secured in the raid of 24 August.

Only a fortnight after the initial *Tirpitz* attack, Barracudas made their operational début in the Pacific war theatre. Between 16 and 21 April 1944, Barracudas of Nos. 810 and 847 Squadrons, embarked in *Illustrious*, joined U.S. Navy dive-bombers in a shattering attack on the Japanese submarine base and oil-tanks at Sabang, Sumatra. Other Barracuda squadrons which made their mark in the Pacific were Nos. 815 and 817 in *Indomitable*, and Nos. 822 and 831 in *Victorious*, all of which were engaged in dive-bombing over Sumatra in the period August–September 1944.

Back in home waters, No. 841 Squadron in *Implacable* was active in a series of anti-shipping strikes off the Norwegian coast from August to October 1944, and other Barracudas did invaluable work on anti-submarine patrol with the smaller escort carriers. To get off these small carrier decks, the Barracuda was equipped with R.A.T.O.G., and some of the squadrons so engaged were No. 821, in *Puncher*, No. 823, in *Atheling*, and No. 815 in *Activity*, *Smiter* and *Fencer*.

With the arrival of VJ-Day, those Barracuda squadrons still operational were rapidly disbanded, and at the beginning of 1946 only three remained. Of these, No. 815 Squadron disbanded in January and No. 821 in February. No. 860 Squadron, with Barracuda IIIs, re-armed with Fireflies in February: this squadron was unusual in that it received its first Barracudas at Ayr on 1 September 1945, after the war ended, subsequently serving in the escort carrier *Nairana*.

After being absent from first-line squadrons of the F.A.A. for almost two years, the Barracuda was revived in December 1947, when No. 815 Squadron re-formed at Eglinton, Northern Ireland. No. 815 Squadron was equipped with 12 Barracuda IIIs taken over from No. 744 Training Squadron. These aircraft, the last Barracudas in first-line service, were eventually superseded by Grumman Avengers in 1953.

UNITS ALLOCATED

No. 810 Squadron (formed February 1943 at Stretton; embarked in *Illustrious* and *Activity*); No. 812 Squadron (formed June 1944 at Stretton; shore-based at Crail and Fern; embarked in *Vengeance*); No. 814 Squadron (formed July 1944 at Stretton; shore-based at Fearn and Macrihanish; embarked in *Venerable*); No. 815 Squadron (formed October 1943 at Lee-on-Solent; embarked in *Indomitable*, *Activity, Smiter* and *Fencer;* also post-war from December 1947 at Eglinton); No. 816 Squadron (formed February 1945 at Lee-on-Solent); No. 817 Squadron (formed December 1943 at Lee-on-Solent; embarked in *Begum, Indomitable* and *Unicorn*); No. 818 Squadron (formed May 1945 at Crimond); No. 820 Squadron (formed January 1944 at Lee-on-Solent; embarked in *Indefatigable*); No. 821 Squadron (formed May 1944 at Stretton; embarked in *Puncher* and *Trumpeter*); No. 822 Squadron (formed August 1943 at Lee-on-Solent; embarked in *Victorious* and *Rajah*); No. 823 Squadron (formed June 1943 at Lee-on-Solent; embarked in *Atheling*); No. 824 Squadron (formed July 1945 at Lee-on-Solent; embarked in *Activity*); No. 825 Squadron (formed July 1945 at Rattray); No. 826 Squadron (formed December 1943 at Lee-on-Solent; embarked in *Indefatigable* and *Formidable*); No. 827 Squadron (formed January 1943 at Stretton; embarked in *Furious, Victorious, Formidable* and *Colossus*); No. 828 Squadron (formed March 1944 at Lee-on-Solent; embarked in *Implacable*); No. 829 Squadron (formed October 1943 at Lee-on-Solent; embarked in *Victorious*); No. 830 Squadron (formed May 1943 at Lee-on-Solent; embarked in *Furious* and *Formidable*); No. 831 Squadron (formed June 1943 at Stretton; embarked in *Victorious* and *Furious*); No. 847 Squadron (formed June 1943 at Lee-on-Solent; embarked in *Illustrious*); No. 860 Squadron (formed September 1945 at Ayr; embarked in *Nairana*); No. 744 Training Squadron (Eglinton).

TECHNICAL DATA (BARRACUDA I, II AND III)

Description (Mks. I and II): Three-seat carrier-borne or shore-based torpedo-bomber and dive-bomber. (T.R. III): Three-seat carrier-borne or shore-based torpedo-reconnaissance aircraft. All-metal stressed skin construction.

Manufacturers: Fairey Aviation Co. Ltd., Stockport, Cheshire. Sub-contracted by Blackburn, Boulton Paul and Westland.

Power Plant (Mk. I): One 1,260-h.p. Rolls-Royce Merlin 30. (Mks. II and III): One 1,640 h.p. Rolls-Royce Merlin 32.

Dimensions (All marks): Span, 49 ft. 2 in. Length, 39 ft. 9 in. Height, 15 ft. 1 in. Wing area, 367 sq. ft.

Weights (Mk. I): Empty, 8,700 lb. Loaded, 11,900 lb. or 13,500 lb. maximum. (Mk. II): Empty, 9,350 lb. Loaded, 13,200 lb. or 14,100 lb. maximum. (Mk. III): Empty, 9,407 lb. Loaded, 13,300 lb. or 14,100 lb. maximum.

Performance: (Mk. I): Maximum speed, 235 m.p.h. at 11,000 ft. Cruising, 138 m.p.h. (economical) or 191 m.p.h. (maximum) at 6,000 ft. Climb, 6·7 mins. to 6,000 ft. Range, 524 miles with 2,000 lb. of bombs; 853 miles with a 1,610-lb. torpedo; 1,320 miles with maximum fuel and no bombs. Service ceiling, 18,400 ft. (Mk. II): Maximum speed, 228 m.p.h. at 1,750 ft. Cruising, 172 m.p.h. (economical) or 193 m.p.h. (maximum) at 5,000 ft. Climb, 6 mins. to 5,000 ft. Range, 524 miles with 1,800 lb. of bombs; 686 miles with a 1,620-lb. torpedo; 1,150 miles with maximum fuel and no bombs. Service ceiling, 16,600 ft. (Mk. III): Maximum speed, 239 m.p.h. at 1,750 ft. Cruising, 170 m.p.h. (economical) or 205 m.p.h. (maximum) at 5,000 ft. Climb, 4½ mins. to 5,000 ft. Range, 684 miles with a 1,572-lb. torpedo; 818 miles with no bombs and 226 gallons of fuel; 1,125 miles with no bombs and 342 gallons of fuel. Service ceiling, 20,000 ft.

Armament: All marks had twin Vickers 'K' guns in rear cockpit. (Mk. I): One 1,610-lb. torpedo or one 1,500-lb. mine below fuselage or four 500-lb. or six 250-lb. bombs below wings. (Mk. II): One 1,620-lb. torpedo or four 450-lb. depth-charges or six 250 lb. bombs. (Mk. III): One 1,572-lb. torpedo or four 250-lb. depth-charges.

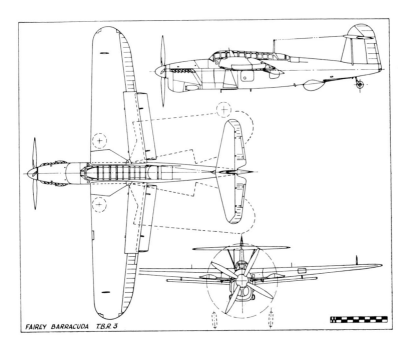

FAIREY BARRACUDA T.B.R.3

Firefly I (Z 1832). (*Chas. E. Brown Photo.*)

Fairey Firefly (F. 1 to N.F. 2)

The Firefly was designed to the Naval Spec. N. 5/40 (a combination of two earlier project tenders by Fairey to Specs. N. 8/39 and N. 9/39) and it carried on the tradition, peculiar to the F.A.A., of the fast two-seater combining the fighter and reconnaissance rôles. This class of aircraft had first been conceived as early as 1926 and embodied in a specification which brought forth the Fairey Fleetwing and Hawker Osprey biplanes. The Osprey served until 1939, and in 1940 the fighter-reconnaissance philosophy was perpetuated by the Fairey Fulmar, the first monoplane of the class and the Firefly's immediate predecessor.

The prototype Firefly (Z 1826) was first flown by C. S. Staniland on 22 December 1941, less than 18 months after the Admiralty had approved the original mock-up.

Designed by Mr. H. E. Chaplin, the Firefly was generally similar to its predecessor but of improved aerodynamic form, with æsthetically pleasing elliptical wings and the much more powerful Griffon engine in place of the Merlin. Fire-power was also vastly improved by the substitution of four 20-mm. guns for the eight machine-guns. It at once commended itself by proving 40 m.p.h. faster than the Fulmar, yet had excellent handling qualities at the lower end of the speed range, so essential in a carrier-borne aircraft. A great feature of the design was the incorporation of fully-retractable Fairey–Youngman flaps which could be extended beneath the trailing-edge, almost horizontal with the line of flight, to improve cruising and manœuvrability characteristics, as well as being lowered at an angle, in the usual way, for take-off and landing requirements.

Three further Firefly prototypes were built: these were Z 1827, flown in March 1942, Z 1828, flown in August 1942, and Z 1829, flown in September 1942. After tests with these aircraft two changes were incorporated: the horn-balanced rudder was modified and metal ailerons replaced the original fabric-covered type.

Following an initial order for 200 aircraft, production of the Firefly I began with Z 1830, which was delivered on 4 March 1943. The parent firm built 297 of these aircraft at their Hayes factory, and the type was also sub-contracted by the General Aircraft Company, which built another 132 at Hanworth. The Firefly F. 1 was followed by the F.R. 1,

A Firefly I shows off its graceful lines. (*Chas. E. Brown Photo.*)

which carried ASH ship and submarine-detection radar under the engine cowling. Fairey built 376 F.R. 1s, the last aircraft (TW 679) being delivered on 23 November 1946. Early production Fireflies in the Mk. 1 range differed from later aircraft in having a low raked front screen-panel with a windscreen wiper and a shallow hood; this was later made taller, the wiper deleted and the bubble hood increased in height to give more head room. This improved the forward view, which was some-what deficient in early Fireflies. Other modifications introduced on the Mk. 1 production line included the addition of fairings to the 20-mm. gun barrels, the deletion of the two-man dinghy stowed inside the rear fuselage in favour of individual K-type seat dinghies and (from the 470th aircraft) the installation of the Griffon XII engine in place of the Griffon IIB.

The next Firefly development was the production of a night-fighter version. This was the N.F. 2 (prototype Z 1831), which had two small radomes containing A.I. Mk. 10 radar mounted well inboard on the wings at either side of the fuselage. The additional equipment for the A.I. observer in the rear cockpit upset the centre of gravity position: this was rectified by lengthening the nose 18 in., inserting an extra bay between the firewall and the front cockpit. Production of the Firefly N.F. 2 ceased after only 37 had been built, because it had been found possible to fit a more compact form of radar in a container beneath the centre section without the need for structural alterations. This enabled the F.R. 1 to be modified for night-fighter duties by conversion on the production line. This variant, the N.F. 1, had shrouded exhausts.

The final operational variant of the Mk. 1 was the Firefly F. 1A, which was the F. 1 converted to F.R. 1 standard by the addition of ASH radar.

Production Fireflies first went aboard an aircraft-carrier in July 1943, and the first operational unit of the F.A.A., No. 1770 Squadron, formed with 12 aircraft at Yeovilton on 1 October 1943. After periods of shore-based service at Grimsetter and Hatston, No. 1770 Squadron's Fireflies embarked in H.M.S. *Indefatigable*, and were operational for the first time over Norway, between 14 and 19 July 1944, during F.A.A. attacks on the German battleship *Tirpitz*. The Fireflies were used in attacks on gun positions and two auxiliary vessels during these operations. Between 18 August and 2 September 1944 Fireflies of No. 1770 Squadron carried out photographic reconnaissance flights over *Tirpitz* and obtained vital information which led to the final destruction of the battleship, by R.A.F. Lancasters, on 12 November 1944.

The second Firefly squadron, No. 1771, formed at Yeovilton on 1 February 1944 and eventually embarked in H.M.S. *Implacable*. No. 1771 Squadron made its first operational sorties in October 1944, and until December its Fireflies were active in armed reconnaissance and anti-shipping strikes along the Norwegian coast.

The first major naval action in which Fireflies took part, however, was with the British carriers operating in the Far East, attached to the East Indies Fleet based on Ceylon. This was the spectacularly successful attack on the Japanese oil refineries in Sumatra, which produced vast quantities of fuel for enemy air and naval operations. Fireflies of No. 1770 Squadron carried out rocket attacks on refineries at Pangkalan Brandan between 1 and 7 January 1945, before the main Fleet action of 24 Jan-

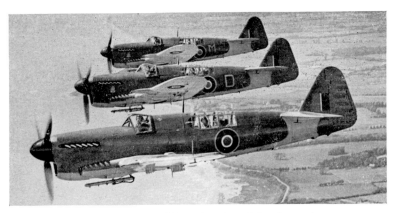

Firefly Is of No. 816 Squadron in echelon formation.

uary, in which 48 Avengers, 16 Hellcats and 32 Corsairs took part as well as the 12 Fireflies of No. 1770 Squadron. The Fireflies were flown off *Indefatigable*, the other carriers engaged being *Indomitable*, *Illustrious* and *Victorious*. The plan of campaign, which worked admirably, was for the fighters to attack enemy airfields and eliminate the fighter defences, thus leaving the way clear for the Avengers and Fireflies to make their strike. The target was the refinery at Pladjoe, Palembang, one of the most important in the Far East. In order to reach it, the Avengers and Fireflies had to dive through a balloon barrage and run the gauntlet of intense anti-aircraft fire, but they pressed home their attack and succeeded in devastating the main buildings of the refinery. On 29 January a similar force repeated the operation, this time against the other Palembang refinery at Songei Gerong. Once again the Avengers and Fireflies (the former with bombs and the latter with rockets) knocked out the target. As some wag remarked at the time, the Fireflies had helped to put the 'bang' into Palembang.

This, the first major action by the F.A.A. against the Japanese, resulted

Firefly N.F. 2 (Z 1875). (*Imp. War Museum Photo.*)

Firefly T. 3 of No. 795 Training Squadron. (*Official Admiralty Photo.*)

in the loss of only 16 aircraft by enemy action: a small enough price to pay for an operation which altered the whole course of the war in the Pacific. Months later the Japanese were still feeling the effects of this curtailment of their oil supplies.

After Sumatra the carriers sailed to Australia, where they joined the British Pacific Fleet, based on Sydney. On 14–15 June 1945 Fireflies of No. 1771 Squadron, in *Implacable*, joined in the attacks on Truk in the Carolina Islands, and on 10 July aircraft of this squadron became the first in the F.A.A. to fly over the Japanese mainland. On 24 July they were joined in the operations against shipping and shore targets among the Japanese islands by Fireflies of No. 1772 Squadron (H.M.S. *Indefatigable*), which had first formed at Burscough on 1 May 1944. During these operations (in preparation for an amphibious landing which was forestalled by the dropping of the atomic bombs) Fireflies had the honour of being the first British aircraft to fly over Tokyo.

One of the first activities in which Fireflies engaged after the Second World War was the dropping of supplies to prisoner-of-war camps in Japan. This operation was carried out by No. 1772 Squadron between 21 and 30 August 1945.

When VJ-Day arrived a total of 658 Fireflies had left the factories (574 of them from Fairey) and the F.A.A. had eight squadrons in being, of which four were with the British Pacific Fleet (Nos. 1770, 1771, 1772 and 1790, the latter night-fighters), and the remainder working up in the United Kingdom. There were also two Fireflies embarked in the escort carrier *Vindex*, with Wildcat VIs of No. 882 Squadron. In Nos. 816 and 822 Squadrons the Fireflies were displacing Barracudas. The remaining home-based squadrons (Nos. 1791 and 1792) were equipped with Firefly night-fighters. Both the home-based night-fighter squadrons and the Fireflies in the Far East had a relatively short post-war existence; all were disbanded by June 1946.

Firefly N.F. 1 (DT 933), the night-fighter conversion of the F.R. 1 with shrouded exhausts and radome beneath the nose. (*Imp. War Museum Photo.*)

A Firefly F.R. 1 (DT 934) aboard a carrier of the British Pacific Fleet in 1945. Eight 60-lb. rocket-projectiles are mounted below the wings. (*Imp. War Museum Photo.*)

Production of the Firefly F.R. 1 continued until the middle of 1946, when it was superseded on the production line by the Mk. 4 (described separately). From October 1945 onwards 11 more squadrons were equipped with Firefly Mk. 1s, mostly in units which had previously flown Barracudas. An exception was No. 805 Squadron, one of the last first-line units to receive the Firefly Mk. 1, which was a fighter squadron previously equipped with Seafires. No. 805 Squadron received its Fireflies at Malta in September 1946.

With the introduction of the Firefly Mk. 4 the earlier marks gradually disappeared from first-line squadrons. Their final period of service was with R.N.V.R. air squadrons from 1947 until about 1950.

No. 805 Squadron (formed September 1946; shore-based at Malta); No. 812 Squadron (formed January 1946; embarked in *Thesus*); No. 814 Squadron (formed January 1946; embarked in *Vengeance*); No. 816 Squadron (formed July 1945 at Woodvale; embarked in *Nairana* and *Theseus*; augmented by four Firefly night-fighters in May 1946; embarked in *Ocean* and *Sydney*); No. 822 Squadron (formed August 1945 at Woodvale; disbanded February 1946); No. 824 Squadron (formed October 1945 at Ayr; disbanded January 1946); No. 825 Squadron (formed January 1946; embarked in *Warrior* of Royal Canadian Navy); No. 826 Squadron (formed January 1946; disbanded February 1946); No. 827 Squadron (formed September 1946; embarked in *Triumph*); No. 837 Squadron (formed November 1945; embarked in *Glory*); No. 860 Squadron (formed February 1946; shore-based at St. Merryn and Dale, transferred to Royal Netherlands Navy in September 1946); No. 861 Squadron (formed September 1946; transferred to Royal Netherlands Navy in February 1947); No. 882 Squadron (two Fireflies added to Wildcats abroad *Vindex* in February 1945; subsequently embarked in *Searcher* and disbanded October 1945); No. 1770 Squadron (formed October 1943 at Yeovilton; embarked in *Indefatigable*; disbanded September 1945); No. 1771 Squadron (formed February 1944 at Yeovilton; embarked in *Implacable*; disbanded September 1945); No. 1772 Squadron (formed May 1944 at Burscough; embarked in *Ruler* and *Indefatigible*; disbanded March 1946); No. 1790 Squadron (formed January 1945 at Burscough; embarked in *Vindex* and *Implacable*; disbanded June 1946); No. 1791 Squadron (formed March 1945 at Lee-on-Solent; shore-based at Inskip, Drem and Burscough; disbanded September 1945); No. 1792 Squadron (formed May 1945 at Lee-on-Solent; shore-based at Inskip and Drem, embarked in *Ocean*; disbanded April 1946); No. 1830 Squadron, R.N.V.R. (formed May 1947 at Abbotsinch). Also Nos. 746, 766 and 771 Training Squadrons and Nos. 792 and 782 Night Fighter Training Squadrons.

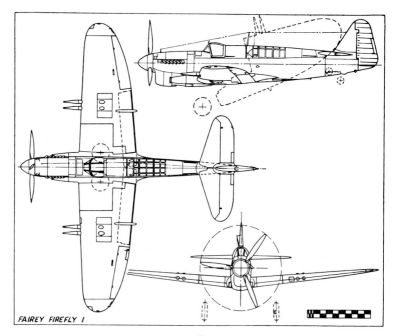

FAIREY FIREFLY I

Description: Two-seat carrier-borne fighter-reconnaissance aircraft. All-metal stressed-skin construction.

Manufacturers: Fairey Aviation Co. Ltd., Hayes, Middlesex and General Aircraft, Ltd., Hanworth, Middlesex.

Power Plant: One 1,730 h.p. Rolls-Royce Griffon IIB or 1,990-h.p. Griffon XII.

Dimensions: Span, 44 ft. 6 in. (13 ft. 3 in. folded). Length, 37 ft. $7\frac{1}{4}$ ins. Height, 13 ft. 7 ins. Wing area, 328 sq. ft.

Weights: Empty, 9,750 lb. Loaded, 14,020 lb.

Performance: Maximum speed, 316 m.p.h. at 14,000 ft. Climb, $2\frac{1}{2}$ mins. to 5,000 ft. and $5\frac{3}{4}$ mins. to 10,000 ft. Maximum range, 1,300 miles. Service ceiling, 28,000 ft.

Armament: Four fixed 20-mm. guns in wings. Provision could be made for eight 60-lb. rocket-projectiles or two 1,000-lb. bombs below the wings.

Barracuda V (RK 558) from Lee-on-Solent. (*Crown Copyright Photo.*)

Fairey Barracuda V

The Barracuda V appeared too late to see action in the Pacific against the Japanese, where it was intended to serve as an interim replacement type prior to the introduction of the Fairey Spearfish. Though superficially similar to the wartime Barracudas (described separately), it was in fact extensively re-engineered and had an improved performance. This resulted from the installation of the Griffon engine in place of the Merlin: it also had increased range due to additional internal fuel capacity.

The installation of the Griffon in a Barracuda had first been planned for the Mk. IV, but this did not get beyond the project stage. The first prototype Barracuda V was a rebuilt Mk. II (P 9976), and it first flew at Ringway on 16 November 1944. A Griffon VII (later VIII) of 1,850 h.p. was installed and the wing-span was increased by 4 ft., the tips being squared and the entire structure re-stressed to give a greater margin of safety in a dive. Another change was the deletion of the third crew position, the rear cockpit being occupied by a navigator/radar operator with no gunnery duties. The prototype was followed by four more conversions (DT 845, PM 944, PM 941 and PM 940) and a small initial production batch, converted from earlier marks (including LS 479 and LS 486), which retained the original type of fin and rudder. Barracudas from RK 530 were built as Mk. Vs and had a large dorsal fillet, giving additional fin area. Late production aircraft (from RK 551) underwent a further tail revision and introduced a tall, pointed rudder.

The first true-built Barracuda V (RK 530) flew on 22 November 1945, but, with the end of the war, contracts had been curtailed and output was limited to about 30, ceasing with RK 574, which was delivered to the Royal Navy on 27 October 1947. The production Barracuda Vs mounted an easily-detachable radome under the port wing and had the up-rated Griffon 37 engine. They were used mostly for training duties by the F.A.A. and did not enter first-line squadrons.

UNITS ALLOCATED

No. 750 Squadron (R.N.A.S., St. Merryn, Cornwall).

Description: Two-seat carrier-borne or shore-based bomber-reconnaissance aircraft. All-metal stressed-skin construction.

Manufacturers: Fairey Aviation Co. Ltd., Stockport, Cheshire.

Power Plant: One 2,020-h.p. Rolls-Royce Griffon 37.

Dimensions: Span, 53 ft. 0½ in. (19 ft. 6 in. folded). Length, 41 ft. 1 in. Height, 13 ft. 2½ in. Wing area, 435 sq. ft.

Weights: Empty, 11,430 lb. Loaded, 15,250 lb. (normal); 16,000 lb. (overload).

Performance: Maximum speed, 253 m.p.h. at 10,000 ft.; 232 m.p.h. at sea level. Climb, 1,400 ft./min.; 8·6 mins. to 10,000 ft.; 13·8 mins. to 15,000 ft. Range, 1,120 miles at 170 m.p.h. without bombs or 600 miles at 163 m.p.h. with 2,000 lb. of bombs. Service ceiling, 24,000 ft.

Armament: No defensive guns. Maximum load of 2,000 lb. of bombs on external racks.

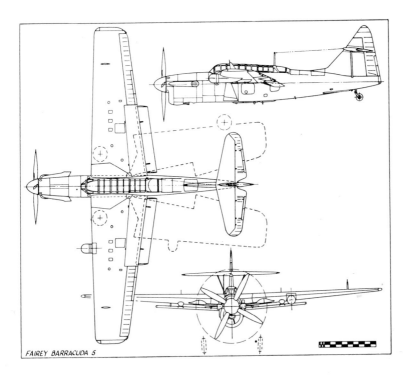

FAIREY BARRACUDA 5

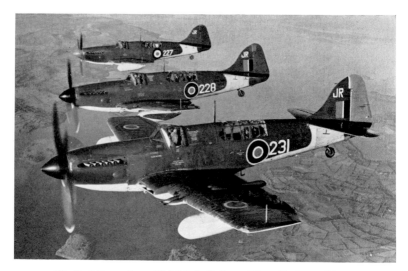

Firefly Mk. 4s from H.M.A.S. *Sydney.* (*Chas. E. Brown Photo.*)

Fairey Firefly (F.R. 4 to A.S. 6)

From 1945, when the fully modified Mk. 4 made its first appearance, the Firefly assumed notably different external characteristics. The wings were clipped, which improved the rate of roll but detracted rather from the appearance, and the beard radiator disappeared, to be replaced by coolant radiators in extensions of the leading-edges of the centre section. A four-bladed Rotol airscrew replaced the earlier three-bladed type, and an extension was made to the leading-edge of the fin, increasing its area and improving stability. To complete the transformation, two large fairings appeared beneath the wings: the port fairing housed auxiliary fuel formerly carried in the centre section and the starboard fairing carried the radar scanner previously mounted below the centre section.

These changes came about as a result of installing the two-speed two-stage supercharged Griffon 74 (Griffon 72 in the prototypes), which improved the high-altitude performance considerably, raising the maximum speed by as much as 70 m.p.h. The original testing of a two-stage Griffon engine was in a converted Firefly Mk. 1 (Z 1855), which, fitted with a Griffon 61 series engine, was re-designated Firefly Mk. 3. This experimental prototype was flown in 1943: it retained similar cowling arrangements to that of the earlier Griffon, resulting in a somewhat bulky nose, which produced unsatisfactory flight characteristics, and the type was abandoned.

In its original form, as flown in 1944, the first prototype Firefly Mk. 4 (a converted Mk. 1, Z 2118) retained the elliptical wing and the original tail assembly. In 1945 it was modified to full Mk. 4 standard, and three more conversions were made from the Mk. 1 airframes (MB 649, Z 1835 and PP 482) for trial installations and further test flying before genuine Mk. 4 production began. The prototypes had the 2,330-h.p. Griffon 72 engine, which was replaced by a 2,245-h.p. Griffon 74 in production aircraft.

The first production Firefly F.R. 4 (TW 687) flew on 25 May 1945, and a total of 160 was built, 120 of which went to the F.A.A. and 40 to the Royal Netherlands Naval Air Service. This figure included a small number of N.F. 4 night-fighters. Some 43 production aircraft were converted on the line from Mk. 1 airframes. The last Firefly Mk. 4 (VH 144) was delivered from the Fairey factory on 9 February 1948. Retrospectively, a number of Firefly Mk. 4s were converted for target-towing duties, being fitted with an M.L. Type G winch under the centre section and designated T.T. 4.

The first F.A.A. squadrons to be equipped with the Firefly Mk. 4 were Nos. 825 and 810, which were re-armed at Eglinton in August and October 1947, respectively. At that time No. 825 Squadron was on detachment to the Royal Canadian Navy.

The Firefly Mk. 4 was followed on the production line by the Mk. 5, the most prolific of the later Fireflies. With this mark the Firefly began to be fitted with varying equipment for specialised rôles, resulting in the sub-variants F.R. 5 for day-fighter-reconnaissance, the N.F. 5 for night-fighting and the A.S. 5 for anti-submarine patrol. The differences between these Fireflies were mainly internal. Altogether, 352 Firefly Mk. 5s were built, of which 14 went to the Royal Netherlands Naval Air Service. The first production Firefly 5 (VT 362) made its original flight on 12 December 1947 and was delivered to the F.A.A. on 9 January 1948. The final Firefly 5 (WB 440) left the Fairey factory on 19 May 1950.

One important change introduced during the life of the Firefly 5 was that of power-folding wings. The first aircraft so modified (VX 414) left the factory on 24 January 1949.

First-line Firefly squadrons of the F.A.A. re-equipped with the Mk. 5 version during 1948 and 1949, the first being No. 814, at Yeovilton in January 1948. The following year war broke out in Korea, and in this conflict, which was to last for two years, Fireflies found themselves in action once again in the Far East. The Far Eastern Fleet of the Royal Navy was at its station off the Korean coast only three days after the fighting started, and within six days was engaged in operations. The first air sortie was flown from the light fleet-carrier *Theseus*, and, from that time onwards, an aircraft-carrier of the Royal Navy, or one of the Commonwealth navies, was constantly in West Korean waters. Though strikes against enemy mine-layers and supply shipping were flown, the major part of the flying was in support of the armies ashore, disrupting enemy supplies and communications. In these bombing and rocket strikes Fireflies shared honours with Hawker Sea Furies, and some remarkable records of intensive operational flying and high serviceability factors were achieved. During the first spell of operations from *Theseus* no aircraft was ever unserviceable for longer than two hours, and no less than 1,300 deck landings were made without a failure or accident of any kind. As the war progressed the light fleet carriers gradually increased their average daily sorties flown from 60 to 120. The Firefly squadrons engaged in the Korean operations were No. 810 (in *Theseus*), No. 812 (in

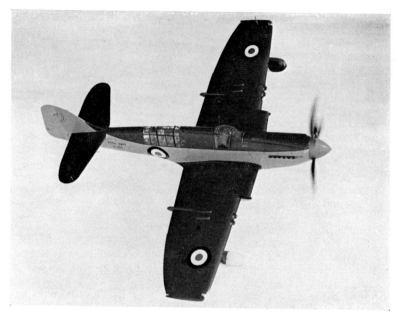

Firefly A.S. 5 (VT 406). (*'Flight' Photo.*)

Glory), No. 817 (in the Australian light fleet carrier *Sydney*), No. 820 (in *Glory*), No. 825 (in *Ocean*) and No. 827 (in *Triumph*). During the severe Korean winters the aircraft frequently operated in arctic weather conditions, with rough seas, snowstorms and temperatures well below freezing. Undaunted, the Fireflies and Sea Furies carried on, and even amidst the most appalling weather of November 1951, *Sydney*'s aircraft flew 270 sorties during air strikes against Hungnam. Her Fireflies (No. 817 Squadron) and Sea Furies (No. 805 Squadron) started many fires in industrial areas and severely damaged harbour and rail communications. In another close-support operation for United Nations troops No. 817's Fireflies demolished four important bridges with 16 bombs. It was during *Sydney*'s period of operations (from November 1951 to January 1952) that one of her Fireflies, flown by Sub-Lt. N. D. MacMillan, R.A.N., completed the 2,000th operational sortie flown from this carrier.

A particularly distinguished record was put up by the 14th Carrier Air Group, comprised of the Fireflies of No. 812 Squadron and the Sea Furies of No. 804 Squadron, embarked in the light fleet carrier *Glory*. This Group flew 4,834 operational sorties in the Korean War for the loss of only 27 aircraft.

Another Firefly 5 squadron, No. 825, was awarded (jointly with its companion Sea Fury squadron, No. 802) the Boyd Trophy for 1952 for its work in Korea from the light fleet carrier *Ocean*. The Fireflies and Sea Furies of *Ocean* surpassed all previous Korean records by achieving 123 sorties in a single day. They expended 6,000 rockets and dropped 4,000 bombs during ground-attack sorties in the close-support rôle.

In 1954 the Fireflies of No. 825 Squadron went into action again in the ground-attack rôle, this time against bandits in Malaya. During these operations they were embarked in the light fleet carrier *Warrior*.

By the time of the Coronation Naval Review at Spithead on 15 June 1953 the Firefly squadrons had been once more re-armed, the Mk. 5 having given way to the Mk. 6. The first Mk. 6s went to No. 814 Squadron at Yeovilton early in 1951. In this version the Firefly was equipped exclusively for anti-submarine duties and was designated A.S. 6. Generally similar to the A.S. 5, the A.S. 6 differed in carrying no armament, and it became the F.A.A.'s leading type of anti-submarine aircraft until the introduction of the Gannet in 1955. Total production of the Firefly A.S. 6, all built at Hayes, was 133. The first Firefly A.S. 6 (WB 505) made its maiden flight on 23 March 1949 and was delivered to the Royal Navy on 26 May 1950. The last A.S. 6 to be built (WJ 121) was delivered on 18 September 1951.

As well as being standard equipment in first-line squadrons (Nos. 812, 814, 817, 820, 825 and 826 all flew A.S. 6s in the Coronation fly-past), the type was widely employed by the anti-submarine squadrons of the R.N.V.R. air divisions. The first of these squadrons to be formed, No.

Firefly A.S. 6s of No. 812 Squadron from *Glory*. (*Official Admiralty Photo*.)

Firefly T.T. 4 (VH 132) from Ford. (*Official Admiralty Photo*.)

Firefly A.S. 6 (WD 917) from Ford. (*Crown Copyright Photo.*)

1830 at Abbotsinch, received A.S. 6s in November 1951 in place of its older Fireflies and, from 1952 onwards, other R.N.V.R. units were supplied with the A.S. 6. Nos. 1830, 1840 and 1841 Squadrons joined the first-line squadrons in the fly-past at Spithead, making the Firefly by far the most predominant F.A.A. aircraft on this historic and impressive occasion.

The Firefly A.S. 6 outlasted the A.S. 7 (described separately) in F.A.A. squadrons to become the last representative of the prolific Firefly family to remain on operational duties. By 1956 the F.A.A.'s anti-submarine force had completed its transition to Gannets and Avengers and the Firefly disappeared from the scene after 13 years of valuable service.

UNITS ALLOCATED

(Firefly Mk. 4): Nos. 810, 812, 814 and 825 Squadrons. Also No. 1840 Squadron, R.N.V.R. (Culham). (Firefly Mks. 5 and/or 6): Nos. 810, 812, 814, 817, 820, 821 (night-fighter), 825 and 826 Squadrons. Also the following R.N.V.R. Squadrons: No. 1830 (Scottish Air Division, Abbotsinch); No. 1840 (Channel Air Division, Ford); No. 1841 (Northern Air Division, Stretton); No. 1842 (Channel Air Division, Ford); No. 1843 (Scottish Air Division, Abbotsinch) and No. 1844 (Midland Air Division, Bramcote). Also No. 737 and 796 Training Squadrons and No. 771 Fleet Requirements Unit, Ford.

TECHNICAL DATA (FIREFLY A.S. 5)

Description: Two-seat carrier-borne anti-submarine reconnaissance and strike aircraft. All-metal stressed-skin construction.
Manufacturers: Fairey Aviation Co. Ltd., Hayes, Middlesex.
Power Plant: One 2,250-h.p. Rolls-Royce Griffon 74.
Dimensions: Span, 41 ft. 2 in. Length, 27 ft. 11 in. Height, 14 ft. 4 in. Wing area, 330 sq. ft.

Weights: Empty, 9,674 lb. Loaded (normal), 13,927 lb.; (maximum), 16,096 lb.

Performance: Maximum speed, 386 m.p.h. at 14,000 ft. Cruising, 220 m.p.h. Climb, 6 mins. 50 secs. to 10,000 ft.; 15½ mins. to 2,0000 ft. Range, 660 miles (with 192 gals.) or 1,300 miles (with 418 gals.). Endurance, 6½ hrs. Service ceiling, 28,400 ft.

Armament: Four fixed 20-mm. guns in wings and provision for sixteen 60-lb. rocket-projectiles or two 1,000-lb. bombs below the wings.

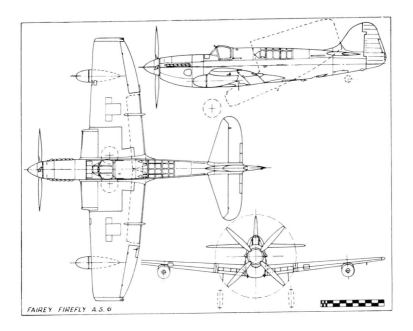

FAIREY FIREFLY A.S. 6

Firefly T. 1 (Z 1980). (*'Flight' Photo.*)

Fairey Firefly Trainer (T. 1 to T. 3)

In 1946, with the Firefly I firmly established as the Royal Navy's standard fighter-reconnaissance aircraft, the Fairey concern turned its attentions to the provision of a dual-control trainer version. This differed fundamentally from the fighter in having the rear (instructor's) cockpit raised 12 in. above the normal position to improve forward vision for landing when flown from the back seat, and in mounting two instead of four 20-mm. guns in the wings. The original Firefly Trainer (MB 750) was taken through its prolonged Service trials during 1947. It was flown by Mr. Duncan Menzies, and was tested at the Admiralty Flying School at Hinstock, the Operational Flying School at Lossiemouth, the Deck-Landing Training School at Milltown and the School of Naval Air Warfare at St. Merryn.

The initial production version, designated Firefly T. 1, was like the prototype in being a conversion of Mk. I airframes. The first of 34 such conversions (MB 473) flew for the first time on 1 September 1947. Only nine of these aircraft carried the two wing-mounted guns; the rest were unarmed. The Firefly T. 1s were used principally as deck-landing conversion trainers.

The next Firefly Trainer was the T. 2, equipped to operate primarily as a tactical weapons trainer. All the Firefly T. 2s mounted two 20-mm. guns in the wings and had gyro gunsights in both cockpits. Fifty-four Firefly T. 2s were delivered, all conversions of Mk. I fighters. The first T. 2 conversion (MB 543) made its maiden flight on 12 August 1949.

The last trainer variant based on the Firefly I airframe was the Firefly T. 3, which first flew in 1951. Firefly T. 3s were conversions of F.R. 1s, and differed from the earlier trainers in having no raised rear cockpit. They carried special equipments for the training of naval air observers in the techniques of anti-submarine warfare and were unarmed. Firefly T. 3s were eventually superseded in this rôle by the Firefly T. 7 around 1953.

Nos. 765 and 781 Training Squadrons; Nos. 1840 and 1842 Squadrons (Ford); Nos. 1830 and 1843 Squadrons (Abbotsinch); No. 1844 Squadron (Bramcote). T.3 to Nos. 781, 795 and 796 Training Squadrons.

TECHNICAL DATA (FIREFLY T. I)

Description: Two-seat dual-control deck-landing conversion trainer. All-metal stressed-skin construction.

Manufacturers: Fairey Aviation Co. Ltd., Stockport, Cheshire.

Power Plant: One 1,735-h.p. Rolls-Royce Griffon II or XII.

Dimensions: Span, 44 ft. 6 in. (13 ft. 6 in. folded). Length, 37 ft. $7\frac{1}{4}$ in. Height, 13 ft. 7 in. Wing area, 328 sq. ft.

Weights: Empty, 9,647 lb. Loaded, 12,300 lb.

Performance: Maximum speed, 305 m.p.h. at 16,500 ft.; 283 m.p.h. at sea level. Climb, 5·75 mins. to 10,000 ft. Range, 805 miles. Service ceiling, 28,000 ft.

Armament: A few aircraft with two 20-mm. guns in wings; rest unarmed.

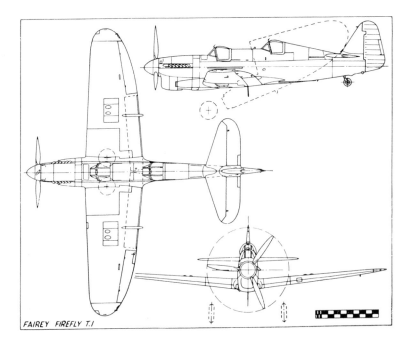

FAIREY FIREFLY T.I

Firefly A.S. 7s of No. 719 Training Squadron. (*'Flight' Photo.*)

Fairey Firefly A.S. 7 and T. 7

The Firefly A.S. 7 was produced as an interim anti-submarine aircraft pending the availability of the Gannet A.S. 1 and subsequently, in its trainer version, became the last variant of the Firefly to be built, excluding radio-controlled target drones. Many airframe changes were incorporated in the Mk. 7, making it readily distinguishable from earlier Fireflies. The full-span wing (though of modified plan-form) was revived and a deep beard radiator, larger than on the original Fireflies, mounted below the nose. Provision was made for a crew of three, with two radar operators in the rear cockpit, which had a large, bulged canopy similar to that of the Gannet. Most noticeable of all the changes was a completely revised tail.

In the event, the Firefly A.S. 7 saw only limited service in first-line squadrons, and production was switched to the T. 7 version, equipped for the training of observers. This variant flew from shore bases with second-line squadrons and had the deck-arrester gear deleted.

The prototype Firefly A.S. 7 (WJ 215) flew on 22 May 1951 and the first production aircraft (WJ 146) on 16 October 1951. A total of 151 (including T. 7s) was built, of which the Hayes factory produced 110 and Stockport 41. The last aircraft (WM 879) was delivered in December 1953.

No. 824 Squadron was the first operational unit to receive the Firefly A.S. 7, and it retained the type until re-equipped with Gannets in February 1955. Firefly A.S. 7s of Nos. 719, 750 and 824 Squadrons took part in the massed fly-past of F.A.A. aircraft in the Coronation Naval Review at Spithead on 15 June 1953.

The last Fireflies to be built by Faireys were 34 pilotless target drone versions of the Mk. 7, designated U. 8, for duties in connection with guided missile development. The first U. 8 (WM 810) flew on 30 December 1953 and the last (WP 354) on 26 March 1956. The latter aircraft was the last of 1,702 Fireflies built since 1941.

Nos. 814 and 824 Squadrons; Nos. 719, 737, 744, 750, 765, 766 and 796 Training Squadrons.

TECHNICAL DATA (FIREFLY A.S. 7)

Description: Anti-submarine search aircraft with a crew of three. All-metal stressed-skin construction.

Manufacturers: Fairey Aviation Co. Ltd., Hayes, Middlesex, and Stockport, Cheshire.

Power Plant: One 1,965-h.p. Rolls-Royce Griffon 59.

Dimensions: Span, 44 ft. 6 in. Length, 38 ft. 3 in. Height, 13 ft. 3 in. Wing area, 342½ sq. ft.

Weights: Empty, 11,016 lb. Loaded, 13,970 lb.

Performance: Maximum speed, 300 m.p.h. at 10,750 ft. Cruising, 257 m.p.h. Climb, 1,550 ft./min. Range, 860 miles at 166 m.p.h. Service ceiling, 25,500 ft.

Armament: None carried. Intended for search rôle only.

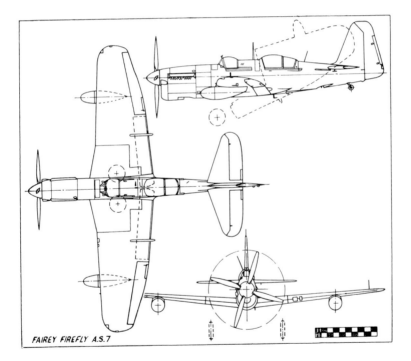

FAIREY FIREFLY A.S.7

Gannet A.S. 1 (XA 391) of No. 820 Squadron. (*'Flight' Photo*.)

Fairey Gannet (Mks. 1 to 5)

The Gannet, which from 1955 became the mainstay of the F.A.A.'s carrier-borne anti-submarine force, was the first aircraft in the world to fly with a double airscrew-turbine unit, providing all the qualities of a twin-engined aircraft with a single-engine configuration. This unusual characteristic offered special advantages for naval aviation. Each half of the Double Mamba engine could be controlled independently, shut down and its airscrew feathered, permitting all the economies of single-engined operation and extending the cruising range during normal patrol. When extra speed was needed, in combat, the thrust of both airscrews was immediately available again. Another advantage derived from the use of contra-rotating co-axial airscrews was that no assymetric problems were encountered as with a normal twin-engined aircraft. Making the Gannet even more suitable for carrier operation was the fact that its Double Mamba engine was designed from the outset to run on kerosene, wide cut turbine fuel or naval diesel fuel. This assisted the Admiralty policy of eliminating petrol stowage in aircraft-carriers.

The Gannet was the first aircraft in F.A.A. squadrons to combine the search and strike rôle: it was provided with an exceptionally capacious weapons bay, aft of which was installed a large retractable radar scanner. It is of interest to note that the Gannet was the first British-built naval aircraft to enter squadron service capable of carrying all its strike weapons (except wing-mounted rocket-projectiles) internally. This included two homing torpedoes: all previous F.A.A. torpedo-carriers had their weapon mounted externally, with the exception of the American-built Grumman Avenger.

The prototype Gannet, then known as the Fairey Type 'Q', was ordered by the Ministry of Supply on 12 August 1946. Like its unsuccessful competitor, the Blackburn Y.B. 1 (also with a Double Mamba), it was built to the requirements of Spec. G.R. 17/45, and the first aircraft (VR 546) was flown by Gp. Capt. Slade at Aldermaston on 19 September 1949. This and the second prototype (VR 557, flown 6 July 1950) were two-seaters: meanwhile in June 1949 a third prototype equipped as a three-seater had been ordered. The first prototype reappeared on 13 March 1951 with a mock-up third cockpit and the radar scanner moved further aft; in June 1951 it was again modified and mounted auxiliary fins on the tailplane. Finally, in December 1951, the bomb-bay was lengthened.

The third prototype (WE 488) made its first flight on 10 May 1951, and was generally similar in appearance to subsequent production aircraft. All three prototypes underwent an intensive development and test programme, and on 19 June 1950, VR 546 was landed aboard H.M.S. *Illustrious* at sea. This was the first occasion on which a turbo-prop aircraft had ever landed aboard a carrier (the Blackburn Y.B. 1 did not achieve this feat until 30 October 1950, also aboard *Illustrious*). During the carrier trials the three Gannet prototypes completed over 250 deck landings.

On 14 March 1951 the Gannet was ordered into quantity production under the 'Super-Priority' scheme, and the first production aircraft (WN 339) was flown by Peter Twiss on 9 June 1953. First production Gannets, designated A.S. 1, mounted the same Double Mamba (100) ASM.D. 1 as the prototypes and were built at Hayes, assembled at Northolt and flown to White Waltham for collection by F.A.A. pilots. From October 1954 Gannet A.S. 1s (beginning WN 370) also came off the Fairey assembly line at Stockport, being test-flown at Ringway.

In October 1953 the first production Gannet A.S. 1 successfully completed its carrier trials (some of them at night) and in April 1954 four Gannets (WN 347, 348, 349 and 350) joined No. 703X Flight of No. 703 Squadron Service Trials Unit at Ford, Sussex, commanded by Lt.-Cdr. F. E. Cowtan. With Service trials completed, the first operational Gannet unit, No. 826 Squadron, formed up at Lee-on-Solent on 17 January 1955. In February 1955 No. 824 Squadron at Eglinton, Northern Ireland, also received Gannets. No. 826 Squadron embarked in the new carrier *Eagle* in May 1955 and No. 824 Squadron in *Ark Royal* in October 1955. In July 1955 the third Gannet squadron, No. 825, received its new equipment at Culdrose, Cornwall.

On 13 April 1956, the Gannet A.S. 4 (beginning XA 412) made its first flight. This aircraft, which succeeded the A.S. 1 in production, differed from the earlier version in having the Double Mamba (101) ASM.D. 3 and in detail changes. Prototype development of the A.S. 4 took place with the converted A.S. 1, WN 372. With the Gannet A.S. 4, the F.A.A. completed its anti-submarine re-equipment programme, and this type supplanted all remaining Firefly A.S. 7s, A.S. 6s and Avengers.

When equipment of first-line squadrons had been fully completed, Gannets were also issued to anti-submarine squadrons of the R.N.V.R. in place of Fireflies. Two squadrons (Nos. 1840 and 1882) had been so equipped when these units disbanded at the beginning of 1957.

From 1955 onwards dual-control trainer versions of the Gannet were also supplied to the F.A.A. The first prototype Gannet T. 2 (WN 365, a converted A.S. 1) made its initial flight on 16 August 1954, and production aircraft began with XA 508. The Gannet T. 2 differed from the A.S. 1 in having no retractable radome, as well as in the installation of dual controls in the observer's cockpit and an additional periscope, retractable when the front hood opened. The second trainer variant, the Gannet A.S. 5, was the dual-control version of the A.S. 4. The first production Gannet T. 5 (XG 882) made its maiden flight on 1 March 1957.

Gannet T. 2 (XA 508) of No. 737 Training Squadron. (*'Flight' Photo*.)

At the S.B.A.C. Show at Farnborough, Hampshire, in September 1957, F.A.A. aircraft participated in strength for the first time, and it fell to 12 Gannets to provide a most effective fly-past in Royal Navy 'anchor' formation. The Gannets were drawn from Nos. 737, 796 and 825 Squadrons.

Early in 1957 it was announced that a further operational version of the Gannet was being developed for service as an airborne early-warning aircraft. Designated Gannet A.E.W. 3, the prototype (XJ 440) made its first flight during the summer of 1958. The Gannet A.E.W. 3 is characterised by a large 'guppy' radome, a modified tail unit, provision for radar operators within the fuselage and a new Double Mamba engine with short jet pipes. Production aircraft are to supersede the American-built Skyraiders in the F.A.A. The A.E.W. 3 appears on page 364.

Gannet T. 5 (XG 883).

No. 703X Flight of No. 703 Service Trials Squadron; No. 719 Training Squadron; No. 737 Training Squadron; No. 771 Fleet Requirements Unit; No. 796 Training Squadron; Nos. 812, 814, 815, 820, 824, 825 and 826 Squadrons. Nos. 1840 and 1842 Squadrons of the R.N.V.R.

TECHNICAL DATA (GANNET A.S. 1 AND A.S. 4)

Description: Carrier-borne anti-submarine search and strike aircraft with a crew of three. All-metal, stressed-skin construction.

Manufacturers: Fairey Aviation Co. Ltd., Hayes, Middlesex, and Stockport, Cheshire.

Power Plant (A.S. 1): One 2,950-e.h.p. Armstrong Siddeley Double Mamba 100. (A.S. 4): One 3,035-e.h.p. Armstrong Siddeley Double Mamba 101.

Dimensions: Span, 54 ft. 4 in. Length, 43 ft. Height, 13 ft. 8½ in. (or 13 ft. 9 in. with power-operated double-hinged wings in folded position).

Weights: Not released.

Performance: Not released.

Armament: Provision in bomb-bay for two homing torpedoes; parachute mines, depth-charges or other weapons. Also provision for 16 60-lb. rocket-projectiles below the wings.

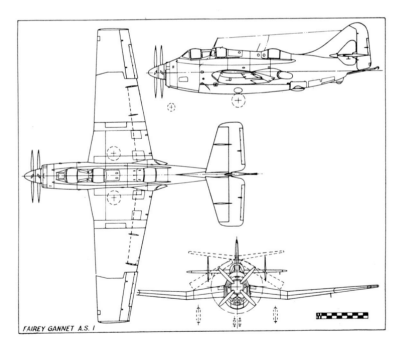

FAIREY GANNET A.S. 1

F. 2A (N 4545) from Felixstowe. (*Imp. War Museum Photo.*)

Felixstowe F. 2A

Though it saw action only during the last year of the First World War, the F. 2A earned a reputation comparable with that of the Sunderland in the Second World War. By virtue of its great endurance and heavy defensive armament, it bore the brunt of the long-range anti-submarine and anti-Zeppelin patrols over the North Sea in 1918 and figured in innumerable fights with German seaplanes; the exploits of Great Yarmouth's boats were typical, and are related at length in C. F. Snowden Gamble's classic, *The Story of a North Sea Air Station.* It established the trend of British flying-boat design for two decades and was a triumphant justification of the pioneer work of John Porte, who had from 1914 devoted himself unceasingly to the development of the flying-boat as a weapon of war.

The F. 2A was the first of the Felixstowe boats to be widely used by the R.N.A.S. The first of the series was the F. 1 (No. 3580), which combined the Porte I type of hull with the wings and tail assembly of a Curtiss H. 4. This was an experimental design only and was not put into quantity production. The success of the Porte I hull was such that it was decided to build a larger one on the same principles which could be married to the wings and tail assembly of the Curtiss H. 12 Large America. The outcome of this idea was the Felixstowe F. 2, the immediate forerunner of the F. 2A. The Porte-type hulls offered greater seaworthiness than had been the case with the Curtiss hulls, yet their method of construction was such that they could be produced by firms with no previous boat-building experience. This was an obvious asset at a period of the war when the need for greater numbers of flying-boats for anti-submarine patrol was becoming urgent.

The first F. 2A flying-boats were delivered late in 1917, and by March 1918 some 160 had been ordered; by the Armistice just under 100 had been completed, and in the immediate post-war period some aircraft ordered under these contracts were converted on the production line to F. 5 flying-boats. The number of F. 2As built would undoubtedly have been greater if a decision had not been taken by the Admiralty to issue extensive contracts for the F. 3, a flying-boat in some respects inferior to the F. 2A. As the F. 2A had originally been intended for operation from sheltered harbours, it was necessary to make some structural modifications to the hull when its use became more widespread and indiscriminate. Nevertheless, the F. 2A stood up well to harsh operational conditions, and such setbacks as it had were due, not to lack of seaworthiness, but rather to the inadequacies of the fuel system, for the windmill-driven piston pumps failed all too frequently.

One of the great advantages of the F. 2A in view of its considerable range (some boats stayed airborne for as long as $9\frac{1}{4}$ hours by carrying extra petrol in cans) was the provision of dual control; this had not been available on earlier types, such as the H. 12. Modifications to the boats to suit the ideas of individual air stations were quite common; one of the most noteworthy was the removal of the cabin for the pilot and second pilot, leaving an open cockpit. This improved both visibility and performance, and from about September 1918 was incorporated in aircraft as they left the works.

F. 2As of the Felixstowe air station inherited from the Curtiss H. 12s the historic 'Spider's Web' patrol system. This patrol began in April 1917, and was centred on the North Hinder Light Vessel, which was used as a navigation mark. Flying-boats operated within an imaginary octagonal figure, 60 sea-miles across, and followed a pre-arranged pattern

F. 2A under tow on a lighter. (*Photo from J. M. Bruce.*)

which enabled about 4,000 square miles of sea to be searched systematic-
ally. One flying-boat could search a quarter of the whole web in about
three hours, and stood a good chance of sighting a U-boat on the surface,
as submarines had to economise on battery power. Moreover, flying-
boats had the advantage over other heavier-than-air anti-submarine aircraft in that they could carry bombs of 230 lb., which could seriously
damage a submarine, even if a direct hit were not secured.

The F. 2A, despite its five-and-a-half tons, could be thrown about the
sky in a 'dog-fight' with enemy seaplanes, and on 4 June 1918 there
occurred one of the greatest air battles of the war, waged near the enemy
coastline, over three hours' flying time from the R.N.A.S. bases at Great
Yarmouth and Felixstowe. The formation of flying-boats, led by Capt.
R. Leckie, consisted of four F. 2As (N 4295 and N 4298 from Great
Yarmouth and N 4302 and N 4533 from Felixstowe) and a Curtiss H. 12.
One F. 2A (N 4533) was forced down before the engagement, due to the
old trouble of a blocked fuel line, but the remaining F. 2As fought with
a force of 14 enemy seaplanes and shot six of them down. During the
action another F. 2A (N 4302) was forced down with a broken fuel pipe,
but a repair was effected, and finally three F. 2As returned triumphantly
to base having suffered only one casualty. Following this action, in which
the danger of being forced down on the sea with fuel-pipe trouble became
only too evident, it was decided to paint the hulls of the F. 2As in distinctive colours for ready recognition. Great Yarmouth boats were painted to
the crews' own liking, and some bizarre schemes resulted; Felixstowe,
on the other hand, imposed a standardised scheme of coloured squares
and stripes. The scheme of each individual F. 2A was charted, and
copies were held by all air and naval units operating off the East Coast.

The F. 2A was also successful against Zeppelins. The most remarkable
of these engagements was on 10 May 1918, when N 4291 from Killingholme, flown by Capts. T. C. Pattinson and A. H. Munday, attacked the

Felixstowe F. 2C flying-boat. (*Imp. War Museum Photo.*)

F. 2A flying-boats on the slipway at a coastal air station of the R.N.A.S.
(*Imp. War Museum Photo.*)

Zeppelin *L. 62* at 8,000 ft. over the Heligoland minefields and shot it
down in flames. Some F. 2As, operating as far afield as Heligoland, were
towed to the scene of action on lighters behind destroyers. This technique
was first employed on 10 March 1918, and was originally part of a scheme
to extend the flying-boats' range so as to mount a bombing offensive on
enemy naval bases.

One variation of the F. 2A was built with the designation F. 2C (N 65);
it had a modified hull of lighter construction and alterations to the front
gun position. Although only one F. 2C was produced, it saw active
service with the R.N.A.S. at Felixstowe and on 24 July 1917 participated
in the successful attack on the U-boat *U.C. 1*, which was sunk by bombing.
The F. 2C, flown by Wg. Cdr. J. C. Porte, the famous flying-boat pioneer,
shared the credit for the destruction of the U-boat with two other flying-
boats in the same formation.

UNITS ALLOCATED

R.N.A.S. coastal air stations at Calshot, Dundee, Felixstowe, Great Yarmouth,
Killingholme, Scapa Flow and Tresco.

TECHNICAL DATA (F. 2A)

Description: Fighting and reconnaissance flying-boat with a crew of four.
Wooden structure, with wood and fabric covering.
Manufacturers: Aircraft Manufacturing Co. Ltd., Hendon (with hulls from
May, Harden & May, Southampton); S. E. Saunders Ltd., Isle of
Wight; Norman Thompson Flight Co., Bognor Regis. Serial numbers
allocated were N 4080 to N 4099, N 4280 to N 4309, N 4430 to N
4504, N 4510 to N 4519, N 5430 to N 5454 and N 4560 to N 4568,
but some aircraft were eventually delivered as F. 5s.
Power Plant: Two 345-h.p. Rolls-Royce Eagle VIII.
Dimensions: Span, 95 ft. 7½ in. Length, 46 ft. 3 in. Height, 17 ft. 6 in.
Wing area, 1,133 sq. ft.
Weights: Empty, 7,549 lb. Loaded, 10,978 lb.

An F. 2A flying-boat on patrol over the North Sea. (*Imp. War Museum Photo.*)

Performance: Maximum speed, 95½ m.p.h. at 2,000 ft.; 80½ m.p.h. at 10,000 ft. Climb, 3 mins. 50 secs. to 2,000 ft.; 39 mins. 30 secs. to 10,000 ft. Endurance (normal), 6 hrs. Service ceiling, 9,600 ft.

Armament: From four to seven free-mounted Lewis machine-guns (in bows, waist positions, rear cockpit and above pilot's cockpit) and two 230-lb. bombs mounted in racks below the bottom wings.

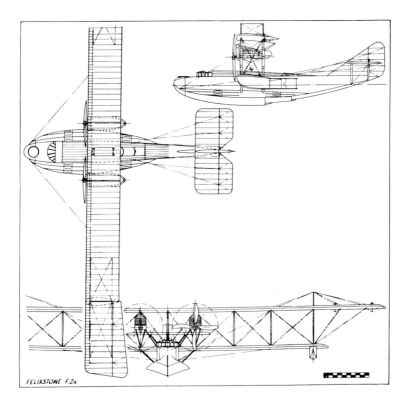

FELIXSTOWE F.2A

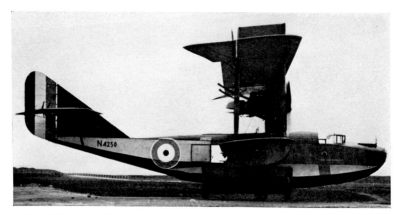

F. 3 (N 4230) built by Dick, Kerr & Co. Ltd. (*Imp. War Museum Photo.*)

Felixstowe F. 3

It is generally conceded that the F. 3, though the subject of large-scale production contracts, which by March 1918 had reached a total of 263, was in many respects the inferior of the F. 2A. Admittedly it could carry twice as many bombs, but it was slower and less manœuvrable, and hence lacked the qualities which had enabled the F. 2A to take on German seaplane fighters in air combat. On the other hand, it was capable of a greater range. These qualities resulted in the F. 3s being sent to coastal air stations where anti-submarine patrols were the order of the day and the likelihood of engagements with enemy fighters or Zeppelins remote.

The prototype F. 3 (N 64) differed from production aircraft in having twin 320-h.p. Sunbeam Cossack engines instead of Rolls-Royce Eagles. It is recorded that it served operationally during 1917–18 with the Royal Naval air station at Felixstowe. It made its maiden flight in February 1917 and was finally written off in May 1918.

Unlike the F. 2A, which served only from home stations, the F. 3 operated extensively in the Mediterranean, and in October 1918 accompanied the Naval attack on Durazzo in Albania. The operational requirements for anti-submarine flying-boats in the Mediterranean area were, in fact, so pressing that manufacture of F. 3 flying-boats was undertaken locally in Malta dockyards. Eighteen were built in Malta between November 1917 and the Armistice.

Not all the F. 3s ordered were built, as, with the end of hostilities, flying-boat contracts were cancelled or heavily curtailed, and at that time only about 100 had been completed. Some were completed as F. 5s and delivered post-war. The serial numbers allocated to contractors are listed below.

UNITS ALLOCATED

Coastal air stations at Cattewater, Felixstowe, Houton Bay and Tresco, Scillies. Also in the Mediterranean.

Description: Anti-submarine patrol flying-boat with a crew of four. Wooden structure, with wood and fabric covering.

Manufacturers: Short Bros., Ltd., Rochester (N 4000 to N 4049); Dick, Kerr & Co. Ltd., Preston (N 4100 to N 4159 and N 4230 to N 4279); Phoenix Dynamo Manufacturing Co. Ltd., Bradford (N 4160 to N 4179, N 4180 to N 4229 and N 4400 to N 4429); Malta Dockyard (N 4310 to N 4321).

Power Plant: Two 345-h.p. Rolls-Royce Eagle VIII.

Dimensions: Span, 102 ft. Length, 49 ft. 2 in. Height, 18 ft. 8 in. Wing area, 1,432 sq. ft.

Weights: Empty, 7,958 lb. Loaded (normal), 12,235 lb.

Performance: Maximum speed, 91 m.p.h. at 2,000 ft.; 86 m.p.h. at 6,500 ft. Climb, 5¼ mins. to 2,000 ft.; 24 mins. to 6,500 ft. Endurance, 6 hrs. Service ceiling, 8,000 ft.

Armament: Four Lewis machine-guns on free mountings and four 230-lb. bombs on racks beneath the wings.

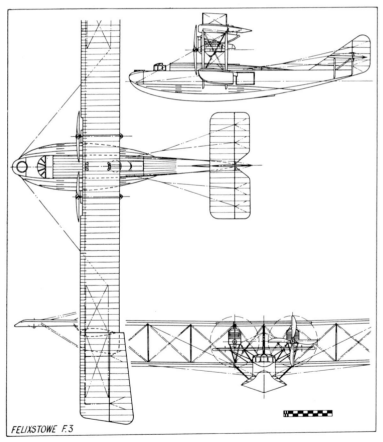

FELIXSTOWE F.3

Sea Gladiator (N 5525). (*'Flight' Photo.*)

Gloster Sea Gladiator

Just as the Gladiator was the last biplane fighter of the R.A.F., so was the Sea Gladiator the last of its kind in the F.A.A. It differed little from its R.A.F. counterpart, except in the installation of catapult points, a deck-arrester hook and a collapsible dinghy in a fairing beneath the fuselage between the undercarriage legs. It first made its appearance in 1938 at a time when the F.A.A. was badly in need of a new carrier fighter to replace the Hawker Nimrods, which had served since 1932.

Sixty Sea Gladiators (N 5500 onwards) were specially built for the F.A.A. There were also 38 interim versions (N 2265 to N 2302) converted from R.A.F. Gladiators. First deliveries (N 5501 to N 5516) were made to the Royal Naval Air Station at Donibristle in February 1939. The Sea Gladiators replaced Nimrods and Ospreys in No. 801 Squadron, and in May 1939 they embarked in H.M.S. *Courageous*. At this period No. 801 Squadron had six Sea Gladiators and three Skuas in *Courageous*; later in the year the squadron went over entirely to Skuas.

During 1940 Sea Gladiators fought both in the North Sea and in the Mediterranean. In August, during the naval bombardment of Bardia, Sea Gladiators of No. 813 Squadron in *Eagle* provided effective fighter protection for the spotting Swordfish, and in the Norwegian campaign Sea Gladiators of No. 804 Squadron in *Glorious* went into action against the *Luftwaffe*, providing fighter patrols whilst ferrying the R.A.F. Gladiators of No. 263 Squadron to Norway. By the close of 1940, however, the Sea Gladiator had been largely superseded as a first-line fighter by the Grumman Martlet.

As is now well known, four Sea Gladiators borrowed from the F.A.A.

and flown by the R.A.F. (N 5519, N 5520, N 5524 and N 5531) formed the sole air defence of Malta from 11 to 28 June 1940. The full story of this epic is told in Kenneth Poolman's book *Faith, Hope and Charity*, the names by which three of these aircraft were known to the Maltese.

No. 801 (Donibristle and *Courageous*); No. 802 (*Glorious*); No. 804 (Hatston, *Glorious* and *Furious*); No. 805 (with Fulmars and Buffalos in Crete); No. 813 (with Swordfish, in *Illustrious* and *Eagle*); No. 885 (with Buffalos, in Egypt) and No. 769 Training Squadron.

TECHNICAL DATA (SEA GLADIATOR)

Description: Single-seat carrier-borne fighter. Metal structure, with fabric and metal covering.
Manufacturers: Gloster Aircraft Co. Ltd., Hucclecote, Gloucester.
Power Plant: One 840-h.p. Bristol Mercury VIIIA.
Dimensions: Span, 32 ft. 3 in. Length, 27 ft. 5 in. Height, 10 ft. 4 in. Wing area, 323 sq. ft.
Weights: Empty, 3,745 lb. Loaded, 5,420 lb.
Performance: Maximum speed, 245 m.p.h. at 15,000 ft. Cruising, 212 m.p.h. at 15,500 ft. Range 425 miles. Endurance, $2\frac{1}{4}$ hrs. Service ceiling, 32,000 ft.
Armament: Four Browning machine-guns: two mounted in fuselage and two in lower wings.

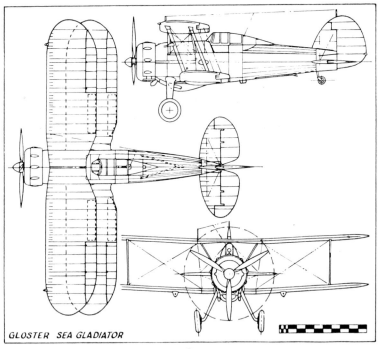

GLOSTER SEA GLADIATOR

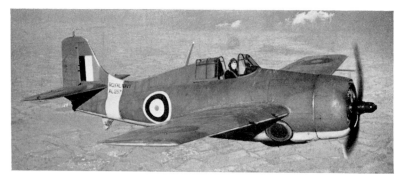

Martlet I (AL 257). (*Imp. War Museum Photo.*)

Grumman Martlet (Mks. I to III)

One of the Grumman Martlet's chief claims to fame is that it was the first type of American fighter in service with British forces to shoot down a German aircraft in the Second World War. This notable event occurred on 25 December 1940 and two Martlets of No. 804 Squadron were involved. Flown by Lt. L. V. Carver, R.N., and Sub-Lt. (A) Parke, R.N.V.R., the Martlets were on patrol over the Home Fleet base at Scapa Flow, when they intercepted and forced down a Junkers Ju 88 attempting to bomb the Fleet. The crew of four from the Ju 88 was captured. So began the Martlet's long and fruitful career with the F.A.A.

The Martlet was the British version of the U.N. Navy and Marine Corps F4F-3, and was ordered for the F.A.A. at the same time that it was accepted for service in the U.S. services. It was known to its manufacturers as the G-36, and was the latest of a long line of successful Grumman fighters for the U.S. Navy, though it differed from all its predecessors in being a monoplane. Grumman's association with U.S. Navy fighters began with their two-seat FF-1 biplane of 1931 and developed through the F2F-1 single-seater of 1935 and the F3F-1, a 1936 derivative. All these biplanes were characterised by the tubby fuselage later to be seen on the F4F monoplane, and were unusual in their day in employing a retractable undercarriage: the 27 FF-1 fighters which went aboard *Ranger* in 1934 were the first aircraft with retractable undercarriage ever seen aboard a carrier.

Grumman's new monoplane fighter made its first flight on 23 December 1937, and in 1940 the U.S. Navy placed an initial contract for 78 F4F-3s, as the production version was designated, to supersede the Grumman F3F-3, which was the last biplane fighter in U.S. Navy squadrons. The F4F-3 was a notable advance in U.S. naval fighters, offering as it did about 310 m.p.h. against the F3F-3 biplane's 270 m.p.h. and four 0·50-calibre guns in place of two of 0·30 calibre. In 1941 the U.S. Navy named the type the Wildcat, but Martlet was retained as the British nomenclature until January 1944.

With the entry of the U.S.A. into the war in December 1941, the Wildcat was the most widely-used fighter aboard U.S. aircraft-carriers, and it also equipped numbers of shore-based units of the U.S. Marine Corps. It was one of the latter units—Marine Fighting Squadron 211—which defended Wake Island so heroically against the Japanese in an action strongly reminiscent of the *Faith, Hope* and *Charity* epic with Sea Gladiators in Malta. In the first Japanese bombing raid on Wake Island on 8 December 1941, eight out of 12 Wildcats were destroyed, but the remaining four fought on in the face of heavy sea and air attacks and succeeded in sinking an enemy cruiser and a submarine, as well as shooting down six aircraft before the last two Wildcats were destroyed as the Japanese landed on 22 December 1941.

With the F.A.A., Martlets first entered service with No. 804 Squadron at Hatston in October 1940, superseding Sea Gladiators. These aircraft were drawn from a batch of 85 Martlet I (AL 236 to AL 262, AX 725 to AX 738, AX 824 to AX 829, BJ 507 to BJ 527 and BJ 554 to BJ 570) which reached Britain during 1940. The Martlet I had fixed wings, a single-row Wright Cyclone engine and mounted four machine-guns. It was followed in 1941 by the Martlet II, which, like all subsequent Martlets and Wildcats down to the Mk. V, was powered by the two-row Pratt and Whitney Twin Wasp engine. By virtue of its folding wings, the Martlet II was the first of the series to be embarked in British aircraft-carriers. It was equivalent to the F4F-3 in U.S. Navy service. Ninety Martlet IIs were built, of which 54 (AJ 100 to AJ 153) were shipped to the Far East (some being lost at sea) and the remaining 36 (AM 964 to AM 999) supplied to the United Kingdom. A further batch of Martlet III fighters was also delivered to Britain, comprising 10 aircraft from British contract (AM 954 to AM 963) and 30 aircraft from a Greek contract. The Martlet III was similar to the Martlet II, except that it had fixed wings, as on the Martlet I.

One of the first units to go to sea with Martlets was No. 802 Squadron, whose aircraft were aboard the small escort carrier H.M.S. *Audacity*, a converted German merchant-ship of 5,600 tons, during her first trip in September 1941, escorting a Gibraltar-bound convoy. On 19 September the Martlets attacked a U-boat with machine-gun fire, forcing it to submerge, and the next day succeeded in shooting down a Focke Wulf Fw 200 four-engined bomber which had been shadowing the convoy. The two Martlets responsible were flown by Sub-Lts. N. H. Patterson and G. R. P. Fletcher. During the second voyage by *Audacity*, in November 1941, No. 802 Squadron's Martlets destroyed four Focke Wulf Fw 200 bombers, and in one day alone flew a total of 30 hrs. On this hectic day the last two Martlets to return to *Audacity* had to land in the dark whilst the ship was rolling 14 degrees.

In May 1942 Martlets of Nos. 881 and 882 Squadrons, both embarked in *Illustrious*, added to their growing reputation as formidable fighting aircraft during operations over Madagascar. On 6 May Martlets patrolled the beaches, carried out tactical reconnaissances for the Army and ground-straffed enemy positions holding up the advance. They also shot down three Potez 63 bombers without loss to themselves. The next day there were numerous air combats between the Martlets and Vichy French Moranes, and in the whole three days of fighting the Martlets shot down

Martlet II (AJ 132) of No. 881 Squadron. (*Imp. War Museum Photo.*)

seven enemy aircraft for the loss of only one, as well as having given the landing parties complete air cover.

In August 1942 Martlets of No. 806 Squadron in *Indomitable* sailed with one of the famous Malta convoys and were in action against Italian bombers over the Mediterranean. The following November, with the Allied invasion of North Africa, Martlets were in the thick of the fighting once more. Again they covered the troops going ashore in assault craft and attacked machine-gun posts along the beaches. It was during these operations that a Martlet of No. 882 Squadron, from *Victorious*, took the surrender of the French fighter airfield at Blida, about 30 miles from Algiers. Whilst on patrol over the airfield, Lt. B. H. C. Nation noticed some French officers signalling. He landed, was greeted by the Commandant, and handed a formal surrender.

As well as operating with great success from carriers, Martlets also took part in the air operations over the Western Desert during December 1942. The unit concerned was No. 805 Squadron, based at Dekheila.

In all these operations the Martlet proved itself a sturdy and reliable aircraft. In the words of one pilot:

'It was manœuvrable and could turn inside any aircraft it met. It dived at 390 to 400 m.p.h. with no trouble at all. The Twin Wasp was a most reliable engine and one Martlet was, apart from routine inspections, never once unserviceable in twelve months of operations. On completion of 190 hours' flying in *Illustrious* its engine was running as well as ever. The heavy calibre guns meant that fifty rounds per gun frequently sufficed to shoot down an enemy aircraft.'

UNITS ALLOCATED

No. 802 (Donibristle, *Argus* and *Audacity*); No. 804 (Hatston); No. 805 (Dekheila, Egypt); No. 806 (*Indomitable*); No. 881 (Lee-on-Solent, *Illustrious* and *Furious*); No. 882 (Donibristle, *Illustrious*, *Archer*, *Formidable* and *Victorious*); No. 888 (*Formidable*); No. 890 (*Battler* and *Argus*); No. 892 (*Battler* and *Archer*); No. 893 (with Fulmars, Donibristle and *Formidable*); No. 894 (U.S.S. *Wolverine* and *Battler*); No. 896 (*Victorious*) and No. 898 (*Victorious*).

Description: Single-seat carrier-borne or shore-based fighter. All-metal stressed-skin construction.

Manufacturers: Grumman Aircraft Engineering Corporation, Bethpage, Long Island, New York.

Power Plant (Mk. I): One 1,200-h.p. Wright Cyclone G-205A. (Mk. II): One 1,200-h.p. Pratt & Whitney Twin Wasp S3C4-G.

Dimensions: Span, 38 ft. Length, 28 ft. 10 in. Height, 9 ft. 2½ in. Wing area, 260 sq. ft.

Weights (Mk. I): Empty, 4,425 lb. Loaded, 5,876 lb. (Mk. II): Empty, 4,649 lb. Loaded, 6,100 lb.

Performance (Mk. I): Maximum speed, 310 m.p.h. Cruising, 257 m.p.h. Climb, 3,300 ft./min. Range, 1,100 miles. Service ceiling, 28,000 ft. (Mk. II): Maximum speed, 315 m.p.h. Cruising, 260 m.p.h. Climb, 3,300 ft./min. Range, 1,150 miles. Service ceiling, 28,000 ft.

Armament (Mk. I): Four fixed 0·50-calibre guns in wings. (Mk. II): Six 0·50-calibre guns in wings.

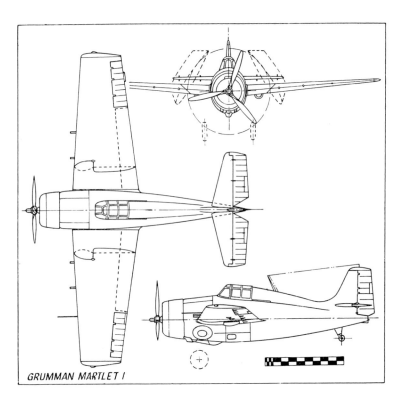

GRUMMAN MARTLET I

Wildcat V (JV 579) in D-Day invasion stripes.

Grumman Wildcat (Mks. IV to VI)

Unlike the earlier Martlets delivered to the F.A.A. in 1940 and 1941, the Martlet IV and subsequent fighters in the series were not bought by the British Government, but were supplied under Lend–Lease arrangements. Both the Martlet IV and V were known as such until January 1944, when the name was changed to Wildcat to conform with U.S. Navy nomenclature. The Wildcat VI, which entered service after this date, was known from the outset under this name. For the sake of simplicity, the name Wildcat is used throughout the following narrative.

The Wildcat IV was the F.A.A. equivalent of the U.S. Navy's F4F-4. It was generally similar to the Mk. II (F4F-3), but had two additional wing guns, making a total of six. The total of aircraft supplied was 220, the serial numbers allocated being FN 100 to FN 319. Deliveries began in 1942.

The Wildcat V, which followed in 1943, was the British equivalent of the U.S. Navy's FM-1, the new designation signifying that the aircraft were built by the Eastern Aircraft Division of the General Motors Corporation, instead of the parent company. Grumman had by this time tapered off Wildcat production (after building about 1,600) in favour of the new Hellcat. Thereafter all Wildcats came from the General Motors plant, where about 5,500 were built before VJ-Day. Total deliveries of the Wildcat V to the F.A.A. amounted to 312 aircraft, with serial numbers JV 325 to JV 636.

Wildcat IV and V fighters served for the most part in MAC-ships, the light escort-carriers converted from merchant ships which made such an invaluable contribution to victory in the Battle of the Atlantic. Some of the later Wildcats, however, also saw action from the larger carriers, notably in *Illustrious* during the Salerno landings, and in *Victorious* for operations in the S.W. Pacific.

In the escort carriers the Wildcats worked mainly in conjunction with Swordfish. Their rôle was to provide fighter protection for convoys and to assist the Swordfish in their rocket strikes on submarines, by diverting the attention of the U-boat's gun-team whilst the strike aircraft made its run. The first squadron equipped with the Wildcat IV was No. 892, which took delivery of six aircraft at Norfolk, Virginia, on 15 July 1942. It subsequently embarked in the escort carriers *Battler* and *Archer*. The Wildcat IVs were joined in 1943 by Wildcat Vs, and by the middle of 1944 there were about 15 squadrons in the escort carrier force flying these fighters. Some of them saw action in the North Russian convoy escorts: Wildcats of No. 813 Squadron (also equipped with 12 Swordfish) shot down two enemy aircraft during the convoy of September 1944. Wildcats from escort carriers were also active in the invasion of S. France by the Allies: No. 882 Squadron, in *Searcher*, flew 167 sorties over the landing-beaches between 15 and 23 August 1944, and others, from No. 881 Squadron, were flown off from *Pursuer*. Wildcats were also called upon to provide fighter escorts for Barracudas during the series of dive-bombing

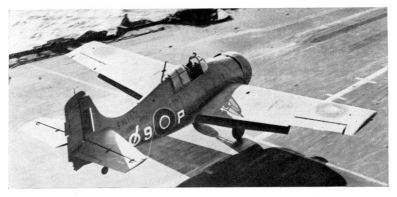

Wildcat IV (FN 142). (*Imp. War Museum Photo.*)

Wildcat VI (JV 642). (*Crown Copyright Photo.*)

raids on *Tirpitz* in 1944, the squadrons engaged being Nos. 881, 896 and 898. In subsequent operations over Norway from *Searcher* No. 898 Squadron Wildcats shot down four Blohm and Voss Bv 138 flying-boats and a Focke Wulf Fw 200, which were engaged on reconnaissance sorties.

During the Allied landings at Salerno in September 1943 Wildcats of Nos. 878 and 890 Squadrons (both embarked in *Illustrious*) maintained constant patrols over the beaches, sharing this task with Seafires from the light escort carriers *Attacker, Battler, Hunter* and *Stalker*.

In June 1944 Wildcats of No. 846 Squadron participated in the widespread fighter activities over the landing-zones during the D-Day operations. A few weeks previously a Wildcat V of this same squadron had shared, with an Avenger and a Swordfish, in the sinking of *U-288*.

Shortly after D-Day a new version of the Wildcat, the Mk. VI, began to enter F.A.A. squadrons. This was the last variant to be supplied for British service, and was the equivalent of the U.S. Navy's FM-2. It could be easily distinguished from earlier Wildcats by reason of its modified tail design, with much taller fin and rudder. The Wildcat VI also marked a return to the Wright Cyclone engine. This Cyclone was a much-improved version incorporating a turbo-supercharger and developing 1,350 h.p.

A total of 370 Wildcat VI fighters was supplied under Lend–Lease, the serial numbers allocated being JV 637 to JV 924, JW 785 to JW 836 and JZ 860 to JZ 889. The Wildcat VI first entered service in the F.A.A. with No. 881 Squadron on 4 July 1944, replacing Wildcat Vs in H.M.S. *Pursuer*. This variant served chiefly in the Far East with the British East Indies and Pacific Fleets.

With the arrival of VJ-Day the Wildcats were all returned to the U.S.A., and by the end of 1945 had disappeared from the F.A.A. scene.

UNITS ALLOCATED

No. 811 Squadron (three Wildcats added to 12 Swordfish in 1943; embarked in *Biter* and *Vindex*); No. 813 Squadron (four Wildcats added to 12 Swordfish, April 1944; embarked in *Campania* and *Vindex*); No. 816 Squadron (six Wildcats added to nine Swordfish, January 1944; embarked in *Chaser* and *Activity*); No. 819 Squadron (three Wildcats added to Swordfish, August 1943; embarked in *Activity*); No. 821 Squadron (six Wildcats added to 12 Barracudas, April 1945; embarked in *Trumpeter*); No. 824 Squadron (six Wildcats added to 12 Swordfish, April 1944; embarked in *Striker*); No. 825 Squadrons (eight Wildcats added to Swordfish —replacing Sea Hurricanes—November 1944; embarked in *Campania*); No. 832 Squadron (four Wildcats added to 15 Avengers, January 1944; embarked in *Illustrious* and *Begum*); No. 833 Squadron (seven Wildcats added to three Swordfish, April 1944; embarked in *Activity*); No. 835 Squadron (six Wildcats added to 14 Swordfish, August 1944; embarked in *Nairana*); No. 842 Squadron (four Wildcats—replacing Seafires—added to 6 Swordfish, November 1943; embarked in *Hunter, Fencer* and *Campania*); No. 845 Squadron (four Wildcats added to 12 Avengers, January 1944; embarked in *Engadine, Emperor* and *Shah*); No. 846 Squadron (four Wildcats added to Avengers, January 1944; embarked in *Tracker, Trumpeter* and *Premier*); No. 849 Squadron (four Wildcats added to 12 Avengers, November 1943; embarked in *Victorious*); No. 851 Squadron (six Wildcats added to 12 Avengers, May 1943; embarked in *Emperor* and *Shah*); No. 853 Squadron (four Wildcats added to 12 Avengers, June 1944; embarked in *Tracker* and *Queen*); No. 878 Squadron (formed with 12 Wildcats at Lee-on-Solent, March 1943; embarked in *Illustrious*); No. 881 Squadron (embarked in *Unicorn, Fencer, Trumpeter, Premier* and *Pursuer*); No. 890 Squadron (formed with six Wildcats at

Halifax, Novia Scotia, June 1942; embarked in *Battler, Argus, Illustrious* and *Atheling*); No. 892 Squadron (formed with six Wildcats at Norfolk, Virginia, July 1942; embarked in *Battler* and *Archer*); No. 896 Squadron (formed with six Wild-cats at Norfolk, Virginia, September 1942; embarked in *Victorious* and *Pursuer*); No. 898 Squadron (formed with 12 Wildcats at Norfolk, Virginia, October 1942; embarked in *Victorious, Searcher, Fencer* and *Striker*); No. 1832 Squadron (formed as light escort-carrier pool at Speke, August 1943; 'A' Flight to *Fencer*, 'B' Flight to *Tracker*, 'C' Flight to *Slinger*, 'D' Flight to *Engadine*, 'E' Flight to *Fencer*, 'F' Flight to *Campania* and 'G' Flight to *Nabob*).

TECHNICAL DATA (WILDCAT IV)

Description: Single-seat carrier-borne fighter. All-metal stressed-skin construction.
Manufacturers: Grumman Aircraft Engineering Corporation, Bethpage, Long Island, New York.
Power Plant: One 1,200-h.p. Pratt & Whitney Twin Wasp R-1830-86.
Dimensions: Span, 38 ft. Length, 28 ft. 11 in. Height, 9 ft. 2½ in. Wing area, 260 sq. ft.
Weights: Empty, 4,649 lb. Loaded, 6,100 lb.
Performance: Maximum speed, 330 m.p.h. at 19,500 ft.; 290 m.p.h. at sea level. Cruising, 297 m.p.h. at 19,500 ft. Initial climb, 3,300 ft./min. Maximum range, 1,150 miles. Service ceiling, 28,000 ft.
Armament: Six fixed 0·50-calibre machine-guns in the wings.

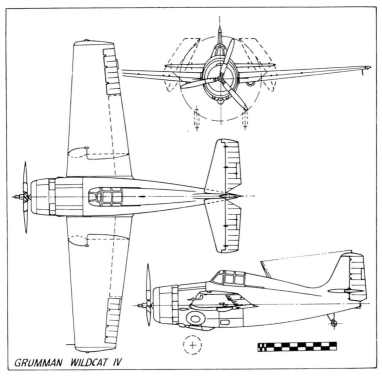

GRUMMAN WILDCAT IV

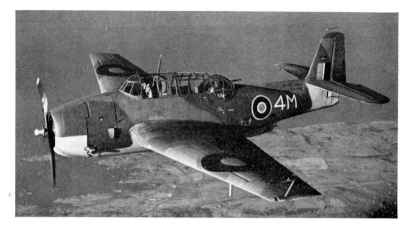

Avenger I (FN 908). (*Chas. E. Brown Photo.*)

Grumman Avenger (Mks. I to III)

Despite a far from encouraging start when first used on operations in the Pacific in 1942, the Grumman Avenger later redeemed itself and, in fact, became one of the outstanding naval aircraft of the Second World War. It was produced in vast quantities, almost 10,000 being built (about 2,200 by the parent firm and the rest by General Motors), of which nearly 1,000 reached the F.A.A. No fewer than 15 first-line squadrons of the F.A.A. received Avengers, and they gave excellent service in a great variety of rôles from shore bases and aboard both escort-carriers and large fleet carriers.

The Avenger first appeared in 1941 with the designation XTBF-1. It was designed by William T. Schwendler as a replacement for the Douglas Devastator, which had been the U.S. Navy's standard torpedo-bomber for a number of years. In general appearance it had many features of the same company's Wildcat fighter: both aircraft were the work of the same designer. Two features made the Avenger outstanding: it was the first single-engined American aircraft to mount a power-operated gun turret, and the first to carry a 22-in. torpedo. The Devastator had been armed with only a 21-in. torpedo.

The first production Avenger, designated TBF-1, left the Grumman factory in February 1942 and less than four months later, in June 1942, six Avengers made their operational début in the now historic Battle of Midway. Operating from a shore base, the Avengers met with a serious reverse; they failed to sink any enemy ships, and five out of six were shot down.

By July 1943 over 1,000 Avengers had been built, and by this time the manufacturing resources of the great General Motors organisation were being devoted to the type, the latter aircraft being distinguished by the designation TBM-1. The Trenton-built TBM Avengers eventually superseded the older Grumman-built T.B.F.s in the U.S. Navy. The final production total was 9,857, comprised of 2,311 TBF-1 and TBF-1C built at Grumman, and 2,882 TBM-1 and TBM-1C, followed by 4,664 TBM-3 and TBM-3E, by General Motors.

Avengers delivered to the F.A.A. were supplied under Lend–Lease arrangements, beginning in 1943. Until January 1944 the British name Tarpon was used: thereafter the original American name was revived as part of an inter-Allied standardisation in designations. The Tarpon I (afterwards Avenger I) was the British equivalent of the U.S. Navy TBF-1, and 402 were delivered, numbered FN 750 to FN 949, JT 773, and JZ 100 to JZ 300. Next came 334 Avenger IIs, equivalent to the U.S. Navy's TBM-1, and numbered JZ 301 to JZ 634. The Avenger III, of which 222 were supplied, introduced the R-2600-20 engine, in place of the R-2600-8 used in previous Marks, and there were other detailed changes, including anti-submarine radar in some aircraft. The Avenger III (JZ 635 to JZ 746 and KE 430 to KE 549) was the F.A.A. equivalent of the U.S. Navy TBM-3 and 3E. A final batch of 70 Avenger IV (KE 540 to KE 609) was also earmarked for Britain, but never delivered.

No. 832 Squadron of the F.A.A., formerly flying Fairey Albacores, was the first to be equipped with Avengers. The squadron took delivery at Norfolk in the U.S.A. on 1 January 1943. In April 1943 No. 832 Squadron's Avengers went aboard the U.S. Navy carrier U.S.S. *Saratoga*, and on 27 June went into action during the landings in the Middle Solomons in the Coral Sea. This is believed to have been the first occasion on which F.A.A. aircraft went into action from an American carrier. Afterwards No. 832's Avengers transferred to the East Indies Fleet, embarking first in *Victorious* and later in *Illustrious*. No. 832 Squadron's last commission (from June 1944 until disbandment on 21 February 1945) was in the escort carrier *Begum*, which protected shipping in the Indian Ocean.

By the end of 1943 there were eight Avenger squadrons with the F.A.A. The squadrons formed up at the U.S. Navy bases at Norfolk, Quonset and Squantam, and the crews familiarised themselves with their aircraft before embarking in escort carriers to be ferried to the United Kingdom. Another five squadrons came into being in this way in 1944: all of them started life with Avengers, having had no previous existence. In the case of the last two squadrons to be formed (No. 820 in October 1944 and No. 828 in February 1945) the Avengers superseded Barracudas.

Although designed primarily as a torpedo-bomber, and widely employed as such by the U.S. Navy, the Avenger in F.A.A. service was rarely engaged in this rôle. Instead it operated as a bomber (with bombs, mines or depth-charges) and as a strike aircraft armed with rocket-projectiles beneath the wings. In home waters Avengers so equipped operated chiefly with escort-carriers or from shore bases on anti-submarine patrol, or occasionally on mine-laying sorties. Shore-based Avengers operated both from Royal Naval air stations and under the control of Coastal Command at R.A.F. stations. The first Avengers to operate in home waters were those of No. 846 Squadron. This unit formed at Quonset on 1 April 1943 and served in turn at R.N.A.S. Hatson, Grimsetter and Machrihanish before embarking in the escort-carrier *Tracker*, together with four Wildcat fighters, on 4 January 1944. On 1 April 1944, whilst escorting a Russian convoy, an Avenger of No. 846 Squadron shared honours with H.M.S. *Beagle* for the sinking of *U-355* in the Arctic. A few days later, on 4 April, an Avenger and a Wildcat V of No. 846 Squadron shared with a Swordfish of No. 819 Squadron (*Activity*) the destruction of *U-288*.

Another Avenger squadron engaged on convoy escort, No. 853, took part in the last trip to North Russia before VE-Day, and on 7–10 May 1945 escorted naval forces to Copenhagen.

With the gradual build-up for D-Day in 1944 a number of Avenger squadrons were added to the anti-shipping strike forces of Coastal Command, starting in April 1944. They joined Albacores and Beaufighters in Operation 'Channel Stop', which was designed to prevent enemy shipping from entering the English Channel, escorted assault convoys and participated in many night attacks on 'E' boats, 'R' boats and minesweepers. On 24 July 1944 an Avenger of No. 850 Squadron, flying from Perranporth, sank a large enemy merchant-ship off Guernsey.

The most spectacular exploits of the F.A.A.'s Avengers were, however, in the Far East with the East Indies and Pacific Fleets. One of the first big operations in which they took part was the attack on the Japanese naval base at Sourabaya, Java, on 19 May 1944. Avengers of Nos. 832 and 845 Squadrons, flying from *Illustrious*, joined U.S. Navy Dauntlesses from *Saratoga* in this remarkably successful raid, which took the Japanese completely by surprise. It was the first time that F.A.A. Avengers had bombed a land target.

During the final phases of the war against Japan, Avengers operated first with the East Indies Fleet based on Ceylon, and, afterwards, with the British Pacific Fleet based on Australia to deal the enemy some smashing blows. In January 1945 Avengers played a major rôle in one of the most important F.A.A. actions of the Second World War: a carefully planned attack on the Japanese oil refineries at Palembang, in Sumatra. These refineries produced a large proportion of the oil needed by the Japanese Navy and aviation fuel by their Air Force. Forty-eight Avengers took part, drawn from Nos. 820, 849, 854 and 857 Squadrons, respectively aboard *Indefatigable*, *Victorious*, *Illustrious* and *Indomitable*; an escort of 32 Corsairs, 16 Hellcats and 12 Fireflies was provided. The attacks were made on 24 and 29 January, and on both occasions the Avengers dived through a balloon barrage to be sure of hitting their targets. Despite intense anti-aircraft fire and strong fighter opposition, the operation was a major success; the Avengers hit their targets fairly and squarely, and both refineries were completely destroyed. This significant victory, the first large-scale action by the F.A.A. against the Japanese, made a vital contribution to ultimate success in the Pacific by depriving the enemy of fuel both for ships and aircraft. As late as May 1945 the refinery at Songei Gerong was still inactive, and the other, at Pladjoe, producing less than half its normal output.

Between March and May 1945 Avengers from the carriers *Illustrious*, *Indefatigable*, *Indomitable*, *Formidable* and *Victorious*, all of the 1st Aircraft Carrier Squadron of the British Pacific Fleet based on Sydney, carried out intensive bombing raids on enemy fighter bases in Formosa and islands south of Japan to assist the American landings in Okinawa. On 24 July 1945 Avengers of No. 848 Squadron (*Formidable*) became the first F.A.A. bombers to attack Japan proper, during a raid on Yokushima airfield,

Avengers of No. 848 Squadron from *Formidable*. (*Imp. War Museum Photo*.)

They were supported in this operation by Avengers of No. 828 Squadron (*Implacable*), which had the previous June seen action in the Battle of Truk, one of the bloodiest operations of the Pacific War. The mainland of Japan remained under attack by Avengers until 15 August 1945, one of the last raids being a strike in the Tokyo area by No. 820 Squadron. With the end of the war Avenger squadrons disbanded rapidly, and by the close of 1945 only two squadrons remained. With the disbandment of No. 828 Squadron on 3 June 1946, Avengers disappeared from front-line squadrons of the F.A.A.

By an unusual turn of events Avengers made their appearance in first-line squadrons once again in 1953, and details of this post-war version, the Avenger A.S. 4, can be found separately.

UNITS ALLOCATED

No. 820 (October 1944 to May 1946; embarked *Indefatigable*); No. 828 (February 1945 to June 1946; shore-based Fearn and *Implacable*); No. 832 (January 1943 to February 1945; embarked *Saratoga*, *Victorious*, *Illustrious* and *Begum*); No. 845

An Avenger of the British Pacific Fleet. (*Imp. War Museum Photo*.)

(February 1943 to October 1945; shore-based Machrihanish and Trincomalee; embarked *Chaser, Engadine, Illustrious, Ameer, Empress, Emperor* and *Shah*); No. 468 (April 1943 to October 1945; shore-based Hatston, Grimsetter, Machrihanish, Burscough, Limavady, Ayr and Crail; embarked *Ravager, Tracker, Trumpeter* and *Premier*); No. 848 (June 1943 to October 1945; shore-based Hatston, Eglinton, Manston, Thorney Island, Dekheila and Nowra; embarked *Trumpeter, Formidable, Illustrious* and *Victorious*); No. 849 (August 1943 to October 1945; shore-based Hatston, Eglinton, Perranporth, St. Eval and Ceylon; embarked *Khedive, Rajah* and *Victorious*); No. 850 (January 1943 to December 1944; shore-based Perranporth, Limavady and Maydown; embarked U.S.S. *Charger* and *Empress*); No. 851 (October 1943 to October 1945; embarked *Emperor* and *Shah*); No. 852 (November 1943 to October 1944; embarked *Nabob, Trumpeter* and *Fencer*); No. 853 (February 1944 to May 1945; embarked *Arbiter, Tracker* and *Queen*); No. 854 (January 1944 to December 1945; shore-based Thorney Island; embarked *Indomitable, Activity* and *Illustrious*); No. 855 (February 1944 to October 1944; shore-based Hawkinge, Manston, Bircham Newton and Docking; embarked *Queen*); No. 856 (March 1944 to June 1945; embarked *Smiter* and *Premier*) and No. 857 (April 1944 to November 1945; embarked *Rajah* and *Indomitable*).

TECHNICAL DATA (AVENGER T.R. I AND T.R. III)

Description: Three-seat carrier-borne or shore-based torpedo-bomber and anti-submarine strike aircraft. All-metal stressed-skin construction.
Manufacturers: Grumman Aircraft Engineering Corporation, Bethpage,

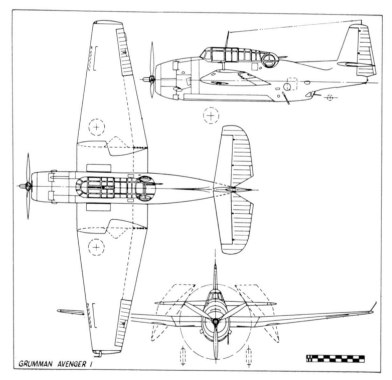

GRUMMAN AVENGER I

Long Island, New York. Sub-contracted by General Motors, Eastern Aircraft Division, Trenton, New Jersey.

Power Plant (Mk. I): One 1,850-h.p. Wright Cyclone GR-2600-8. (Mk. III): One 1,750-h.p. Wright Cyclone R-2600-20.

Dimensions: Span, 54 ft. 2 in. Length, 40 ft. Height, 15 ft. 8 in. Wing area, 490 sq. ft.

Weights (Mk. I): Empty, 10,600 lb. Loaded, 16,300 lb. (Mk. III): Empty, 10,700 lb. Loaded, 16,400 lb.

Performance (Mk. I): Maximum speed, 259 m.p.h. at 11,200 ft.; 247 m.p.h. at sea level. Cruising, 171 m.p.h. at 5,000 ft. Climb, 4·3 mins. to 5,000 ft. Range, 1,020 miles (normal) and 1,910 miles (maximum, with no bombs and extra fuel). Service ceiling, 23,000 ft. (Mk. III): Maximum speed, 262 m.p.h. at 16,600 ft.; 257 m.p.h. at 5,300 ft. Cruising, 174 m.p.h. at 5,000 ft. Climb, 3·8 mins. to 5,000 ft. Range 1,000 miles with 2,000 lb. of bombs or 2,230 miles with no bombs and extra fuel. Service ceiling, 25,000 ft.

Armament: Two fixed 0·05-calibre guns in the wings, one 0·30-calibre gun in ventral position and one 0·50-calibre gun in dorsal turret. Provision inside bomb-bay for one 22-in. torpedo of 1,921 lb. or one 1,600-lb. torpedo, or one 1,000-lb. bomb or four 500-lb. bombs. Eight 60-lb. rocket-projectiles below the wings.

Hellcat I (FN 376). (*Chas. E. Brown Photo.*)

Grumman Hellcat

The Hellcat was designed as a replacement for the Wildcat in U.S. Navy fighter squadrons and it succeeded the earlier type on the Grumman production lines in 1942. It was originally created as a private venture as a result of close collaboration between Grumman's engineering staff and U.S. Navy pilots with extensive experience of air combat with the Japanese. The outcome was a fighter which, whilst following the general lines of its predecessor, was nearly 50 m.p.h. faster and possessed a much superior rate of climb. Fire-power remained unchanged, but more ammunition could be carried, range and ceiling were improved and the protective armour plating for the pilot was much augmented. The most notable change in external appearance was the re-positioning of the wings lower down the fuselage, enabling the undercarriage to be retracted into the centre section instead of the fuselage, as on the mid-wing Wildcat. By this method a much wider undercarriage track was obtained, improving ground handling. The high-placed cockpit was designed to give good vision, and an unusual feature was the three degrees of down-thrust in the engine installation, which gave a tail-down attitude in flight.

The prototype Hellcat, designated XF6F-1, was first flown on 26 June 1942 and differed from production aircraft in having a Curtiss Electric airscrew with a large spinner. This was replaced in production Hellcats by the Hamilton Standard Hydromatic airscrew. The transition from the prototype to the production stage was achieved remarkably quickly, and the first production Hellcat was delivered in November 1942, less than a year after design had first begun. Hellcats remained in production for three years and over 10,000 were built.

Early in 1943 Hellcats were made available to Great Britain under

Lend–Lease arrangements, and deliveries continued until the end of the war, a total of 1,182 being allocated. These comprised 252 Hellcat I (originally known as the Gannet I in British service until standardisation of names was introduced), and 930 Hellcat II. The Hellcat I was the British equivalent of the U.S. Navy's F6F-3, with the Double Wasp R-2800-10 engine, and the Hellcat II the equivalent of the F6F-5 with R-2800-10W engine. Some 74 of the Hellcat IIs were equipped for night-fighter duties, and could be distinguished by means of a radome mounted on the starboard wing and a midnight-blue paint scheme in place of the orthodox British camouflage. These aircraft were the British equivalent of the U.S. Navy's F6F-5N. The Hellcat Is were allocated the serial numbers FN 320 to FN 449 and JV 100 to JV 221; the Hellcat IIs JV 222 to JV 324, JW 700 to JW 784, JW 857 to JW 899, JX 670 to JX 999, JZ 775 to JZ 827, JZ 890 to JZ 999, KD 103 to KD 160 and KE 118 to KE 265.

Hellcats first entered service with the F.A.A. on 1 July 1943, when No. 800 Squadron re-equipped from Sea Hurricanes. No. 800 Squadron's Hellcats first saw operational service during anti-shipping strikes off the Norwegian coast after embarkation in the light escort-carrier *Emperor*, in December 1943. In April 1944 they joined the fighter forces covering the attack on *Tirpitz* in Kaafiord. A later strike on *Tirpitz*, in August 1944, was escorted by Hellcats of No. 1840 Squadron embarked in *Furious*.

Most of the Hellcat's F.A.A. service, however, was with the British Pacific Fleet in the Far East. By the end of 1944 Hellcats serving in this theatre of operations were with No. 800 Squadron in *Emperor*, No. 808 Squadron in *Khedive*, No. 888 Squadron in *Empress*, No. 1839 Squadron in *Indomitable*, No. 1840 Squadron in *Indefatigable* and No. 1844 Squadron in *Indomitable*. Hellcats of No. 808 Squadron were in action off the Malayan coast from October 1944 and on 2 May 1945 those of No. 800 Squadron provided fighter cover during the capture of Rangoon. No. 888 Squadron specialised in photographic reconnaissance work, and, between 22 February and 7 March 1945, their Hellcats completed 22 reconnaissance

Hellcat II of the British Pacific Fleet. (*Imp. War Museum Photo.*)

Hellcat II (JX 822) carrying two 500-lb. bombs. (*Crown Copyright Photo.*)

sorties over the Kra Isthmus, Penang and Northern Sumatra. Earlier, No. 1839 Squadron's Hellcats had also been active over Sumatra.

During the F.A.A.'s first major action against the Japanese, the attack on the oil refineries in Sumatra in January 1945, Hellcats played an important part. Flying from the carrier *Indomitable*, Hellcats of Nos. 1839 and 1844 Squadrons provided close escort during the early strike on Pangkalan Brandan, and again in the large operations against Palembang on 24 and 29 January 1945. For these latter the 16 Hellcats were joined by 32 Corsairs of Nos. 1830 and 1833 Squadrons from *Illustrious*.

No. 1844 Squadron's Hellcats were in action again in air operations over the Sakashima Islands between 26 March and 20 April 1945, and during May were fighting over Formosa.

Meanwhile, from January 1945, Hellcats had been replacing Wildcats in the light escort-carrier force building up in readiness for the invasion of Japan. Nos. 896 and 898 Squadrons re-equipped with Hellcats at Wingfield, South Africa, in January 1945, and No. 881 Squadron followed in April. Also formed in April 1945 was the first Hellcat night-fighter squadron (No. 892) at Eglinton, Northern Ireland. It was joined by a second night-fighter squadron (No. 891) in June, but both units were too late to see any operational service before the war ended, though No. 892 served briefly in the post-war light fleet carrier *Ocean*.

Only two of the 12 squadrons of Hellcats which were serving with the F.A.A. on VJ-Day survived into 1946; these were No. 892 and No. 888, which disbanded in April and August 1946 respectively. Like other Lend–Lease aircraft, the Hellcats were returned to the U.S.A., but one or two examples were still to be seen at Royal Naval air stations for a number of years after the war. One of these (KE 209) was still being flown by Capt. J. A. Ivors, the commanding officer of the Royal Naval air station Lossiemouth, as late as April 1953.

UNITS ALLOCATED

No. 800 Squadron (equipped July 1943; embarked in *Emperor*); No. 808 Squadron (equipped October 1944; embarked in *Khedive* and *Emperor*); No. 881 Squadron (formed April 1945); No. 885 Squadron (equipped August 1944; embarked in *Ruler*); No. 888 Squadron (equipped June 1944; embarked in *Indefatigable*, *Empress*, *Emperor* and *Ameer*); No. 889 Squadron (equipped June 1945); No. 891

Squadron (equipped June 1945); No. 892 Squadron (equipped April 1945; embarked in *Ocean*); No. 896 Squadron (equipped January 1945; embarked in *Ameer* and *Empress*); No. 898 Squadron (equipped January 1945; embarked in *Attacker* and *Pursuer*); No. 1839 Squadron (formed November 1943; embarked in *Indomitable* and *Begum*); No. 1840 Squadron (formed March 1944; embarked in *Indefatigable*, *Furious*, *Formidable* and *Speaker*); No. 1844 Squadron (formed December 1943; embarked in *Begum* and *Indomitable*); No. 1847 Squadron (formed February 1944).

TECHNICAL DATA (HELLCAT II)

Description: Single-seat carrier-borne day- or night-fighter. All-metal stressed-skin construction.

Manufacturers: Grumman Aircraft Engineering Corporation, Bethpage, Long Island, New York.

Power Plant: One 2,000-h.p. Pratt & Whitney Double Wasp R-2800-10W.

Dimensions: Span, 42 ft. 10 in. (16 ft. 2 in. folded). Length, 33 ft. 7 in. Height, 14 ft. 5 in. Wing area, 334 sq. ft.

Weights: Empty, 9,212 lb. Loaded, 12,727 lb. (normal) or 13,753 lb. (maximum).

Performance: Maximum speed, 371 m.p.h. at 17,200 ft.; 331 m.p.h. at sea level. Economical cruising, 159 m.p.h. Initial climb, 3,410 ft./min. Range, 1,040 miles at 159 m.p.h. (normal) or 1,530 miles at 161 m.p.h. (with maximum fuel of 332 gallons). Service ceiling, 36,700 ft.

Armament: Six fixed 0·50-calibre machine-guns in wings. Provision for six 60-lb. rocket-projectiles under outer wing panels or two 1,000-lb. bombs beneath the centre section.

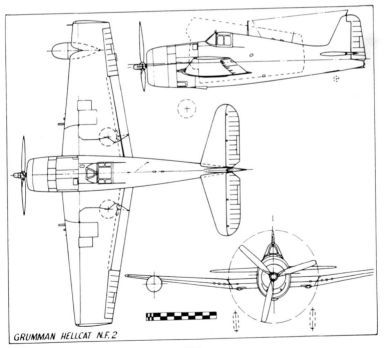

GRUMMAN HELLCAT N.F.2

Avenger A.S. 4 (XB 444) from Ford. (*Crown Copyright Photo.*)

Grumman Avenger A.S. 4

As related in the earlier narrative on the Grumman Avenger in wartime service with the F.A.A., the last first-line squadron relinquished its Avenger IIIs in June 1946 and the intended deliveries of Avenger IVs (KE 540 to KE 609) never materialised. However, early in 1953 it was announced in the House of Commons, during the presentation of the Navy Estimates, that the Avenger was to enter service again in the Royal Navy. The Avengers were to strengthen the anti-submarine force, which at that time was at a low ebb, as the new Fairey Gannet was then some distance away from squadron service and did not in fact reach a first-line unit until July 1955.

The post-war Avengers were supplied under the Mutual Defence Assistance Programme and were of the TBM-3E and TBM-3C type as used by the U.S. Navy. Avengers remained in first-line service with the U.S. Navy until superseded by the Grumman S2F-1 Sentinel in June 1954. Those supplied to Britain (commencing XB 296) were modified to take special electronics equipment and given the designation A.S. 4. The first shipment arrived at Glasgow in the carrier *Perseus* on 30 March 1953, and in May 1953 entered service with No. 815 Squadron, replacing Barracudas.

About 80 Avenger A.S. 4s were delivered to the F.A.A., all of them built by the Eastern Aircraft Division of General Motors, and the type was also made available during the same period to the Royal Canadian Navy, the Royal Netherlands Navy and the Japanese Navy. Avengers of No. 815 Squadron and No. 881 (R.C.N.) Squadron participated in the Coronation Naval Review fly-past at Spithead on 15 June 1953, and the type remained in first-line squadrons until supplanted by Gannets in 1955.

Later, Avengers superseded Fireflies in several squadrons of the R.N.V.R. air divisions and remained with this force until its disbandment.

No. 815 Squadron, No. 820 Squadron, No. 831 Squadron (with Sea Venoms), No. 881 Squadron, R.C.N., No. 1830 Squadron (Scottish Air Division, R.N.V.R., Abbotsinch), No. 1841 Squadron (Northern Air Division, R.N.V.R., Stretton) and No. 1844 Squadron (Midland Air Division, R.N.V.R., Bramcote).

TECHNICAL DATA (AVENGER A.S. 4)

Description: Three-seat carrier-borne or shore-based anti-submarine strike aircraft. All-metal stressed-skin construction.

Manufacturers: General Motors, Eastern Aircraft Division, Trenton, New Jersey.

Power Plant: One 1,750-h.p. Wright Cyclone R-2600-20.

Dimensions: Span, 54 ft. 2 in. Length, 40 ft. Height, 15 ft. 8 in. Wing area, 490 sq. ft.

Weights: Empty, 10,700 lb. Loaded, 16,761 lb.

Performance: Maximum speed, 261 m.p.h. Cruising, 151 m.p.h. Range, 1,130 miles. Service ceiling, 22,600 ft.

Armament: Provision for 2,000 lb. of bombs or depth-charges and eight 60-lb. rocket-projectiles below the wings.

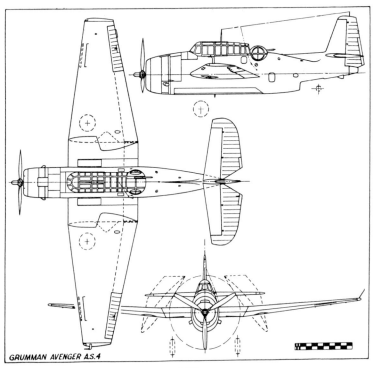

GRUMMAN AVENGER A.S.4

O/100 of the R.N.A.S. at Manston. (*Photo from H. H. Russell.*)

Handley Page O/100

It is not always appreciated that the Admiralty was the first of the British Service Departments to recognise the potentialities of the large aeroplane for long-range bombing work, and that it made its requirements known to the industry as early as December 1914. The O/100, the forerunner of the much better known O/400, was the outcome of this policy and the answer to Commodore Murray F. Sueter's classic request, when Director of the Air Department of the Admiralty, for a 'bloody paralyser' of an aeroplane.

The prototype O/100, with an enclosed cabin for the crew, flew for the first time at Hendon on 18 December 1915. Later the cabin was removed and, also, most of the armour plating. Deliveries of production aircraft to the R.N.A.S. began in September 1916, and the first front-line unit to receive the type was the Fifth Naval Wing at Dunkirk in November 1916. The third O/100 for the R.N.A.S. was delivered to the enemy intact on 1 January 1917, due to a navigational error.

Apart from a solitary night raid by an O/100 of the Third Wing on 16/17 March 1917, the O/100s were at first employed in their original intended rôle of oversea patrols off the Belgian coast, Later they concentrated almost exclusively on night-bombing raids against U-boat bases, rail centres and Gotha aerodromes. By the end of 1917 the R.N.A.S. had four squadrons of O/100s in action, including Naval 'A' Squadron—later No. 16 (Naval) Squadron—which joined the 41st Wing at Ochey, the nucleus of the Independent Force for strategic raids against targets in southern Germany. These O/100s first operated on the night of 24/25 October 1917 with F.E. 2b's of No. 100 Squadron, R.F.C.

In June 1917 an O/100 flown by Sqn. Cdr. K. S. Savory went overseas to Mudros in the Aegean, and on 9 July succeeded in bombing Constantinople. During this raid the enemy battle-cruiser *Goeben* was attacked with eight 112-lb. bombs

Forty-six O/100s were built, the airframe numbers being 1455 to 1466 and 3115 to 3142 for Eagle-engined aircraft and B 9446 to B 9451 for Cossack-engined versions.

Nos. 7 and 7A (later No. 14 Naval) of the R.N.A.S. 5th Wing at Dunkirk;
R.N.A.S. 3rd Wing at Luxeuil; 'A' Squadron (later No. 16 Naval) at Ochey;
R.N.A.S. Mudros (one aircraft).

TECHNICAL DATA (O/100)

Description: Heavy night-bomber with a crew of four. Wooden structure,
   fabric covered.
Manufacturers: Handley Page, Ltd., Cricklewood, London.
Power Plant: Two 266-h.p. Rolls-Royce Eagle II or two 320-h.p. Sunbeam
   Cossack.
Dimensions: Span, 100 ft. Length, 62 ft. $10\frac{1}{4}$ in. Height, 22 ft. Wing area,
   1,648 sq. ft.
Weights: Empty, 8,000 lb. (approx.). Loaded, 14,000 lb. (approx.).
Performance: Maximum speed, 85 m.p.h. (approx.).
Armament: Up to five free-mounted Lewis machine-guns in nose, amidships
   and ventral positions and a bomb-load comprised of 16 112-lb. bombs.

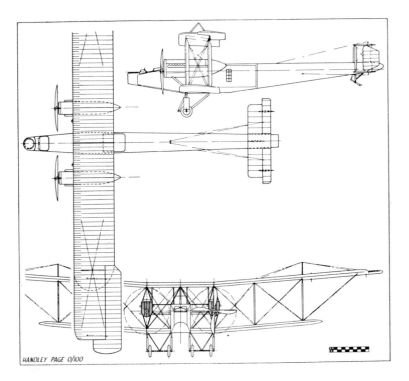

HANDLEY PAGE O/100

Nimrod II (K 4620) of No. 800 Squadron. (*Air Ministry Photo.*)

Hawker Nimrod

The Nimrod was introduced in the F.A.A. in 1932 as a replacement for the well-tried Fairey Flycatcher, which had by then been the standard carrier-borne fighter for almost a decade. Although a naval counterpart of the R.A.F.'s Fury interceptor, it was quite a distinct type and differed in having wings of greater span and special equipment, such as flotation boxes in the wings and fuselage, producing a slightly reduced performance.

Orginally named the Norn, the Nimrod was descended by way of the N. 21/26 private venture aircraft from the Hawker Hoopoe (N 237) in the same way as the Fury was related to the F. 20/27. Both these earlier prototypes bore a marked resemblance to their descendants, except that they were powered by radial engines. The prototype Nimrod (S 1577) was powered by a Kestrel IS and was first flown by F./Lt. P. W. S. Bulman in the autumn of 1930. Later it was modified to take a Kestrel II.MS and in this form was first flown by P. G. Lucas on 21 September 1931. A second prototype (S 1578) appeared with twin floats. Production of the Nimrod I began in October 1931, and 42 were built, including S 1619 to S 1630 and K 2823 to K 2840. From March 1934 the Nimrod II was built (beginning K 2909), and 36 of this variant were delivered ending with K 5058, the last Nimrod, completed in November 1935. The Nimrod II differed from the Mk. I in having sweep-back on both upper and lower wings, a modified tail unit and an arrester hook. It also had an up-rated Kestrel engine.

Nimrods superseded Flycatchers in Nos. 402, 408 and 409 Fleet Fighter Flights in 1932, and afterwards served with Nos. 800, 801 and 802 Squadrons, each of which had two flights of Nimrods and one flight of Osprey two-seaters. Nimrods were still serving with No. 802 Squadron in *Glorious* as late as May 1939, but by the outbreak of war the type had disappeared from front-line squadrons, where it had been supplanted by the Skua and the Sea Gladiator.

UNITS ALLOCATED

No. 402 Flight (*Courageous*); No. 408 Flight (*Glorious*); No. 409 Flight; No. 800 Squadron (*Courageous*); No. 801 Squadron (*Furious*); No. 802 Squadron (*Glorious*). No. 1 Flying Training School, Leuchars, for catapult training. Base Training Squadron, Gosport.

TECHNICAL DATA (NIMROD I AND II)

Description: Single-seat carrier-borne fighter. All-metal structure with metal and fabric covering.
Manufacturers: Hawker Aircraft, Ltd., Kingston-on-Thames, Surrey.
Power Plant (Mk. I): One 525-h.p. Rolls-Royce Kestrel II.MS. (Mk. II): One 640-h.p. Rolls-Royce Kestrel V.
Dimensions: Span, 33 ft. 6¼ in. Length, 26 ft. 11¾ in. Height, 9 ft. 9 in. Wing area, 298½ sq. ft.
Weights: Empty, 3,065 lb. Loaded, 4,258 lb.
Performance (Mk. I): Maximum speed, 181 m.p.h. at 13,120 ft.; 159½ m.p.h. at 3,280 ft. Cruising, 145 m.p.h. (Mk. II): Maximum speed, 195 m.p.h. at 14,000 ft. Climb, 1,640 ft./min.; 2·2 mins. to 3,280 ft.; 12 mins. to 16,400 ft. Endurance, 1·65 hrs. at 10,000 ft. Service ceiling, 26,000 ft.
Armament: Two fixed, synchronised Vickers guns.

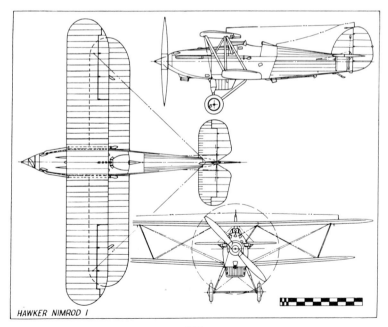

HAWKER NIMROD I

Osprey I (S 1682). (*Air Ministry Photo.*)

Hawker Osprey

The advent of the Osprey in the F.A.A. in 1932 saw the introduction of a hitherto unknown class aboard aircraft-carriers—the fast, two-seat fighter-reconnaissance aircraft. The Osprey inherited its performance from the Hart day-bomber, of which it was the deck-landing variant, and was available both with land undercarriage and as a twin-float seaplane to be catapulted from capital ships and cruisers.

The original Osprey, first flown in the summer of 1930, was the Hart prototype (J 9052) converted to the requirements of Spec. O.22/26, to which the Fairey Fleetwing was also designed. It incorporated folding wings, flotation gear and other naval equipment and was included in the composite flight of new types aboard H.M.S. *Eagle* when it visited the Argentine for the British Empire Trade Exhibition in March 1931. Production of Ospreys began in June 1932 with a batch of 28 Mk. Is (S 1677 onwards and K 2774 onwards) and continued with 16 Mk. IIs and 39 Mk. IIIs (S 1699 onwards, K 3615 onwards and K 4322 to K 4338). All these Ospreys had the Kestrel IIMS engine; with the Osprey IV (K 5742 to K 5767) the up-rated Kestrel V was substituted. The last of 110 Ospreys for the F.A.A. (K 5767) was delivered in October 1935.

The first units equipped with Ospreys were Nos. 404 and 409 Flights in November 1932, formerly with Flycatchers. From June 1933 Ospreys joined Nimrod single-seat fighters in Nos. 800, 801 and 802 Squadrons, each of which had three Ospreys and nine Nimrods. No. 801 Squadron later converted to nine Ospreys and No. 803 Squadron was, from the outset, an all-Osprey unit. In November 1938 No. 803 Squadron embarked its six Ospreys in the new carrier *Ark Royal* for its shake-down cruise, and remained until superseded by Skuas in 1939. Three Ospreys of No. 800 Squadron also served in *Ark Royal*.

As a seaplane, the Osprey replaced Fairey IIIFs in No. 407 Flight of the

Home Fleet's 2nd Cruiser Squadron in November 1932, and by 1935 Ospreys had supplanted IIIFs in all catapult flights.

UNITS ALLOCATED

Catapult Flights: No. 403 (5th Cruiser Squadron, China); No. 406 (E. Indies); No. 407 (2nd Cruiser Squadron, Home Fleet); No. 443 (W. Indies and S. Africa); No. 444 (Capital ships, Home Fleet); No. 447 (1st Cruiser Squadron, Mediterranean Fleet). *Carrier-borne:* Nos. 404 and 409 Flights; No. 800 Squadron (*Courageous* and *Ark Royal*); No. 801 Squadron (*Furious*); No. 802 Squadron (*Glorious*); No. 803 Squadron (*Eagle, Hermes* and *Ark Royal*). Also No. 24 Squadron, R.A.F., for communications duties.

TECHNICAL DATA (OSPREY IV)

Description: Two-seat carrier-borne or seaplane fighter-reconnaissance aircraft. Metal (stainless steel) structure, metal and fabric covered.
Manufacturers: Hawker Aircraft, Ltd., Kingston-on-Thames, Surrey.
Power Plant: One 640-h.p. Rolls-Royce Kestrel V.
Dimensions: Span, 37 ft. (15 ft. $7\frac{1}{4}$ in. folded). Length, 29 ft. 4 in. (31 ft. $9\frac{3}{4}$ in. as seaplane). Height, 10 ft. 5 in. (12 ft. 5 in. as seaplane). Wing area, 339 sq. ft.
Performance (Landplane): Maximum speed, 176 m.p.h. at 13,120 ft.; 161 m.p.h. at 6,560 ft. Cruising, 109 m.p.h. Climb, 1,625 ft./min. Endurance, $2\frac{1}{4}$ hrs. Service ceiling, 25,000 ft. (Seaplane): Maximum speed, 169 m.p.h. Climb, 1,300 ft./min. Service ceiling, 22,000 ft.
Armament: One fixed Vickers gun and one movable Lewis gun.

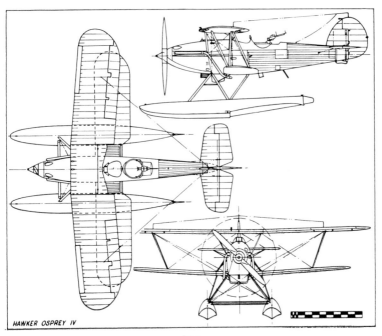

HAWKER OSPREY IV

Sea Hurricane I (P 3090). (*Chas. E. Brown Photo.*)

Hawker Sea Hurricane

The Sea Hurricane arrived on the F.A.A. scene in 1941, and it was the first British single-seat monoplane fighter to be used aboard aircraft-carriers of the Royal Navy. Until the introduction of the Seafire in 1942, the Sea Hurricane was the fastest of the F.A.A.'s fighters, and it proved a most welcome addition to its contemporaries, the American Grumman Martlet and the two-seat Fairey Fulmar. Its contribution to the war at sea was twofold, for it was used not only from carriers but also as a catapult fighter from the decks of merchant ships. In this way it effectively countered the threat of the Focke Wulf Fw 200 Condor four-engined bombers, which were being used against shipping increasingly until the 'Catafighter' scheme was initiated.

The Sea Hurricane IA, the first version to appear, was specially pro-duced for the 'Catafighter' scheme, and had catapult spools only. The second version, with both catapult spools and a deck-arrester hook, was the Sea Hurricane IB. These aircraft, and all other variants of the Sea Hurricane, were conversions from existing Hurricane land-fighters, and no Sea Hurricanes were built as such. Many of the earlier Sea Hurricanes were converted from Battle of Britain veterans which had already seen a good deal of operational flying with the R.A.F. The Sea Hurricane IA and IB were followed by the Mk. IC, with four 20-mm. guns in the wings, and the Mk. IIC, which introduced the Merlin XX engine. The Sea Hurricane IIC was equipped for carrier operations, but had no catapult points. The final variant was the Sea Hurricane XIIA, which was the conversion from the Canadian-built Hurricane with a Packard–Merlin XXIX engine. No precise records exist for the number of Sea Hurricanes supplied to the F.A.A., but it is known that contracts for at least 800 con-versions were issued. The last Sea Hurricane to be delivered, in August 1943, was the Austin-built aircraft NF 717. Some Sea Hurricanes were subsequently converted back to land-fighter standard as Hurricane IICs. The great majority of the Sea Hurricane conversion work was undertaken by General Aircraft Ltd. in 1941–42. The Sea Hurricane differed little from its land counterpart, and the modifications were for the most part limited to the local reinforcement of the airframe to withstand the extra loads imposed by catapult accelerations and, in the case of deck-landing aircraft, the sudden decelerations when the hook picked up the arrester wires on deck. Although a scheme was prepared for a Hurricane with folding wings, this modification was never incorporated, and all Sea Hurricanes had fixed wings.

The Sea Hurricanes aboard merchant ships were at first flown by F.A.A. pilots: later the task was taken over by R.A.F. personnel. The first success came on 3 August 1941, when a Sea Hurricane of No. 804 Squadron, flown by Lt. R. W. H. Everett, R.N.V.R., shot down a Focke Wulf Fw 200 Condor after being catapulted from H.M.S. *Maplin*. For this achievement Lt. Everett was awarded the D.S.O. H.M.S. *Maplin* was one of the fleet of naval catapult ships, introduced in the summer of 1941, to supplement the work of the original catapult-armed merchantmen which had been operating since the spring of 1941. The first F.A.A. pilot to be catapulted from one of these C.A.M. ships was Sub-Lt. M. A. Birrell, who had previously fought with the R.A.F. in the Battle of Britain. All the catapult pilots of the F.A.A. were volunteers, and maintenance was by naval ratings.

Although the catapulted Sea Hurricanes were successful in reducing the number of bombing attacks on convoys, there was a major disadvantage in the scheme in that the aircraft could not return to the ship, and if, as was frequently the case, they were not within flying distance of a shore base, the pilot had to face the perils of parachuting into the sea as near to the convoy as possible, in the hope of being rescued by a passing vessel. This situation was slightly improved by the fitting of two 45-gallon auxiliary tanks beneath the wings of the Sea Hurricanes in the later stages of the scheme.

An advancement on the naval catapult ship for the protection of convoys

Sea Hurricane ready for catapulting aboard a merchant ship. (*Imp. War Museum Photo.*)

was the small escort-carrier, converted as a 'flat top' from a merchant ship. These merchant aircraft-carriers, or MAC-ships, were to prove the most effective way of providing close air cover for convoys, particularly in the middle stretches of the Atlantic beyond the range of Coastal Command's land-based anti-submarine aircraft. Each MAC-ship carried its quota of fighters and anti-submarine aircraft, though no hangar accomodation was provided and the aircraft remained parked aft.

Sea Hurricanes did particularly valuable service aboard MAC-ships on the arduous Russian convoys. No. 802 Squadron, which had flown Martlets in the first of the merchant carriers, *Audacity*, re-formed at Yeovilton in February 1942 with six Sea Hurricanes and embarked in *Avenger*, joining six more Sea Hurricanes of No. 883 Squadron, which had also formed at Yeovilton the previous October. *Avenger*'s Sea Hurricanes, together with three Swordfish, played a vital rôle in protecting convoy P.Q. 18, which sailed from Loch Ewe for North Russia on 2 September 1942. This operation was typical of many which were to follow. It was the first in which an escort-carrier had been provided: the previous Russian convoy P.Q. 17 had been badly mauled by German aircraft from Norway and Finland through lack of air cover. With convoy P.Q. 18 it was a different story: the Sea Hurricanes of Nos. 802 and 883 Squadrons together shot down five enemy aircraft and damaged 17 others. Four Sea Hurricanes were lost, but three of the pilots were saved.

Meanwhile aboard the larger aircraft-carriers Sea Hurricanes were playing their part in the hard-fought battles over the Mediterranean as convoys made the bitterly-contested voyage to the relief of Malta. One of the largest of these convoys was that of August 1942, for which a fighter cover of 70 Sea Hurricanes, Fulmars and Martlets was provided by the carriers *Victorious*, *Indomitable* and *Eagle*. The Sea Hurricanes were those of No. 800 Squadron (*Indomitable*), No. 801 Squadron (*Eagle*) and No. 885 Squadron (*Victorious*). It was during this voyage that *Eagle* met her end, being torpedoed by U-boats. Yet, in spite of this loss, the F.A.A. enjoyed one of their greatest victories during three days of air fighting against a force of about 500 German and Italian bombers, torpedo-carriers and escorting fighters.

Sea Hurricane IC (V 6741). (*Imp. War Museum Photo.*)

Sea Hurricane IIC (NF 717). (*Imp. War Museum Photo.*)

Sea Hurricanes, aided by the Fulmars and Martlets, shot down 39 enemy aircraft and damaged many more for the loss of only eight of their own number. Time and time again they drove off attacking forces of Cant Z. 1007 and Junkers Ju 88 aircraft, and one pilot alone (Lt. R. J. Cork, D.S.C.) shot down three German and three Italian aircraft in his Sea Hurricane. Faced with such skill and determination, the enemy aircraft could make little impression and, against all the odds, the convoy got through.

The Malta convoy of August 1942 was one of the last major actions in which Sea Hurricanes operated from large aircraft-carriers: during the North African invasion in November 1942 the Seafire was predominant. But Sea Hurricanes continued to give good service in the escort-carriers, and No. 891 Squadron, in *Dasher*, did in fact contribute to the North African landings.

By the close of 1943 the Sea Hurricane had largely disappeared from front-line units of the F.A.A., being superseded by Seafires and Hellcats in the large carriers and by Wildcats in the escort-carriers.

UNITS ALLOCATED

No. 800 Squadron (July 1942 to June 1943; embarked in *Indomitable*, *Biter* and *Unicorn*); No. 801 Squadron (August 1941 to August 1942; embarked in *Argus* and *Eagle*); No. 802 Squadron (re-equipped February 1942; embarked in *Avenger*); No. 803 Squadron (re-equipped May 1941; shore-based in Palestine and Western Desert); No. 804 Squadron (re-equipped with both Sea Hurricanes and Fulmars in February 1941; embarked in *Pegasus*, *Eagle*, *Argus*, *Furious* and *Dasher*); No. 806 Squadron (May 1941 to December 1941; embarked in *Formidable*); No. 811 Squadron (July 1941 to November 1941: two Sea Hurricanes added to 14 Chesapeakes, shore-based); No. 813 Squadron (two Sea Hurricanes added to nine Swordfish); No. 824 Squadron (six Sea Hurricanes added to nine Swordfish in October 1943; embarked in *Striker*); No. 825 Squadron (six Sea Hurricanes added to nine Swordfish in July 1943; embarked in *Vindex*); No. 835 Squadron (six Sea Hurricanes added to Swordfish in July 1943; embarked in *Chaser* and *Nairana*); No. 877 Squadron (formed in April 1943 for local air defence at Tanga, East Africa: disbanded December 1943); No. 880 Squadron (January 1941 to August 1942; embarked in *Furious* and *Indomitable*); No. 883 Squadron (formed October 1941; embarked in *Avenger*); No. 885 Squadron (December 1941 to August 1942; embarked in *Victorious*); No. 889 Squadron (with Fulmars, Egypt, January–

Sea Hurricane IB with arrester hook extended. (*Imp. War Museum Photo.*)

Sea Hurricanes aboard an aircraft-carrier. (*Imp. War Museum Photo.*)

February 1942); No. 891 Squadron (formed July 1942; embarked in *Dasher*); No. 895 Squadron (November 1942 to April 1943; shore-based at Stretton); No. 897 Squadron (December 1942 to April 1943; shore-based at Stretton).

TECHNICAL DATA (SEA HURRICANE IIC)

Description: Single-seat carrier-borne fighter. Metal structure with metal and fabric covering.

Manufacturers: Hawker Aircraft, Ltd., Kingston-on-Thames, Surrey.

Power Plant: One 1,460-h.p. Rolls-Royce Merlin XX.

Dimensions: Span, 40 ft. Length, 32 ft. 3 in. Height, 13 ft. 3 in. Wing area, 258 sq. ft.

Weights: Empty, 5,800 lb. Loaded, 7,800 lb.

Performance: Maximum speed, 342 m.p.h. at 22,000 ft. Cruising, 212 to 292 m.p.h. at 20,000 ft. Climb, 9·1 mins. to 20,000 ft. Range, 460 miles (normal) or 970 miles with auxiliary tanks. Service ceiling, 35,600 ft.

Armament: Four 20-mm. guns in the wings.

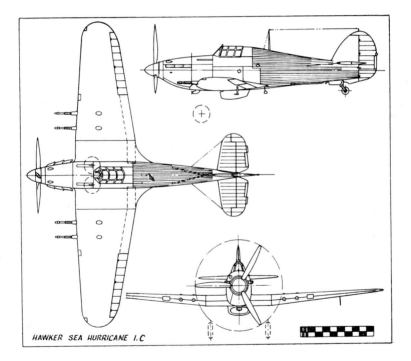

HAWKER SEA HURRICANE I.C

Sea Fury F.B. 11 (VX 639) from Culdrose. (*Crown Copyright Photo.*)

Hawker Sea Fury

The Sea Fury was the F.A.A.'s last piston-engined fighter in first-line squadrons, where it served from 1947 until 1954, and some were still operating with No. 1834 Squadron of the R.N.V.R. air divisions when these units were disbanded early in 1957. It was also the first British naval aircraft in regular service with power-folding wings.

The prototype Sea Fury (SR 661) was a navalised version of the Fury I, which had been designed to Spec. F. 2/43 as an intended replacement for the Tempest in the R.A.F. Deck-landing trials with SR 661 (which had a sting-type arrester hook but fixed wings) took place aboard H.M.S. *Ocean* in October 1945. Two subsequent prototypes (SR 666 and VB 857) incorporated folding wings, and were followed by the first production Sea Fury F. 10 (TF 895), which flew on 30 September 1946. Fifty Sea Fury F. 10s (TF 895 to TF 944) were built to Spec. 22/43 and were followed by 615 Sea Fury F.B. 11s, the last of which (WZ 641) was delivered in November 1952.

Sea Furies first entered service with No. 807 Squadron (formerly Seafires) at Eglinton in August 1947, and in May 1948 the first F.B. 11 unit, No. 802 Squadron, formed at the same station. By the time that the Korean War broke out in 1950 the Sea Fury was the F.A.A.'s leading single-seat fighter, and it fought with distinction throughout the campaign. Sea Fury squadrons engaged were No. 802 (in *Ocean*), No. 807 (in *Theseus*), Nos. 801 and 804 (in *Glory*) and Nos. 805 and 808 (in *Sydney*). Although used chiefly in conjunction with Fireflies for ground-attack duties, using bombs and rockets, the Sea Furies also fought the much faster MIG 15 jet-fighters, the first victory being claimed by Lt. P. Carmichael of No. 802 Squadron.

Sea Furies first entered R.N.V.R. service in November 1951, when they replaced Seafire 17s in No. 1832 Squadron. Another R.N.V.R. air squadron, No. 1831, took its Sea Furies to Malta in May 1952, being the first of the reserve units to do their annual training overseas.

UNITS ALLOCATED

Nos. 801, 802, 804, 805, 807, 808 (Australian), 871 (Canadian) and 898 Squadrons. Nos. 738 and 764 Training Squadrons. Nos. 1831, 1832, 1833, 1834, 1835 and 1836 Squadrons, R.N.V.R.

TECHNICAL DATA (SEA FURY F.B. 11)

Description: Single-seat carrier-borne fighter-bomber. All-metal stressed-skin construction.
Manufacturers: Hawker Aircraft, Ltd., Kingston-on-Thames, Surrey.
Power Plant: One 2,550-h.p. Bristol Centaurus 18.
Dimensions: Span, 38 ft. 4¾ in. (16 ft. 1 in. folded). Length, 34 ft. 8 in. Height, 15 ft. 10½ in. Wing area, 280 sq. ft.
Weights: Empty, 9,240 lb. Loaded, 12,500 lb.
Performance: Maximum speed, 460 m.p.h. at 18,000 ft.; 415 m.p.h. at 30,000 ft. Climb, 10·8 mins. to 30,000 ft. Range, 700 miles at 30,000 ft., or 1,040 miles with two 90-gallon drop-tanks.
Armament: Four fixed 20-mm. guns in wings and provision for 12 60-lb. rocket-projectiles or two 1,000-lb. bombs below the wings.

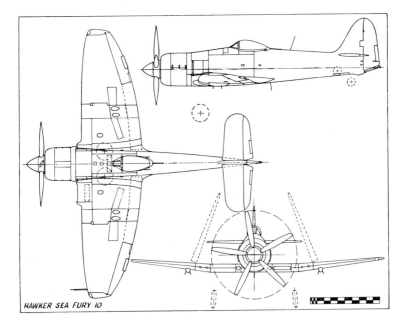

HAWKER SEA FURY 10

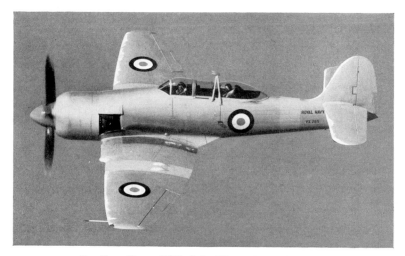

Sea Fury T. 20 (VX 285). (*Crown Copyright Photo.*)

Hawker Sea Fury T. 20

The Sea Fury T. 20 was a straightforward two-seat dual-control trainer adaptation of the Sea Fury single-seat fighter. Basically similar to the fighter, the T. 20 had a second cockpit for the instructor connected to the front cockpit by a long Perspex fairing, each cockpit being provided with an individual sliding canopy. Whereas the fighter had four 20-mm. guns in the wings, the T. 20 mounted only two, so as to permit the installation in the wing of equipment displaced from the fuselage by the second cockpit. Another feature peculiar to the trainer was the installation of a mirror on a tripod between the cockpits; this enabled the instructor to see the reflector gunsight over the head of his pupil during air-firing exercises.

The prototype Sea Fury T. 20 (VX 818) made its first flight on 15 January 1948, some 15 months after the first production Sea Fury fighter had flown. Deliveries of the production version of the Sea Fury Trainer proceeded concurrently with fighters. Total production of the type amounted to 60 aircraft, the last (WG 656) being delivered to the Royal Navy in March 1952.

Sea Fury T. 20s were used by second-line squadrons of the F.A.A., providing operational training at Culdrose, Cornwall, for pilots who had previously graduated through the R.A.F. Flying Training School at Syerston and more advanced instruction at Lossiemouth. Later, with the introduction of Sea Fury fighters in the squadrons of the R.N.V.R., the T. 20 was issued to reserve units as a conversion trainer. Sea Fury Trainers were on the strength of the Northern Air Division at Stretton, the Scottish Air Division at Abbotsinch, and the Southern Air Division at Benson and Yeovilton.

Nos. 1830, 1831, 1832, 1834, 1835, 1836 and 1843 Squadrons, R.N.V.R. No. 738 Training Squadron.

TECHNICAL DATA (SEA FURY T. 20)

Description: Two-seat dual-control advanced trainer. All-metal stressed-skin construction.

Manufacturers: Hawker Aircraft, Ltd., Kingston-on-Thames, Surrey.

Power Plant: One 2,480-h.p. Bristol Centaurus 18.

Dimensions: Span, 38 ft. 4¾ in. Length, 34 ft. 7 in. Height, 12 ft. 3½ in. Wing area, 280 sq. ft.

Weights: Empty, 8,697 lb. Loaded, 11,930 lb.

Performance: Maximum speed, 445 m.p.h. at 20,000 ft.; 415 m.p.h. at 7,500 ft.; 370 m.p.h. at sea level. Climb, 4,300 ft./min.; 1·3 mins. to 5,500 ft.; 4·05 mins. to 15,000 ft.; 5·65 mins. to 20,000 ft. Range, 1,630 miles.

Armament: Two 20-mm. guns mounted in wings.

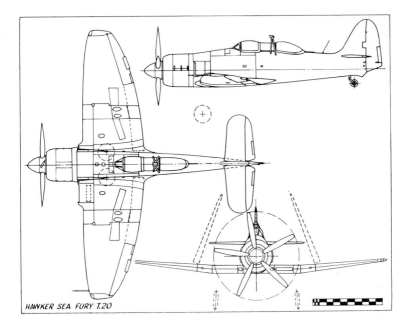

HAWKER SEA FURY T.20

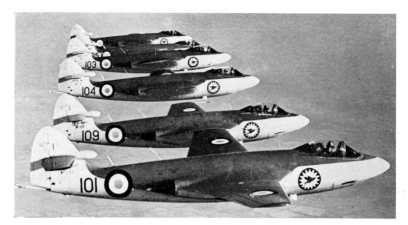

Sea Hawk F.G.A. 4s of No. 898 Squadron. (*'Flight' Photo.*)

Hawker Sea Hawk

The Sea Hawk first entered F.A.A. squadrons in 1953, superseding the Attacker jet fighter and the Sea Fury piston-engined fighters. Its basic design stemmed from that of Hawker's first jet fighter, the P. 1040, which was adapted for carrier-borne interceptor duties to Spec. N. 7/46. Three prototypes were ordered in February 1946, and the first (VP 413) flew on 31 August 1948. The first production Sea Hawk F. 1 (WF 143) flew in November 1951, and differed from the prototypes in having its wing-span increased from 36 ft. 6 in. to 39 ft., an increase in tailplane area, a revised cockpit canopy and a Nene 101 engine in place of the Nene 2 or 4. Initial aircraft were built by Hawker, but from WF 162 production was by Armstrong Whitworth, who built all subsequent Sea Hawks. The acorn fairing at the junction of tailplane and fin appeared early in 1953. About 100 Sea Hawk F. 1s were built.

The Sea Hawk F. 1 was succeeded by the F. 2, which introduced power-boosted ailerons, and the F.B. 3, which had a strengthened wing for external loads. The first Sea Hawk F. 2 (WF 240) flew on 24 February 1954, and the first F.B. 3 (WF 280) on 13 March 1954. The last production version was the F. (GA) 4, equipped for the close-support rôle, the first example of which (WV 792) flew on 26 August 1954. The Sea Hawk F.B. 5 and F. (GA) 6 were retrospective conversions of the F.B. 3 and F. (GA) 4 respectively, fitted with the Nene 103 engine.

Sea Hawks first entered service with No. 806 Squadron at Brawdy in March 1953, subsequently embarking in *Eagle*. Sea Hawks with a carrier task force provided close support for the Anglo-French landings in Egypt in November 1956, being flown by Nos. 800, 802, 804, 810, 897 and 899 Squadrons from the carriers *Albion*, *Eagle* and *Bulwark*.

In September 1957 five red-painted Sea Hawks of No. 738 Training Squadron provided a spectacular demonstration of formation aerobatics at the S.B.A.C. Display at Farnborough, rivalling that of the R.A.F.'s famed Hunter team of No. 111 Squadron.

UNITS ALLOCATED

Nos. 800, 801, 802, 803, 804, 806, 807, 810, 811, 892, 897, 898 and 899 Squadrons. Also Nos. 1832, 1835 and 1836 Squadrons of the R.N.V.R. air divisions and Nos. 736 and 738 Training Squadrons.

TECHNICAL DATA (SEA HAWK F. (GA) 6)

Description: Single-seat carrier-borne ground-attack fighter. All-metal stressed-skin construction.

Manufacturers: Sir W. G. Armstrong Whitworth Aircraft Ltd., Baginton, Coventry.

Power Plant: One 5,400-lb thrust Rolls-Royce Nene 103.

Dimensions: Span, 39 ft. (13 ft. 4 in. folded). Length, 39 ft. 8 in. Height, 8 ft. 8 in. Wing area, 278 sq. ft.

Weight: Loaded, approximately 10,000 lb.

Performance: Maximum speed, 630 m.p.h. (approx.) at sea level. Climb, 9,000 ft./min. (approx.). Range, over 1,400 miles with drop-tanks.

Armament: Four fixed 20-mm. guns in fuselage and provision for 10 rocket-projectiles and two 500-lb. bombs below the wings in addition to two 75-gallon drop-tanks.

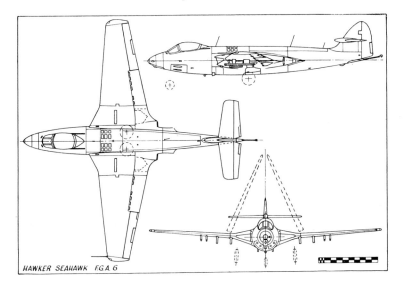

HAWKER SEAHAWK F.G.A. 6

Henri Farman F. 22. (*Imp. War Museum Photo.*)

Henri Farman

The name of the Henri Farman pusher biplane appears in some of the earliest annals of British naval aviation. It is recorded that on 27 August 1914 seaplanes Nos. 97 and 156 of the R.N.A.S. led the Battle Fleet to sea. The seaplanes in question were Henri Farmans and, indeed, many of the aircraft of this type supplied to the R.N.A.S. before the outbreak of war were fitted with twin floats as shown in the three-view drawing. Both landplanes and seaplanes were built in England by the Aircraft Manufacturing Company at Hendon, and all were powered by the 80-h.p. Gnome, with the exception of No. 115, which had a 100-h.p. Renault.

The first R.N.A.S. unit to go overseas, the Eastchurch squadron commanded by Wg. Cdr. C. R. Samson, flew to Ostend with nine assorted types, one of which was a Henri Farman landplane. In March 1915 this unit became No. 3 Squadron, R.N.A.S., and was sent to the Eastern Mediterranean to participate in the Dardanelles campaign with eight Henri Farmans, two B.E.2Cs, two B.E.2s, two Sopwith Tabloids, a Breguet and three Maurice Farmans. Of all these types, the Henri Farmans were the least useful, for they lacked the power to lift a useful bomb-load, and were too slow and difficult to maintain in the field. They were used as single-seaters for reconnaissance; a further six which arrived in May were promptly returned to England as being valueless for first-line duties. Re-engined with the 140-h.p. Canton Unné, the Henri Farman was distinctly better, and served as a bomber with the R.N.A.S. in the Aegean from July 1915 onwards. This version, the F. 27, was of steel construction, and it was with this type that Wg. Cdr. Samson dropped a 500-lb. bomb (the biggest of the war at that date) on a Turkish barracks during a flight from Imbros on 18 December 1915. The Farman F. 27 is illustrated on page 13 of the introduction.

Some of the earliest bombing attacks on submarines and Zeppelin sheds were made by Henri Farmans of the R.N.A.S. in Belgium. On the night of 6/7 June 1915, F./Sub-Lt. J. S. Mills of No. 1 Wing destroyed *L.Z. 38* in its shed at Evere with four 20-lb. bombs. On 26 August 1915 Sqn. Cdr. A. W. Bigsworth of No. 2 Wing attacked a U-boat six miles off Ostend

and, on 28 November 1915, F./Sub-Lt. Viney claimed to have blown a
U-boat in half with two well-aimed 65-lb. bombs, but this feat was never
officially recognised.

Eastchurch squadron, which became No. 3 Squadron, R.N.A.S., in March 1915
and No. 3 Wing, R.N.A.S., in June 1915. Also Nos. 1 and 2 Squadrons (later Nos.
1 and 2 Wings), R.N.A.S.

TECHNICAL DATA (HENRI FARMAN F. 20)

Description: Two-seat reconnaissance, bombing and training aircraft.
Wooden structure, fabric covered.
Manufacturers: Henri and Maurice Farman, Billancourt (Seine), France.
Sub-contracted by Aircraft Manufacturing Co. Ltd., Hendon.
Power Plant: One 80-h.p. Gnome.
Dimensions: Span, 44 ft. 9 in. Length, 26 ft. 6 in. Height, 12 ft. Wing area,
375 sq. ft.
Weights: Empty, 820 lb. Loaded, 1,440 lb.
Performance: Maximum speed, 60 m.p.h. at sea level. Climb, 18½ mins. to
3,000 ft. Endurance, 3 hrs.
Armament: None standardised, but some aircraft fitted with a Lewis gun in
front cockpit.

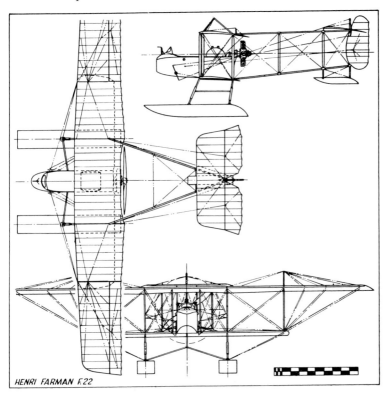

HENRI FARMAN F.22

Sea Prince C. 1 (WF 137). (*Crown Copyright Photo.*)

Hunting Percival Sea Prince

The Royal Navy was the first of the Services to order a military version of the Percival Prince civil feeder liner and executive transport, which first made its appearance in August 1948. The first Sea Prince, as the naval version was named, emerged almost three years before the R.A.F.'s Pembroke.

The first Sea Prince C. Mk. 1 (WF 136) made its maiden flight on 24 March 1950, and was equipped for special communications duties. It was followed by two further C. Mk. 1s; one was fitted out as an 'Admiral's Barge' V.I.P. transport, and the other was a standard eight-seater for the use of the naval staff of the Joint Services Mission in Washington, D.C. This latter aircraft was delivered by air across the North Atlantic, via Iceland, Greenland, Newfoundland and Canada. The three Sea Prince C. Mk. 1s were similar in most respects to the Prince Series II. The maker's designation was P. 66.

The next production version was the Sea Prince T. Mk. 1 (see three-view), which met the Royal Navy's requirement for a 'flying classroom'. This version introduced a number of changes, such as a lengthened nose to accommodate radar, a long-stroke twin-wheel undercarriage leg and longer engine nacelles. The interior of the fuselage was fitted out to accommodate three pupils, and a comprehensive range of wireless and radar equipments for the training of observers in navigation and the techniques of anti-submarine warfare. The first Sea Prince T. Mk. 1 (WF 118) made its initial flight at Luton, on 28 June 1951, and a total of 41 aircraft of this type was built.

The last version of the Sea Prince was the C. Mk. 2 which was a communications version of the T. Mk. 1, and four of these were delivered. The first C. Mk. 2 (WM 756) flew on 1 April 1953 and the last (WJ 350) was delivered to the Royal Navy on 3 September 1953.

UNITS ALLOCATED

No. 750 Squadron (R.N.A.S. Culdrose); No. 781 Squadron: Junior Air Officers' Course (R.N.A.S. Lee-on-Solent).

Description: Navigation and anti-submarine trainer with a crew of two and three pupils. All-metal stressed-skin construction. Maker's designation, P. 57

Manufacturers: Hunting Percival Aircraft Ltd., Luton, Beds.

Power Plant: Two 550-h.p. Alvis Leonides 125.

Dimensions: Span, 56 ft. Length, 46 ft. 4 in. Height, 16 ft. 1 in. Wing area, 365 sq. ft.

Weights: Empty, 8,850 lb. Loaded, 11,850 lb.

Performance: Maximum speed, 223 m.p.h. at 2,000 ft. Cruising, 183 m.p.h. at 11,000 ft. Climb, 1,400 ft./min. Range, 400 nautical miles. Service ceiling, 22,000 ft.

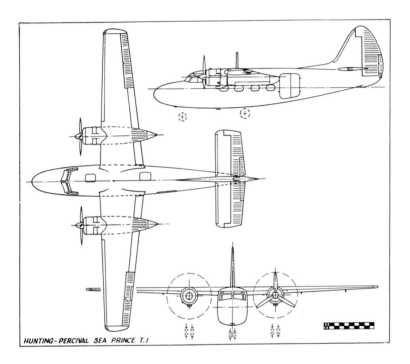

HUNTING-PERCIVAL SEA PRINCE T.I

Maurice Farman Shorthorn (N 6310) of the R.N.A.S. (*Photo. from F. Cheesman.*)

Maurice Farman Shorthorn

Both the Maurice Farman Shorthorn and the Longhorn (see Appendix) were being supplied to the R.N.A.S. by the Aircraft Manufacturing Company at Hendon before the First World War. Among the first 200 official serial numbers allotted by the Admiralty for naval aircraft, the S. 7 Longhorn made its first appearance as No. 23, and the S. 11 Shorthorn as No. 29. The latter was a twin-float seaplane (as shown in the three-view drawing), and was stationed at Great Yarmouth from June 1913. Another of the early Shorthorn seaplanes appeared on strength at Cromarty in July 1913.

The Longhorn and the Shorthorn (the latter distinguished by the absence of a forward elevator) had been introduced to the British flying services as trainers at the Central Flying School as early as 1912, and they continued to serve in this rôle with both the R.F.C. and the R.N.A.S.

Whereas the Longhorn was used only as a trainer, the Shorthorn also saw operational service for reconnaissance and bombing. Of the R.N.A.S.'s first-line strength of 40 landplanes and 31 seaplanes on 4 August 1914, four were Maurice Farman landplanes fitted with 70-h.p. Renault engines and three others Maurice Farman seaplanes, with either 70-h.p. or 100-h.p. Renault engines. The celebrated Commander C. R. Samson, in his entertaining book *Fights and Flights*, speaks of a Maurice Farman which he flew with a 130-h.p. Canton Unné engine. This aircraft (No. 1241) completed 120 hrs. of operational flying on the Western Front before going out to the Dardanelles in 1915 and, on 21 December 1914, made the first night flight of the war by either side. On this occasion it carried 18 16-lb. bombs which it dropped on enemy batteries near Ostend.

Three Maurice Farmans, one the famous No. 1241 and the others with 100-h.p. Renaults, accompanied Samson's No. 3 Squadron, R.N.A.S., to the Dardanelles and did a lot of useful bombing over the Turkish lines.

The last Shorthorns delivered to the R.N.A.S. were 20 built as trainers by the Eastbourne Aviation Company. The R.N.A.S. used 90 Shorthorns in all.

With Wg. Cdr. Samson's unit in Belgium, later No. 3 Squadron R.N.A.S., at Dardanelles.

TECHNICAL DATA (S. 11 SHORTHORN)

Description: Two-seat reconnaissance and bombing aircraft, also used for training. Wooden structure, fabric covered.

Manufacturers: Henri and Maurice Farman, Billancourt (Seine), France. Sub-contracted by Aircraft Manufacturing Co. Ltd., Hendon, Eastbourne Aviation and others.

Power Plant: One 70-h.p. or 100-h.p. Renault.

Dimensions: Span, 53 ft. Length, 30 ft. 8 in. Height, 10 ft. 4 in. Wing area, 561 sq. ft.

Weights: Empty, 1,441 lb. Loaded, 2,046 lb.

Performance: Maximum speed, 66 m.p.h. at sea level. Climb, 15 mins. to 3,000 ft. Endurance, $3\frac{3}{4}$ hrs.

Armament: No defensive armament normally carried. Light bomb-load below wings.

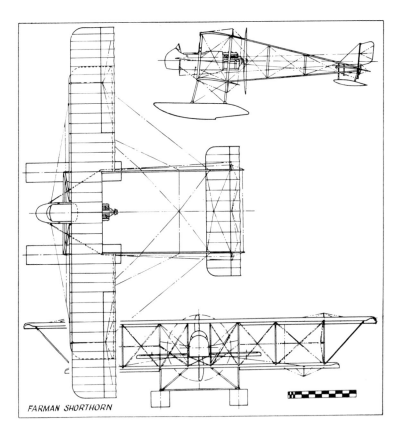

FARMAN SHORTHORN

Monitor T.T. II (NP 407). (*'The Aeroplane' Photo.*)

Miles Monitor

The Monitor high-speed target-tug was designed to meet the requirements of Air Ministry Spec. Q 9/42, which called for a twin-engined aircraft capable of towing drogues or winged targets of 16 ft. or 32 ft. span at 300 m.p.h. and with an endurance of 3 to 4 hrs. The prototype Monitor Mk. 1 (NF 900) made its first flight at Woodley, Berkshire, on 5 April 1944. It was afterwards destroyed in an accident and replaced by two further prototypes, NP 404 and NP 405. The original plan to build Monitors for the R.A.F. was eventually abandoned, and the type was taken over by the Royal Navy, where a requirement existed for an aircraft capable of simulating dive-bombing attacks on warships at speeds up to 400 m.p.h. Suitably modified, and equipped with hydraulic dive-brakes, the Monitor emerged as the T.T. Mk. II, which also differed from the Mk. I in having a Miles manually-operated dorsal cupola in place of the Beaufighter-type dorsal blister. At one period of the Monitor's development it had been planned to introduce other Beaufighter components, such as wings and undercarriage assembly, but this scheme was cancelled.

The Monitor T.T. Mk. II entered production for the Royal Navy in the autumn of 1945, but the original contracts had been reduced with the end of the war and, finally, only 20 were completed (NP 406 to NP 425), not all of which were delivered. The Monitors served only briefly with Fleet Requirements Units before being superseded by the Mosquito T.T. 39.

Despite its brief service, the Monitor is interesting historically as being the first twin-engined aircraft to be designed specifically for target-towing work, and its hydraulic winch marked a great technical advance on the older type of wooden windlass, which could not be operated at speeds much above 150 m.p.h.

TECHNICAL DATA (MONITOR T.T. II)

Description: High-speed target tug with a crew of two. Wings of wooden construction with plywood skin; fuselage and tail assembly of all-metal stressed-skin construction.

Manufacturers: Miles Aircraft, Ltd., Woodley, Reading, Berks.

Power Plant: Two 1,750-h.p. Wright R-2600-31 Double-Row Cyclone.
Dimensions: Span, 55 ft. 3 in. Length, 46 ft. 8 in. Height, 13 ft. 9 in. Wing area, 500 sq. ft.
Weights: Empty, 15,723 lb. Loaded, 21,056 lb.
Performance: Maximum speed, 360 m.p.h. at 20,000 ft. Cruising, 300 m.p.h. at 20,000 ft. Climb, 5 mins. to 10,000 ft. Range, 1,000 miles.

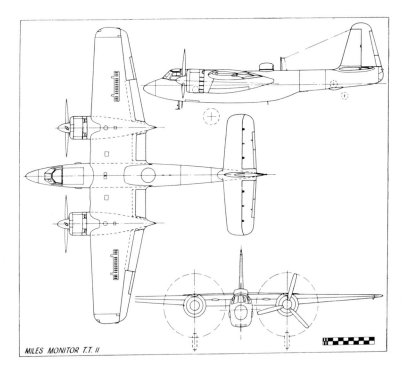

MILES MONITOR T.T. II

Morane Parasol (No. 3253) flown by Warneford. (*Imp. War Museum Photo.*)

Morane-Saulnier Type L

The Morane-Saulnier Company was one of the pioneer firms of the French aircraft industry. The Type 'L' two-seat monoplane, more generally known as the Morane Parasol, made its first appearance in 1913, and was at once ordered by the French Army. At the end of 1914, when French aircraft were eagerly sought by the British Government, the Morane Parasol was also acquired for the R.N.A.S., and 25 (Nos. 3239 to 3263) were delivered. The R.N.A.S. thus became the first of the British flying services to use the type, though the later version, Type 'LA', was subsequently adopted by the R.F.C. for artillery observation duties during 1916–17.

The name of the Morane Parasol will forever be associated with the remarkable feat of F./Sub-Lt. R. A. J. Warneford, who was flying an aircraft of this type, No. 3253, when he destroyed the Zeppelin *L.Z. 37* over Bruges on 7 June 1915. Warneford, a member of No. 1 Squadron, R.N.A.S., had set off from Dunkirk to bomb Berchem Ste. Agathe, but was diverted from his task by the sight of a Zeppelin, which he chased, though under heavy machine-gun fire from its gondolas. Eventually he outclimbed the Zeppelin and reached 11,000 ft, from which height he dived to drop six 20-lb. bombs on the *L.Z.* 37's envelope. The Zeppelin exploded and went down in flames; meanwhile a broken petrol pipe forced Warneford to land inside enemy lines, where he stayed for 35 mins. before he effected a repair and flew back. This was the first time that a Zeppelin had been destroyed in the air, and for his achievement Warneford was awarded the V.C., being the second airman to be so decorated.

Apart from this outstanding incident, the career of the Morane Parasol with the R.N.A.S. was not particularly distinguished. In addition to its service in Belgium, Wg. Cdr. E. L. Gerrard's No. 2 Wing had six Moranes on strength during the Dardanelles operations. The Moranes had scant success, chiefly because their Le Rhone engines picked up the fine sand so easily.

No. 1 Squadron, later No. 1 Wing, R.N.A.S., at Dunkirk and No. 2 Squadron, later No. 2 Wing, R.N.A.S., at Dunkirk and Imbros.

TECHNICAL DATA (MORANE TYPE 'L')

Description: Two-seat reconnaissance aircraft, frequently used as a single-seater by the R.N.A.S. Wooden structure, fabric covered. Maker's designation: M.S. 3.

Manufacturers: Morane-Saulnier Soc. de Constructions Aeronautiques, Paris.

Power Plant: One 80-h.p. Le Rhone.

Dimensions: Span, 34 ft. Length, 20 ft. 9 in. Height, 11 ft. 5 in. Wing area, 172 sq. ft.

Weight: Loaded, 839 lb.

Performance: Maximum speed 76 m.p.h. Climb, 345 ft./min.

Armament: No standard armament, though rifles could be carried and bomb-racks were improvised in the field.

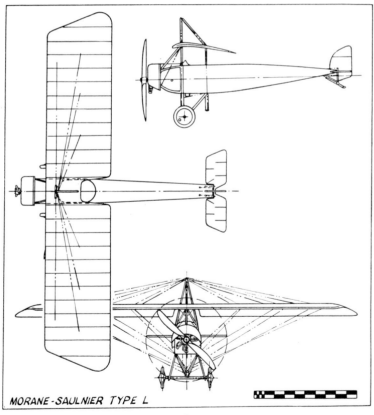

MORANE-SAULNIER TYPE L

Nieuport 24 (N 5875) of the R.N.A.S. (*Photo from J. M. Bruce.*)

Nieuport Scout

In its various guises, the Nieuport Vee-strutter sesquiplane scout was one of the most famous aircraft of the First World War, and will always be associated with the brilliant exploits of such pilots as Ball and Bishop of the R.F.C., and Navarre and Nungesser of the French Air Force. With the R.N.A.S., Nieuport Scouts first entered service in 1915. Wg. Cdr. C. R. Samson's No. 3 Wing in the Dardanelles received six with 80-h.p. Le Rhone engines (Type 11) in July 1915. This version is illustrated in the Appendix. Samson flew one personally and recorded in his memoirs that 'it climbed like a witch'. It was in the Dardanelles campaign, flying a Nieuport Scout, that Sqn. Cdr. R. Bell Davies won the second V.C. awarded to a R.N.A.S. pilot. This was on 19 November 1915, when he landed under enemy fire to rescue the pilot of a Henri Farman who had been forced down behind the enemy lines.

It was with R.N.A.S. fighting squadrons on the Western Front, however, that the Nieuport Scout really came into its own. By this time, 1916, the Type 17 with a 110-h.p. Le Rhone engine was available, to be followed by the Type 24 with round-sided, streamlined fuselage, both of which served the R.N.A.S. The Type 24 had a 120-h.p. Le Rhone. As early as 29 March 1916 four R.N.A.S. Nieuports from Eastchurch had been lent by the Admiralty to the R.F.C. to protect artillery observation aircraft on the Western Front, and on 10 June 1916 a unit known as 'A' Squadron, comprised of two flights of Nieuport Scouts under Sqn. Cdr. F. K. Haskins, was detached from No. 1 Wing at St. Pol and sent to Furnes, where it became the first homogeneous fighting unit of the R.N.A.S.

From then until 1917, when replaced by Sopwith Pups and Triplanes, Nieuport Scouts fought with distinction, defending the Dunkirk base, escorting bombers, shooting down enemy seaplanes and (with Sqn. Cdr. G. R. Bromet's famous No. 8 Naval Squadron) in support of the R.F.C. on the Somme. They also shot down German kite balloons which were spotting for the Tirpitz battery, using Le Prieur rockets fired from the interplane struts.

Nos. 1, 2, 3, 6, 8, 9, 10 and 11 (Naval) Squadrons on the Western Front and No. 3 Wing, R.N.A.S., in Dardenelles campaign.

TECHNICAL DATA (NIEUPORT 17)

Description: Single-seat fighting scout. Wooden structure, fabric covered.

Manufacturers: Soc. Anonyme des Etablissements Nieuport, Issy-le-Molineax (Seine), France.

Power Plant: One 110-h.p. Le Rhone.

Dimensions: Span, 27 ft. 3 in. Length, 19 ft. 6 in. Height, 7 ft. Wing area, 158 sq. ft.

Weights: Empty, 825 lb. Loaded, 1,233 lb.

Performance: Maximum speed, 107 m.p.h. at 6,500 ft.; 101 m.p.h. at 10,000 ft. Climb, $5\frac{1}{2}$ mins. to 6,500 ft.; 9 mins. to 10,000 ft. Endurance, 2 hrs. Service ceiling, 17,400 ft.

Armament: One fixed Lewis gun mounted above the top wing firing clear of the airscrew disc. Later a synchronised Vickers gun was mounted above the cowling. Provision for four Le Prieur rockets on each 'vee' strut.

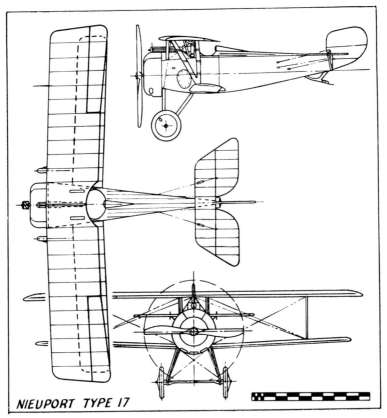

NIEUPORT TYPE 17

Nieuport 12 (N 9233) built by Beardmore. (*Imp. War Museum Photo.*)

Nieuport Two-Seater

In common with the Nieuport Scout, which it closely resembled in general configuration, the Nieuport two-seater was widely used by the R.N.A.S. as well as the R.F.C.

Officially designated the Nieuport Type 12, the two-seater, as might be expected, was of somewhat larger overall dimensions than the Scout and accommodated pilot and observer in closely-coupled cockpits, the pilot being seated immediately beneath the centre section and the observer-gunner level with the trailing edge. Some Nieuport 12s in R.N.A.S. service, however, dispensed with the rear gunner and were flown as single-seaters from the front cockpit, a single Lewis gun being mounted above the top wing to fire above the airscrew disc, as on the normal Scouts. Nieuports modified in this way were in action with Wg. Cdr. Samson's No. 3 Wing in the Dardanelles campaign until the end of 1915.

The original batches of Nieuport two-seaters in British service were purchased from the French industry, but later the type was built in Britain. The British-built Nieuports differed from the earlier model (shown in the three-view drawing) in having a fixed fin and a fully circular cowling instead of the cutaway type. Fifty were built for the Admiralty by Beardmore in 1916, the serial numbers being Nos. 9201 to 9250. Later, some of these aircraft (Nos. 9213 to 9232) were transferred to the R.F.C. as A 5183 to A 5202. Altogether the R.N.A.S. received 194 Nieuport two-seaters: 72 had the 130-h.p. Clerget engine and the remainder the 110-h.p. Clerget.

The Nieuport two-seaters did some good work with the Dunkirk wing in combat with German aircraft along the Belgian coast. A typical engagement was that of 14 December 1915 when F./Sub-Lt. C. W. Graham, with Sub-Lt. A. S. Ince as observer, shot down a German seaplane in flames which was attempting to bomb an Allied merchant steamer stranded on a sandbank. The Nieuport crew were forced down in the sea, but were rescued by the mine-sweeper *Balmoral*.

No. 1 Wing, R.N.A.S., Dunkirk; No. 2 Wing, R.N.A.S., Imbros; No. 3 Wing, R.N.A.S., Dardanelles; No. 7 (Naval) Squadron, Petite Synthe; No. 10 (Naval) Squadron (first with No. 1 Wing at Dunkirk and later with No. 4 Wing co-operating with the R.F.C.).

TECHNICAL DATA (NIEUPORT 12)

Description: Two-seat fighting, reconnaissance and bombing aircraft. Wooden structure, fabric covered.

Manufacturers: Soc. Anonyme des Etablissements Nieuport, Issy-le-Molineax (Seine), France. Sub-contracted by Wm. Beardmore & Co. Ltd, Dalmuir, Dumbartonshire.

Power Plant: One 110-h.p. or 130-h.p. Clerget.

Dimensions: Span, 29 ft. 7½ in. Length, 23 ft. 11¼ in. Height, 8 ft. 9 in. Wing area, 236½ sq. ft.

Weights: Empty, 1,210 lb. Loaded, 2,026 lb.

Performance: Maximum speed, 78 m.p.h. at 5,000 ft. Climb, 14 mins. to 6,500 ft. Endurance, 3 hrs. Service ceiling, 13,000 ft.

Armament: Single free-mounted Lewis gun in rear cockpit for observer or single fixed Lewis gun above top wing when flown as single-seaters.

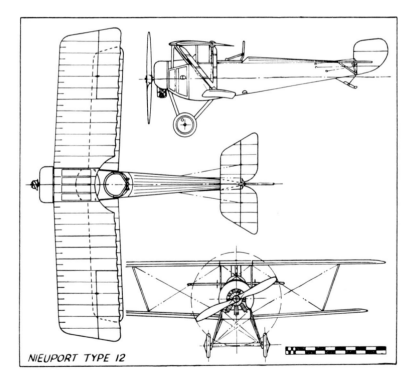

NIEUPORT TYPE 12

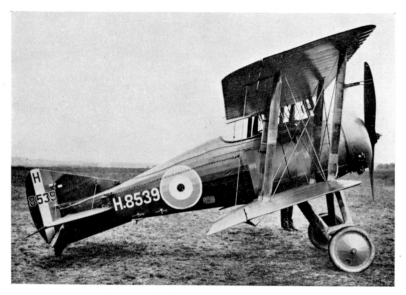

Nightjar (H 8539). (*Air Ministry Photo.*)

Nieuport Nightjar

The Nightjar was the first new type of single-seat fighter to be used aboard British aircraft-carriers after the end of the First World War. It remained in service for only a brief period, from 1922 to 1924, and was followed by the Parnall Plover and Fairey Flycatcher.

Like its F.A.A. contemporary, the Parnall Panther spotter-reconnaissance aircraft, the Nightjar was powered by the Bentley B.R. 2 rotary engine, and it was this feature that distinguished it from the closely related Nieuport Nighthawk, as used by the R.A.F., which had an Armstrong Siddeley Jaguar or Bristol Jupiter radial engine. Many Nightjars were, in fact, straight conversions from Nighthawk airframes after that type had been declared obsolete in 1923. Three examples of Nightjars converted from Nighthawks were H 8535, H 8539 and J 6930. The total number of Nightjars produced was 22.

The Nightjar was but one of a series of fighters produced by the Gloucestershire company after the original Nieuport Nighthawk design had been taken over in 1920. Differing only in detail, these fighters were known as the Mars series. The Mars II, III and IV were supplied in quantity to the Japanese Navy, where they were known as the Sparrowhawk I, II and III respectively. The Mars IV (the only version with a radial instead of a B.R. 2 engine) was the Nighthawk, and the Mars X became the Nightjar. The Nightjar differed from earlier Mars fighters in having an undercarriage of wider track and longer stroke, with arrester hooks on the axle to engage fore-and-aft wires on the carrier deck.

Details of the Nightjar's Service record are sparse, but the type is known to have served with No. 203 Squadron during the Chanak (Turkish) crisis of 1922 and, afterwards, remained with this squadron until it disbanded at Leuchars on 1 April 1923. Nightjars were also embarked in H.M.S. *Argus* and served with a training flight at Leuchars in 1923. Six Nightjars served with No. 401 Flight until replaced by Flycatchers in 1924.

No. 203 Squadron (Leuchars)and No. 401 Flight (*Argus*).

TECHNICAL DATA (NIGHTJAR)

Description: Single-seat carrier-borne fighter. Wooden structure, fabric covered.
Manufacturers: Gloucestershire Aircraft Co. Ltd., Cheltenham.
Power Plant: One 230-h.p. Bentley B.R. 2.
Dimensions: Span, 28 ft. Length, 19 ft. 2 in. Height, 9 ft. 7 in. Wing area, 270 sq. ft.
Weight: Loaded, 2,165 lb.
Performance: Maximum speed, 108 m.p.h. at 6,500 ft.; 93 m.p.h. at 10,000 ft.; 90 m.p.h. at 15,000 ft. Climb, 20 mins. to 15,000 ft. Endurance, 2 hrs. at 3,000 ft. Service ceiling, 15,000 ft.
Armament: Two fixed, synchronised Vickers guns.

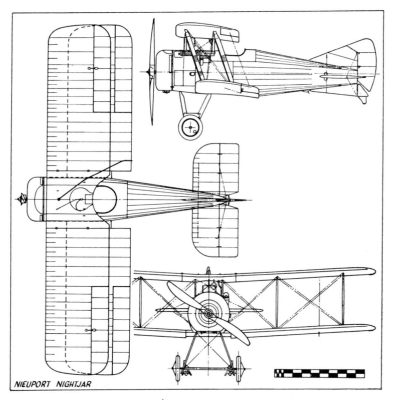

NIEUPORT NIGHTJAR

N.T. 4A (N 2742) of the R.N.A.S. (*Imp. War Museum Photo.*)

Norman Thompson N.T. 4

The Norman Thompson N.T. 4 is perhaps the least known of all the large flying-boats employed on coastal patrol by the R.N.A.S. in the First World War. It never enjoyed the fame that attended the American Curtiss boats, or the Felixstowe series, but nevertheless was responsible for a good deal of routine anti-submarine reconnaissance from a string of bases between Calshot and Scapa Flow.

The N.T. 4 was the first new design to appear after the old White and Thompson Company changed its name to the Norman Thompson Flight Company in October 1915, and its emergence coincided with the Curtiss H. 4. For this reason, in the somewhat haphazard custom of those days, it was known by the name of 'America', and later changed to 'Small America', in the same way as the Curtiss. This may account for the obscurity in which its operational record is shrouded, as there may have been some confusion between the two types in official archives.

A feature of the N.T. 4 was the completely enclosed accommodation for the crew. In the earlier version the view was poor and the cabin was progressively improved, so that in the late production models the cabin-top was glazed as well as the sides.

The first batch of aircraft (Nos. 8338 to 8343) were fitted with two 150-h.p. Hispano-Suiza engines. Subsequent machines had 200-h.p. geared Hispanos, were designated N.T. 4A and were allotted the serial numbers 9061 to 9064, N 2140 to N 2159 and N 2740 to N 2759. Production ceased in the summer of 1918.

One of the N.T. 4 flying-boats (No. 8338) was the subject of an interesting experiment in armament. It was fitted with a Davis two-pounder recoil-less gun mounted above the cabin. The installation was never embodied in production aircraft.

UNITS ALLOCATED

R.N.A.S. coastal air stations at Calshot, Cattewater, Dundee, Felixstowe, Invergordon, Killingholme and Scapa Flow.

TECHNICAL DATA (N.T. 4A)

Description: anti-submarine reconnaissance flying-boat with a crew of four. Wooden structure, with wood and fabric covering.
Manufacturers: Norman Thompson Flight Co. Ltd., Bognor Regis, Sussex.
Power Plant: Two 200-h.p. Hispano-Suiza.
Dimensions: Span, 78 ft. 7 in. Length, 41 ft. 6 in. Height, 14 ft. 10 in. Wing area, 936 sq. ft.
Weights: Empty, 4,572 lb. Loaded, 6,469 lb.
Performance: Maximum speed, 95 m.p.h. at 2,000 ft.; 91 m.p.h. at 10,000 ft. Climb, 3 mins. 50 secs. to 2,000 ft.; 31 mins. 5 secs. to 10,000 ft. Service ceiling, 11,700 ft.
Armament: Possibly provision for free-mounted Lewis gun firing through a side window and racks for bombs beneath lower wings.

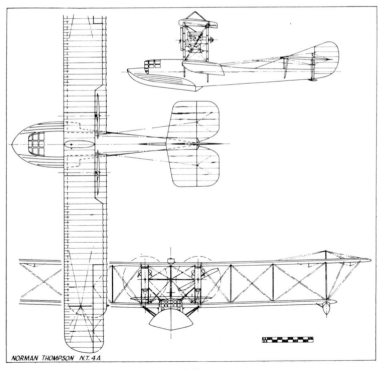

NORMAN THOMPSON N.T. 4A

Panther (N 7511) built by Bristol. (*Air Ministry Photo.*)

Parnall Panther

The Panther was one of the first British aircraft designed specifically for operation from aircraft-carriers. It was the work of Mr. Harold Bolas, formerly with the Air Department of the Admiralty, and met the requirements of the Admiralty Spec. N. 2A for a two-seat deck-landing reconnaissance aircraft. The first prototype (N 91) made its appearance in 1917 and was followed by five other prototypes (N 92 to N 96). It was unorthodox in a number of respects: it had a monocoque fuselage, a form of construction not then very common, and to conserve space aboard ship the fuselage was made to fold, being hinged just aft of the rear cockpit so that the rear fuselage and tail assembly could be swung to starboard. The pilot and observer were mounted unusually high; this gave the pilot an excellent forward view for deck-landing, but restricted entry to the cockpit which had to be reached through a hole in the top wing.

Two other features of the Panther, which added to its somewhat singular appearance, were the flotation air bags fitted beneath the bottom wings at either side of the undercarriage, and the hydrovane to prevent the aircraft nosing over in the event of a forced descent in the sea.

The original order for 300 Panthers was reduced to 150 with the Armistice, and these aircraft (N 7400 to N 7549) were built by Bristol (then British and Colonial) at Filton during 1919 and 1920. The Panthers equipped Fleet Spotter Reconnaissance Flights aboard *Argus* and *Hermes* at a period when longitudinal arrester wires supporting hinged wooden flaps were in vogue. The aircraft itself carried hooks on the axle. This system was far from satisfactory and caused a lot of accidents; R. R. Money in his book *Flying and Soldiering* claims that, during a 1924 training period in *Argus*, only five landings out of six escaped mishap. Although the Panthers handled well in the air, their Bentley engines needed careful nursing and demanded frequent attention. Be that as it may, the Panther was a great pioneer of early deck-flying, and remained in first-line service with the F.A.A. as late as 1926 with No. 442 Flight at Leuchars. Panthers were finally superseded by the Fairey IIID.

No. 421 Fleet Spotter Flight (Gosport); Nos. 441 and 442 Fleet Spotter Reconnaissance Flights (Leuchars). Aircraft-carriers *Argus* and *Hermes*.

TECHNICAL DATA (PANTHER)

Description: Two-seat carrier-borne spotter-reconnaissance aircraft. Wooden structure with wood and fabric covering.
Manufacturers: Parnall & Sons, Bristol. Sub-contracted by the British & Colonial Aeroplane Co. Ltd., Filton, Bristol.
Power Plant: One 230-h.p. Bentley B.R. 2.
Dimensions: Span, 29 ft. 6 in. Length, 24 ft. 11 in. (14 ft. 6 in. folded). Height, 10 ft. 6 in. Wing area, 336 sq. ft.
Weights: Empty, 1,328 lb. Loaded, 2,595 lb.
Performance: Maximum speed, $108\frac{1}{2}$ m.p.h. at 6,500 ft.; 103 m.p.h. at 10,000 ft. Climb, 2 mins. 20 secs. to 20,00 ft.; 17 mins. 5 secs. to 10,000 ft. Endurance, $4\frac{1}{2}$ hrs. Service ceiling, 14,500 ft.
Armament: One free-mounted Lewis machine-gun in rear cockpit.

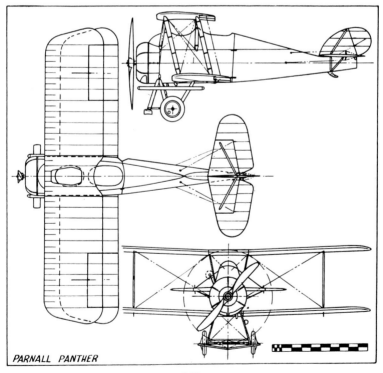

PARNALL PANTHER

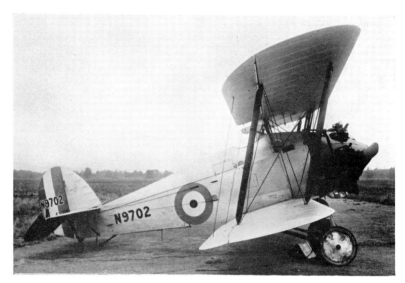

Plover (N 9702). (*Air Ministry Photo.*)

Parnall Plover

Having established themselves as designers of naval aircraft with their Panther two-seat spotter, the Parnall concern produced in 1922 the Plover single-seat fighter. Like its more successful competitor, the Fly-catcher, the Plover met an Air Ministry specification for a deck-landing fighter, capable of superseding the Nieuport Nightjar and utilising either the Bristol Jupiter or Armstrong Siddeley Jaguar radial engine. As might be expected, the Plover bore many points of resemblance to its Fairey rival, but it never earned the same favour and disappeared into obscurity after a very short life with the F.A.A.

The Plover was designed by Harold Bolas (who was also responsible for the Panther), and three prototypes were built, numbered N 160, N 161 and N 162. The first two Plovers had the 436-h.p. Jupiter engine, and the third aircraft a 385-h.p. Jaguar. Like the Flycatcher, the Plover was also available as amphibian, with wheels projecting from the bottom of twin floats, and N 161 appeared in this guise. One of the Plovers was exhibited in the New Types Park at the R.A.F. Display at Hendon in 1923.

Small-scale production of the Plover (with the Jupiter engine) took place in 1923, when six aircraft entered service with Nos. 403 and 404 Fleet Fighter Flights as contemporaries of the six Nightjars with No. 401 Flight, and six Flycatchers with No. 402 Flight. The Flycatcher soon proved its superiority and the following year superseded the Plovers as well as the Nightjars. The Plover's rapid eclipse was possibly due to structural weakness: R. R. Money recalls in his book *Flying and Soldiering* an incident at Leuchars in 1924 when a Plover on test had its centre section collapse during aerobatics. The unfortunate pilot had no parachute, but by skilful flying contrived to crash-land the Plover on a moor near the mouth of the River Eden.

No records have survived of Plover production quantities, but the earliest to be photographed was N 9608, and it is likely that the batch continued to No. 9615 as the first production Flycatcher was N 9616. The existence of a later batch is indicated by the aircraft illustrated, N 9702.

UNITS ALLOCATED

Nos. 403 and 404 Fleet Fighter Flights.

TECHNICAL DATA (PLOVER)

Description: Single-seat carrier-borne fighter available either as a landplane or an amphibian. Wooden structure, fabric covered.
Manufacturers: George Parnall & Co. Ltd., Park Row, Bristol.
Power Plant: One 436-h.p. Bristol Jupiter IV.
Dimensions: Span, 29 ft. Length, 23 ft. Height, 12 ft. Wing area, 306 sq. ft.
Weights: Empty, 2,035 lb. Loaded, 2,984 lb.
Performance: No details available.
Armament: Twin, synchronised Vickers machine-guns.

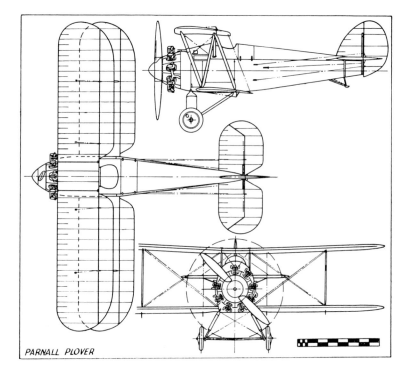

PARNALL PLOVER

Short Type 184 (No. 8076) with 240-h.p. Sunbeam, built by Short. (*Imp. War Museum Photo.*)

Short Type 184 Seaplane

In any history of the development of British naval aviation the Short Type 184 must occupy an honoured place. It was to the First World War what the Swordfish became in the Second World War; both types made history as torpedo-carrying aircraft and earned reputations in every theatre of war for solid reliability. More than 650 Short Type 184 seaplanes were built for the R.N.A.S. They served at practically every coastal air station round Great Britain, as well as in the Mediterranean, the Aegean, the Red Sea, in Mesopotamia and on the French coast. The most important fact about the Short Type 184, however, is that it was the first aircraft in the world to sink an enemy ship at sea by means of a torpedo attack. It was also the only aircraft to play an active part in the Battle of Jutland.

As was the case with a number of key types of British naval aircraft, the Short Type 184 owed its existence to the fertile brain of Commodore Murray F. Sueter (later Rear-Adm. Sir Murray Sueter), who was Director of the Air Department of the Admiralty in the formative years of the R.N.A.S. Commodore Sueter, from the earliest days a keen advocate of the torpedo as a R.N.A.S. weapon, had had his hand strengthened by the success of the experiment, on 28 July 1914, when a 14-in. Whitehead torpedo of 810 lb. had been dropped from a Short seaplane with 160-h.p. Gnome engine. With the outbreak of war, Commodore Sueter pressed his theories about the value of a powerful torpedo-carrying seaplane, and talked over his plans with Shorts. The outcome, early in 1915, was the Short Type 184. It took its designation from the curious Admiralty custom of those days whereby types were referred to by the number allocated to the first aircraft. Later, the type became known in general service by the more colloquial '225', which was the horse-power of the engine, though more powerful engines were subsequently fitted.

Some of the first Short 184s delivered to the R.N.A.S. (including the original No. 184) went aboard the seaplane carrier *Ben-my-Chree* to serve in the Dardanelles campaign from June 1915. Within a few weeks it seemed that the optimism about the torpedo had been justified, for, on 12 August, F./Cdr. C. H. K. Edmonds made his historic flight, during which he sank an enemy ship. Flying from the Gulf of Xeros, he spotted a large vessel in the Straits, glided down from 800 ft. to 15 ft., and launched his Whitehead torpedo at a range of 300 yds., striking the ship abreast the mainmast. On 17 August F./Cdr. Edmonds took his Short seaplane out again and repeated his success; his torpedo hit one of three steamers making for Ak Bashi Liman. The steamer was set on fire and had to be towed back to Constantinople, a burnt-out hulk. Meanwhile, F./Lt. G. B. Dacre in another Short 184 had succeeded in sinking a large steam tug whilst taxying on the water after a forced descent due to engine failure.

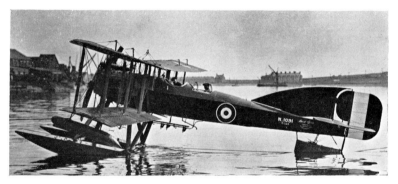

Short Type 184 (N 1091) with 240-h.p. Renault, built by Short. (*Short Bros. Photo.*)

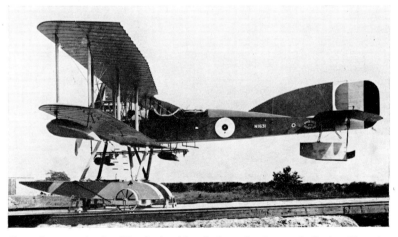

Short Improved 184 (N 1631) with 260-h.p. Sunbeam, built by Phoenix. (*Imp. War Museum Photo.*)

Afterwards he coaxed his Short into the air again under heavy Turkish fire.

These early successes with air-launched torpedoes were not to be repeated, but the Shorts from *Ben-my-Chree* were far from inactive. They performed a vital reconnaissance function, spotting for a naval monitor which shelled enemy transports, and bombing Turkish harbours. On 8 November 1915 Short seaplanes bombed the railway bridge over the River Maritza, and they were still hammering away at enemy communications as late as 27 August 1916, when Cdr. C. R. Samson (who had taken over command of *Ben-my-Chree* the previous May) led a raid on Chikaldir Bridge, with F./Cdr. England and Lt. Clemson in the other Shorts. As Cdr. Samson recalls in his book *Fights and Flights*, these raids were not without their difficulties; engines gave a lot of trouble due to overheating, as the coolant water boiled readily in the hot climate.

In February 1916 five Short 184s were sent to Mesopotamia, where they operated from the River Tigris. During the siege of Kut they dropped supplies to the garrison, each seaplane carrying about 250 lb. of food.

In home waters Short 184s did a vast amount of routine anti-submarine patrol, and on one occasion (9 November 1916) even participated in a night-bombing raid on Ostend and Zeebrugge. For these operations they flew from coastal air stations, but they were also embarked in seaplane carriers, and it was one of these latter aircraft that achieved immortality in the Battle of Jutland. The Short 184 in question (No. 8359, a Westland-built aircraft) was serving in *Engadine* and operating with the Battle Cruiser Fleet under Sir David Beatty. Piloted by F./Lt. F. J. Rutland (who later pioneered the flying of Pups from gun-turret launching platforms), and with Assistant Paymaster G. S. Trewin as observer, the Short took off just after 3 p.m. on 31 May 1916. Within 40 mins. it had reported the presence and course of three enemy cruisers and ten destroyers. To make this observation, the Short had to fly low, under enemy gun-fire, as the clouds were at 900 ft. and the visibility was poor. Continued bad weather made further air activity impracticable during the Battle of Jutland, and *Engadine* returned to Rosyth on 2 June. Limited as it was, the reconnaissance of 31 May was a milestone in naval air warfare equal in significance to the torpedo attack of the previous August.

The Short 184 was progressively improved throughout its career, some of the changes being introduced by the sub-contracting firms, of which there were many. In 1915, after only 12 Short 184s had been completed by the parent company, contracts were issued to S. E. Saunders Ltd., Mann, Egerton & Co. Ltd., Westland, the Phoenix Dynamo Company and Frederick Sage & Co. Ltd. Some of these firms had never previously built aircraft; nevertheless the first sub-contracted aircraft (from Sage) was ready in September 1915, and was followed by deliveries from Mann, Egerton in November 1915 and from Westland's and Phoenix early in 1916. Meanwhile the type continued in production at Shorts, and still more contractors were brought in later. As mentioned earlier, total production reached over 650, of which more than 300 were still in service in October 1918.

The power of the Short 184 was progressively increased from the 225-h.p. of the original Sunbeam to the 275-h.p. of the Sunbeam Maori III. This latter engine was fitted in some late production models, which could be

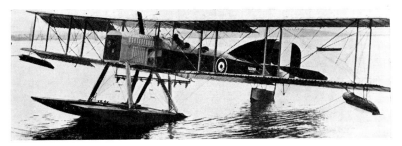

Short 184 'Dover Type' (N 1098) with 260-h.p. Sunbeam and nose radiator, built by Short. (*Short Bros. Photo.*)

distinguished by their twin exhaust stacks. Other standard installations were the 240-h.p. Sunbeam, the 240-h.p. Renault and the 260-h.p. Sunbeam.

The late production 260-h.p. Short became known as the Dover type; it differed from its fore-runners in having a car-type radiator immediately behind the airscrew and dispensed with the ugly box-type radiator above or at the sides of the engine which had characterised other Short 184s. Most of the later Short 184s had a bomb-beam below the fuselage, between the float struts, and a Scarff ring for the observer in the aft cockpit.

UNITS ALLOCATED

R.N.A.S. coastal air stations (the squadrons are those which the stations became after the R.N.A.S. had been incorporated administratively in the R.A.F. after 1 April 1918): Bangor (No. 244, disbanded 22 January 1919), Bembridge (No. 253, disbanded 5 May 1919), Calshot (No. 240, disbanded 15 May 1919), Cattewater (No. 237, disbanded 15 May 1919), Dover (No. 233, disbanded 15 May 1919), Dundee (No. 257, disbanded 30 June 1919), Felixstowe, Fishguard (No. 245, disbanded 10 May 1919), Great Yarmouth (No. 229, disbanded 31 December 1919), Hornsea (No. 248, disbanded 6 March 1919 and No. 251, disbanded 30 June 1919), Killingholme (No. 249, disbanded 8 October 1919), Newhaven (No. 242, disbanded 15 May 1919), Newlyn (No. 235, disbanded 22 February 1919), Pembroke (No. 255, disbanded 14 January 1919), Portland (No. 241, disbanded 18 June 1919), Prawle Point (No. 254, disbanded 22 February 1919), Torquay (No. 239, disbanded 15 May 1919), Tresco (No. 234, disbanded 15 May 1919), Tynemouth (No. 252, disbanded 30 June 1919), Westgate (No. 219, disbanded 7 February 1920), and Westward Ho (No. 260, disbanded 22 February 1919). Overseas at: Alexandria, Basra, Cherbourg (No. 243, disbanded 15 March 1919), Dunkirk, Malta (No. 266, disbanded 1 September 1919), Mudros, Otranto (No. 271, disbanded 9 December 1918), Port Said (No. 269, disbanded 15 November 1919), Santa Maria di Leuca and Suda Bay. Seaplane carriers: *Anne, Ben-my-chree, Campania, City of Oxford, Empress, Engadine, Furious, Nairana, Pegasus, Raven II, Riviera* and *Vindex*.

TECHNICAL DATA (SHORT 184)

Description: Two-seat reconnaissance, bombing and torpedo-carrying seaplane. Wooden structure, fabric covered.
Manufacturers: Short Bros., Rochester, Kent (Nos. 184, 185, 841 to 850, 8031 to 8105, N 1080 to N 1099, N 1580 to N 1589). Sub-contracted

by Brush Electrical Engineering Co. Ltd., Loughborough (N 1660 to
N 1689, N 2600 to N 2629, N 2630 to N 2659, N 2790 to N 2819,
N 9060 to N 9099 and N 9260 to N 9289); Mann, Egerton & Co. Ltd.,
Norwich (Nos. 8344 to 8355); Phoenix Dynamo Manufacturing Co.
Ltd., Bradford (Nos. 8368 to 8378, N 1630 to N 1659 and N 1740 to
N 1759); Robey & Co. Ltd., Lincoln (Nos. 9041 to 9060, N 1220 to
N 1229, N 1260 to N 1279, N 1820 to N 1839, N 2820 to N 2849,
N 9000 to N 9059 and N 9290 to N 9305); Frederick Sage & Co. Ltd.,
Peterborough (Nos. 8380 to 8391, 9065 to 9084, N 1130 to N 1139,
N 1230 to N 1239, N 1590 to N 1599 and N 1780 to N 1799); S. E.
Saunders, Ltd., Isle of Wight (Nos. 8001 to 8030, N 1140 to N 1149,
N 1600 to N 1624 and N 1760 to N 1774); Supermarine Aviation Works,
Ltd., Southampton (N 9170 to N 9181); Westland Aircraft Works,
Yeovil (Nos. 8356 to 8367) and J. Samuel White & Co. Ltd., Isle of
Wight (N 1240 to N 1259, N 2950 to N 2999 and N 9100 to N 9139).
Power Plant: One 225-h.p. or 240-h.p. or 260-h.p. Sunbeam; 240-h.p.
Renault or 275-h.p. Sunbeam Maori III.
Dimensions: Span, 63 ft. 6¼ in. Length, 40 ft. 7½ in. Height, 13 ft. 6 in.
Wing area, 688 sq. ft.
Weights (with 260-h.p. Sunbeam): Empty, 3,703 lb. Loaded, 5,363 lb.
Performance (with 260-h.p. Sunbeam): Maximum speed, 88½ m.p.h. at
2,000 ft.; 84 m.p.h. at 6,500 ft. Climb, 8 mins. 35 secs. to 2,000 ft.;

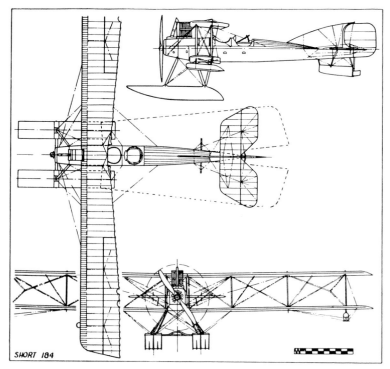

SHORT 184

33 mins. 50 secs. to 6,500 ft. Endurance, 2¾ hrs. Service ceiling, 9,000 ft.

Armament: One free-mounted Lewis machine-gun aft and provision for one 14-in. torpedo or various loads of bombs up to a maximum of 520 lb.

A Short Type 184 in flight. (*Imp. War Museum Photo.*)

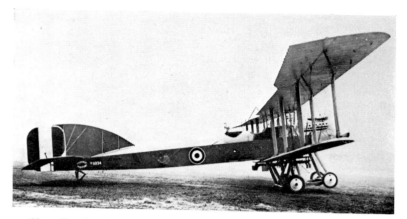

Short Bomber (No. 9834) built by Phoenix. (*Imp. War Museum Photo.*)

Short Bomber

As will be evident from its appearance, the Short Bomber was a landplane adaptation of the famous Short Type 184 seaplane. The prototype (No. 3706) was produced to meet the requirements of an Admiralty competition of 1915 for a bomber offering good range and load-carrying properties, for even at this early stage the R.N.A.S. was turning it attention to the possibilities of strategic bombing. The prototype had two-bay wings, but all production aircraft had three-bay wings of increased span. The fuselage, too, was lengthened on later production aircraft, though early batches had a short fuselage, as in the drawing. Contracts for over 80 Short Bombers were placed, of which 36 were by Short Brothers (Nos. 9306 to 9340), 15 by Sunbeam (Nos. 9356 to 9370), 20 by Mann, Egerton (Nos. 9476 to 9495), six by Parnall (Nos. 9771 to 9776) and six by Phoenix (Nos. 9831 to 9836). The Sunbeam Company fitted the 225-h.p. Sunbeam engine in their aircraft: otherwise the 250-h.p. Rolls-Royce was standard.

The Short Bomber first entered service with No. 7 Squadron, R.N.A.S. Four of the new Shorts (250-h.p. engines) joined 18 other bombers of the 4th and 5th Naval Wings in a raid on the Ateliers de la Marine and the Slyken Electric Power Station at Ostend on the night of 15 November 1916. Each Short carried eight 65-lb. bombs, twice the bomb-load of the accompanying Caudrons, but well below the aircraft's total capacity of 900 lb. No. 7's Short Bombers continued to raid enemy naval installations throughout the winter of 1916–17, until superseded by Handley Page O/100s when the Squadron moved to Coudekerque in April 1917.

Early in 1916 15 Short Bombers (together with 20 Sopwith 1½ Strutter bombers) were earmarked for the initial equipment of the new R.N.A.S. bombing unit known as No. 3 Wing, based at Luxeuil in the Nancy area, but ambitious plans for raids on German industry were seriously hampered by the need to transfer aircraft to the hard-pressed R.F.C., at the request of Gen. Trenchard. It is not known to what extent the Shorts eventually participated in the No. 3 Wing raids which began on 12 October 1916.

No. 7 Squadron of No. 5 Wing, R.N.A.S., Coudekerque, and No. 3 Wing, R.N.A.S., Luxeuil.

TECHNICAL DATA (SHORT BOMBER)

Description: Two-seat long-range bomber. Wooden structure, fabric covered.

Manufacturers: Short Bros., Rochester. Sub-contracted by Mann, Egerton & Co. Ltd. of Norwich; Parnall & Sons Ltd. of Bristol; the Phoenix Dynamo Manufacturing Co. Ltd. of Bradford, and the Sunbeam Motor Car Co. Ltd. of Wolverhampton.

Power Plant: One 225-h.p. Sunbeam or 250-h.p. Rolls-Royce Eagle.

Dimensions: Span, 85 ft. Length, 45 ft. Height, 15 ft. Wing area, 870 sq. ft.

Weights: Loaded, 6,800 lb.

Performance: Maximum speed, $77\frac{1}{2}$ m.p.h. at 6,500 ft. Climb, 45 mins. to 10,000 ft. Endurance, 6 hrs. Service ceiling, 9,500 ft.

Armament: One free-mounted Lewis gun in rear cockpit. Bomb-load of four 230-lb. or eight 112-lb. bombs on racks below wings.

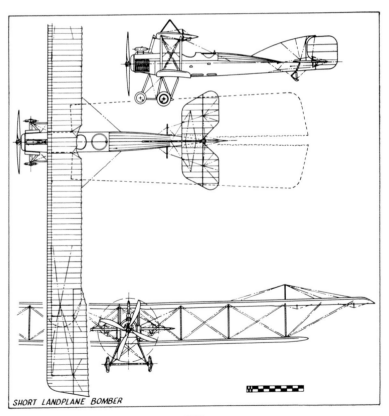

SHORT LANDPLANE BOMBER

Short Admiralty Type 827 of the R.N.A.S. (*Imp. War Museum Photo.*)

Short 827/830 Seaplane

Very similar in appearance to the Short 166 Seaplane (see Appendix), the Short 827/830 was of somewhat smaller dimensions and had two alternative power plants. The Type 827 could be more readily distinguished from the Type 166 in that it had an in-line Sunbeam engine, whereas the Type 830 had a Salmson water-cooled radial as in the Type 166. The Type 830 is depicted in the three-view general arrangement drawing and the Type 827 in the photograph.

The Admiralty's first contract for 12 aircraft was placed in the summer of 1914: it covered six Type 827s (Nos. 822 to 827) and six Type 830s (Nos. 819 to 821 and 828 to 830). Ultimately, the Type 827 predominated and over 100 were ordered, against the score or so of the Type 830. The Short 827 enjoyed a remarkably long operational life, for it served from 1915 until the Armistice.

Unlike the Short 830, which was built by the parent firm only, the Short 827 was manufactured by four firms in addition to Short Bros. and, indeed, 12 aircraft of this type (Nos. 8550 to 8561) were the first aircraft ever built by Fairey before they turned to their own designs. Fairey-built 827s were tested at Hamble by the Australian pilot Sydney Pickles.

Both the Short 827 and 830 were used from seaplane carriers, from R.N.A.S. coastal air stations and overseas. In March 1916 four Short 827s accompanied four Voisins to Zanzibar to form a unit which became No. 8 (Naval) Squadron. They did much useful work in the East African campaign and a number of successful attacks were planned after photographic reconnaissance by a Short 827 operating from the seaplane carrier *Manica*. Short 827s operated in Mesopotamia from September 1915 and in December two were converted as landplanes to bomb the Turks advancing on Kut al Imara.

The following year, on 25 April 1916, a Short 827 from Great Yarmouth bombed the German warships that were shelling Lowestoft.

256

No. 8 (Naval) Squadron, East Africa. R.N.A.S. coastal air stations at Calshot, Dundee, Great Yarmouth, Isle of Grain and Killingholme. Seaplane carriers *Ben-my-Chree*, *Engadine*, *Manica* and *Raven II*. Armed merchant vessels *Himalaya* and *Laconia*. R.N.A.S. units at Basra and Otranto.

TECHNICAL DATA (SHORT 827)

Description: Two-seat reconnaissance and bombing seaplane. Wooden structure, fabric covered.

Manufacturers: Short Bros., Rochester. Sub-contraced by Brush Electrical Engineering Co. Ltd. of Loughborough; Fairey Aviation Co. Ltd. of Hayes; Parnall & Sons Ltd. of Bristol and Sunbeam Motor Car Co. of Wolverhampton.

Power Plant: One 150-h.p. Sunbeam Nubian.

Dimensions: Span, 53 ft. 11 in. Length, 35 ft. 3 in. Height, 13 ft. 6 in. Wing area, 506 sq. ft.

Weight: Loaded, 3,400 lb.

Performance: Maximum speed, 61 m.p.h.

Armament: One free-mounted Lewis machine-gun. Bomb-racks below fuselage.

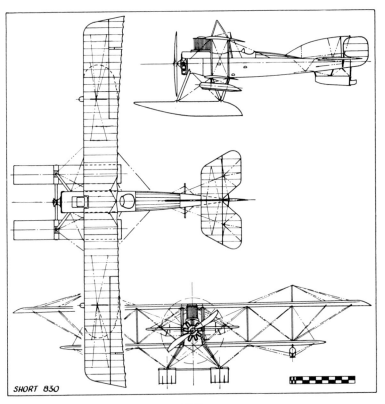

SHORT 830

Short Type 320 (N 1498) built by Short. (*Imp. War Museum Photo.*)

Short 320 Seaplane

The Short 320 was the last of many types of Short seaplane to enter service during the First World War. It was also the largest, since it was designed to combine long range with sufficient weight-lifting capacity to carry the new Mk. IX 18-in. torpedo of 1,000 lb.

The designation of the Short 320 derived from its 320-h.p. Sunbeam Cossack engine, though the original version had a Sunbeam of only 310 h.p. The prototypes (Nos. 8317 and 8318) made their first flights in 1916 and were followed by a production contract for 25 aircraft in January 1917. At this time the Admiralty was giving increasing attention to the claims of the Mediterranean, where U-boats based in the Adriatic called for more air patrols. As an immediate step, six Short 225s were transferred from Dundee air station to this theatre, and plans were finalised for attacks by torpedo-carrying seaplanes on the Austrian fleet at Pola. It was decided that the new Otranto base should have 12 Short 320s on its strength when these became available and two more were to be established at a torpedo school based in Malta.

The first attack by the Italian-based Short 320s was launched on 2 September 1917, when six aircraft, carrying their 18-in. torpedoes, were towed by motor launches to a point 50 miles south of Traste Bay, where they were to take off for a raid on submarines lying off Cattaro. The operation proved abortive; by a great misfortune it was robbed of success by gales and heavy seas which sprang up on 3 September.

For some unexplained reason, no further attacks of this kind were made, though a series of experiments with torpedo drops at Calshot in February 1918 proved very successful. By 31 March 1918 the R.N.A.S. had received 110 Short 320s and when the war ended there were 50 still in service: 30 of these were in the Mediterranean. Thereafter, with more interest being shown in the carrier-borne landplane for torpedo work, the Short 320 soon disappeared from the scene. Some of the last remained with No. 268 Squadron, which served at Malta until disbanded in October 1919.

R.N.A.S. coastal air stations at Calshot, Felixstowe, Great Yarmouth, Isle of Grain and Killingholme; No. 6 Wing (Otranto and Brindisi); No. 268 Squadron and Torpedo School (Malta).

TECHNICAL DATA (SHORT 320)

Description: Two-seat anti-submarine patrol or single-seat torpedo-carrying seaplane. Wooden structure, fabric covered.

Manufacturers: Short Bros., Rochester. Sub-contracted by the Sunbeam Motor Car Co. Ltd., Wolverhampton.

Power Plant: One 310-h.p. or 320-h.p. Sunbeam Cossack.

Dimensions: Span, 75 ft. Length, 45 ft. 9 in. Height, 17 ft. 6 in. Wing area, 810 sq. ft.

Weights (with torpedo): Empty, 4,933 lb. Loaded, 7,014 lb.

Performance (with torpedo): Maximum speed, $72\frac{1}{2}$ m.p.h. at 1,200 ft. Climb, 12 mins. to 2,000 ft. Service ceiling, 3,000 ft.

Armament: One free-mounted Lewis machine-gun above front cockpit level with wing. One 18-in. torpedo or two 230-lb. bombs below the fuselage.

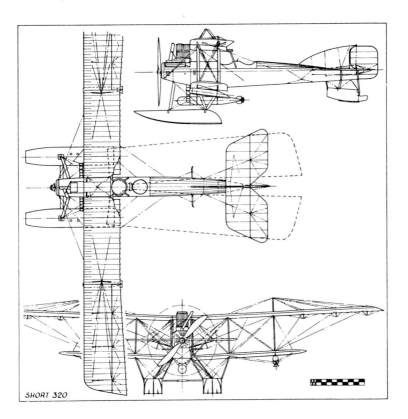

SHORT 320

Sturgeon T.T. 2 (TS 486). (*Official Admiralty Photo.*)

Short Sturgeon

The Sturgeon was the first twin-engined aircraft designed specifically for naval use to enter service with the F.A.A.; the Monitor, Sea Mosquito and Sea Hornet were all conversions of aircraft designed originally for the R.A.F. It was originally intended as a reconnaissance-bomber for operation from *Ark Royal* and *Hermes* class aircraft-carriers, being designed to Spec. S. 11/43, and the first prototype (RK 787) flew in 1946. With changed operational requirements in the post-war period, the Sturgeon never entered production as a first-line aircraft, but was modified instead for high-speed target-towing duties to a new specification, Q 1/46.

The new variant was known as the Short S.A. 2 Sturgeon T.T. Mk. 2, and two prototypes were built (VR 363 and VR 371), the first flight being made on 1 September 1949. The Sturgeon T.T. 2 was fully equipped for deck-landing and had power-operated folding wings and a lengthened nose to accommodate photographic equipment. The F.A.A. took delivery of 23 Sturgeon T.T. 2s, (TS 475 to TS 497); the first production aircraft flew on 8 June 1950. These aircraft were used from carriers for Fleet gunnery practice, for air-to-air firing exercises, photographic marking and radar calibration.

After some years of useful service, it was decided to use Sturgeons from shore-based units only, and accordingly modifications were undertaken on 19 aircraft for the new rôle. The new variant, the Short S.B. 9 Sturgeon T.T. Mk. 3 (see three-view), reverted to the short nose of the original Sturgeon and had manually folding wings; the deck-landing gear was deleted. The last of the 19 Sturgeon T.T. 3s was delivered to the F.A.A. on 22 May 1957. Most of them served at the Royal Naval air station, Hal Far, Malta, where they were used by No. 728 Squadron, a Fleet Requirements Unit.

TECHNICAL DATA (STURGEON T.T. 2)

Description: High-speed carrier-borne target-tug with a crew of two. All-metal stressed-skin construction.

Manufacturers: Short Bros. & Harland, Ltd., Queens Island, Belfast, Northern Ireland.

Power Plant: Two 1,660-h.p. Rolls-Royce Merlin 140S.

Dimensions: Span, 59 ft. 9 in. (22 ft. 5 in. folded). Length, 48 ft. $10\frac{1}{2}$ in. Height, 13 ft. $2\frac{1}{2}$ in. Wing area, 564 sq. ft.

Weights: Empty, 17,647 lb. Loaded, 22,350 lb.

Performance: Maximum speed, 370 m.p.h.; 356 m.p.h. at 24,200 ft.; 302 m.p.h. at 15,000 ft.; 248 m.p.h. with 32 ft. span winged target; 262 m.p.h. with sleeve target. Range, 1,600 miles. Endurance, $3\frac{1}{4}$ hrs., including 1 hr. with 32-ft. winged target. Service ceiling, 35,700 ft.; 32,900 ft. with 32-ft. winged target.

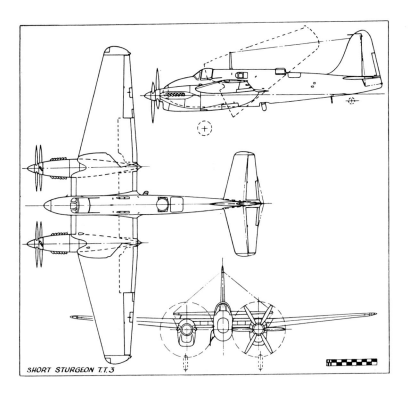

SHORT STURGEON T.T.3

Tabloid single-seat scout. (*Imp. War Museum Photo.*)

Sopwith Tabloid

The Tabloid was one of the most outstanding aircraft produced in Great Britain before the outbreak of war in 1914. By the standards of those days, its top speed of over 90 m.p.h. and its climb of 1,200 ft. per min. placed it in a class of its own, and it caused a sensation when demonstrated in public for the first time by Harry Hawker, at Hendon on 29 November 1913. The prototype seated two, side-by-side, but subsequent Tabloids were single-seaters, including the seaplane flown to victory in the 1914 Schneider Trophy contest by Howard Pixton.

The military potential of the Tabloid was immediately apparent and production for the Naval and Military Wings of the R.F.C. began early in 1914. By October 1914 the R.N.A.S. possessed only three Tabloids, yet in that month the type struck a telling blow at the enemy. On the 8th Sqn. Cdr. Spenser Gray and F./Lt. R. L. G. Marix took off from Antwerp, then under bombardment by the enemy, in Tabloids Nos. 167 and 168 to bomb Zeppelin sheds at Cologne and Dusseldorf. Mist prevented Spenser Gray from finding his target, so he bombed Cologne railway station, but Marix's success was complete. He dived on the sheds at Dusseldorf and bombed from 600 ft. Within 30 seconds flames had risen to 500 ft.; the new Zeppelin $Z. IX$ had been destroyed, the first to fall a victim to a British aircraft.

Between October 1914 and June 1915, a further 36 Tabloids were built and delivered to the R.F.C. and R.N.A.S. The naval Tabloids served with Wg. Cdr. Samson's Eastchurch squadron in Belgium, as already mentioned, and later with Samson's No. 3 Squadron, R.N.A.S., in the Dardanelles campaign. Others served aboard the seaplane-carrier *Ark Royal* in the same campaign, and at least one Tabloid was on the strength of the R.N.A.S. station at Great Yarmouth.

Description: Single-seat scouting and bombing aircraft. Wooden structure, fabric covered.

Manufacturers: Sopwith Aviation Co. Ltd., Kingston-on-Thames.

Power Plant: One 100-h.p. Gnome Monosoupape.

Dimensions: Span, 25 ft. 6 in. Length, 20 ft. 4 in. Height, 8 ft. 5 in. Wing area, 241 sq. ft.

Weights: Empty, 730 lb. Loaded, 1,120 lb.

Performance: Maximum speed, 92 m.p.h. at sea level. Climb, 1 min. to 1,200 ft. Endurance, $3\frac{1}{2}$ hrs.

Armament: One Lewis machine-gun mounted on the centre section or at the side of the fuselage. A small load of 20-lb. bombs could be carried.

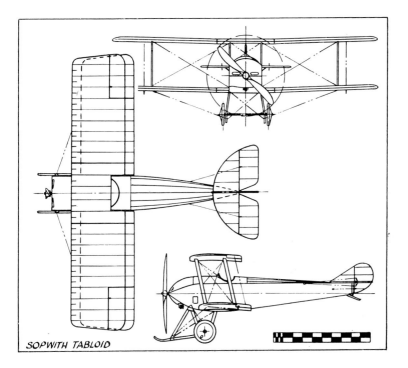

SOPWITH TABLOID

Schneider (No. 3734) with wing warping. (*Imp. War Museum Photo.*)

Sopwith Schneider

The Schneider was so named because it was directly descended from the Sopwith Tabloid seaplane which had been used by Mr. Howard Pixton to win the Schneider Trophy contest for Great Britain at Monaco on 20 April 1914. The little Tabloid performed magnificently; its average speed was over 86 m.p.h., and in an extra two laps after finishing the race Pixton reached 92 m.p.h., which was then a world's record for seaplanes.

It was natural that with the outbreak of war the R.N.A.S. should adopt this fine seaplane, and production began in November 1914 with an order for 12 aircraft, Nos. 1436 to 1447. The early R.N.A.S. Schneiders differed little from Pixton's Tabloid. The same 100-h.p. Monosoupape Gnome engine was used, housed in a curious bull-nosed cowling which became a characteristic feature of the Schneider and in fact distinguished the type from the later Baby. Early aircraft had a triangular fin and employed wing-warping; later an enlarged, curved fin and normal ailerons were introduced, as in the three-view drawing. Subsequent orders were for 24 Schneiders (Nos. 1556 to 1579) and 100 (Nos. 3707 to 3806), and the final production total was 160, five of which remained in commission in March 1918.

During 1915 repeated attempts were made to use Schneiders to intercept Zeppelins over the North Sea. The seaplanes were carried in light cruisers, paddle-steamers such as *Killingholme* and *Brocklesby*, and in the seaplane-carriers *Ben-my-Chree* and *Engadine*. Scant success attended these sorties; frequently the seaplanes could not take off due to heavy seas, or the floats broke up in the water. A remedy was sought by fitting two-wheeled dollies beneath the floats, enabling the Schneiders to operate from the short flying-off deck of carriers so equipped. The first successful take-off using this device was from *Campania* on 6 August 1915. The Schneider was flown by F./Lt. W. L. Welsh.

Overseas, Schneiders did an immense amount of useful work, both

264

reconnaissance and fighting, in the eastern Mediterranean and the Red Sea. They saw service in the Dardanelles campaign, flying from *Ark Royal*, and as late as 21 November 1916 a Schneider, flown by F./Sub-Lt. A. F. Brandon, shot down an enemy aircraft over Mudros.

R.N.A.S. coastal air stations at Calshot, Dundee, Dunkirk, Felixstowe, Fishguard, Great Yarmouth, Killingholme, Scapa Flow and Westgate. Seaplane carriers: *Anne, Ark Royal, Ben-my-Chree, Campania, Empress, Engadine,* and *Raven II.* R.N.A.S. stations in Aegean, Egypt and Mediterranean. Also used experimentally aboard submarine *E. 22.*

TECHNICAL DATA (SCHNEIDER)

Description: Single-seat scouting seaplane. Wooden structure, fabric covered.
Manufacturers: Sopwith Aviation Co. Ltd., Kingston-on-Thames.
Power Plant: One 100-h.p. Gnome Monosoupape.
Dimensions: Span, 25 ft. 8 in. Length, 22 ft. 10 in. Height, 10 ft. Wing area, 240 sq. ft.
Performance: No details available, but probably similar to Sopwith Tabloid (which see).
Armament: One Lewis machine-gun firing through aperture in centre section and provision for one 65-lb. bomb below fuselage.

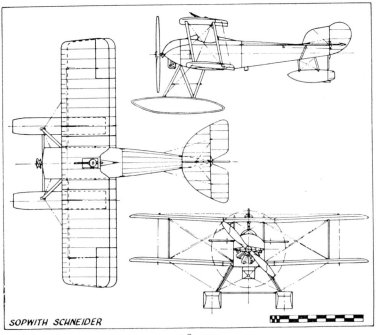

SOPWITH SCHNEIDER

Baby (N 2070) built by Blackburn. (*Imp. War Museum Photo.*)

Sopwith Baby

The Sopwith Baby was a development of the Schneider, from which it differed in having the more powerful 110-h.p. Clerget engine in place of the Gnome Monosoupape, the bull-nosed cowling of the earlier aircraft being replaced by an open-fronted cowling of more orthodox pattern. Another improvement was the installation of a synchronised Lewis gun above the fuselage, though some Babies retained the original type of gun-mounting with the Lewis inclined upwards through the top wing. The first batch of 100 Babies (Nos. 8118 to 8217) were built by Sopwith and delivered between September 1915 and July 1916. The first five aircraft of this batched retained the 100-h.p. Gnome engine, as did No. 8199. The rest had the 110-h.p. Clerget, and this engine was retained when Baby production was transferred to the Blackburn Company.

The first Blackburn Baby (N 300) was followed by 70 production aircraft with 110-h.p. Clerget engines (N 1010 to N 1039, N 1060 to N 1069 and N 1100 to N 1129) and 115 with the 130-h.p. Clerget engine (N 1410 to N 1449 and N 2060 to N 2134). It had originally been planned to fit the Bentley A.R. 1 from N 1410, but these engines were not available in time. The first batch of 130-h.p. Babies differed from the others in having Ranken anti-Zeppelin darts fitted instead of a machine-gun.

In the same way as the Schneiders, Babies operated from seaplane-carriers in the North Sea and in the Mediterranean. They also flew on fighter patrols from Dunkirk until superseded by Sopwith Pups in July 1917. In the various Middle East campaigns, Babies were frequently used in bombing raids. *Ben-my-Chree*'s Babies attacked the Chikaldir railway bridge in December 1916, and, in November, those from the carrier *Empress* took part in the Palestine fighting. Bombing raids on Zeppelin bases from home waters were less successful. In an attack on the Tondern

266

airship base from the carriers *Engadine* and *Vindex* on 4 May 1916 only one out of 11 Babies succeeded in bombing the target.

R.N.A.S. coastal air stations at Calshot, Dundee, Dunkirk, Felixstowe, Fishguard, Great Yarmouth, Killingholme, Scapa Flow and Westgate. Seaplane carriers *Ben-my-Chree, Campania, City of Oxford, Empress, Engadine, Furious, Manxman, Peony, Raven II, Riviera* and *Vindex.* R.N.A.S. stations at Alexandria, Otranto, Port Said, Santa Maria di Leuca, Suda Bay and Thasos.

TECHNICAL DATA (BABY)

Description: Single-seat scouting and bombing seaplane. Wooden structure, fabric covered.

Manufacturers: Sopwith Aviation Co. Ltd., Kingston-on-Thames. Subcontracted by the Blackburn Aeroplane & Motor Co. Ltd., Leeds.

Power Plant: One 110-h.p. or 130-h.p. Clerget.

Dimensions: Span, 25 ft. 8 in. Length, 23 ft. Height, 10 ft. Wing area, 240 sq. ft.

Weights (with 130-h.p. Clerget): Empty, 1,226 lb. Loaded, 1,715 lb.

Performance (with 130-h.p. Clerget): Maximum speed, 100 m.p.h. at sea level. Climb, 35 mins. to 10,000 ft. Endurance, $2\frac{1}{4}$ hrs.

Armament: One Lewis machine-gun and provision for two 65-lb. bombs. Ranken darts replaced the Lewis gun on some aircraft.

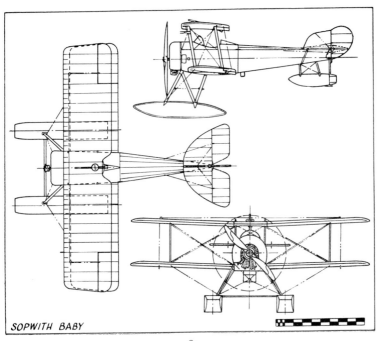

SOPWITH BABY

A 1½ Strutter of the R.N.A.S. (*Imp. War Museum Photo.*)

Sopwith 1½ Strutter

The claims of the Sopwith 1½ Strutter to historical fame are many. It was, of course, the first of the Sopwith breed to achieve widespread use as a fighting aeroplane and hence the precursor of a justly renowned series. In addition to this it was the first British aeroplane to enter service already equipped with a synchronising gear, enabling the fixed front gun to fire between the revolving blades of the airscrew, and also the first two-seater which gave the pilot a chance to use his gun effectively as well as the observer. It thus established what came to be a classic formula, that of the two-seat fighter, later exemplified in the Bristol Fighter and the Hawker Demon.

Nor did the 1½ Strutter's pioneering tendencies end here. In 1916, with the 3rd Wing of the R.N.A.S. at Luxeuil, 1½ Strutters became the first British aircraft ever to take part in bombing raids of an avowedly strategic nature, attacking German industrial centres and providing, as it were, a prelude to the heavier blows struck later by the squadrons of the R.A.F.'s Independent Force. Finally, in the sphere of shipboard flying, it was a 1½ Strutter that became the first two-seater to take off from a British warship, in April 1918.

The Admiralty had from the earliest beginnings of the R.N.A.S. shown interest in the products of the Sopwith Company, and it was therefore only logical that the 1½ Strutter should be first ordered for naval service, though it later entered the R.F.C. as well. The prototype (No. 3686) was completed at the end of 1915, and first deliveries of R.N.A.S. Strutters began early in 1916, against an Admiralty contract for 150. Some of the first to enter service equipped part of No. 5 Wing at Coudekerque in April 1916. No. 5 Wing was formed in March 1916 for long-range bombing duties and was equipped primarily with Caudrons and Farmans. The 1½ Strutters were able to provide a welcome escort, as well as operating in the bombing rôle themselves. As related in the narrative on the Caudron G. IV, a 1½ Strutter was on 2 August 1916 used to control a No. 5 Wing bombing formation by firing Very lights, a sort of forerunner of the master bomber technique of the Second World War. A few days later, on 9 August, two of No. 5 Wing's 1½ Strutters flown by F./Sub-Lts. R. H. Collet and D. E. Harkness made bombing attacks on the Zeppelin sheds at Evere and Berchem Ste. Agathe; another attack followed on 25 August, this time on the sheds at Cognelee. Subsequently the 1½ Strutters of No. 5 Wing participated in many important raids on enemy aerodromes and ammunition dumps, as well as naval targets such as U-boat bases and the Tirpitz battery.

Meanwhile, plans for the establishment of No. 3 Wing, R.N.A.S. (which was to have received 20 1½ Strutters by 1 July 1916), had been delayed due to the Admiralty's agreement to forgo its Strutters in favour of the R.F.C., which was desperately short of aircraft with which to fight the Battle of the Somme. Eventually No. 3 Wing's 1½ Strutters started their raids in October 1916 and, though severely hampered by winter weather conditions, bombed industrial targets at Hagendingen, Oberndorf, Dillingen and other towns in the Saar where the Admiralty believed steel for U-boats was being manufactured in large quantities. It is interesting to note that No. 3 Wing's base at Luxeuil was close to Belfort, from whence the R.N.A.S. Avros had taken off in November 1914 to raid Friedrichshafen.

Two distinct versions of the 1½ Strutter were supplied to the R.N.A.S., where the type was officially known as the Sopwith Type 9700. As well as the normal two-seater, the R.N.A.S. used a single-seater bomber without the rear cockpit, with provision for 12 bombs stowed internally. It is recorded that, of some 550 1½ Strutters ordered for the R.N.A.S., about 420 were two-seaters and the remainder single-seaters.

Although by 1917 the 1½ Strutter was outclassed as a fighting aircraft on the Western Front, it continued to give extensive service with the R.N.A.S. in other theatres of war. The R.N.A.S. was, in fact, the only service to operate the type outside France. In Macedonia, particularly, the naval Strutters saw a lot of action in bombing raids between April and September 1917, when they hit targets such as aerodromes, ammunition dumps and railway communications behind the enemy lines on the Struma.

Single-seat 1½ Strutters of the R.N.A.S. (*Photo from H. H. Russell.*)

The Sopwith 1½ Strutter's versatility extended also to anti-submarine patrols, both in home waters and in the Mediterranean area. The home-based patrols started in April 1917 and those in the Mediterranean in June 1917. On 17 September 1917 a 1½ Strutter based at Otranto succeeded in sinking a U-boat by attacking it with a 65-lb. delayed-action bomb.

At the Armistice some 170 Sopwith 1½ Strutters remained in service with the R.A.F. and nearly 40 of these were at sea with the Grand Fleet. Indeed, when, in March 1918, H.M.S. *Furious* was made the flagship of the Flying Squadron of the Grand Fleet her complement included 14 1½ Strutters. For deck flying the 1½ Strutter was used both with the normal wheeled undercarriage and with a special skid undercarriage first developed in trials at the Isle of Grain; the latter version usually had a hydrovane mounted at the front end of the skids to prevent the aircraft nosing over if forced into the sea. This device, as well as the inflatable air-bags located either side of the engine nacelle, remained a feature of naval aircraft until

1½ Strutters of No. 3 Wing, R.N.A.S. (*Imp. War Museum Photo.*)

1½ Strutter takes off from gun-turret platform. (*Imp. War Museum Photo.*)

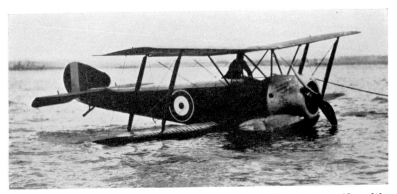

A 1½ Strutter undergoing flotation tests with inflatable air-bags. (*Imp. War Museum Photo.*)

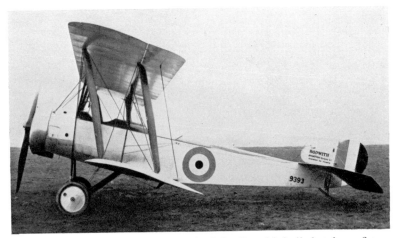

An R.N.A.S. 1½ Strutter (No. 9393) of the Sopwith-built batch 9376 to 9425. (*Imp. War Museum Photo.*)

about 1923, when flotation equipment was mounted inside the rear fuselage instead.

Numerous experiments in deck-flying were made with 1½ Strutters. One aircraft (N 5601) fitted with skids was flown off a railed deck aboard H.M.S. *Vindex*, and the first successful landing aboard H.M.S. *Argus* using the early form of deck arrester gear was made by Wg. Cdr. Bell-Davies, V.C., in a 1½ Strutter. A further development of 1918 was the introduction of 1½ Strutters for two-seat reconnaissance duties aboard capital ships. This involved flying off a short platform mounted above the forward gun turret and became standard practice aboard battle cruisers after the first successful take-off had been achieved from the Australian warship H.M.A.S. *Australia* by Capt. F. M. Fox on 4 April 1918, carrying an observer and full wireless equipment.

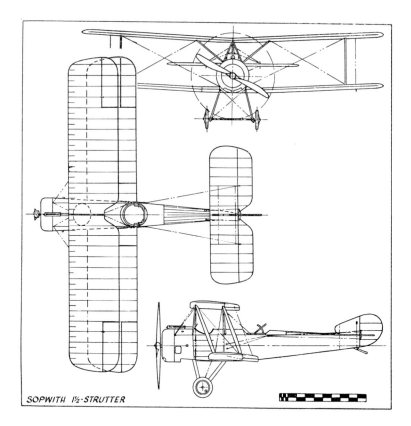

SOPWITH 1½-STRUTTER

Nos. 2, 4, 5, 7 and 8 Squadrons, R.N.A.S. (Western Front); Macedonian units: 'A' Squadron (Thasos), 'B' Squadron (later No. 23 (Naval)) (Mitylene), 'C' Squadron (later No. 20 (Naval)) (Imbros and Mudros), 'D' Squadron (Stavros), 'E' Squadron (Hadzi Junas) and 'F' Squadron (Amberkoj). R.N.A.S. coastal air stations at Dover, Great Yarmouth, Mullion, Otranto, Pembroke and Prawle Point. R.N.A.S. training schools at Cranwell and Manston. Aircraft-carriers: *Argus*, *Furious* and *Vindex*. Battleships: *Australia*, *Barham*, *Queen Elizabeth* and *Repulse*.

TECHNICAL DATA (1½ STRUTTER)

Description: Single-seat bomber, or two-seat bomber, fighting and reconnaissance aircraft for shore-based or carrier-borne operations. Wooden structure, fabric covered.

Manufacturers: Sopwith Aviation Co. Ltd., Kingston-on-Thames (Nos. 9376 to 9425, 9651 to 9750, 9892 to 9897, N 5080 to N 5179, N 5500 to 5537 and N 5550 to N 5559). Sub-contracted by: Mann, Egerton & Co. Ltd., Norwich (N 5200 to N 5219, N 5220 to N 5249 and N 5630 to N 5654) and Westland Aircraft, Yeovil (N 5600 to N 5624).

Power Plant: One 110-h.p. or 130-h.p. Clerget.

Dimensions: Span, 33 ft. 6 in. Length, 25 ft. 3 in. Height, 10 ft. 3 in. Wing area, 346 sq. ft.

Weights (two-seater with 110-h.p. Clerget): Empty, 1,259 lb. Loaded, 2,149 lb. (single-seater with 130-h.p. Clerget): Empty, 1,316 lb.

Performance (two-seater with 110-h.p. Clerget): Maximum speed, 106 m.p.h. at sea level; 92 m.p.h. at 12,000 ft. Climb, 1 min. 20 secs. to 1,000 ft.; 10 mins. 50 secs. to 6,500 ft.; 20 mins. 25 secs. to 10,000 ft. Endurance, 4½ hrs. (single-seater with 130-h.p. Clerget): Maximum speed, 102 m.p.h. at 6,500 ft. Climb, 12 mins. 40 secs. to 6,500 ft.; 24 mins. 35 secs. to 10,000 ft. Service ceiling, 13,000 ft.

Armament (single-seat bomber): One Vickers machine-gun forward and four 65-lb. bombs. (Two-seater): One Vickers machine-gun forward and one Lewis machine-gun aft. Two 65-lb. bombs for anti-submarine patrol.

A Pup takes off from H.M.S. *Manxman*. (*Imp. War Museum Photo.*)

Sopwith Pup

Although the Sopwith Pup was used both by the R.N.A.S. and the R.F.C. it was, like its immediate predecessor the 1½ Strutter, pioneered in service by naval squadrons on the Western Front. As early as May 1916 a Pup was on trial with Naval 'A' Squadron at Furnes and by the following September was in squadron service with the R.N.A.S., fully three months before the first R.F.C. squadron went into action with Pups.

The Pup was known officially as the Sopwith Scout and chronologically occupies a position between the 1½ Strutter and the Triplane. It had many qualities to recommend it: it was at once a superior fighting aeroplane and a thoroughly delightful flying machine. As a fighting scout it maintained its ascendancy from the autumn of 1916 until about the middle of 1917: it proved more than a match for the German Albatros and earned the respect of even the most skilful enemy pilots. Due largely to its low wing loading, the Pup could hold its height better than any Allied or enemy aircraft of its day and retained its excellent manœuvrability to an altitude of about 15,000 ft. These qualities are the most remarkable in view of the low power output of the Le Rhone rotary, even by the standards of 1916.

In keeping with the traditional association of the Sopwith Company and the Admiralty, the Pup prototype (No. 3691) which emerged in February 1916, and the five succeeding prototypes (Nos. 9496, 9497, 9898, 9899 and 9900), were all delivered to the R.N.A.S. The first production contracts were placed with William Beardmore & Co., and as their first Pup was numbered 9901, the official designation Sopwith Type 9901 was adopted in accordance with the Admiralty custom. It is estimated that about 290 Pups were used by the R.N.A.S., including a number transferred from R.F.C. contracts.

R.N.A.S. Pups first entered service in quantity with No. 1 Wing

274

(formerly No. 1 Squadron, which it became again on 3 December 1916) and by 24 September 1916 had claimed their first victim when F./Sub-Lt. S. J. Goble shot down an L.V.G. two-seater. At about this period the R.F.C., which had suffered heavy casualties during the Battle of the Somme, began to look for reinforcements, and on 25 October 1916 the famous No. 8 (Naval) Squadron under Sqn. Cdr. G. R. Bromet was formed for this purpose. Its equipment at first consisted of six Pups, six Nieuports and six 1½ Strutters; later the Pup was standardised throughout. Naval Eight operated from Vert Galand, and was the first complete R.N.A.S. squadron to work with the Army on the Western Front. The squadron operated with the R.F.C. until 7 February 1917, when it was relieved by No. 3 (Naval) Squadron, also equipped with Sopwith Pups, and returned to the Dunkirk command. During its three months with the R.F.C., Naval Eight destroyed 14 enemy aircraft and drove down another 13 out of control. Until re-equipped with Camels in July 1917, No. 3 (Naval) Squadron's Pups flew and fought with great distinction, and by the middle of June had accounted for no fewer than 80 enemy aircraft. Such was their renown, in fact, as a fighting unit that enemy pilots frequently avoided combat with them. On returning to naval command in June 1917, No. 3 (Naval) Squadron was relieved by No. 9 (Naval) Squadron, which was attached to the R.F.C. until 28 September 1917. Very shortly after joining the Army command, No. 9 (Naval) exchanged its six Pups and nine Triplanes for Sopwith Camels.

Meanwhile another R.N.A.S. unit, No. 4 (Naval) Squadron at Bray Dunes, had been occupied exclusively on naval work. First equipped with Pups in March 1917, No. 4 (Naval) Squadron engaged in offensive patrols, escort duties and the protection of naval units from air attack. Their fighting efficiency was just as high as that of the better-publicised Pup squadrons attached to the R.F.C. On 12 May 1917, for example, seven of No. 4 (Naval)'s Pups shot down five Albatros scouts in a dogfight near Zeebrugge with no losses to themselves.

Another more directly naval use for the Pup was in the protection of merchant shipping and in escorting the slower seaplanes on reconnaissance work. From May 1917 Pups were flown from Walmer for this purpose, and in July 1917 superseded Baby Seaplanes at St. Pol. Pups remained with the Seaplane Defence Flight until supplanted by Camels in September 1917; in common with the Walmer Pups, they were provided with air-bags to enable them to float if forced down in the sea.

The brilliance of the Pup's fighting record over the Western Front tends to overshadow its other activities. If this were not so it would probably be best remembered for its equally important rôle in the development of deck-flying in the R.N.A.S. At the beginning of 1916 it was decided to introduce Pups in place of Baby seaplanes aboard seaplane-carriers such as *Campania* and *Manxman* which had a short flying-off deck but no provision for landing-on. Until the advent of this scheme, landplanes had never been used from carriers, and the problem at once arose of how to keep the Pup afloat when it alighted alongside its mother ship. This was solved by fitting emergency flotation bags below the lower wings. These were developed after experiments at the Isle of Grain and proved more efficient than the earlier type of air-bag installed inside the rear fuselage.

Having established itself on the early carriers (which had a flying-off

Pup with skid undercarriage on carrier with longitudinal arrester wires.
(*Imp. War Museum Photo.*)

deck about 200 ft. long), the Pup was then used to initiate two further
developments in naval aviation; namely, the take-off from short platforms
mounted above the gun turrets of warships and the successful return to a
ship's deck instead of the inconvenient ditching. The Pup was the first
aeroplane to achieve either of these feats. The first of them goes to the
credit of F./Cdr. F. J. Rutland, who succeeded in flying a Pup off the
20-ft. platform of the light cruiser H.M.S. *Yarmouth* in June 1917. The
second feat was achieved on 2 August 1917 when Sqn. Cdr. E. H. Dunning
became the first man in history to land an aircraft on the deck of an
aircraft-carrier. The experiment took place aboard H.M.S. *Furious*, and
its success was all the more remarkable in view of the fact that at this
period the idea of a continuous flying-deck along the full length of a ship
was unheard of and Dunning was forced to manœuvre his Pup round the
superstructure and funnels of *Furious* and somehow contrive to get down
on the 228-ft. flight-deck mounted forward. This he did with great
resource, and with the aid of a deck party who seized rope toggles beneath
the wings and fuselage to bring the Pup to rest, as at this period there were
no arrester devices either. Sad to relate, this great pioneer was killed a few
days later when attempting a third landing aboard *Furious*.

Both these successful experiments led rapidly to wider operational uses
for the Pup. Many other light cruisers were equipped in the same way as
H.M.S. *Yarmouth*, and the value of the scheme was confirmed on 21
August 1917, when F./Sub-Lt. B. A. Smart took off from *Yarmouth*, then
cruising off the Danish coast, and shot down the Zeppelin *L. 23* in flames.

On 1 October 1917 the Pup was flown from a battle cruiser for the first
time, when Sqn. Cdr. F. J. Rutland took off from a platform aboard H.M.S.
Repulse. This marked yet another step forward, for this platform was on a
turntable and it enabled the Pups to be launched into wind without the
warship diverting from its course: the original platforms had been fixed.

By this time it was clear that the real future of naval aviation lay with
the aircraft-carrier proper, and work went ahead to provide H.M.S.
Furious with an aft landing-on deck at the same time that Pups were being

A Pup with the R.N.A.S. at Dunkirk. (*Photo from H. H. Russell.*)

used at the Isle of Grain for early experiments with deck-arrester gear. The original scheme (curiously prophetic of the system re-introduced in the nineteen-thirties) was to utilise transverse cables across the deck which would be engaged by a hook dangling below the rear fuselage. This was first tried out on a Pup (No. 9497), but did not work out in practice, and the Pups which eventually went aboard H.M.S. *Furious* in 1918 were fitted with a rigid skid undercarriage in place of wheels. In place of the transverse arrester wires were fore-and-aft wires which engaged 'dog-lead' clips on the Pup's undercarriage. Although aircraft with skids eventually gave way once again to those with wheeled undercarriages, the fore-and-aft arrester wires persisted in aircraft-carriers until finally abandoned in the mid nineteen-twenties. The Pups with skids were re-designated Sopwith Type 9901s by the Admiralty. At the end of the war 10 of these aircraft were serving with aircraft-carriers and there were also 13 other Pups with the Grand Fleet being used for gun-turret platform take-offs from battleships and cruisers.

UNITS ALLOCATED

No. 1 Wing, R.N.A.S., and Nos. 3, 4, 8, 9 and 12 (Naval) Squadrons (Western Front); Naval 'C' Squadron (Imbros); Seaplane Defence Flight (St. Pol); R.N.A.S. coastal air stations at Dover, Great Yarmouth, Port Victoria and Walmer; R.N.A.S. training schools at Cranwell and Manston. Aircraft-carriers: *Argus*, *Campania*, *Furious* and *Manxman*. Warships with flying-off platforms: *Caledon*, *Cassandra*, *Cordelia*, *Dublin*, *Repulse* and *Yarmouth*.

TECHNICAL DATA (PUP)

Description: Single-seat fighting scout for shore-based or shipboard duties. Wooden structure, fabric covered.

Manufacturers: Sopwith Aviation Co. Ltd., Kingston-on-Thames (Prototypes and N 5180 to N 5199, N 6460 to N 6479). Sub-contracted by Wm. Beardmore & Co. Ltd., Dalmuir, Dunbartonshire (Nos. 9901 to 9950 and N 6430 to N 6479).

The first production Pup built by Sopwith for the R.N.A.S., N 5180. (*Imp. War Museum Photo.*)

A Pup fitted with skids and early arrester gear. (*Imp. War Museum Photo.*)

Power Plant: One 80-h.p. Le Rhone.

Dimensions: Span, 26 ft. 6 in. Length, 19 ft. $3\frac{3}{4}$ in. Height, 9 ft. 5 in. Wing area, 254 sq. ft.

Weights: Empty, 787 lb. Loaded, 1,225 lb.

Performance: Maximum speed, $111\frac{1}{2}$ m.p.h. at sea level; 103 m.p.h. at 9,000 ft.; 85 m.p.h. at 15,000 ft. Climb, 2 mins. to 2,000 ft.; 14 mins. to 10,000 ft.; 35 mins. to 16,100 ft. Endurance, 3 hrs. Service ceiling, 17,500 ft.

Armament: One fixed, synchronised Vickers machine-gun forward was standard on Pups used over the Western Front. Those flown from ships had a single Lewis machine-gun firing upwards through the centre or eight Le Prieur rockets mounted on the interplane struts, or both.

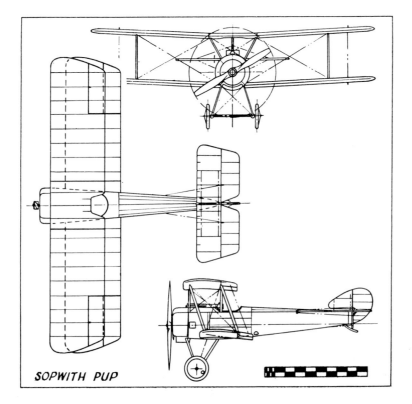

SOPWITH PUP

Triplane (N 6290) of No. 8 (Naval) Squadron. (*Photo from H. H. Russell.*)

Sopwith Triplane

The Sopwith Triplane was one of the great successes of the First World War. Its unusual configuration bestowed such qualities as a remarkable rate of roll and a fast climb, both invaluable in air combat. It was used only by the R.N.A.S., and it gained complete ascendancy over the Western Front during the heavy aerial fighting of 1917.

In the Sopwith chronology the Triplane bridged the gap between the Pup and the Camel, and the first prototype (N 500) did Service trials with Naval 'A' Fighting Squadron at Furnes in June 1916. Production Triplanes entered service with No. 1 and 8 (Naval) Squadrons in February 1917 and with No. 10 (Naval) Squadron in May. Some remarkable engagements were fought by such redoubtable Triplane pilots as Sqn. Cdr. C. Draper, D.S.C., of 'Naval Eight' and F./Sub-Lt. Raymond Collishaw of 'Naval Ten'. The Triplanes of Collishaw's 'B' Flight (named *Black Death, Black Maria, Black Roger, Black Prince* and *Black Sheep*) became the terror of the enemy: between May and July 1917 they destroyed 87 German aircraft. Collishaw personally accounted for 16 in 27 days and shot down the German ace Allmenroder on 27 June.

The Triplane's career was glorious but brief. It remained in action for only seven months; in November 1917 the Camel had supplanted it in squadrons. Total deliveries to the R.N.A.S. amounted to about 140, including transfers from R.F.C. contracts in exchange for naval Spads. Over 90 Triplanes were built by Sopwith to original Admiralty contracts (N 5420 to N 5494 and N 6290 to N 6309); the rest came from sub-contractors. The last Triplane (N 5912), delivered on 19 October 1917, survives to the present day.

From February 1917 Triplanes had a smaller tailplane of 8-ft. span instead of the original Pup-type of 10-ft. span. This accompanied the change to a 130-h.p. engine and improved diving characteristics.

Nos. 1, 8, 9, 10 and 12 (Naval) Squadrons, Western Front. One aircraft (N 5431) used by 'E' Squadron of No. 2 Wing, R.N.A.S., in Macedonia.

TECHNICAL DATA

Description: Single-seat fighting scout. Wooden structure, fabric covered.

Manufacturers: Sopwith Aviation Co. Ltd., Kingston-on-Thames. Sub-contracted by Clayton & Shuttleworth, Ltd., Lincoln, and Oakley, Ltd., Ilford.

Power Plant: One 110-h.p. or 130-h.p. Clerget.

Dimensions: Span, 26 ft. 6 in. Length, 18 ft. 10 in. Height, 10 ft. 6 in. Wing area, 231 sq. ft.

Weights: Empty, 1,101 lb. Loaded, 1,541 lb.

Performance (with 130-h.p. Clerget): Maximum speed, 117 m.p.h. at 5,000 ft. Climb, 25 mins. to 16,000 ft. Endurance, 2¾ hrs. Service ceiling, 20,500 ft.

Armament: One fixed, synchronised Vickers machine-gun was standard, but a few aircraft had twin Vickers.

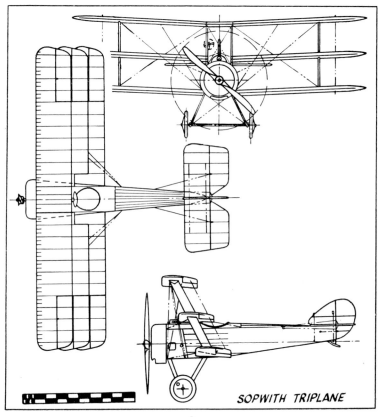

SOPWITH TRIPLANE

F. 1 Camel of No. 9 (Naval) Squadron. (*Photo from H. H. Russell.*)

Sopwith F. 1 Camel

The Camel is generally conceded to have been the greatest British fighting scout of the First World War; it destroyed the record total of 1,294 enemy aircraft. The Camels in R.N.A.S. service accounted for 386 of these. Its manœuvrability became a legend and was matched only by the Fokker Triplane. The installation of twin Vickers guns contributed to its success; it was the first British fighter to be so equipped.

Five Camels from the R.N.A.S. station at Dunkirk were the first to see action, on 4 July 1917, when they attacked a formation of Gothas returning from a raid over England. By the end of July No. 6 (Naval) Squadron had gone over completely from Nieuports to Camels and Nos. 8 and 9 (Naval) Squadrons were also getting Camels in place of Triplanes. All the original F. 1 Camels for the R.N.A.S. had 130-h.p. Clerget engines; later the 150-h.p. Bentley B.R. 1 was substituted, and eventually became the more common installation in naval Camels.

The exploits of naval Camels fighting over the Western Front rivalled those of their R.F.C. counterparts. In August 1917, for example, a Camel of 'Naval Eight' made one of the first successful night ground-attack sorties by a British fighter and destroyed a kite-balloon shed by gun-fire. The R.N.A.S. Camels were for long periods placed at the disposal of the Army and attached to the R.F.C.; at other times they reverted to Naval command and flew fleet patrols to protect the ships of the Belgian Coast Barrage from enemy air attack. From 1 April 1918 the naval Camel squadrons became part of the R.A.F. officially, but they retained their naval identity until their disbandment, for the most part in 1919.

It fell to a Bentley-powered Camel of No. 209 Squadron (formerly No. 9 Naval) to take part in one of the most dramatic air fights of the First World War. This historic event was on 21 April 1918, when the celebrated von Richthofen (80 victories) was shot down by Capt. A. R. Brown.

The F. 1 Camel was also used in limited numbers by the R.N.A.S. in Italy and the Aegean, at coastal air stations in the United Kingdom and at Cranwell, where a two-seat version of the Camel was also flown.

Clerget-Camel to Nos. 6, 8 and 9 (Naval) Squadrons (Western Front) and Bentley-Camel to Nos. 1, 3, 4, 8, 9, 10 and 13 (Naval) Squadrons which from April 1918 became Nos. 201, 203, 204, 208, 209, 210 and 213 Squadrons, R.A.F.

TECHNICAL DATA (F. I CAMEL)

Description: Single-seat fighting scout. Wooden structure, fabric covered.

Manufacturers: Sopwith Aviation, Kingston-on-Thames. Sub-contracted by Boulton & Paul (Norwich); British Caudron (Cricklewood); Clayton & Shuttleworth (Lincoln); Hooper (London); March, Jones & Cribb (Leeds); Nieuport & General Aircraft (Cricklewood); Portholme Aerodrome (Huntingdon); Ruston, Proctor (Lincoln).

Power Plant: One 130-h.p. Clerget or 150-h.p. Bentley B.R. 1.

Dimensions: Span, 28 ft. Length, 18 ft. 9 in. with Clerget and 18 ft. 6 in. with B.R. 1. Height, 8 ft. 6 in. Wing area, 231 sq. ft.

Weights (with 130-h.p. Clerget): Empty, 929 lb. Loaded, 1,453 lb.

Performance (with 130-h.p. Clerget): Maximum speed, 115 m.p.h. at 6,500 ft. Climb, 20 mins. 40 secs. to 15,000 ft. Endurance, $2\frac{1}{2}$ hrs. Service ceiling, 19,000 ft.

Armament: Twin fixed, synchronised Vickers machine-guns and capacity for four 25-lb. bombs below wings.

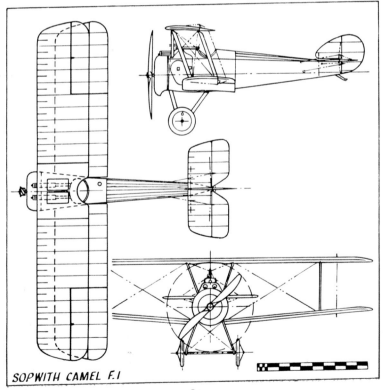

SOPWITH CAMEL F.I

2F. 1 Camel (N 7136) built by Beardmore. (*Imp. War Museum Photo.*)

Sopwith 2F. 1 Camel

Unlike the F. 1 Camel, which served both the R.N.A.S. and R.F.C., the 2F. 1 was designed specifically as a shipboard fighter and, to this end, incorporated a number of features that distinguished it from the earlier Camel. The fuselage was made in two parts, the rear half being detachable just behind the cockpit: this conserved space aboard ship. Another distinguishing feature was the use of steel tubular centre-section struts instead of the wide wooden struts of the F. 1.

The prototype 2F. 1 Camel (N 5) flew in March 1917, and the production aircraft that followed were built by the Beardmore concern; additional contracts with the Fairey Aviation Company and Pegler & Co. Ltd. of Doncaster were subsequently cancelled.

The main operational function of the 2F. 1 Camels was to intercept Zeppelins over the North Sea. For this purpose they were carried in numerous warships, where they were flown from platforms mounted above gun turrets in the same way as the Pups they superseded. They were also flown from aircraft-carriers such as *Furious*. Yet another means of getting the Camels to the scene of operations was from lighters towed by destroyers of Harwich Force; the first successful take-off by this method was achieved by Lt. S. D. Culley on 31 July 1918. A few days afterwards, on 10 August the same officer shot down the Zeppelin *L. 53* whilst flying from a lighter. It was the last Zeppelin to be destroyed in air combat.

Another method of attacking Zeppelins was to bomb them in their sheds —a technique much favoured by the R.N.A.S. from the earliest days of the war. In June 1918 a specially trained force of 2F. 1 Camels joined *Furious* for an audacious strike on the airship sheds at Tondern. Escorted by the First Light Cruiser Squadron, *Furious* flew off seven Camels on 17 July 1918. Six of the Camels, each carrying two 50-lb. bombs, succeeded in reaching Tondern and the Zeppelins *L. 54* and *L. 60* were destroyed.

By October 1918 there were 129 2F. 1 Camels in service and 112 were carried in ships of the Grand Fleet. Camels aboard *Argus* took part in some of the earliest experiments with deck-arrester gear in 1919.

Aircraft-carriers *Argus*, *Eagle*, *Furious* and *Pegasus*; also battle cruisers and light cruisers. R.N.A.S. stations at Cranwell, Donibristle, Felixstowe, Great Yarmouth (No. 212 Squadron, including experiments with air launch from airship R. 33), Manston and Port Victoria.

TECHNICAL DATA (2F. I CAMEL)

Description: Single-seat ship-board fighting scout. Wooden structure, fabric covered.

Manufacturers: Wm. Beardmore & Co. Ltd., Dalmuir, Dumbartonshire.

Power Plant: One 130-h.p. Clerget or 150-h.p. Bentley B.R. 1.

Dimensions: Span, 26 ft. 11 in. Length, 18 ft. 8 in. Height, 9 ft. 1 in. Wing area, 221 sq. ft.

Weights (with B.R. 1): Empty, 1,036 lb. Loaded, 1,530 lb.

Performance (with B.R. 1): Maximum speed, 124 m.p.h. at 6,500 ft. Climb, 25 mins. to 15,000 ft. Service ceiling, 17,300 ft.

Armament: One fixed, synchronised Vickers gun above the fuselage and one Lewis gun above the wing centre section. Provision for two 50-lb. bombs in racks below the wings.

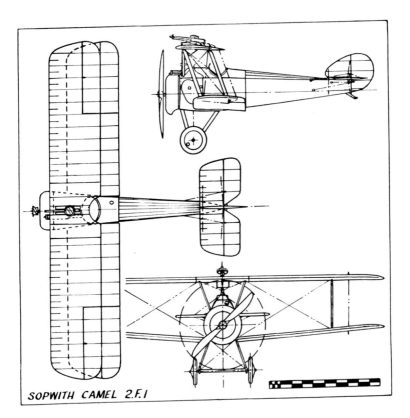

SOPWITH CAMEL 2.F.1

Cuckoo (N 6971) built by Blackburn. (*Photo. from J. M. Bruce.*)

Sopwith Cuckoo

The Cuckoo was something of a landmark in British naval aircraft design; it was the first landplane torpedo-carrier capable of operation from a flying-deck. Before the advent of the Cuckoo the torpedo could be carried only by seaplanes which were severely restricted in their capabilities. They suffered not only the weight handicap of their floats, but also the inability to operate from any but the calmest of seas. The idea of using a landplane first came from that staunch advocate of the torpedo, Commodore Murray Sueter, who made the suggestion to Sopwith in October 1916.

The prototype Sopwith T. 1 (N 74), later christened Cuckoo, first made its appearance in June 1917, powered by a 200-h.p. Hispano-Suiza engine. After trials at the Isle of Grain, a production order for 100 aircraft (N 7000 to N 7099) was awarded to the Fairfield Engineering Company at Glasgow in September 1917. In February 1918 a further 100 Cuckoos were ordered; 50 from Pegler of Doncaster (N 6900 to N 6949) and 50 from Blackburn (N 6950 to N 6999). The Blackburn-built Cuckoos were the first to be delivered; N 6950 emerged in July 1918 and was followed by the first Fairfield Cuckoo in September and the first Pegler Cuckoo in October. At the Armistice just over 90 Cuckoos had been delivered and contracts for 350 placed. Many of these were cancelled, but limited production continued during 1919 of a Mk. II version which had a Wolseley Viper engine in place of the Sunbeam Arab of the Mk. I.

The Cuckoo first entered service with the Torpedo Aeroplane School at East Fortune, where pilots were trained for the operational squadron which joined the Fleet on 7 October 1918, and embarked in H.M.S. *Argus* on 19 October. The Armistice intervened before the squadron could prove itself in action.

Cuckoos served for a number of years in aircraft-carriers and with shore-based torpedo squadrons. They were finally withdrawn when No. 210 Squadron disbanded at Gosport in April 1923.

No. 185 (East Fortune) and No. 210 (Gosport). Aircraft-carriers *Argus*, *Eagle* and *Furious*.

TECHNICAL DATA (CUCKOO MK. I)

Description: Single-seat carrier-borne or shore-based torpedo-carrier. Wooden structure, fabric covered.

Manufacturers: Sopwith Aviation Co. Ltd., Kingston-on-Thames. Sub-contracted by Blackburn Aeroplane & Motor Co. Ltd., Leeds; Fairfield Shipbuilding & Engineering Co. Ltd., Glasgow; Pegler & Co. Ltd., Doncaster.

Power Plant: One 200-h.p. Sunbeam Arab.

Dimensions: Span, 46 ft. 9 in. Length, 28 ft. 6 in. Height, 10 ft. 8 in. Wing area, 566 sq. ft.

Weights: Empty, 2,199 lb. Loaded, 3,883 lb.

Performance: Maximum speed, $103\frac{1}{2}$ m.p.h. at 2,000 ft.; 98 m.p.h. at 10,000 ft. Climb, 4 mins. to 2,000 ft.; 31 mins. to 10,000 ft. Endurance, 4 hrs. Service ceiling, 12,100 ft.

Armament: One 18-in. Mk. IX torpedo carried below the fuselage.

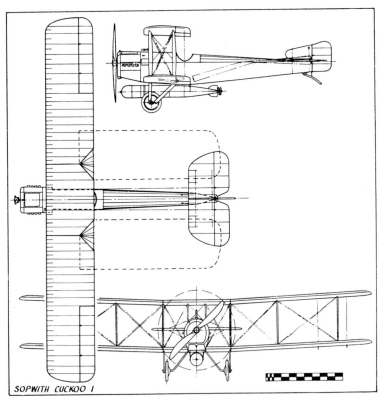

SOPWITH CUCKOO I

Seagull III (N 9647). (*Air Ministry Photo.*)

Supermarine Seagull III

Supermarine began its long association with marine aircraft with the A.D. flying-boat (see Appendix) of 1916, and this was followed by the Baby single-seat flying-boat and the Sea King fighter amphibian which first appeared at Olympia in 1920. In 1921 the Seal deck-landing amphibian fleet spotter was produced, and this was further developed to become the Seagull, ordered in quantity by the Air Ministry in 1922. Both the Seal and Seagull differed from their predecessors in having a tractor layout: all earlier Supermarine flying-boats and amphibians had favoured the pusher arrangement.

The prototype Seagull (N 158) was exhibited at the R.A.F. Display at Hendon in 1922 and deliveries of production aircraft (in and around N 9642 to N 9647) followed in 1923. Unlike the Seagull I and II, the Seagull III production version had its fuel-tanks located under the top mainplane centre section: those of the earlier marks were inside the hull behind the pilot. The Seagull III was the first single-engined flying-boat to employ gravity feed, and the removal of the tanks from the hull permitted free access between the front and rear crew positions. Two further developments of the Seagull were the Mk. IV and a closely-related type known as the Sheldrake, but neither of these aircraft was produced in quantity. The Seagull IV had twin fins and rudders and was fitted with Handley Page slots. The Seagull V was a much later design which appeared in 1933 and eventually became the Walrus.

The only unit of the F.A.A. to employ the Seagull III was No. 440 (Fleet Reconnaissance) Flight, which equipped with the type in 1923. No. 440 Flight's six Seagulls were based in the aircraft-carrier *Eagle* and served mainly in the Mediterranean area. They remained active for only a short period, being superseded in No. 440 Flight by Fairey IIIDs in 1925. With the replacement of the Seagull, the spotter amphibian as a class disappeared from the F.A.A. for a decade until it was revived in the shape of the Walrus.

In 1926, six Seagull IIIs were delivered to the R.A.A.F., where they equipped a special flight which carried out a photographic survey of the Great Barrier Reef.

TECHNICAL DATA (SEAGULL III)

Description: Three-seat carrier-borne amphibian for spotter-reconnaissance duties. Wooden structure, with fabric-covered wings and wooden hull.
Manufacturers: Supermarine Aviation Works (Vickers) Ltd., Southampton.
Power Plant: One 450-h.p. Napier Lion V.
Dimensions: Span, 46 ft. Length, 37 ft. Height, 12 ft. Wing area, 593 sq. ft.
Weights: Empty, 3,897 lb. Loaded, 5,668 lb.
Performance: Maximum speed, 108 m.p.h. at sea level. Climb, 11 mins. to 5,000 ft.
Armament: One Lewis machine-gun mounted amidships, aft of the wings.

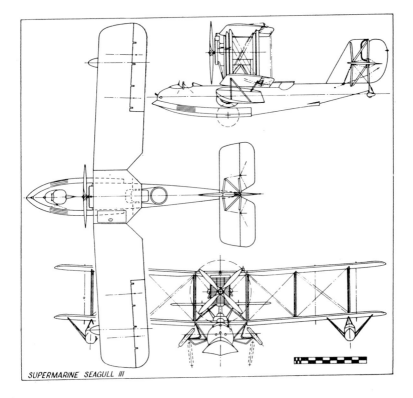

SUPERMARINE SEAGULL III

Walrus II (W 2743) being hoisted aboard. (*Imp. War Museum Photo.*)

Supermarine Walrus

The Walrus amphibian, known universally as the 'Shagbat', enjoyed a reputation in the F.A.A. rivalled only by that of its contemporary, the Swordfish. Both these aircraft, biplanes in a monoplane age, attracted their share of ridicule from the less well-informed who judged only by appearances and knew little of their solid virtues. Naval pilots, who knew better, sang their praises, and their loyalties remained unshaken. They had good reason to praise the Walrus, for it proved its dependability through 10 years of F.A.A. service, flying in every imaginable climate, from the Arctic to the tropics, and performing a remarkable range of duties which on one occasion (during operations in the Red Sea) even included dive-bombing. Predominantly, however, the Walrus was a spotter-reconnaissance aircraft, and its first duty was to be 'the eyes of the Fleet'. Embarked as a catapult aircraft in warships and cruisers, the Walrus performed this rôle all over the world, from the Arctic to the Falkland Islands, from West Africa to Madagascar and from Aden to Ceylon. One of the functions of the Walrus was searching out commerce raiders and one squadron (No. 710) was active on these duties only five days after the outbreak of war in 1939 from a base at Freetown, guarding the approaches to West Africa.

When the Walrus first appeared in 1933 it was known as the Seagull V, but it was a very different aircraft from the earlier Seagull amphibians of the 'twenties. Whereas its F.A.A. predecessor, the Seagull III, was a tractor amphibian of wholly wooden construction, the Seagull V had a pusher engine, a metal hull and offered enclosed accommodation for the pilot and navigator. Moreover, it was stressed for catapulting, and in fact became the first amphibian in the world to be catapulted from a warship with full military load. The prototype Seagull V (K 4797) was first flown on 21 June 1933 and was designed as a private venture by R. J. Mitchell, who later achieved fame for his creation of the Spitfire. First ordered by the Australian Government, who retained the name Seagull V, the type was adopted for the F.A.A. under the name Walrus, after trials had taken place aboard H.M.S. *Nelson* in 1935. Prototype testing was in the hands of No. 702 Catapult Flight.

The initial Air Ministry contract was placed in May 1935 to Spec. 2/35 and was for 12 Walrus I aircraft, K 5772 to K 5783. In 1936 orders for 204 more aircraft were placed to Spec. 37/36, including K 8338 to K 8345 and L 2169 to L 2336. After 287 Walrus I amphibians had been built by Supermarine, production was transferred to Saunders–Roe to enable the parent firm to concentrate on Spitfires. Saunders–Roe built a further 453 before production ceased in January 1944. The Saro-built Walrus differed from the Supermarine version in having a wooden instead of a metal hull and in a number of details such as the substitution of a tail wheel for the original skid and the installation of the Pegasus VI engine in place of the Pegasus IIM2. With these alterations, the Walrus became the Mk. II.

From July 1936, when F.A.A. catapult flights were re-organised in the '700' series, Walruses served in battleships and cruisers as contemporaries of Swordfish and, later, of Seafox floatplanes. In some flights the equipment was mixed: No. 702 Flight with the 2nd Battle Squadron had two Seals (later replaced by Swordfish) and one Walrus. The 4th and 8th Cruiser Squadrons also had mixed flights comprised of Walruses and Seafoxes. In January 1940 all catapult units in warships were combined to form No. 700 Squadron, which had on its strength 42 Walruses, 11 Seafoxes and 12 Swordfish.

Walrus being catapulted from a warship. (*Imp. War Museum Photo.*)

Mention has already been made of the valuable work done by Walruses of No. 710 Squadron off the West African coast from September 1939. During the Norwegian campaign catapult aircraft proved their worth again, spotting for naval bombardments and carrying out anti-submarine and convoy patrols. On 18 April 1940 a squadron of Walruses commanded by Cdr. R. S. D. Armour was established at Harstad, in Northern Norway, where it was used to ferry British and French naval and military officers in a region where communications facilities ashore were otherwise non-existent. Before its re-embarkation in *Ark Royal* on 8 May, Cdr. Armour's squadron completed over 200 communications flights, as well as carrying out a bombing attack on German troop concentrations at Solfolla.

This bombing raid was not an isolated instance of the Walrus assuming more offensive capabilities, for on 18 November 1940, H.M.S. *Dorsetshire*'s Walrus was catapulted off armed with bombs for a raid on Italian Somaliland. After hitting enemy fuel supplies, the Walrus went on to spot for the ship's guns during a bombardment of the port of Dante.

Another notable occasion when a Walrus directed a naval bombardment was during an attack by the Royal Navy on Genoa in February 1941. During this action a Walrus circled the town at only 600 ft. plotting and reporting the fall of the British shells, and returned to its ship completely unscathed. The following month another Walrus made important reconnaissances during the Battle of Matapan.

Perhaps one of the most daring escapades to the credit of the Walrus was during the siege of Tobruk in North Africa, when one of these remarkable aircraft alighted in the harbour at night under fire from the enemy to deliver urgent supplies.

In 1942 the hard-worked Walruses of the seaplane-carrier *Albatross*, which had started the war off the West African coast, moved into the Indian Ocean for trade protection duties, and in October played a useful rôle spotting for the guns during the occupation of Madagascar.

In addition to its work with the F.A.A., the Walrus was also extensively used from 1941 onwards by the R.A.F., mainly for air–sea rescue duties, and many pilots shot down in the sea owe their life to rescue by a Walrus. Flying near enemy coasts, risking interception, and frequently alighting in mine-infested waters, the Walruses did heroic work which received little publicity at the time.

From 1944 onwards the Walrus was gradually superseded in the F.A.A. by the Sea Otter, but some remained in service with No. 1700 Squadron until after VJ-Day. They operated with the East Indies Fleet and were based at Trincomalee in Ceylon.

The Walrus will long be remembered by naval pilots, if only for the unforgettable noise made by its 18 open exhaust ports, and its flying characteristics have never been better described than by Terence Horsley in his book *Find, Fix and Strike*:

'Turns are made with slow dignity, as one might imagine a 60-seater bus on a smooth road. Pipes and tobacco come out, the transparent panel is slid over our heads, but the side window is left open for fresh air. The engine makes a steady roar but sufficiently above and behind us to make conversation possible. On a rough day the Walrus behaves more like a cow than a bus—a very friendly cow however. She wallows in the trough

F.A.A. Walruses on a training flight. (*Imp. War Museum Photo.*)

of the rough airs as a heifer knee deep in a boggy meadow. Her driver has a certain amount of heavy work to do in pushing the wheel around but he is reassured by the steady roar of the one and only Pegasus engine.'

UNITS ALLOCATED

Catapult Flights: No. 702 (2nd Battle Squadron); No. 711 (1st Cruiser Squadron); No. 712 (2nd Cruiser Squadron); No. 714 (4th Cruiser Squadron); No. 715 (5th Cruiser Squadron); No. 718 (8th Cruiser Squadron); No. 720 (New Zealand Division). *Catapult Squadrons:* No. 700 (January 1940 to March 1944); No. 701 (formed May 1940); No. 710 (August 1939 to October 1943); No. 711 (1938 to September 1944); No. 712 (1938 to August 1944); No. 714 (1938 to August 1944). *Training Squadrons:* Nos. 737, 740, 749, 751, 753, 754 and 763. *Air-sea Rescue:* No. 1700 Squadron (May 1945 to June 1946).

TECHNICAL DATA (WALRUS)

Description: Spotter-reconnaissance amphibian for carrier-borne or cata-pult duties. Crew of three. Metal hull and composite wood and metal wings, fabric covered.

Manufacturers: Supermarine Aviation Works (Vickers) Ltd., Southampton, Hants. Sub-contracted by Saunders–Roe Ltd., Isle of Wight.

Power Plant: One 775-h.p. Bristol Pegasus II. M2 or VI.

Dimensions: Span, 45 ft. 10 in. (17 ft. 11 in. folded). Length, 37 ft. 3 in. Height, 15 ft. 3 in. Wing area, 610 sq. ft.

Weights: Empty, 4,900 lb. Loaded, 7,200 lb.

Performance: Maximum speed, 135 m.p.h. at 4,750 ft. Cruising, 95 m.p.h. at 3,500 ft. Initial climb, 1,050 ft./min. Range, 600 miles. Service ceiling, 18,500 ft.

Armament: One Vickers K gun in bows and either one or two Vickers K guns amidships, both cockpits with Scarff rings. Provision for light bombs below the wings.

Ratings fold the wings of a Walrus aboard a carrier. (*Imp. War Museum Photo.*)

Walrus I (K 8541) seen at Mount Batten in 1937.

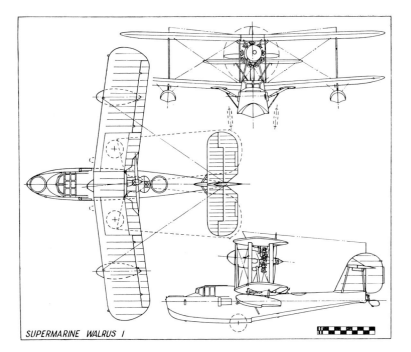

SUPERMARINE WALRUS I

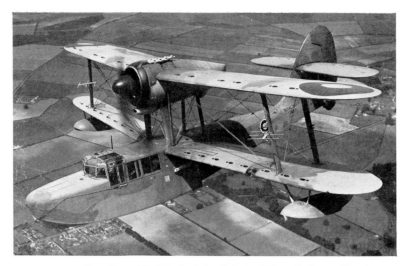

Sea Otter (JM 831) of the F.A.A. (*Chas. E. Brown Photo.*)

Supermarine Sea Otter

The Sea Otter first entered service with the F.A.A. in 1944, where it superseded the Walrus for air–sea rescue duties and general communications
work. It was employed both in aircraft-carriers and at shore establishments and outlived its more famous predecessor by five or six years to
become the last biplane in squadron service with the F.A.A. With the
adoption of the helicopter for rescue and communications work from 1950
onwards the Sea Otter gradually disappeared from the Royal Navy and
no more amphibians were used.

As the last of a long line of biplane amphibians designed by Supermarine,
the Sea Otter marked a reversion to the tractor layout which had characterised the Seagull III used by the F.A.A. in the 'twenties. Of generally
cleaner design than the Walrus, it had more speed, better range and improved handling characteristics on the water. The prototype (K 8854)
was designed to Spec. S. 7/38 and first flew in August 1938. After further
development to Specs. S. 14/39 and 12/40, it entered production at the
Saunders–Roe factory, which completed its first Sea Otter in July 1943.
Production ceased in July 1946 after 290 Sea Otters had been delivered.

Sea Otters first served with No. 1700 Squadron of the F.A.A., which
took delivery of six aircraft at Lee-on-Solent in November 1944, subsequently embarking in the escort-carrier *Khedive*. When the war ended,
No. 1700's Sea Otters were shore-based at Trincomalee in Ceylon, being
attached to the East Indies Fleet.

UNITS ALLOCATED

No. 1700 Squadron (formed November 1944 at Lee-on-Solent; embarked in
Khedive, Stalker, Emperor and *Ameer*); No. 1701 Squadron (formed February 1945

at Lee-on-Solent; embarked in *Begum*; shore-based at Maryborough, Australia and Hong Kong, attached to Pacific Fleet); No. 1702 Squadron (formed June 1945 at Lee-on-Solent; embarked in *Trouncer*; shore-based at Hal Far, Malta, Greece and Bizerta on mine-spotting duties); No. 1703 Squadron (formed August 1945 at Lee-on-Solent). Also No. 772 Fleet Requirements Unit.

TECHNICAL DATA (SEA OTTER II)

Description: Carrier-borne or shore-based air–sea rescue and communications amphibian with a crew of three/four. Metal hull and composite wings, fabric covered.

Manufacturers: Saunders–Roe, Ltd., East Cowes, Isle of Wight.

Power Plant: One 855-h.p. Bristol Mercury XXX.

Dimensions: Span, 46 ft. Length, 39 ft. 5 in. Height, 16 ft. 2 in. Wing area, 610 sq. ft.

Weights: Empty, 6,805 lb. Loaded, 10,000 lb.

Performance: Maximum speed, 150 m.p.h. at 5,000 ft. Cruising, 100 m.p.h. Climb, 870 ft./min.; 6·2 mins. to 5,000 ft. Range (normal), 565 miles; (maximum), 725 miles. Service ceiling, 16,000 ft.

Armament: Two Vickers K guns amidships and one Vickers K gun in bows.

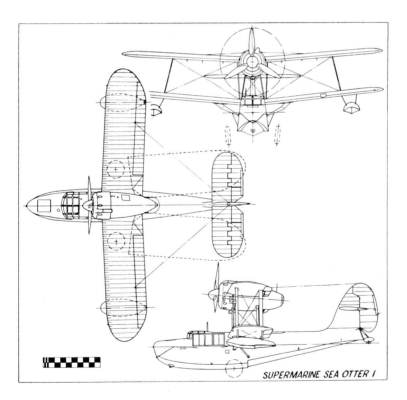

SUPERMARINE SEA OTTER I

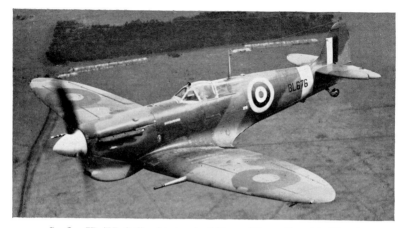

Seafire IB (BL 676) with tropical filter. (*Crown Copyright Photo.*)

Supermarine Seafire
(Merlin variants)

The decision to adopt the Spitfire for carrier-borne service with the F.A.A. was taken in 1941 after the Sea Hurricane had proved its value both in carriers and with the catapult fighter units. The Sea Hurricane had shown that a high-performance land-fighter could be safely flown from a carrier deck: this caused a revolution in naval thinking, and it was a logical step to seek a fighter of even higher performance, such as the Spitfire. The original tests were carried out with a standard Spitfire VB, which had been fitted with an arrester hook under the rear fuselage and trials took place aboard *Illustrious* late in 1941. The pilot of this original 'Hooked Spitfire' was Cdr. H. P. Bramwell, D.S.O., D.S.C., and trials included catapult take-offs as well as normal carrier operations.

With the success of these trials, work went ahead with the conversion of Spitfires into Seafires prior to the production of Seafires proper, which had been built as such. The original conversions (from Spitfire VBs) were known as Seafire IBs and, apart from the introduction of a retractable 'V' frame arrester hook, were almost identical to their land-fighter counterparts. As with the R.A.F.'s Spitfire VB, some of the Seafire IBs had clipped wings and a beard-type tropical filter under the nose. Conversion work was undertaken by Air Service Training Ltd., at Hamble, and others were modified on the production line at the Supermarine factory. About 140 Spitfires were converted into Seafire IBs and in addition a small batch of 48 Seafire IBs were built as such by Cunliffe–Owen Aircraft Ltd. All the Seafire IBs had fixed wings and the 'B' type Spitfire wing with two 20-mm. guns and four machine-guns. The engine was a Merlin 45, 46, 50, 50A, 55 or 56, varying according to the Spitfire converted. The earliest known example of a Spitfire VB converted to a Seafire IB is P 7909, subsequent

298

conversions being in the serial number ranges with P, X, AA, AB, AD, AR, BL and BM prefixes. The Seafire IBs built by Cunliffe–Owen could be distinguished by serial numbers with NX and PA prefixes.

The next variant of the Seafire was the Mk. IIC, which was generally similar to the Seafire IB, except for the use of the 'C' type Spitfire wing and some reinforcement of the airframe to permit the installation of catapult spools. The 'C' type wing (as fitted to the Spitfire VC) could mount four 20-mm. guns or any of the earlier combinations of armament. Two versions of the Seafire IIC were built: the F. IIC by Supermarine and the L. IIC by Westland. The latter was specially produced for low-altitude operations and mounted the Merlin 32 engine, which drove a four-blade airscrew instead of the three-blade type seen on all earlier Seafires. Total production of the Seafire IIC was 262 by Supermarine and 110 by Westland. Serial numbers had NM, MA, MB and LR prefixes The final

Seafire L. IIC lands aboard *Furious*. (*Imp. War Museum Photo.*)

Seafire F. IIC (MB 156) of No. 885 Squadron. (*Imp. War Museum Photo.*)

variant of the Seafire IIC was a photographic-reconnaissance version which mounted one vertical and one oblique camera.

With the introduction of the Seafire III, the major Merlin-engined version, a manually-folding wing appeared on the Seafire for the first time, improving deck handling and enabling hangar lifts to be utilised. The trial installations aircraft for the folding wing was a converted Seafire IIC (MA 970), and this became in effect the Seafire III prototype. Large-scale manufacture of the Seafire III was undertaken by Cunliffe–Owen Aircraft Ltd. and Westland Aircraft Ltd. and total production reached 1,220 aircraft. Of these, Cunliffe–Owen built 350 between November 1943 and July 1945. All but the first 20 Cunliffe–Owen Seafire IIIs had four-blade airscrews, and the revised tropical filter appeared on the 90th and subsequent aircraft. Provision for a 30-gal. flush-fitting drop-tank below the fuselage was made from the 130th aircraft onwards, and the final 129 aircraft by Cunliffe–Owen were fitted with two F. 24 cameras and designated F.R. III. The Seafire L.F. III was the low-altitude variant corresponding to the earlier L.F. IIC. All Seafire IIIs could be fitted with rocket-assisted take-off (R.A.T.O.G.) equipment, first tested on the Seafire IIC MB 141. They appeared both with clipped and full-span wings and could carry either two 250-lb. bombs under the wings or a 500-lb. bomb beneath the fuselage.

Seafires first entered service with No. 807 Squadron in June 1942, followed by No. 801 Squadron in September 1942. Both these squadrons embarked their Seafires in *Furious* in time to participate in Operation Torch, the Allied invasion of North Africa in November 1942. This operation, the first in which Seafires took part and the largest naval action of the war to that date, was an Anglo-American venture in which the American troops captured Casablanca whilst British forces took Oran and Algiers. The Seafires were in action from daybreak on 8 November, when they escorted a strike force of Albacores and made low-flying attacks on enemy airfields. During these attacks they were engaged by Vichy–French Dewoitine D. 520 fighters. In the dogfight which followed, Sub-Lt. G. C.

Seafire III (LR 765).

Baldwin, D.S.C., shot down one of the Dewoitines: this was the first air victory claimed by a Seafire. Later, another Dewoitine was shot down by a Seafire during tactical reconnaissance of La Senia and Lourmel airfields. An amusing story is told of one Seafire pilot who landed alongside an American tank column to find out his whereabouts, later rejoining his carrier safely.

By the end of 1942 the F.A.A. had six squadrons of Seafires, mostly armed with the Mk. IIC. Nos. 801 and 807 had been joined by Nos. 808, 884 and 887 (formerly with Fulmars) and No. 880 (formerly with Sea Hurricanes). The following year, as Seafire production mounted, Nos. 809, 886, 894, 895, 897 and 899 Squadrons also received the type: additionally six Seafires were allotted to each of Nos. 833, 834, 842 and 879 Squadrons in the escort-carriers.

Following the success of the F.A.A.'s fighters in providing cover for the landings in North Africa, they were once again allotted this responsible task in the even greater amphibious assault almost a year later, known as Operation Avalanche. This was the Allied landing in the Gulf of Salerno, which took place in September 1943. Naval air support was provided by the escort-carriers *Attacker*, *Battler*, *Hunter* and *Stalker* and the Fleet carriers *Formidable* and *Illustrious*. Seafires were the principal types of fighter used in this fiercely-fought action, and those of Nos. 807, 809, 833, 834, 879, 894, 897 and 899 Squadrons were all engaged.

Typical of the work done by the Seafires at Salerno was the achievement of No. 879 Squadron. This unit, which had equipped with Seafire IIIs at Stretton in March 1943, flew no less than 75 offensive patrols over the landing beaches in the period 9 to 13 September 1943: it was operating from the escort-carrier *Attacker*. The following June No. 879 Squadron disembarked at Orvieto and joined the Desert Air Force for Army support and tactical reconnaissance duties.

Both the landings in North Africa and at Salerno had been covered in the inital phases exclusively by F.A.A. fighters as land-based fighters were out of range. The same situation obtained during Operation Dragoon, the Allied invasion of the south of France in August 1944. Once again the escort-carriers and the Seafires were active: the British sector of the beach was covered by aircraft from *Attacker*, *Emperor*, *Khedive*, *Hunter*, *Pursuer* and *Searcher*. Seafire IIIs of No. 807 Squadron, which had flown with No. 879 Squadron from shore bases in Italy since June 1944, operated from the escort-carrier *Hunter*. Also present were Seafire IIIs of No. 809 Squadron (in *Stalker*) and No. 899 Squadron. No. 899 Squadron completed 201 sorties from *Khedive* during the period 15 to 23 August 1944.

Mention had already been made of the tactical reconnaissance duties performed by Seafires with the Desert Air Force in Italy. With the Allied invasion of northern France in June 1944, Seafires also formed part of the Second Tactical Air Force, operating with the Air Spotting Pool of No. 34 (Photographic Reconnaissance) Wing, which contained Nos. 808, 885, 886 and 897 Squadrons of the F.A.A. as well as two Spitfire squadrons, Nos. 26 and 63. These units were among the first to operate from the hastily improvised air strips established in the face of enemy fire soon after troops had landed in Normandy. The Seafires remained shore-based with the Second Tactical Air Force until the middle of July, when they returned to naval command.

Seafire III, showing the wing-folding arrangement. (*Vickers Photo.*)

Seafires played their part in a number of the celebrated attacks on the German battleship *Tirpitz* during 1944. In the first Barracuda strike, during April, Seafires of No. 801 Squadron operated from the carrier *Furious*, joining Hellcats and Corsairs to provide fighter protection. Later, during an attack on 22 August, Seafires of No. 894 Squadron shot down two enemy aircraft. This squadron's Seafire IIIs had had the unusual task the previous spring of escorting Typhoon fighter-bombers of the R.A.F. on raids from Culhead, Somerset.

In 1945, when the F.A.A.'s striking power was concentrated in the Far East for the final phases of the war against Japan, the Seafire III was serving with eight squadrons in this theatre. Nos. 807, 809, 879 and 899 Squadrons were in the escort-carriers *Hunter*, *Stalker*, *Attacker* and *Chaser*, whilst Nos. 801 and 880 were in *Implacable* and Nos. 887 and 894 in *Indefatigable*. No. 807 Squadron provided fighter cover for the invasion of Rangoon and Penang, and the Seafires of *Indefatigable* joined in the large fighter escort for the brilliant attacks on the Japanese oil refineries in Sumatra by Avengers and Fireflies. In March–April 1945 Pacific Fleet Seafires were in action over the Sakishima Islands, in June at Truk and by August were flying over the Japanese mainland.

At the time of VJ-Day Seafires equipped 12 first-line squadrons of the F.A.A.: all but four were still flying the Mk. III, which had been in action since 1943. If the war had continued, the Seafire IIIs would have been superseded by the Griffon-engined versions of the Seafire, more details of which appear in the following pages. In the event, the Griffon-engined Seafires were almost wholly post-war types in the F.A.A., with the exception of the Seafire XVs of Nos. 802, 803, 805 and 806 Squadrons, which were working up in the United Kingdom preparatory to Pacific service when the war ended.

The Seafire III remained only briefly in first-line squadrons after the war and finally disappeared when Nos. 887 and 894 Squadrons disbanded in March 1946.

No. 801 (re-equipped September 1942: embarked in *Furious* and *Implacable*); No. 805 (re-equipped July 1945); No. 807 (re-equipped June 1942: embarked in *Furious*, *Battler* and *Hunter*); No. 808 (re-equipped December 1942: embarked in *Battler* and *Hunter*); No. 809 (re-equipped April 1942: embarked in *Unicorn*, *Stalker* and *Attacker*); No. 833 (six Seafires added to nine Swordfish June 1943: embarked in *Stalker*); No. 834 (Six Seafires added to Swordfish April 1943: embarked in *Hunter* and *Battler*); No. 842 (six Seafires added to six Swordfish July 1943: embarked in *Fencer*); No. 879 (re-equipped March 1943: embarked in *Attacker*); No. 880 (re-equipped August 1942: embarked in *Argus*, *Indomitable*, *Stalker*, *Furious* and *Implacable*); No. 884 (re-equipped November 1942: embarked in *Argus*); No. 885 (re-equipped August 1942: embarked in *Formidable*); No. 886 (re-equipped March 1943: embarked in *Attacker*); No. 887 (re-equipped December 1942: embarked in *Unicorn*, *Indefatigable* and *Implacable*); No. 889 (re-equipped April 1944: shore-based Ceylon); No. 894 (re-equipped March 1943: embarked in *Illustrious*, *Indefatigable* and *Implacable*); No. 895 (re-equipped April 1943); No. 897 (re-equipped April 1943: embarked in *Unicorn* and *Stalker*); No. 899 (formed January 1943: embarked in *Indomitable*, *Hunter*, *Khedive* and *Chaser*). Also No. 728 Fleet Requirements Unit at Malta; No. 770 Training Squadron at Drem and No. 775 Fleet Requirements Unit at Alexandria.

TECHNICAL DATA (SEAFIRES I TO III)

Description: Single-seat carrier-borne fighter, fighter-bomber or tactical reconnaissance aircraft. All-metal stressed-skin construction.

Manufacturers: Supermarine Division of Vickers–Armstrongs Ltd., Southampton. Sub-contracted by Cunliffe–Owen Aircraft, Ltd., and Westland Aircraft, Ltd.

Power Plant (Mks. IB and F. IIC): One 1,340-h.p. Rolls-Royce Merlin 45 or 46. (L. IIC): One 1,640-h.p. Rolls-Royce Merlin 32. (F. III): One 1,470-h.p. Rolls-Royce Merlin 55. (F.R. II and L.F. III): One 1,585-h.p. Rolls-Royce Merlin 55M.

Dimensions: Span, 36 ft. 8 in. Length, 30 ft. Height, 11 ft. 2 in. Wing area, 242 sq. ft.

Weights (IB): Empty, 5,000 lb. Loaded, 6,700 lb. (F. IIC): Empty, 5,300 lb. Loaded 7,000 lb. (F. III): Empty, 5,400 lb. Loaded, 7,100 lb. (F.R. III): Empty, 5,400 lb. Loaded, 7,200 lb.

Performance (IB): Maximum speed, 365 m.p.h. at 16,000 ft. Cruising, 215 m.p.h. or 310 m.p.h. at 20,000 ft. Climb, 7·6 mins. to 20,000 ft. Range, 492 miles (normal) or 770 miles with drop tank. Service ceiling, 36,400 ft. (L. IIC): Maximum speed, 333 m.p.h. at 5,000 ft. Cruising, 188 m.p.h. or 282 m.p.h. at 5,000 ft. Climb, 1·7 mins. to 5,000 ft. Range, 493 miles (normal) or 755 miles with drop tank. Service ceiling, 32,000 ft. (F. III): Maximum speed, 352 m.p.h. at 12,250 ft. Cruising, 218 m.p.h. at 20,000 ft. Climb, 8·1 mins. to 20,000 ft. Range, 465 miles (normal) or 725 miles with drop tank. Service ceiling, 33,800 ft. (F.R. III): Maximum speed, 341 m.p.h.

at 6,000 ft. Cruising, 173 m.p.h. or 259 m.p.h. at 5,000 ft. Climb, 2·1 mins. to 5,000 ft. Range, 508 miles (normal) or 771 miles with drop tank. Service ceiling, 31,500 ft.

Armament (IB): Two 20-mm. guns and four 0·303 guns in wings. No bombs. (F. IIC and subsequent variants): Two 20-mm. guns and four 0·303 guns in wings and provision for one 500-lb. bomb under fuselage or two 250-lb. bombs under wings.

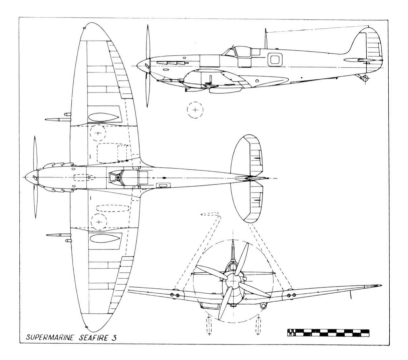

SUPERMARINE SEAFIRE 3

Seafire XVII (SX 194) from Lee-on-Solent. (*Crown Copyright Photo.*)

Supermarine Seafire
(Griffon variants)

Griffon-engined Seafires were just entering service with the F.A.A. when when the Second World War came to an end. If the war had continued for a few months longer, the Seafire XV would have superseded the Seafire III in carriers of the British Pacific Fleet. As events turned out, however, the Seafire XV saw only a brief period of service with squadrons based in the United Kingdom before VJ-Day and subsequent Griffon-engined Seafires did not enter the F.A.A. until the post-war years.

The Seafire XV, the first Griffon variant, was developed to Spec. N. 4/43 and the first three prototypes were NS 487, NS 490 and NS 493. These aircraft flew in 1944, and production Seafire XVs were manufactured by Cunliffe–Owen Aircraft Ltd., who built 134, and by Westland Aircraft Ltd., who built 250. Apart from the installation of the Griffon VI engine, the Mk. XV also differed from earlier Seafires in having increased fuel capacity, with tanks inside the wings, and from the 51st aircraft the sting-type arrester hook was standardised. This hook was mounted in the extreme tail, and the bottom of the rudder had to be cut away to accommodate it. It eventually replaced the old type V frame hook on most naval aircraft. All Seafire XVs (and subsequent marks except 45 and 46) had the folding wing incorporated as standard, and R.A.T.O.G. (rocket-assisted take-off gear) was added from the 75th aircraft. Cunliffe–Owen Seafire XVs could be distinguished by serial numbers with a PR prefix: those built by Westland had serial numbers in the SR and SW ranges.

The Seafire XV first entered service with No. 802 Squadron at Arbroath in May 1945, subsequently embarking in the carriers *Premier*, *Berwick* and *Vengeance*. Other squadrons to receive the type were No. 803, seconded to the Royal Canadian Navy for service in *Warrior*, and Nos. 805 and 806, which saw service in the post-war light fleet-carriers *Ocean* and *Glory*.

The first type of Seafire to enter the F.A.A. after the close of the Second World War was the Mk. XVII, which joined No. 883 Squadron at

Arbroath in September 1945. This squadron was also seconded to the Royal Canadian Navy and eventually disbanded in February 1946. The Seafire XVII was a refinement of the Mk. XV, and the prototype (NS 493) which flew in 1945 was in fact a conversion of the third prototype Seafire XV. It differed from the earlier variant in having a clear-view bubble hood and a cutaway rear fuselage and was built in two versions: the F. XVII and the F.R. XVII. The Seafire XVII also had more fuel capacity than the Mk. XV, as a 33-gal. tank was mounted in the rear fuselage. In the fighter-reconnaissance version, however, this was removed to make way for two F. 24 cameras, one vertical and one oblique. Total production of the Seafire XVII was 232, of which Cunliffe–Owen Aircraft Ltd. built 20 with SP serial prefixes and Westlands the remainder with SW and SX serial prefixes.

The Seafire XVII eventually proved to be the longest-lived of the post-war variants and, after retirement from first-line squadrons, continued to give good service with air squadrons of the R.N.V.R. and with training squadrons. One of the latter retained the last Seafires in naval service.

Whilst the Seafire XV and XVII were in production, development work proceeded at the Cunliffe–Owen factory with a F.A.A. version of the Spitfire Mk. 21, designated Seafire 45. This Seafire was produced to the requirements of Spec. N. 7/44 and the prototype (TM 379) was a converted Spitfire F. 21. Alterations included the fitting of naval radio equipment, a stinger-type arrester hook and modified undercarriage leg fairings and tail wheel-guard to facilitate the use of arrester wires. The Seafire 45 also differed from the earlier Griffon variants in mounting the Series 61/85 engine and in having four 20-mm. guns as standard. The new Griffon engine resulted in a change to a five-bladed airscrew or a six-bladed counter-rotating type, the latter being fitted for a period to the prototype and also on a number of production aircraft. As the Seafire 45 emerged as the war ended, production was limited to 50 aircraft, all of which were built by the Vickers–Armstrongs factory at Castle Bromwich. The Seafire 45 never became operational, but it served with No. 778 Squadron at Ford from October 1946.

Just as the Spitfire 21 became the Seafire 45 when modified for naval service, so did the Spitfire 22 become the Seafire 46. This variant was generally similar to its predecessor, but introduced the bubble-hood and cutaway rear fuselage. It appeared both with a five-blade airscrew and six-blade contra-rotating airscrews, the majority having the latter, and could also be seen with two types of tail assembly. Early Seafire 46s had the original tail, but later aircraft incorporated the revised fin and rudder of increased area as used on the Spiteful and Spitfire 24. The prototype Seafire 46 (TM 383) was converted from the second prototype Seafire 45. It was followed by a small production batch of 24 aircraft (LA 541 to LA 564) from the South Marston factory, the original contract for 200 having been curtailed. A few Seafire 46s were fitted with a single oblique F. 24 camera behind the pilot and designated F.R. 46. The Seafire 46, like the Mk. 45, did not enter first-line squadron service with the F.A.A., but it equipped No. 781 Training Squadron at Lee-on-Solent from March 1947 and in July 1947 was issued to No. 1832 R.N.V.R. Squadron at Culham.

The final version of the Seafire to enter service was the Mk. 47, the

Seafire XV (SW 847). (*Chas. E. Brown Photo.*)

Seafire 45 (LA 428). (*Vickers Photo.*)

naval version of the Spitfire 24. This differed from the Mks. 45 and 46 in that it was fully navalised, with folding wings: those of the Seafire 45 and 46 were fixed. The Seafire 47's wing fold differed from all preceding Seafires in having a hinge at only one point in the mainplane panel. The entire wing folded upwards just outboard of the wheel wells: the wing tips did not fold back as on earlier Seafires. The six-bladed contra-rotating airscrew, bubble hood and Spiteful-type tail assembly was standard on all Seafire 47s: externally it was identical with the later production Seafire 46s except for the re-positioning of the carburettor air intake as a lip just behind the spinner and the use of the short-barrel Hispano guns. Internally, fuel capacity was increased by the installation of a 33-gal. tank in the rear fuselage and, for maximum range, this could be augmented by a 90-gal. flush-fitting drop tank below the fuselage and two 23-gal. blister tanks under the mainplanes. This gave the Seafire 47 a grand total of 289 gals. of fuel and bestowed a range of about 940 miles—greater than that of any other Seafire variant.

The prototype Seafire 47 (PS 944) was followed by production aircraft from the South Marston, Swindon, factory of Supermarine, most of which were fitted out for fighter-reconnaissance and designated F.R. 47. A contract was placed for 150 Seafire 47s but only 90 of these were built. The last Seafire (Mk. 47, serial VR 972) was delivered in March 1949.

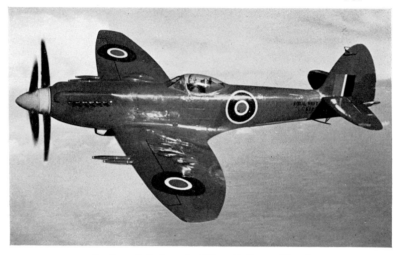

Seafire 46 (LA 542). (*Chas. E. Brown Photo.*)

Seafire 47 (VP 447), showing wing-folding arrangement. (*Vickers Photo.*)

Seafire 47 of No. 800 Squadron takes off for a sortie during the Korean War.
(*Official Admiralty Photo.*)

The Seafire 47 first entered service in the F.A.A. with No. 804 Squadron at Ford in February 1948. It eventually joined other first-line squadrons, including No. 800 Squadron, which received Seafire 47s at Donibristle in April 1949 and subsequently embarked in the light fleet-carrier *Triumph*. From October 1949 until February 1950 No. 800 Squadron took part in rocket strikes against bandit hideouts in Malaya. With the outbreak of war in Korea in June 1950 *Triumph* sailed for Okinawa and No. 800 Squadron's aircraft became the only Seafires to take part in the Korean War. They had a distinguished record, flying 360 sorties comprised of 245 offensive fighter patrols and 115 ground-attack operations.

With the emergence of the Attacker, the F.A.A.'s first operational jet fighter, the Seafire 47 was superseded in first-line squadrons from 1951, but it continued to operate with air squadrons of the R.N.V.R., alongside the older Seafire 17s. The last squadron to use Seafire 47s was No. 1833 (Midland Air Division) at Bramcote: they were finally supplanted by Hawker Sea Furies in 1952.

Credit for being the last Seafire in service must, however, be awarded to the Seafire 17. The only remaining unit of Seafires in the F.A.A., No. 764 Training Squadron, was finally retired at Yeovilton on 23 November 1954.

UNITS ALLOCATED

(Seafire XV): No. 802 (re-equipped at Arbroath, May 1945: embarked in *Premier*, *Berwick* and *Vengeance*); No. 803 (re-equipped June 1945: embarked in *Warrior* with Royal Canadian Navy); No. 804 (re-formed at Eglinton, October 1946: embarked in *Theseus* and *Ocean*); No. 805 (re-equipped March 1946: embarked in *Ocean*); No. 806 (re-formed August 1945: embarked in *Berwick* and *Glory*). (Seafire XVII): No. 800 (re-formed October 1946: embarked in *Triumph*); No. 802; No. 803; No. 805 (re-equipped April 1947: retained until arrival of Sea Furies in August 1948); No. 807 (re-equipped December 1945: embarked in *Implacable* and *Vengeance*); No. 883 (re-equipped at Arbroath, September 1945: to Royal Canadian Navy, disbanded February 1946); No. 1831 (formed at Stretton, June 1947: retained until arrival of Sea Furies in August 1951); No. 1832 (formed at Culham in July 1947: retained until arrival of Sea Furies in November 1951); No. 1833 (formed at Bramcote in August 1947: retained until arrival of Sea Furies in

1952). (Seafire 45): No. 778 (Ford). (Seafire 46): No. 781 (Lee-on-Solent); No. 1832 (Culham and Benson, 1947–52). (Seafire 47): No. 800 (re-equipped April 1949 at Donibristle: embarked in *Triumph*); No. 804 (re-equipped February 1948 at Ford: embarked in *Glory*); No. 1833 (Bramcote, 1947 to 1952).

TECHNICAL DATA (SEAFIRE XV TO 47)

Description: Single-seat carrier-borne fighter, fighter-bomber or fighter-reconnaissance aircraft. All-metal stressed-skin construction.

Manufacturers: Supermarine Division of Vickers–Armstrongs Ltd., Castle Bromwich and South Marston, Swindon. Mks. XV and XVII sub-contracted by Cunliffe–Owen Aircraft Ltd., and Westland Aircraft Ltd.

Power Plant (Mks. XV and XVII): One 1,850-h.p. Rolls-Royce Griffon VI. (Mks. 45 and 46): One 2,035-h.p. Rolls-Royce Griffon 61 or 2,375-h.p. Rolls-Royce Griffon 85. (Mk. 47): One 2,375-h.p. Rolls-Royce Griffon 85.

Dimensions (Mks. XV and XVII): Span, 36 ft. 10 in. Length, 32 ft. 3 in. Height, 10 ft. 8 in. Wing area, 242 sq. ft. (Mks. 45 and 46): Span, 36 ft. 11 in. Length, 33 ft. 7 in. Height, 12 ft. 9 in. Wing area, 244 sq. ft. (Mk. 47): Span, 36 ft. 11 in. Length, 34 ft. 4 in. Height, 12 ft. 9 in. Wing area, 244 sq. ft.

Weights (Mks. XV and XVII): Empty, 6,200 lb. Loaded, 8,000 lb. (Mk. 45): Empty, 7,100 lb. Loaded, 9,400 lb. (Mk. 46): Loaded, 9,730 lb. (Mk. 47): Empty, 7,625 lb. Loaded (normal), 10,200 lb. (maximum), 11,615 lb.

Performance (Mk. XV): Maximum speed, 383 m.p.h. at 13,500 ft. Cruising, 255 m.p.h. or 334 m.p.h. at 20,000 ft. Climb, 7 mins. to 20,000 ft. Range, 430 miles (normal) or 640 miles (with auxiliary tank). Service ceiling, 35,500 ft. (Mk. XVII): Maximum speed, 387 m.p.h. at 13,500 ft. Cruising, 260 m.p.h. or 339 m.p.h. at 20,000 ft. Climb,

Seafire 46 (LA 561) of No.1832 Squadron from Culham   (*'Flight' Photo.*)

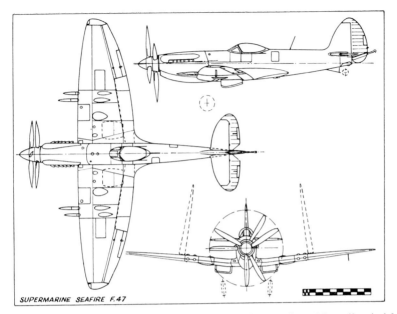

7·2 mins. to 20,000 ft. Range, 435 miles (normal) or 860 miles (with auxiliary tanks). Service ceiling, 35,200 ft. (Mk. 45): Maximum speed, 438 m.p.h. at 25,000 ft. Cruising, 272 m.p.h. or 345 m.p.h. at 20,000 ft. Climb, 7·4 mins. to 20,000 ft. Range, 435 miles (normal) or 740 miles (with auxiliary tanks). Service ceiling, 41,000 ft. (Mk. 47): Maximum speed, 452 m.p.h. at 20,500 ft.; 405 m.p.h. at 10,700 ft.; 382 m.p.h. at sea level. Climb, 4,800 ft./min. at sea level. Range, 400 miles (normal) or 940 miles (with auxiliary tanks). Service ceiling, 43,100 ft.

Armament (Mk. XV): Two 20-mm. guns and four 0·303 guns (Mk. XVII): Two 20-mm. guns and four 0·303 guns plus eight 60-lb. rocket-projectiles below the wings. (Mk. 45 and 46): Four 20-mm. guns. Provision for one 500-lb. bomb below fuselage. (Mk. 47): Four 20-mm. guns plus eight 60-lb. rocket-projectiles below the wings. Provision for three 500-lb. bombs, one below fuselage and two below wings.

Attacker F. 1 (WA 497). (*Vickers Photo.*)

Supermarine Attacker

The Attacker has a special place in F.A.A. history as the first jet fighter to be standardised in first-line squadrons. It was originally conceived as a land-fighter for the R.A.F., and work began on its design in October 1944. Produced to Spec. E. 10/44, the first prototype (TS 409) flew at Chilbolton on 27 July 1946. It incorporated the Spiteful's laminar flow wing and was the first aircraft to use the Rolls-Royce Nene turbojet. No R.A.F. orders materialised, but the second and third prototypes (to Spec. E. 1/45) had long-stroke undercarriages, lift spoilers and deck-arrester hooks to meet naval requirements. The first naval prototype (TS 413) flew on 17 June 1947 and carrier trials were concluded aboard H.M.S. *Illustrious* in October 1947. Production contracts for the F.A.A. were placed in November 1949 and the first aircraft (WA 486) flew on 5 April 1950. A total of 145 Attackers was built for the F.A.A., the last aircraft (WZ 302) being delivered in 1953. The Attacker F. 1 and F.B. 1 with the Nene 3 was succeeded (from WK 319) by the F.B. 2 which had the Nene 102 engine and modified ailerons and cockpit hood. Initial production aircraft did not have the dorsal fin extension, which first appeared early in 1951. Sixty-one Attacker F. 1 and F.B. 1s were built, and 84 F.B. 2s.

Attackers first entered service with No. 800 Squadron at Ford on 22 August 1951: this was the pioneer operational jet squadron of the F.A.A. Standard equipment in service included Martin–Baker ejector seat, R.A.T.O.G., accelerator hooks in the wheel bays and a somewhat cumbersome 250-gal. drop tank below the fuselage. By the time of the Naval Review at Spithead in 1953, Attackers equipped Nos. 800, 803 and 890 Squadrons as well as No. 736 Training Squadron, all of which participated in the Fly-past. In 1954 Nos. 800 and 803 Squadrons re-armed with Sea Hawks and No. 890 Squadron with Sea Venoms and the Attacker passed from first-line service. However, it continued to serve with air squadrons of the R.N.V.R. from 1955 until their disbandment early in 1957. No. 1831 Squadron received Attackers in exchange for Sea Furies at Stretton on 14 May 1955, becoming the first jet squadron of the R.N.V.R.

Nos. 800, 803 and 890 Squadrons and No. 736 Training Squadron. Also No. 1831 Squadron (Northern Air Division, Stretton) and No. 1833 Squadron (Midland Air Division, Bramcote), R.N.V.R.

TECHNICAL DATA (ATTACKER F. I)

Description: Single-seat carrier-borne fighter. All-metal stressed-skin construction.

Manufacturers: Supermarine Division of Vickers–Armstrongs Ltd., South Marston, Swindon, Wilts.

Power Plant: One 5,100-lb. thrust Rolls-Royce Nene 3.

Dimensions: Span, 36 ft. 11 in. Length, 37 ft. 6 in. Height, 9 ft. 11 in. Wing area, 226 sq. ft.

Weights: Empty, 8,434 lb. Loaded (normal), 11,500 lb.

Performance: Maximum speed, 590 m.p.h. at sea level; 583 m.p.h. at 10,000 ft.; 561 m.p.h. at 20,000 ft.; 538 m.p.h. at 30,000 ft. Cruising, 355 m.p.h. Climb, 6,350 ft./min. at sea level; 6·6 mins. to 30,000 ft. Range, 590 miles (normal) or 1,190 miles (with auxiliary ventral tank). Service ceiling, 45,000 ft.

Armament: Four 20-mm. guns in wings. F.B. 1 also equipped for eight 60-lb. rocket-projectiles or two 1,000-lb. bombs below wings.

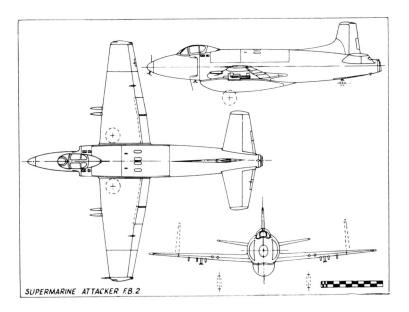

SUPERMARINE ATTACKER F.B.2

Scimitar F. 1 (XD 212). (*Vickers Photo.*)

Supermarine Scimitar

The Scimitar was the first swept-wing single-seat fighter to be produced
for the F.A.A. and also the first to be capable of supersonic flight, attained
in a shallow dive. It was also the first F.A.A. aircraft equipped to carry an
atomic bomb. Designed to meet the requirements of Naval Spec. N. 113D,
the Scimitar first appeared as the Supermarine Type 544, a development
of the Type 525 (VX 138) which first flew on 27 April 1954. This had
been preceded by two earlier straight-winged prototypes with a butterfly
tail, the Type 508 (VX 129), which first flew on 31 August 1951, and the
Type 529 (VX 136), which first flew on 29 August 1952. The first prototype Type 544 (WT 854) made its maiden flight on 20 January 1956. The
second and third prototypes (WT 859 and WW 134) flew later the same
year.

The Scimitar prototype differed from the earlier Type 525 in a number
of respects. Its fuselage was redesigned on the area rule principle; it had
a longer nose and larger air intakes. Also new was the long dorsal spine,
terminating in an intake. Blown flaps, tested experimentally in the Type
525, became standard in the Scimitar. This innovation reduces the safe
approach speed, an obvious advantage for carrier operation, and also
lowers the speed at which catapult launches of this very heavy aircraft
must be made. The system is operated by high-pressure air fed from each
Avon compressor to the top surface of the wing-flaps: the effect is to delay
the onset of turbulence over the wing at high angles of attack and low
speeds. Another innovation in the Scimitar is the Fairey power-operated
control system, the first of its kind in a British naval aircraft.

An initial contract for over 100 Scimitars was placed on behalf of the
Admiralty, and the first production aircraft (XD 210) flew on 11 January
1957. Meanwhile, carrier trials had been successfully completed in H.M.S.
Ark Royal, the first deck-landings having taken place in April 1956.

Capable of low-level attacks at supersonic speeds with tactical nuclear
weapons, high-level interception with air-to-air guided missiles, or fighter-

reconnaissance at extreme ranges, the Scimitar represented a sensational advance on the Sea Hawk, which it superseded as the F.A.A.'s standard single-seat strike fighter. The first Scimitars reached No. 700X Trials Flight for intensive flying trials in August 1957 at Ford, and the first operational squadron was formed at Lossiemouth in June 1958, afterwards embarking in H.M.S. *Victorious*.

TECHNICAL DATA (SCIMITAR F. I)

Description: Single-seat carrier-borne strike fighter or fighter-reconnaissance aircraft. All-metal stressed-skin construction.

Manufacturers: Supermarine Division of Vickers–Armstrongs Ltd., South Marston, Swindon, Wilts.

Power Plant: Two Rolls-Royce Avon 200 series.

Dimensions: Span, 37 ft. 2 in. Length, 56 ft. 2 in. Height, 15 ft.

Weights: Not released.

Performance: Not released.

Armament: Four 30-mm. Aden guns in fuselage and provision for de Havilland Firestreak guided missiles below the wings. Alternatively, bombs or rocket-projectiles can be carried below the wings. For extreme range two 100-gal. and two 250-gal. tanks replace ordnance loads below wings: otherwise there is provision for air-to-air refuelling by nose probe.

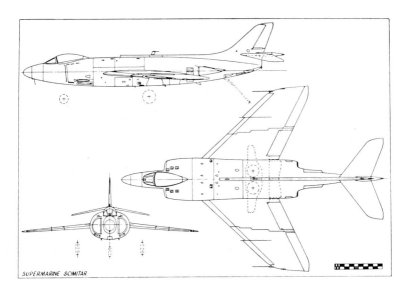

SUPERMARINE SCIMITAR

Chesapeake I dive-bombers.

Vought–Sikorsky Chesapeake

The Chesapeake was the British version of the Vought V-156, which was first designed by R. B. Beisel in 1935 as a scout-bomber for the U.S. Navy with the designation XSB2U-1. The prototype made its first flight on 5 January 1936 and the type was subsequently built for the U.S. Navy under the designations SB2U-1, SB2U-2 and SB2U-3. It supplanted the SBU-1, a Vought biplane scout-bomber which had served for a number of years with the 1st, 2nd and 3rd Scouting Squadrons, and was in fact one of the first monoplane types with the U.S. Navy, where the biplane lingered longer than in the U.S. Army Air Corps.

In 1938 the Vought V-156 was offered for export sales and attracted the attention of the French Government, who ordered it for their Naval Air Service. Deliveries had begun when France was defeated in 1940, and a number of aircraft fell into German hands. It is reputed that a number were used by the *Luftwaffe* for raids on Dover, though there is no official confirmation of this.

With the French capitulation, Britain ordered 50 V-156-B1s, the residue of the French contract, and allotted the airframe serial numbers AL 908 to AL 957. These aircraft, named Chesapeake I, differed from the French V-156-F3 in having four instead of one forward-firing guns and in certain details such as the installation of the British-type arrester gear. Chesapeakes first arrived in Britain early in 1941, and were used for a time by No. 728 Squadron at Arbroath after assembly at the Burtonwood Aircraft Repair Depot, near Liverpool. The first operational squadron to be equipped was No. 811 at Lee-on-Solent, which received 14 Chesapeakes and two Sea Hurricanes on 14 July 1941. In the event, the Chesapeake proved unsuitable for escort-carrier work, for which it had been intended, due to its long take-off run. It was thereafter relegated to training duties in the F.A.A., though with the U.S. Marine Corps it saw active service in the Pacific until 1942 with VMSB-131 and VMSB-231 under the name Vindicator. Some Vindicators served in the carrier *Lexington*.

UNITS ALLOCATED

No. 728 (R.N.A.S. Arbroath) and No. 811 (R.N.A.S. Lee-on-Solent).

Description: Two-seat carrier-borne or land-based dive-bomber. Metal structure, with metal and fabric covering.

Manufacturers: Vought–Sikorsky Aircraft Division of the United Aircraft Corporation, Stratford, Connecticut.

Power Plant: One 750-h.p. Pratt & Whitney Twin Wasp Junior SB4-G.

Dimensions: Span, 42 ft. Length, 33 ft. $11\frac{3}{4}$ in. Height, 9 ft. $9\frac{1}{2}$ in. Wing area, 305 sq. ft.

Weights: Empty, 4,500 lb. Loaded, 6,500 lb.

Performance: Maximum speed, 257 m.p.h. at 11,000 ft. Cruising, 210 m.p.h. Initial climb, 1,545 ft./min. Range, 700 miles. Service ceiling, 28,200 ft.

Armament: Four fixed machine-guns forward and one free-mounted gun aft. Bomb-load of 1,500 lb. comprised of three 500-lb. or 12 116-lb. bombs.

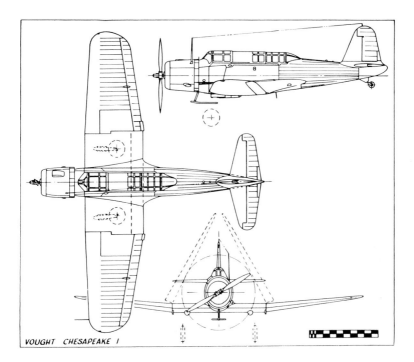

VOUGHT CHESAPEAKE I

Kingfisher seaplane (FN 678). (*Chas. E. Brown Photo.*)

Vought–Sikorsky Kingfisher

The Kingfisher was designed by R. B. Beisel as an observation scout for the U.S. Navy under the designation XOS2U-1, and made its first flight in 1939. Production aircraft were delivered to the U.S. Navy from 1940 onwards with the designations OS2U-1, OS2U-2 and OS2U-3, and over 1,800 were built. The parent company delivered 1,525 of the seaplane version and a further 300 landplanes emerged from the Naval Aircraft Factory under the designation OS2N-1. U.S. Navy Kingfishers gave excellent service in the Pacific and figured in a number of spectacular rescue operations, including a successful search for Capt. Eddie Rickenbacker at the end of 1942. Rickenbacker and his companions, lost in the South Pacific, were rescued by a Kingfisher pilot, who taxied across 40 miles of rough sea to bring them to safety. On another occasion, during the first American attack on the Japanese in the Aleutians, Kingfishers went into action as dive-bombers, each carrying a bomb-load 50% in excess of their normal armament.

With the F.A.A. the Kingfisher was the second Vought–Sikorsky type to enter service. It first appeared in Great Britain in the summer of 1942; the previous year the F.A.A. had received a batch of Vought–Sikorsky Chesapeake dive-bombers. Like the Curtiss Seamew, the Kingfisher was supplied under Lend–Lease arrangements. A total of 100 (FN 650 to FN 749) reached the F.A.A., where they were used both as landplanes and seaplanes.

The first unit to be equipped with Kingfishers in the F.A.A. was No. 703 Squadron, which had 11 seaplanes on its strength. Subsequently Kingfishers saw service as catapult-launched reconnaissance aircraft at sea with armed merchant cruisers, and as trainers with F.A.A. establishments in the West Indies.

Description: Two-seat reconnaissance aircraft, with interchangeable land or float undercarriage, suitable for catapult launch from warships. All-metal structure, with metal and fabric covering.

Manufacturers: Vought–Sikorsky Aircraft Division of the United Aircraft Corporation, Stratford, Connecticut.

Power Plant: One 450-h.p. Pratt & Whitney Wasp Junior R-985-SB3.

Dimensions: Span, 35 ft. 11 in. Length (seaplane), 33 ft. 7¾ in.; (landplane), 30 ft. 1 in. Height (seaplane), 14 ft. 8 in.; (landplane), 13 ft.

Weights (Seaplane): Empty, 3,335 lb. Loaded, 4,980 lb. (Landplane): Empty, 2,915 lb. Loaded, 4,619 lb.

Performance (Seaplane): Maximum speed, 171 m.p.h. Cruising, 152 m.p.h. Climb, 960 ft./min. Range, 908 miles. Service ceiling, 18,200 ft. (Landplane): Maximum speed, 172 m.p.h. Cruising, 147 m.p.h. Range, 900 miles.

Armament: One fixed 0·30 calibre gun forward and one free-mounted gun aft. Provision for 240 lb. of bombs externally below wings.

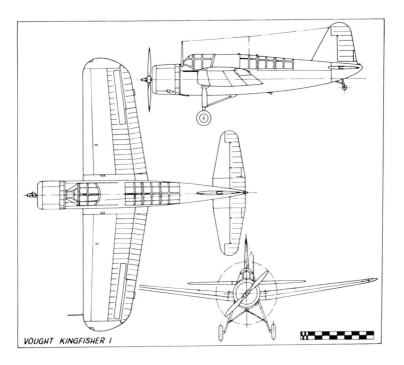

VOUGHT KINGFISHER I

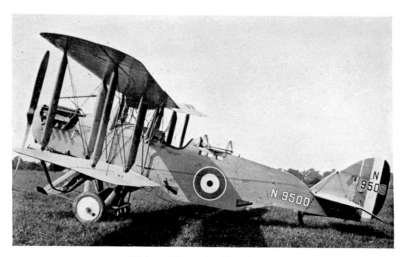

Walrus (N 9500). (*Westland Photo.*)

Westland Walrus

The Westland Walrus was one of the curious collection of ugly ducklings used on Fleet spotting duties in the years immediately following the First World War. It was the first British aeroplane designed for naval duties after the Armistice and the prototype first flew in 1920. It first entered squadron service in 1921 and was still employed on first-line duties at the end of 1925, together with the Parnall Panther, the Avro Bison and the Blackburn Blackburn.

The Walrus was the outcome of an Air Ministry plan to effect financial economies in the lean 'twenties by adapting the R.A.F.'s D.H. 9A day-bomber into a three-seat deck-landing aircraft. The first stage in this transformation was the alteration of the fuselage to accommodate an observer in a third cockpit, behind the gunner, and a large ventral bulge was added to provide the observer with a prone position. This prototype (J 6585) was produced by Armstrong Whitworth and was known as the Tadpole: it differed from the production Walrus in retaining the original Liberty engine with frontal radiator. In the Walrus proper (all built by Westland) the Napier Lion engine was substituted and additional modifications included folding wings, emergency flotation bags, a jettisonable under-carriage fitted with a hydrovane, jaws on the spreader bars to engage fore-and-aft arrester wires and an arrangement to convert the fuel-tank, if required, into an additional flotation chamber. In both the Tadpole and the Walrus the original stagger of the D.H. 9A's wings was heavily reduced, and the final result was to produce one of the ugliest imaginable aeroplanes, which, according to all accounts, handled extremely badly.

At least one Walrus (J 9523) was later fitted with horn-balanced ailerons and an oleo undercarriage. Total output of the Walrus amounted to 36, N 9500 to N 9535 inclusive.

The Walrus first entered service with No. 3 Squadron, R.A.F., at Leuchars in 1921, being superseded by the Avro Bison when the squadron moved to Gosport in 1922. In 1923 the Walrus joined Nos. 420 and 421 Fleet Spotter Flights, each of which had six aircraft at Gosport. At the end of 1925 No. 420 Flight re-equipped with Blackburn Blackburns and No. 421 Flight with Avro Bisons.

No. 3 Squadron, R.A.F. (Leuchars); No. 420 Flight (Gosport); No. 421 Flight (Gosport).

TECHNICAL DATA (WALRUS)

Description: Three-seat carrier-borne spotter-reconnaissance aircraft. Wooden structure, with wood and fabric covering.
Manufacturers: Westland Aircraft, Ltd., Yeovil, Somerset.
Power Plant: One 450-h.p. Napier Lion II.
Dimensions: Span, 45 ft. 10 in. Length, 30 ft. Height, 11 ft. 7 in. Wing area, 496 sq. ft.
Weights: Loaded, 4,994 lb.
Performance: Maximum speed, 124 m.p.h. Climb, 10 mins. to 9,840 ft.
Armament: One Vickers gun forward and one Lewis aft on a Scarff ring.

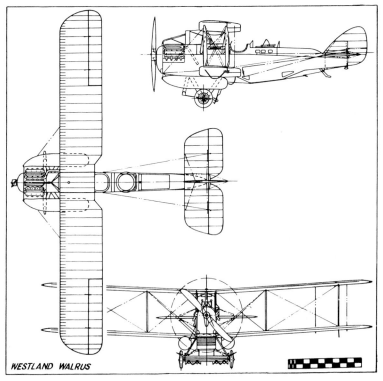

WESTLAND WALRUS

Wyvern S. 4 (WN 334) of No. 831 Squadron. (*'Flight' Photo.*)

Westland Wyvern S. 4

The Wyvern, which was the first Westland-designed aircraft used in the F.A.A. since the Walrus of the 'twenties, had more than the average share of teething troubles: nearly seven years elapsed between the maiden flight and the equipment of the first operational squadron. This is not surprising when it is realised that its three successive power plants (Eagle, Clyde and Python) were all new and untried engines. The final hurdle was the problem of adapting the Python and the huge eight-bladed contra-rotating airscrew for the special techniques demanded by deck-flying: this was eventually solved in 1953 by the installation of the Rotol inertia controller.

Originally designed to Spec. N. 11/44, the Wyvern was from the outset intended for turboprop power, but as such engines did not become available until 1948 the five prototype and ten pre-production T.F. 1s were fitted with the Rolls-Royce Eagle piston engine. The first Wyvern (TS 371) flew on 12 December 1946. The first turboprop Wyverns, designated T.F. 2, were produced to Spec. N. 12/45 and flew in 1949. The Wyvern T.F. 1 and T.F. 2 are described in the Appendix.

The first Wyvern to reach operational status was the S. 4, originally T.F. 4 until this designation was abolished in 1953. The S. 4 (which first flew in May 1951) featured a cut-back engine cowling to permit cartridge starting, stiffened cockpit canopy, modified aileron tabs and auxiliary tail fins on a dihedral tailplane. The last seven T.F. 2s (VW 880 to VW 886) were completed to S. 4 standards and followed by 90 production S. 4s, beginning VZ 745.

The Wyvern S. 4 first entered service with No. 813 Squadron (formerly Firebrands) in May 1953 and was shore-based until 1954, when it embarked first in *Eagle* and later in *Albion*. The second Wyvern squadron was No. 827, which embarked in *Eagle* in May 1955. Finally, in November 1955, Nos. 830 and 831 Squadrons re-formed with Wyverns at Ford, Sussex, joining *Eagle* in April 1956. Both these squadrons flew their Wyverns operationally on ground-attack sorties during the Anglo-French intervention in Egypt in November 1956.

Modifications introduced retrospectively after the Wyvern had entered service included a flat, bullet-proof windscreen in place of the original curved type, perforated air-brakes below the centre section and provision for wing tip fuel-tanks as fitted to the Venom.

UNITS ALLOCATED

Nos. 813, 827, 830 and 831 Squadrons. Also No. 700 Squadron (Fleet Trials Unit) and Nos. 703 and 764 Training Squadrons.

TECHNICAL DATA (WYVERN S.4)

Description: Single-seat carrier-borne strike aircraft. All-metal stressed-skin construction.

Manufacturers: Westland Aircraft Ltd., Yeovil, Somerset.

Power Plant: One 4,110-e.h.p. Armstrong Siddeley Python A.S.P. 3.

Dimensions: Span, 44 ft. (20 ft. folded). Length, 42 ft. 3 in. Height, 15 ft. 9 in. Wing area, 355 sq. ft.

Weights: Empty, 15,608 lb. Loaded, 21,200 lb. (normal) or 24,500 lb. (maximum).

Performance: Maximum speed, 383 m.p.h. at sea level. Cruising, 343 m.p.h. at 20,000 ft. Climb, 2,350 ft./min. at sea level. Range, 904 miles. Service ceiling, 28,000 ft.

Armament: Four 20-mm. guns in wings and provision for 16 rocket-projectiles or a single torpedo or three 1,000-lb. bombs.

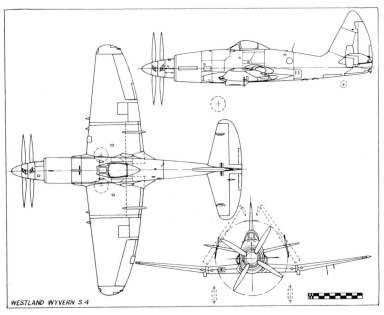

WESTLAND WYVERN S.4

Dragonfly H.R. 3 (WG 668) aboard *Bulwark*. (*Official Admiralty Photo*.)

Westland–Sikorsky Dragonfly

The Royal Navy was quick to appreciate the value of the helicopter, and its No. 705 Helicopter Squadron, formed at Gosport in 1950, was probably the first all-helicopter squadron to be formed outside the U.S.A. Initial experiments had taken place with American-built Hoverflies (see Appendix) some five years previously, but the Westland–Sikorsky Dragonfly was the first British-built helicopter to serve with the Royal Navy, and this type was chosen as the initial equipment of the pioneer No. 705 Squadron.

The Dragonfly, also supplied to the R.A.F., was the British-built version of the American Sikorsky S-51, for which the Westland concern acquired the manufacturing rights in 1947. The total production of Dragonflies built for the Royal Navy, the R.A.F. and for civil use amounted to 133. The initial production version for the Royal Navy was the Dragonfly H.R. Mk. I, which had a three-blade rotor of composite construction and was equipped for a general utility and rescue rôle. One was fitted experimentally with a four-blade metal rotor. This was followed by the principal production variant for the Royal Navy, the Dragonfly H.R. Mk. 3, which differed in having a three-blade metal rotor and a hydraulic servo-control mechanism. The last Dragonfly H.R. 3 for the Royal Navy (WP 504) was delivered on 28 September 1953.

Dragonflies were used extensively aboard aircraft-carriers, both for ship-to-shore communications flying and for 'plane-guard' duties, hovering in attendance during deck-flying operations to provide rapid air–sea rescue facilities if needed. In this latter rôle they superseded the destroyer's traditional duties, proving at once more efficient and more economical. Two Dragonflies were also issued to every coastal air station of the Royal Navy, where they supplanted the well-tried Sea Otter amphibian in the air–sea rescue rôle. Naval Dragonflies took part in many civilian rescue operations and did valiant work in Holland during the floods of 1953. In

June 1953 12 Dragonflies were accorded the honour of leading the massed fly-past of aircraft in the Royal Naval Coronation Review at Spithead.

With the introduction of the more powerful and capacious Whirlwind, the Dragonfly was gradually transferred to training duties. In 1957 it was announced that many naval Dragonflies were to be modified at the Westland factory to become Widgeons. The Widgeon is described and illustrated in the Appendix.

UNITS ALLOCATED

No. 705 Squadron (Gosport and Lee-on-Solent).

TECHNICAL DATA (DRAGONFLY H.R. 3)

Description: Carrier-borne or shore-based air–sea rescue and communications helicopter. Crew of two.
Manufacturers: Westland Aircraft, Ltd., Yeovil, Somerset.
Power Plant: One 550-h.p. Alvis Leonides 50.
Dimensions: Rotor diameter, 49 ft. Length, 57 ft. 6½ in. Height, 12 ft. 11 in.
Weights: Empty, 4,397 lb. Loaded, 5,870 lb.
Performance: Maximum speed, 103 m.p.h. Cruising, 81 m.p.h. Climb, 970 ft./min. Service ceiling, 13,500 ft.

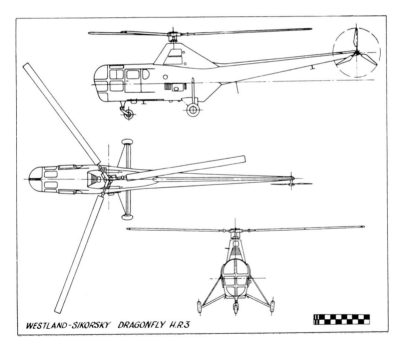

WESTLAND-SIKORSKY DRAGONFLY H.R.3

Whirlwind H.A.R. 7 (XG 586). (*Westland Photo.*)

Westland–Sikorsky Whirlwind
(H.A.R. 1 to H.A.S. 7)

The Whirlwind, British-built version of the American Sikorsky S-55 helicopter, first entered service with the Royal Navy, but was eventually adopted by the R.A.F. and Army as well. The prototype Whirlwind H.A.R. 1 (XA 862) first flew on 15 August 1953 and the first 10 production aircraft were delivered to the F.A.A. for service with No. 705 Squadron. They were not, however, the first S-55 helicopters to join the Royal Navy, as they had been preceded in service by American-built H.A.R. 21 and H.A.S. 22 aircraft (see Appendix) delivered at the end of 1952 under M.D.A.P. arrangements.

The small production batch of Whirlwind H.A.R. 1 (XA 862 to XA 871) was followed by the second naval version, the H.A.R. 3, which differed from the earlier model in having the 700-h.p. Wright Cyclone R-1300-3 engine instead of the 600-h.p. Pratt and Whitney Wasp R-1340-40. The H.A.R. 3 also had a slightly lengthened nose, and the first two prototypes were XJ 393 and XJ 394, originally numbered XD 363 and XD 364.

On 28 August 1955 the prototype Whirlwind H.A.R. 5 (XJ 396) made its maiden flight. This was the first version of the Whirlwind to employ a British power plant, the Alvis Leonides Major. The H.A.R. 5s all incorporated the modified tail cone and rear pylon, producing a droop of 3° on the tail boom and offering greater clearance of the main rotor blades. This modification was first tested on the H.A.R. 3, XJ 402. Also new on the H.A.R. 5 was the horizontal tail stabiliser: earlier versions had pronounced anhedral.

Final version of the Whirlwind for the F.A.A. was the H.A.S. 7, the prototype of which (XG 589) flew for the first time on 17 October 1956. Whereas the H.A.R. 1, 3 and 5 had been equipped only for non-combat rôles such as search and rescue and communications, the H.A.S. 7 was designed for first-line duties in the anti-submarine rôle and was in fact the first British helicopter for this kind of work. Equipment included radar and dipping Asdic, for submarine detection, and suitable strike weapons. First deliveries of the H.A.S. 7 were made to the Helicopter Flight of No. 700 Squadron in June 1957, and the first operational squadron was No. 820, equipped at Eglinton on 21 January 1958.

Whirlwinds were used both at shore stations and aboard aircraft-carriers of the Royal Navy and, in addition to the duties already enumerated, conducted experiments in airborne minesweeping with a large hook slung beneath the tail rotor boom.

TECHNICAL DATA (WHIRLWIND H.A.S. 7)

Description: Carrier-borne or shore-based anti-submarine helicopter with a crew of three. All-metal construction.
Manufacturers: Westland Aircraft Ltd., Yeovil, Somerset.
Power Plant: One 750-h.p. Alvis Leonides Major 755/1.
Dimensions: Rotor diameter, 53 ft. Length, 41 ft. 8½ in. Height, 15 ft. 4½ in.
Weights: Empty, 5,170 lb. Loaded, 7,800 lb.
Performance: Maximum speed, 109½ m.p.h. at sea level. Maximum inclined climb at sea level, 910 ft./min. Hovering ceiling, 9,400 ft. Range, 435 miles.
Armament: Details not released.

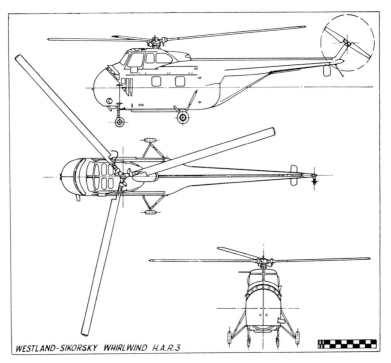

WESTLAND-SIKORSKY WHIRLWIND H.A.R.3

Wessex (XL 722). (*Westland Photo.*)

Westland–Sikorsky Wessex

Produced as a replacement in the F.A.A. for the Westland–Sikorsky Whirlwind, the Wessex was the first helicopter in the world to be manufactured in quantity with a free gas turbine as its power plant. It was developed from the American Sikorsky S-58, used as a 16-seat transport by the U.S. Army and as an anti-submarine helicopter by the U.S. Navy under the designations H-34A, HSS-1 and HUS-1. Unlike the British version, the original S-58 was powered by an orthodox piston engine, a 1,525-h.p. Wright R-1820-84.

The prototype Wessex (XL 722) was an imported S-58 airframe modified to take the Napier Gazelle gas-turbine engine. It made its first flight at Yeovil on 17 May 1957, after a series of ground running tests of the Gazelle engine with the helicopter tethered. The first of the engine runs took place on 22 March 1957. The maiden flight lasted 65 mins. and speeds up to 144 m.p.h. were attained.

The Wessex is the first helicopter ordered for the F.A.A. to have been designed from the outset as an anti-submarine aircraft. It is fitted with an automatic pilot and its armament includes an anti-submarine homing weapon. It can also be used, like its predecessors, for search and rescue and communications duties. Compared with its piston-engined counterpart, the Wessex carries a higher disposable load as well as being smoother and quieter. All these benefits derive from the Gazelle engine, which also enables the Wessex to be airborne from a cold start within 45 secs., and finally eliminates the necessity to carry petrol as well as kerosene in aircraft-carriers. This latter point is important to the Royal Navy, as jet engine fuel can be stowed in ships' tanks in the same way as ships' boiler fuel, leading to economies in storage space.

Description: Anti-submarine patrol and search and rescue helicopter. All-
metal structure.

Manufacturers: Westland Aircraft, Ltd., Yeovil, Somerset.

Power Plant: One Napier Gazelle.

Dimensions: Length, 65 ft. 9 in. (38 ft. 2 in. with tail folded). Height, 15 ft.
10 in.

Weights: Empty, 7,600 lb. Loaded, 12,600 lb.

Performance: Maximum speed, 144 m.p.h. at sea level. Cruising, 103 m.p.h.
Climb, 1,650 ft./min. Range, 610 miles. Hovering ceiling, 7,000 ft.

Armament: Details not released, but could presumably include air-to-sea
guided missiles as used in U.S. Navy version.

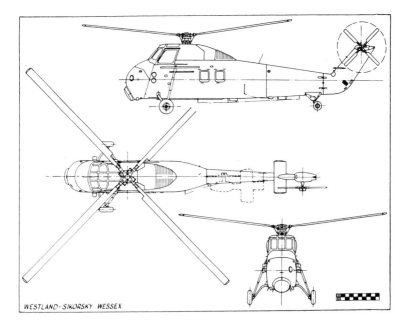

WESTLAND- SIKORSKY WESSEX

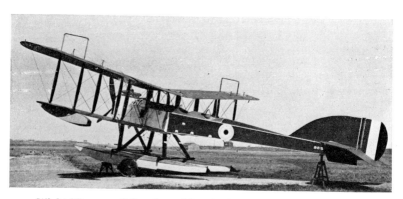

Wight 'Converted' Seaplane (No. 9853). (*Imp. War Museum Photo.*)

Wight 'Converted' Seaplane

The Wight 'Converted' Seaplane was descended from a single-engined landplane bomber (N 501) of 1916 which did not enter production. It was the third type of Wight seaplane to be used in numbers by the R.N.A.S., the others being the Pusher Seaplane of 1913 and the Admiralty Type 840 of 1915, both of which are described and illustrated in the Appendix.

As its name indicated, the Seaplane was a straightforward adaptation of the Bomber, and apart from the undercarriage differed only in minor details such as the installation of double-acting ailerons and modified king-posts on the top wing. The same Rolls-Royce Eagle engine was retained in the first production 'Converted' Seaplanes, but the later batches had a Sunbeam Maori.

Although it was not used in such large numbers as some other types of R.N.A.S. seaplanes, the Wight 'Converted' put in a great deal of work on overseas patrols, and one of them can claim to have destroyed a U-boat, the first to be sunk in the English Channel by direct air attack from a British aircraft. The submarine in question was the *UB-32* and the date was 18 August 1917. The Wight 'killed' its quarry with its first 100-lb. bomb. It was operating from the R.N.A.S. Station at Cherbourg and was flown by F./Sub-Lt. C. S. Mossop and Air Mechanic A. E. Ingledew.

A total of 50 Wight 'Converted' Seaplanes was ordered for the R.N.A.S., but only 37 were built, as it was decided to standardise on the Short 184. The serial numbers allocated were 9841 to 9860, N 1280 to N 1289 and N 2180 to N 2199.

Only a handful of 'Converted' Seaplanes remained at R.N.A.S. Stations by the Armistice. Official records listed seven on 31 October 1918.

R.N.A.S. Stations at Calshot, Cherbourg (later No. 243 Squadron), Dover (later No. 233 Squadron) and Portland.

Description: Two-seat anti-submarine patrol seaplane. Wooden structure
    with fabric covering.

Manufacturers: J. Samuel White & Co., East Cowes, Isle of Wight.

Power Plant: One 322-h.p. Rolls-Royce Eagle VI or 265-h.p. Sunbeam
    Maori.

Dimensions: Span, 65 ft. 6 in. Length, 44 ft. 8½ in. Height, 16 ft. Wing
    area, 715 sq. ft.

Weights: Empty, 3,758 lb. with Eagle engine and 3,957 lb. with Maori
    engine. Loaded, 5,556 lb. with Eagle engine and 5,394 lb. with
    Maori engine.

Performance (Eagle engine): Maximum speed, 84½ m.p.h. at 2,000 ft.;
    82½ m.p.h. at 6,500 ft. Climb, 4 mins. 20 secs. to 2,000 ft.; 42½ mins.
    to 10,000 ft. Endurance, 3½ hrs. Service ceiling, 9,600 ft.

Armament: One Lewis machine-gun on Scarff mounting aft and provision
    for four 100-lb. or 112-lb. bombs below the wings.

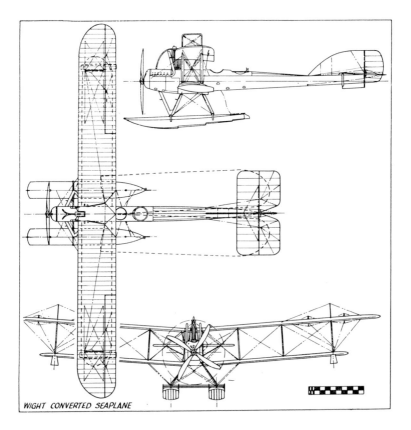

WIGHT CONVERTED SEAPLANE

Other types of aircraft in service with the Royal Flying Corps (Naval Wing), the Royal Naval Air Service and the Fleet Air Arm from 1912 to 1958

This section deals with all British naval aircraft (including those of foreign origin) not otherwise described and illustrated in the main text. It includes:

(i) Early naval types used only in small quantities. This category embraces the less important aircraft of the 1914–18 period and also the miscellaneous types which were included in the standard numbering system for British Service aircraft introduced during 1912. The Admiralty was allotted the numbers 1 to 200, 801 to 1600, 3001 to 4000 and 8001 to 9999.

(ii) Aircraft of all periods used for training duties, or other second-line rôles such as transport or target-towing, but not designed primarily for naval purposes.

(iii) Variants of first-line types.

(iv) First-line aircraft supplied in limited numbers but with no actual operational service to their credit.

(*Imp. War Museum Photo.*)

A.D. FLYING-BOAT

Two-seat patrol flying-boat designed by the Air Department of the Admiralty and constructed by Pemberton–Billing, Ltd. (later Supermarine), at Woolston, Southampton. First flown 1917. Prototypes (1412 and 1413) followed by 27 production aircraft (N 1290, N 1520 to N 1529, N 1710 to N 1719 and N 2450 to N 2455). One 150-h.p. or 200-h.p. Hispano–Suiza engine, loaded weight 3,327 lb. and 3,567 lb. respectively. Span, 50 ft. 4 in. Length, 30 ft. 7 in. Max. speed, 100 m.p.h. at 2,000 ft. Climb, 30 mins. to 10,000 ft. Endurance, $4\frac{1}{2}$ hrs.

(*Imp. War Museum Photo.*)

AIRSPEED ENVOY

Twin-engined development of Courier first flown in 1934. Envoy (P 5629) illustrated was one of several used during 1939–45 for communications duties by the Royal Navy. Two 350-h.p. Armstrong Siddeley Cheetah IX engines and loaded weight of 6,600 lb. Max. speed, 203 m.p.h. Climb, 1,250 ft./min. Range, 620 miles. Service ceiling, 22,000 ft.

AIRSPEED OXFORD

Military training development of the Envoy, first flown 1937. Used predominantly by the R.A.F. but also entered service with the F.A.A. during 1939–45. Naval example illustrated is R 6180. Two 370-h.p. Armstrong Siddeley Cheetah X engines and loaded weight of 8,000 lb. Max. speed, 188 m.p.h. Climb, 960 ft./min. Service ceiling, 19,500 ft. Span, 53 ft. 4 in. Length, 34 ft. 6 in.

ALCOCK SCOUT

Devised but not flown by F./Lt. J. W. Alcock (later to achieve fame in the Vimy Atlantic crossing of 1919), this single-seat scout was operated by No. 2 Wing of the R.N.A.S. at Mudros in 1917–18. It was comprised of components from the Sopwith Triplane and Pup and had a 100-h.p. Monosoupape or 110-h.p. Clerget engine. Armament was twin Vickers machine-guns. No other details available.

(Photo from H. H. Russell.)

ARMSTRONG WHITWORTH F.K. 10

Small numbers of this unconventional two-seat quadruplane were delivered to the R.N.A.S. in 1917, including N 511, N 512 and N 514. They were built under licence by the Phoenix Dynamo Manufacturing Company of Bradford. The first naval F.K. 10 was equipped as a two-seat fighter and the second as a bomber. One 130-h.p. Clerget engine. Loaded weight, 2,019 lb. Max. speed, 84 m.p.h. at 6,500 ft. Service ceiling, 10,000 ft. Span, 27 ft. 10 in. Length, 22 ft. 3 in.

ARMSTRONG WHITWORTH METEOR T.T. 20

The Meteor T.T. 20 is a special target-tug conversion from the Meteor N.F. 11 for the use of Fleet Requirements Units. Modification began at the Armstrong Whitworth factory at the end of 1957, and the first Meteor T.T. 20s will enter service with the F.A.A. late in 1958. Two Rolls-Royce Derwent turbojet engines. Span, 43 ft. Length, 48 ft. 6 in.

(*Imp. War Museum Photo.*)

AVRO 500

Two-seater used for training by both the Naval and Military Wings of the
R.F.C. from 1912 onwards. Used by R.N.A.S. flying school at Chingford
after outbreak of war in 1914. Naval Wing allotted Nos. 41, 51 to 53, 94,
and 150. One 50-h.p. Gnome engine and loaded weight of 1,300 lb.
Max. speed, 62 m.p.h. Span, 36 ft. Length, 29 ft.

(*Photo from J. M. Bruce.*)

AVRO 503

Avro's first seaplane, produced in May 1913. Few only supplied to
R.N.A.S., one of which (No. 16, illustrated) was converted as a landplane
and flown at Eastchurch Naval air station, where it was used for training.
One 100-h.p. Gnome engine and a loaded weight of about 2,200 lb.
Span, 50 ft. Length, 33 ft. 6 in.

AVRO 510

Two-seat patrol seaplane used by R.N.A.S. coastal air stations from 1914 onwards. Allotted Nos. 130 to 134. One 150-h.p. Sunbeam engine and loaded weight of 2,800 lb. Max. speed, 70 m.p.h. Climb, 15 mins. to 3,000 ft. Endurance, $4\frac{1}{2}$ hrs. Span, 63 ft. Length, 38 ft.

AVRO 519

Two only (Nos. 8440 and 8441) supplied to the R.N.A.S. in 1916. So far as is known, the type saw no operational service. Originally built as a two-seater, a single-seat version (No. 8441) is illustrated: it had folding wings. One 150-h.p. Sunbeam Nubian engine.

AVRO ANSON

No Ansons were supplied to the Royal Navy directly by the manufacturers but some (like the Mk. I, DJ 331, illustrated) were handed over by the R.A.F. and used post-war for the training of air observers. Two 350-h.p. Armstrong Siddeley Cheetah IX engines and a loaded weight of 8,000 lb. Max. speed, 188 m.p.h. at 7,000 ft. Climb, 720 ft./min. Range, 790 miles. Service ceiling, 19,000 ft. Span, 56 ft. 6 in. Length, 42 ft. 3 in.

B.E. 2A

The B.E. 2A served with both the Military and Naval Wings of the R.F.C. from 1912 onwards. Naval Wing was allotted Nos. 46, 47, 49 and 50, the latter aircraft becoming the favourite mount of the famed Cdr. Samson. It accompanied the Eastchurch Squadron to Belgium in August 1914 and operated there until February 1915, when it was returned to England. Later it served again with Samson in the Dardanelles region. One 70-h.p. Renault engine and a loaded weight of 1,600 lb. Max. speed, 70 m.p.h. at sea level. Climb, 5 mins. to 7,000 ft. Endurance, 3 hrs. Service ceiling, 10,000 ft. Span, 38 ft. 7½ in. Length, 29 ft. 6½ in.

B.E. 2E

Two-seat Corps reconnaissance aircraft, a development of the B.E. 2C and B.E. 2D, used mainly by the R.F.C. but some 95 were transferred to the R.N.A.S. for service at training schools such as Cranwell. Some of the R.N.A.S. trainers had the 75-h.p. Rolls-Royce Hawk engine instead of the standard 90-h.p. R.A.F. 1A. Loaded weight, 2,100 lb. Max. speed, 90 m.p.h. at sea level. Climb, 53 mins. to 10,000 ft. Endurance, 4 hrs. Service ceiling, 9,000 ft. Span, 40 ft. 9 in. Length, 30 ft. 6 in.

B.E. 8

Commonly known as 'The Bloater', the B.E. 8 was used from 1912 as a trainer at the Central Flying School and one example was still serving with No. 3 Flight, R.N.A.S. Westgate, in July 1915. One 80-h.p. Gnome engine. Max. speed, 70 m.p.h. at sea level. Climb, 10½ mins. to 3,000 ft. Span, 39 ft. 6 in. Length, 27 ft. 3 in.

BEECH TRAVELLER

Five-seat communications aircraft used by U.S. Army as UC-43 and U.S. Navy as GB-1. Lend–Lease deliveries totalled 105, majority to the Royal Navy. Serial numbers were FL 653 to FL 670, FZ 428 to FZ 439 and FT 461 to FT 535. One 450-h.p. Pratt and Whitney Wasp Junior engine and loaded weight of 4,250 lb. Max. speed, 198 m.p.h. Climb, 1,400 ft./min. Range, 700 miles. Service ceiling, 25,000 ft. Span, 32 ft. Length, 26 ft.

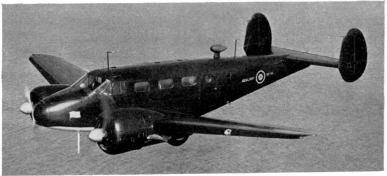

BEECH EXPEDITER

Six–eight-seat communications aircraft used by the U.S. Army as UC-54A and U.S. Navy as the JRB-1. Lend–Lease deliveries totalled 430, about 80 to the Royal Navy. Photograph shows Expediter II KP 110 of the batch KP 100 to KP 124. Other Expediters were FT 975 to FT 996, FR 879 to FR 883, HD 752 to HD 776. Two 450-h.p. Pratt and Whitney Wasp Junior engines and loaded weight of 7,850 lb. Max. speed, 230 m.p.h. at sea level. Climb, 1,850 ft./min. Range, 900 miles. Service ceiling, 27,000 ft. Span, 47 ft. 8 in. Length, 34 ft. 3 in.

(*Air Ministry Photo.*)

BLACKBURN BLACKBURN TRAINER

This side-by-side dual-control trainer variant of the Blackburn fleet spotter (described in the main text) was known to the F.A.A. as the Bull. Contemporary accounts allege that the drag was such with the side-by-side cockpit that the take-off run was increased to 600 yds., requiring the whole length of Leuchars aerodrome to get airborne. Once in the air, it took 10 mins. to reach 1,000 ft.

(*Imp. War Museum Photo.*)

BLACKBURN SHARK SEAPLANE

Twin-float version of the Shark, described and illustrated in the main text. Length increased to 38 ft. 5 in. with floats fitted, otherwise technical details similar to landplane.

342

BLACKBURN FIREBRAND I

The Firebrand was designed to Spec. N. 11/40 and the prototype (DD 804) flew on 27 January 1942. The second prototype (DD 810) did deck-landing trials aboard H.M.S. *Illustrious* in February 1943. A third prototype (DD 815) and nine production Firebrand F. Mk. I fighters were built, all powered by the Napier Sabre engine. A production aircraft (DK 363) is illustrated.

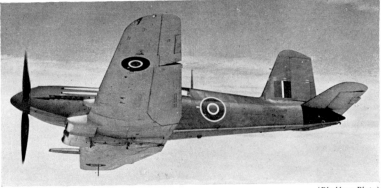

(Blackburn Photo.)

BLACKBURN FIREBRAND II

The Firebrand II had the centre section widened by 18 in. to accommodate a torpedo between the wheel bays. The prototype (DD 810 rebuilt and numbered NV 636) flew on 31 March 1943 and 12 production aircraft followed. A production Firebrand T.F. Mk. II (DK 378) is illustrated. One Napier Sabre III engine.

BLACKBURN FIREBRAND III

This Firebrand variant was the immediate forerunner of the Mk. IV (described in the main text), and most of the 25 production Firebrand IIIs were subsequently converted to Firebrand IVs. The first prototype (DK 372) is illustrated. First flight was on 21 December 1943 and a second prototype (DK 373) was also built. The Firebrand III, the first variant with a radial engine, mounted the Bristol Centaurus IX and had a smaller fin and rudder than the Mk. IV

BLACKBURN N.A. 39

Mention was made of this new naval strike aircraft in the Navy Estimates 1957/58, and it was stated that it would have considerable range and the ability to carry nuclear weapons. It is designed for operation either from aircraft-carriers or shore bases and is powered by two de Havilland Gyron Junior turbojets. The photograph shows the first prototype, XK 486, which made its maiden flight at the R.A.E. Bedford on 30 April 1958.

(*Air Ministry Photo.*)

BLERIOT TYPE XI

Fundamentally similar to the aircraft used by Louis Bleriot for his historic crossing of the English Channel in 1909, this type was used by both the Naval and Military Wings of the R.F.C. and subsequently by the R.N.A.S. from 1912 to early 1915. Some 25 are believed to have entered naval service. One 80-h.p. Gnome engine and a loaded weight of 1,388 lb. Max. speed, 66 m.p.h. at sea level. Climb, 230 ft./min. Span, 34 ft. 3 in. Length, 27 ft. 6 in.

(*Imp. War Museum Photo.*)

BLERIOT PARASOL

This was a development of the earlier Bleriot XI. Served with the R.F.C. and R.N.A.S. in small numbers during 1914–15.

(*Photo from Peter Moss.*)

BOREL SEAPLANE

One of the first seaplanes used for British naval flying, the Borel was of
French manufacture and was first purchased by the British Government
in 1912. At least eight were in service with the Naval Wing before 1914,
including Nos. 37, 48, 83, 84, 85, 86, 87 and 88. No. 48 was embarked in
H.M.S. *Hermes* for the Fleet manœuvres of July 1913 and at about the
same period Lt. A. M. Longmore (later Air Chief Marshal Sir Arthur
Longmore) piloted Admiral Jellicoe in a Borel at Cromarty naval air
station. The Borel was powered by an 80-h.p. Gnome engine.

(*Imp. War Museum Photo.*)

BOULTON PAUL DEFIANT TARGET-TUG

These aircraft, shore-based, were used by Fleet Requirements Units
between 1942 and 1945. The aircraft illustrated operated from H.M.S.
Spurwing, Sierra Leone, and are seen over Freetown Harbour. No. 733
Squadron was one of the F.A.A. Units equipped with the Defiant. One
1,260-h.p. Rolls-Royce Merlin XX engine. Max. speed, 260 m.p.h. at
20,000 ft. Span, 39 ft. 4 in. Length, 35 ft. 4 in.

BOULTON PAUL SEA BALLIOL T. 21

Deck-landing version of the R.A.F.'s Balliol trainer. The first prototype (VR 599) flew in October 1952 and 30 Sea Balliols were delivered to the F.A.A. with the serial numbers WL 715 to WL 734 and WP 324 to WP 333 inclusive. The last Sea Balliol was delivered on 7 December 1954. The Sea Balliol illustrated is WL 723. Units equipped with Sea Balliols were No. 781 Squadron at Lee-on-Solent and No. 1843 Squadron, R.N.V.R., at Abbotsinch. One 1,280-h.p. Rolls-Royce Merlin 35 engine and a loaded weight of 8,410 lb. Max. speed, 288 m.p.h. Climb, 1,790 ft./min. Service ceiling, 32,500 ft. Span, 39 ft. 4 in. Length, 35 ft. 1½ in.

(Imp. War Museum Photo.)

BREGUET DE CHASSE

This early type of Breguet biplane was used by the Naval Wing of the R.F.C. from 1912 onwards. The first to be purchased from France (No. 6) was delivered to Eastchurch in August 1912 and early in 1914 was stationed at Felixstowe. Originally fitted with the 80-h.p. Chenu engine, it later had the 110-h.p. Canton Unne installed. About 15 were used by R.N.A.S.

347

(*Photo from J. M. Bruce.*)

BREGUET TYPE V CONCOURS

Thirty-five of these large pusher biplanes were used by the R.N.A.S.: 25 were purchased from France and 10 built under licence by the Grahame-White concern with the designation G.W. 19. The Grahame-White aircraft had a 250-h.p. Rolls-Royce engine.

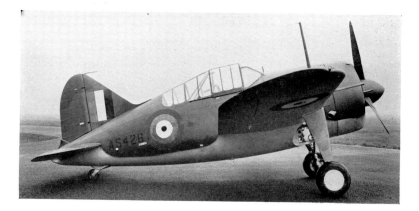

BREWSTER BUFFALO

Although used chiefly by the R.A.F., some examples of this American fighter saw action (together with Fairey Fulmars) with No. 805 Squadron of the F.A.A. during the defence of Crete in March 1941. One 1,200-h.p. Wright Cyclone engine and a loaded weight of 6,840 lb. Max. speed, 313 m.p.h. at 13,500 ft. Climb, 2,070 ft./min. Range, 650 miles. Service ceiling, 30,500 ft. Span, 35 ft. Length, 26 ft.

BRISTOL BOXKITE

First appeared in June 1910 and used by the R.F.C. from its formation in May 1912. Six (Nos. 942 to 947 inclusive) ordered by the Admiralty remained in service at R.N.A.S. training schools at Eastbourne, Eastchurch and Hendon until about the middle of 1915. One 50-h.p. Gnome engine and a loaded weight of 900 lb. Max. speed, 40 m.p.h. Span, 46 ft. 6 in. Length, 38 ft. 6 in. At least one Boxkite was fitted with flotation bags.

BRISTOL T.B. 8

First flown in 1913. The first T.B. 8 for the Admiralty, delivered in January 1914, had twin floats: subsequent aircraft were landplanes. No. 153, illustrated, was delivered to Eastchurch in March 1914. Forty-five T.B. 8 landplanes went to the R.N.A.S. (including 14 diverted from the R.F.C.) and served until 1916. Two served with Eastchurch Squadron at Ostend and Dunkirk and four with No. 1 Squadron at Gosport and Newcastle-on-Tyne. Others were used at Hendon. One 80-h.p. Gnome, Le Rhone or Clerget engine. Loaded weight, 1,665 lb. Max. speed, 75 m.p.h. Climb, 11 mins. to 3,000 ft. Span, 37 ft. 8 in. Length, 29 ft. 3 in.

(Imp. War Museum Photo.)

BRISTOL BEAUFIGHTER II

This version of the Beaufighter, with two 1,280-h.p. Rolls-Royce Merlin XX engines, was used by various Fleet Requirements Units of the F.A.A. between 1941 and 1945. The aircraft illustrated belonged to No. 779 Squadron, based at Gibraltar. Other units with Beaufighter IIs were Nos. 721, 723, 775 and 789 Squadrons. Max. speed, 330 m.p.h. Range, 1,500 miles. Span, 57 ft. 10 in. Length, 41 ft. 8 in.

(Photo R. C. Shelley.)

BURGESS GUNBUS

Thirty-six of these pusher biplanes (Nos. 3657 to 3681 and 8258 to 8268) were purchased from the U.S.A. by the Admiralty in 1915. Some of them were test-flown at Hendon, but they were not a success and never entered squadron service. They went into storage at the White City and were finally condemned in May 1916. The power plant was a single 140-h.p. Sturtevant engine.

(*Imp. War Museum Photo.*)

CAPRONI CA 41 TRIPLANE

Six examples of this three-engined triplane bomber were purchased from Italy for the R.N.A.S., but were not, so far as is known, used operationally. They had the serial numbers N 526 to N 531 inclusive: N 527 is illustrated.

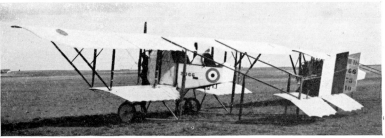

Imp. War Museum Photo.)

CAUDRON G. III

The R.N.A.S. used 124 of these aeroplanes, mostly for training purposes at Vendome in France. The G. III was the single-engined forerunner of the G. IV (see main text) and a few examples (Nos. 45, 55, 56 and 57) were in service as seaplanes with coastal air stations prior to 1914. No. 55, an amphibian, was embarked in H.M.S. *Hermes* at Great Yarmouth in July 1913 and operated from the forward flying-off deck. The pre-war Caudrons had a 80-h.p. or 100-h.p. Gnome engine. Later examples, like No. 3066 illustrated, mounted the 100-h.p. Anzani engine. Loaded weight, 1,619 lb. Max. speed, 70 m.p.h. Climb, 20 mins. to 6,500 ft. Service ceiling, 10,000 ft. Span, 43 ft. 5 in. Length, 22 ft. 6 in.

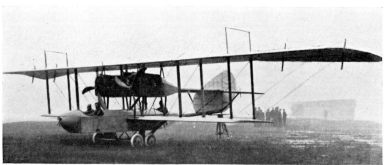

(*Imp. War Museum Photo.*)

CURTISS TWIN CANADA

One hundred of these bombers were ordered for the R.N.A.S. in 1915 (Nos. 9500 to 9599), but the contract was subsequently cancelled. One example (No. 3700) was eventually delivered in November 1916. Designed by Curtiss and built in Canada, the Twin Canada had two 160-h.p. Curtiss XV engines.

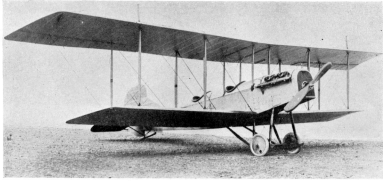

(*Peter M. Bowers Photo.*)

CURTISS R-2 and R-4

One hundred ordered for the R.N.A.S. in 1915 (Nos. 3445 to 3544) for reconnaissance duties. The type proved unsuccessful because its 160-h.p. Curtiss XV engine was unreliable, but a few are believed to have served for armament training duties until as late as 1918. Nos. 3455 and 3459 went to the R.N.A.S. at Luxeuil and Nos. 3462, 3463 and 3464 to Mudros.

(*Imp. War Museum Photo.*)

CURTISS JN-3

The JN-3 was the forerunner of the more famous JN-4 Jenny trainer, and six (Nos. 1362 to 1367) were ordered for the R.N.A.S. in 1914; deliveries followed in March 1915. A further 79 (Nos. 3345 to 3423) was produced to Admiralty orders by the parent firm and 12 (Nos. 8392 to 8403) by Curtiss (Canada) at Toronto. All were fitted with the 90-h.p. Curtiss OX-5 engine.

(*Imp. War Museum Photo.*)

CURTISS JN-4

The celebrated 'Jenny' trainer, used both by the R.F.C. and R.N.A.S. The Admiralty ordered 250, but only 80 entered service with the R.N.A.S. One hundred were transferred to the R.F.C. and 70 were not delivered. The original R.N.A.S. trainers were allotted the serial numbers 8802 to 8901. One 90-h.p. Curtiss OX-5 engine. Loaded weight, 2,130 lb. Max. speed, 70 m.p.h. at 6,500 ft. Climb, 10 mins. to 3,000 ft. Span, 43 ft. 9 in. Length, 27 ft. 4 in. The JN-4 illustrated was photographed in 1917.

CURTISS HELLDIVER

Twenty-six of these dive-bombers, serialled JW 100 to JW 125, were delivered to the F.A.A. under Lease–Lend arrangements. Nine Helldivers were used to form No. 1820 Squadron at Squantum, U.S.A., on 1 April 1944. They were shipped to the United Kingdom in H.M.S. *Arbiter*, but saw no operational service and were disbanded on 15 December 1944. The F.A.A.'s Helldivers were built by the Canadian Car and Foundry factory and were equivalent to the U.S. Navy's SBW-1B. JW 117 is illustrated. One 1,650-h.p. Wright Double Row Cyclone engine. Loaded weight, 12,256 lb. Max. speed, 284 m.p.h. Climb, 2,500 ft./min. Range, 695 miles. Service ceiling, 23,000 ft. Span, 47 ft. Length, 39 ft. 2 in.

CURTISS–WANAMAKER TRIPLANE

Twenty of these enormous triplane flying-boats were ordered from the U.S.A. for the equipment of the R.N.A.S. in 1915. They were intended to carry a crew of six and to be heavily armed for anti-Zeppelin patrols over the North Sea. They were allotted the serial numbers 3073 to 3092, but in the event only one (No. 3073) reached the R.N.A.S., in 1916. Power was provided by four 250-h.p. Curtiss engines.

(*Photo from J. M. Bruce.*)

DEPERDUSSIN MONOPLANE

This type, one of the earliest products of the French aircraft industry, was to be seen at most of the pre-1914 flying meetings. A number entered service with the Naval Wing of the R.F.C. from 1912 onwards and were used both as landplanes and seaplanes. No. 7 was acquired in July 1912 and flown from Lake Windermere: its engine was a 70-h.p. Gnome. Others were Nos. 22, 30, 36 and 44, all with the 80-h.p. Anzani engine. The example illustrated has the early Naval Wing serial number M. 1 on its rudder.

DE HAVILLAND MOTH

Illustrated is J 9107, a Cirrus-Moth converted to Gipsy Moth standard, being employed for deck-landing training. A number of Moths were employed by the F.A.A. for this purpose prior to 1939.

(*Imp. War Museum Photo.*)

DE HAVILLAND QUEEN BEE

The Queen Bee, a special radio-controlled version of the Tiger Moth for anti-aircraft gunnery practice, first flew in January 1935 and subsequently entered service both with the R.A.F. and the F.A.A. The seaplane version was catapulted from warships and employed on Fleet gunnery exercises. The Queen Bee remained in production until 1943 and a total of 420 was built. The aircraft illustrated, K 5114, is a Mk. II.

(*Air Britain Photo.*)

DE HAVILLAND TIGER MOTH

Tiger Moths served with the Royal Navy for a variety of duties and NM 148 is illustrated in post-war livery. As late as 1956, the F.A.A. acquired XL 714, XL 715, XL 716 and XL 717, previously with the civil registrations G-AOGR, G-AOIK, G-AOIL and G-AOXG respectively. One 130-h.p. D.H. Gipsy Major engine. Loaded weight, 1,770 lb. Max. speed, 109 m.p.h. at 1,000 ft. Climb, 673 ft./min. Range, 302 miles. Service ceiling, 13,600 ft. Span, 29 ft. 4 in. Length, 23 ft. 11 in.

DE HAVILLAND FLAMINGO

The D.H. 95 Flamingo, which was just entering service as a civil airliner in 1939, was taken over by the R.A.F. and some also served with the Royal Navy. Naval Flamingoes were operated by No. 782 Squadron at Donibristle on services to the Orkneys, the Shetlands and Northern Ireland during 1939–45. One of No. 782 Squadron's aircraft, *Merlin VI*, is illustrated. Two 930-h.p. Bristol Perseus XVI engines. Loaded weight, 17,600 lb. Max. speed, 239 m.p.h. Range, 1,210 miles. Span, 70 ft. Length, 51 ft. 7 in.

(Crown Copyright Photo.)

DE HAVILLAND DOMINIE

F.A.A. Dominies were, like their counterparts in the R.A.F., used for training and communications duties from 1940 onwards and some remained in service post-war until as late as 1958. A total of 65 entered the Royal Navy between April 1940 and December 1946. The earliest intakes were commandeered civil aircraft (Rapides), but later the Admiralty placed their own contracts for the military version and also acquired some on transfer from the R.A.F. The Dominie illustrated, HG 708, entered service in April 1945 and has the markings of the Royal Naval Air Station, Culham. Two 200-h.p. D.H. Gipsy Six engines. Loaded weight, 5,500 lb. Max. speed, 157 m.p.h. at 1,000 ft. Range, 570 miles. Capacity for ten as a communications aircraft.

DE HAVILLAND MOSQUITO VI

The Mosquito VI fighter-bomber entered service with the F.A.A. when it equipped the re-formed No. 811 Squadron at Ford in September 1945. It remained shore-based, not being equipped for carrier operations, and gave No. 811 Squadron the Mosquito experience it needed before rearming with the Sea Mosquito T.R. 33 in August 1946. A Mosquito VI of No. 811 Squadron (TE 720) is illustrated. Two 1,230-h.p. Rolls-Royce Merlin XXI engines. Loaded weight, 21,600 lb. Max. speed, 380 m.p.h. at 13,000 ft. Range, 1,205 miles. Service ceiling, 36,000 ft. Span, 54 ft. 2 in. Length, 40 ft. 6 in.

(*Photo: Colin Bruce.*)

DE HAVILLAND MOSQUITO T. 3

A number of these two-seat dual-control trainers were handed over to the F.A.A. by the R.A.F. and the example illustrated (VT 626) has the markings of the Royal Naval Air Station, Brawdy. Two Rolls-Royce Merlin 25 engines. Total of 314 built.

('*Flight*' Photo.)

DE HAVILLAND MOSQUITO T.T. 39

High-speed shore-based naval target-tug produced to Spec. Q 19/45 and converted from the Mosquito B. XVI by General Aircraft Ltd. of Feltham, Middlesex. Modifications included lengthened nose, addition of dorsal cupola, and installation of winch gear. Entered service with Fleet Requirements Units from 1948. Example illustrated is PF 606. Two 1,650-h.p. Rolls-Royce Merlin 72/73 or 76/77 engines. Loaded weight, 23,000 lb. Max. speed, 280 m.p.h. (with 32-ft. span target) or 292 m.p.h. (with 16-ft. span target) or 299 m.p.h. (with small sleeve target). Endurance of 1 hr. with 32-ft. target. Span, 54 ft. 2 in. Length, 43 ft. 4 in.

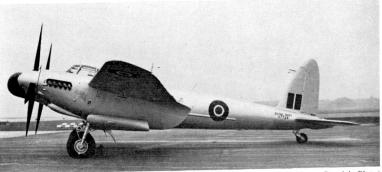

(*Crown Copyright Photo.*)

DE HAVILLAND SEA MOSQUITO T.R. 37

This was a developed version of the T.R. 33 (see main text), six of which were delivered to the F.A.A., beginning with VT 724 illustrated. Fitted with British A.S.V. radar and an enlarged nose to accommodate larger scanner. Two Rolls-Royce Merlin 25 engines. Max. speed, 345 m.p.h. at sea level and 383 m.p.h. at 20,000 ft. Range, 1,100 miles.

DE HAVILLAND SEA HORNET P.R. 22

Photographic reconnaissance version of the Sea Hornet, 23 of which were delivered to the F.A.A. Generally similar to the Sea Hornet F. 20 described in the main text, but fitted with two F. 52 cameras for day reconnaissance or one Fairchild K. 19B camera for night reconnaissance. Loaded weight, 16,804 lb. (night duties) or 18,230 lb. (day duties). Max. speed, 467 m.p.h. at 22,000 ft. Range, 2,050 miles. Service ceiling, 37,500 ft.

DE HAVILLAND SEA VAMPIRE T. 22

F.A.A. version of the R.A.F.'s Vampire T. 11. Production began with XA 100 in 1954 and ended with XG 777 in May 1955. Total of 73 delivered to the Royal Navy. The Sea Vampire T. 22 first entered service with No. 749 Squadron at Lossiemouth and was also used by Nos. 736, 738, 764 and 781 second-line squadrons as well as by air divisions of the R.N.V.R. The aircraft illustrated have the markings of Royal Naval Air Station, Lossiemouth and belong to No. 736 Squadron. One 3,500-lb. thrust D.H. Goblin 35 turbojet engine. Loaded weight, 11,150 lb. Max. speed, 538 m.p.h. at sea level. Climb, 4,500 ft./min. Range, 840 miles. Span, 38 ft. Length, 34 ft. 5 in.

360

DE HAVILLAND SEA DEVON C. 20

The F.A.A. equivalent of the R.A.F.'s Devon, the Sea Devon C. 20 eight-seat light transport was first acquired for the Royal Navy in 1955. Initially, 10 Sea Devons were delivered, the serial numbers being XJ 319 to XJ 324 and XJ 347 to XJ 350. The aircraft illustrated is XJ 347. Three more were added later. The Sea Devons equipped the F.A.A.'s Southern Communications Squadron (part of No. 781 Squadron) based at Lee-on-Solent. Two 340-h.p. D.H. Gipsy Queen 70 engines. Loaded weight, 8,500 lb. Max. speed, 210 m.p.h. at 8,000 ft. Span, 57 ft. Length, 39 ft. 3 in.

DOUGLAS BOSTON

Three examples of this American light bomber were used for second-line duties at Fleet Requirements Units in 1940–41: their serial numbers were BD 121, BD 122 and BL 227. They were similar in all respects to the R.A.F. Bostons. Two 1,200-h.p. Pratt and Whitney Twin Wasp engines. Max. speed, 295 m.p.h. Span, 61 ft. 4 in. Length, 46 ft. 11¾ in.

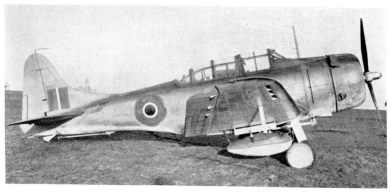

DOUGLAS DAUNTLESS

Nine of these dive-bombers, equivalent to the U.S. Navy's SBD-5, were delivered to the F.A.A. and received the designation Dauntless D.B. Mk. I in January 1945. Their serial numbers were JS 997 to JS 999 and JT 923 to JT 928. The aircraft illustrated is JS 997. They were never used operationally. One 950-h.p. Wright Cyclone engine. Loaded weight, 9,519 lb. Max. speed, 255 m.p.h. at 14,000 ft. Climb, 1,428 ft./min. Range, 773 miles. Service ceiling, 25,200 ft. Span, 41 ft. 6 in. Length, 33 ft. Nearly 6,000 of these famous dive-bombers had been built for the U.S. Navy, U.S. Marine Corps and U.S.A.A.F. when production ceased in July 1944.

FAIREY IIIA

The Fairey IIIA was a landplane conversion of the earlier N. 10 twin-float seaplane and fifty were built for the R.N.A.S. with the serial numbers N 2850 to N 2899. They were fitted either with wheels or skids and were intended to operate as carrier-borne aircraft for reconnaissance duties with the Grand Fleet. Relatively few saw active service and by 1919 all the IIIAs had been declared obsolete. One 260-h.p. Sunbeam Maori II engine. Loaded weight, 3,694 lb. Max. speed, $109\frac{1}{2}$ m.p.h. at sea level. Climb, 10 mins. to 6,500 ft. Endurance, $4\frac{1}{2}$ hrs. Service ceiling, 15,000 ft. Span, 46 ft. 2 in. Length, 31 ft.

FAIREY IIIB

The Fairey IIIB was designed for bombing duties to the requirements of the Admiralty's N. 2B specification. Generally similar to the IIIA, it was built as a seaplane only and had pronounced overhang on the top wing. Twenty-five IIIBs were built, beginning N 2230, and a few entered service at coastal air stations before the Armistice. One 260-h.p. Sunbeam Maori II engine. Loaded weight, 4,892 lb. Max. speed, 95 m.p.h at 2,000 ft. Climb, 17 mins. 50 secs. to 6,500 ft. Endurance, $4\frac{1}{2}$ hrs. Service ceiling, 10,300 ft. Span, 62 ft. 9 in. Length, 37 ft. 1 in.

FAIREY SPEARFISH

Designed as a replacement for the Barracuda, the Spearfish was too late to see war service. It was built to Spec. O. 5/43 and the prototype (RA 356) first flew on 5 July 1945. A production order for 40 Spearfish T.B.D. Mk. I, in hand at Stockport in 1946, was subsequently cancelled, but one production aircraft (RN 241, illustrated) was flown as well as the second and third prototypes, RA 360 and RA 363. One Spearfish was still flying with the Carrier Trials Unit at Ford (earlier at Lee-on-Solent) until the summer of 1952. One 2,320-h.p. Bristol Centaurus 58, 59 or 60 engine. Loaded weight, 22,083 lb. Max. speed, 292 m.p.h. at 14,000 ft. Climb, 12 mins. 40 secs. to 15,000 ft. Range, 1,036 miles. Service ceiling, 25,000 ft. Span, 60 ft. 3 in. Length, 44 ft. 7 in.

FAIREY GANNET A.E.W. 3

This is the airborne early warning version of the Gannet, designed to supersede the Douglas Skyraider in the F.A.A. The photograph shows a model of the aircraft: the prototype had yet to make its first flight at the time of writing.

(Imp Wa Museum Photo

FARMAN F. 40

Fifty of these aeroplanes (usually known as Horace Farmans) entered service with the R.N.A.S. They were frequently fitted with Le Prieur rockets on the interplane struts (as on the example illustrated). Mention is made of the type in the book *The Story of a North Sea Air Station*, where it is related that Horace Farmans were flown directly from the works at Paris to Great Yarmouth, one of the pilots involved being Sqn. Cdr. C. H. Chichester-Smith (now a director of the Fairey Aviation Company). The Farman F. 40 was also used by No. 5 Wing of the R.N.A.S. One 135-h.p. Renault engine.

(*Imp. War Museum Photo.*)

F.B.A. FLYING-BOAT

Some 116 of these small two-seat flying-boats served with the R.N.A.S. for training purposes in the 1914–18 war. Thirty-two were provided by the original French manufacturers and 80 were built in Britain by the Norman Thompson and Gosport Aviation concerns. Another four (N 1075 to N 1078) were handed over by Italy and used by the R.N.A.S. at Orranto. The Norman Thompson aircraft were numbered from N 1040 onwards and the Gosport-built boats from N 2680 onwards.

(*'Flight' Photo.*)

FLANDERS B.2

Designed by the British pioneer aircraft constructor Howard Flanders, this biplane was first flown in 1912 and was purchased by the Admiralty on the outbreak of war in 1914. It subsequently flew at the R.N.A.S. Station, Great Yarmouth, with the serial number 918. It had a 70-h.p. Gnome rotary engine when in R.N.A.S. service. Span, 41 ft. Length, 31 ft. 10 in.

(*Admiralty Photo.*)

GLOSTER METEOR III

The aircraft illustrated (EE 387) was one of two Meteor IIIs fitted with Derwent V engines in short nacelles and arrester hooks. They were used for special investigations into the problems of jet flying aboard carriers and operated for a period in H.M.S. *Implacable.* The other naval Meteor III was EE 337.

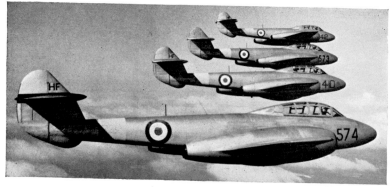

(*Admiralty Photo.*)

GLOSTER METEOR T. 7

The Meteor T. 7 dual-control jet trainer was adopted by the F.A.A. as well as the R.A.F., but used in smaller numbers than its contemporary, the Sea Vampire T. 22. The aircraft illustrated display the markings of the Royal Naval Air Station, Hal Far, Malta, otherwise known as H.M.S. *Falcon.* The F.A.A. Meteor T. 7s were shore-based only and not fitted for deck-flying. They served with No. 759 and other second-line squadrons. Two 3,600-lb. thrust Rolls-Royce Derwent 5 or 8 engines. Max. speed, 585 m.p.h. Climb, 7,600 ft./min. Service ceiling, 35,000 ft. Span, 37 ft. 2 in. Length, 43 ft. 6 in.

(Photo from J. M. Bruce.)

GRAHAME-WHITE TYPE XV

Known as the Type 1600 in R.N.A.S. service (the prototype, No. 1600, is illustrated), this pusher biplane was extensively used as a trainer in the first part of the First World War, operating at the Royal Naval air station at Chingford as well as other schools. The R.N.A.S. received about 80, serial numbers 3151 to 3162, 3607 to 3616, 8305 to 8316 and 8752 to 8801. It was fitted with an 80-h.p. Gnome or Le Rhone rotary engine.

(Photo: A. J. Jackson.)

GRUMMAN WIDGEON

Fifteen of these small amphibians, supplied from the U.S.A. under Lease–Lend, were used by the Royal Navy for communications duties mainly in the West Indies between 1943 and 1945. In British service the type was originally known as the Gosling. The serial numbers allocated were FP 455 to FP 469, and FP 456 is illustrated. Two 200-h.p. Ranger engines. Loaded weight, 4,500 lb. Max. speed, 164 m.p.h. Climb, 1,000 ft./min. Range, 775 miles. Service ceiling, 15,500 ft. Span, 40 ft. Length, 31 ft.

(*Photo from J. M. Bruce.*)

HANDLEY PAGE TYPE 'G'

First flown in 1913, this biplane was unusual in having wings with a curved swept-back leading-edge. It was acquired by the Admiralty soon after the outbreak of war in 1914 and served with the R.N.A.S. for training and Home Defence duties at Hendon and Chingford until August 1915. It had the serial number 892. One 100-h.p. Anzani engine. Max. speed, 73 m.p.h. at sea level. Span, 44 ft. Length, 25 ft. 1 in.

(*Imp. War Museum Photo.*)

HAWKER NIMROD SEAPLANE

The Nimrod fighter, described in the main text, was also available as a twin-float seaplane as illustrated. The Nimrod in the photograph is the second Mk. I, serial number S 1578.

HAWKER HUNTER TRAINER

Ordered both for the F.A.A. and the R.A.F., this side-by-side two-seat dual trainer version of the Hunter made its first flight on 8 July 1955. One Rolls-Royce Avon Series 200 turbojet engine. Span, 33 ft. 7 in. Length, 48 ft. 9 in.

('*The Aeroplane*' *Photo.*)

HILLER HTE-2

Twenty of these small two-seat training helicopters were supplied to the Royal Navy in 1950 under M.D.A.P. arrangements. Serial numbers allocated were XB 474 to XB 481 and XB 513 to XB 524. The Hillers were used mainly by No. 705 Squadron of the F.A.A. One 200-h.p. Franklin engine. Loaded weight, 2,500 lb. Max. speed, 84 m.p.h. Rotor diameter, 35 ft. Length, 40 ft.

(*Imp. War Museum Photo.*)

H.R.E. 2 SEAPLANE

Designed as a two-seat seaplane for the Naval Wing of the R.F.C. by the Royal Aircraft Factory in 1913. Despite its intended purpose (the designation signified 'Hydro Reconnaissance Experimental') it was first flown as a landplane, was unsuccessful as a seaplane, and reverted finally to landplane form. With the serial number 17, the H.R.E. 2 was still in service with the R.N.A.S. when war broke out in 1914. One 70-h.p. or 100-h.p. Renault engine. Span, 45 ft. 3½ in. Length, 32 ft. 3 in.

(*Photo from Sir Murray Sueter.*)

MANN EGERTON TYPE B

This seaplane was a modified version of the Short 184, previously built by Mann, Egerton of Norwich to Admiralty contracts. Mann, Egerton built 10 of their own Type B (Nos. 9085 to 9094 inclusive) and they were delivered to the R.N.A.S. in 1916, seeing service at Calshot. The Type B No. 9085 is illustrated. The engine was a 225-h.p. Sunbeam.

MARTIN MARYLAND

The Maryland light bomber, supplied to Britain from the U.S.A. in 1940, was used mainly by the R.A.F., but a few examples (including AR 720, AR 736 and AR 740) found their way to the F.A.A., where they were used for photographic reconnaissance and target-towing duties from shore bases. It was a Maryland of No. 771 Squadron which on 22 May 1941 took off from Hatston (H.M.S. *Sparrowhawk*) in the Orkneys in appalling weather conditions to report that *Bismark* and *Prinz Eugen* had put to sea from their Norwegian fiord. On this information the Home Fleet put to sea in pursuit. The crew of the Maryland on this historic flight consisted of Lt. N. E. Goddard, R.N.V.R., and Cdr. G. A. Rotheram, O.B.E., R.N. The Maryland had two 1,200-h.p. Pratt and Whitney Twin Wasp engines and a maximum speed of 278 m.p.h. at 11,800 ft. Service ceiling, 26,000 ft. Span, 61 ft. 4 in. Length, 46 ft. 8 in.

MAURICE FARMAN LONGHORN

The Maurice Farman S. 7 Longhorn preceded the S. 11 Shorthorn (described in the main text) and could be readily distinguished by the presence of the forward elevator mounted on outriggers ahead of the nacelle. About 16 Longhorns were in service with the Naval Wing of the R.F.C. before 1914; some had twin floats and operated at coastal seaplane stations. From 1915 the Longhorn served mainly for training purposes. The pre-1914 Longhorns were built by the Aircraft Manufacturing Company Ltd.; the later trainers by the Brush, Robey and Phoenix Dynamo concerns. Brush built Nos. 8921 to 8940 with a 70-h.p. Renault engine and N 5030 to N 5059 with the 80-h.p. Renault. Robey built N 5000 to N 5016 with the 75-h.p. Rolls-Royce Hawk engine and the same power plant was used in the batches N 5330 to N 5349 and N 5750 to N 5759 (one of which is illustrated) built by the Phoenix Dynamo Manufacturing Company of Bradford. The Longhorn had a maximum speed of 59 m.p.h. at sea level. Span, 51 ft. Length, 37 ft. 3 in. Loaded weight, 1,887 lb.

(*Imp. War Museum Photo.*)

MILES MAGISTER

Many F.A.A. pilots took their *ab initio* flying instruction on this type during the Second World War. One 130-h.p. de Havilland Gipsy Major engine. Loaded weight, 1,900 lb. Max. speed, 132 m.p.h. at 1,000 ft. Span, 33 ft. 10 in. Length, 24 ft. 7½ in.

(*'The Aeroplane' Photo.*)

MILES MASTER I

Six of these advanced trainers entered service with the F.A.A., where they were used during the early war period. One 715-h.p. Rolls-Royce Kestrel XXX engine. Max. speed, 226 m.p.h. at 15,000 ft. Climb, 1,500 ft./min. Service ceiling, 28,000 ft. Span, 39 ft. Length, 30 ft. 5 in.

(*Imp. War Museum Photo.*)

MILES MARTINET

This target-tug was widely used by the F.A.A. at its Fleet Requirements Units at home and abroad from 1943. The naval Martinets illustrated were serving at Gibraltar. F.A.A. units with Martinets on strength were Nos. 722, 723, 725, 726, 728, 733, 770, 771, 775, 776, 789, 792 and 794 Squadrons. One 870-h.p. Bristol Mercury XX or XXX engine. Loaded weight, 6,600 lb. Max. speed, 237 m.p.h. at 15,000 ft. Span, 39 ft. Length, 30 ft. 11 in.

(*Photo from J. M. Bruce.*)

MORANE–SAULNIER TYPE BB BIPLANE

A few examples of this French two-seat biplane entered service with the R.N.A.S. in 1915–16 and a naval aircraft (No. 3683) is illustrated. No. 4 Squadron, R.N.A.S., is recorded as having used the Morane Biplane. The engine was an 80-h.p. Le Rhone rotary.

NIEUPORT 11 SCOUT

An account of the Nieuport Scouts appears in the main text, where the Nieuport 17 is shown in the drawing and the Nieuport 24 in the photograph. The earliest of these Nieuports used by the R.N.A.S., the Type 11, is illustrated above. The aeroplane shown belonged to No. 1 Wing of the R.N.A.S.

NIEUPORT SEAPLANE

At least 12 of these early seaplanes were used by the R.N.A.S., the serial numbers being 3187 to 3198. Two of them, Nos. 3194 and 3197, were employed for the training of seaplane pilots on Lake Windermere.

(*Imp. War Museum Photo*)

NORMAN THOMPSON N.T. 2B

Two-seat dual-control training flying-boat used by the R.N.A.S. in 1917–18. It entered service at Calshot, Felixstowe and Lee-on-Solent, and 79 were still on charge at the time of the Armistice. It was built under licence by S. E. Saunders Ltd. of Cowes and the Supermarine Aviation Works as well as by the parent company. The example illustrated (N 2569) is one of the later production versions built by Norman Thompson and is fitted with a 200-h.p. Hispano–Suiza engine. Earlier versions had the 160-h.p. Beardmore or the 200-h.p. Sunbeam Arab engines. Max. speed with the Arab engine was 85 m.p.h. at 2,000 ft. and the service ceiling 11,400 ft. Loaded weight, 3,169 lb. Span, 48 ft. 4¾ in. Length, 27 ft. 4½ in.

NORTH AMERICAN HARVARD

The Harvard III was the version of this widely-used trainer mainly used by the F.A.A., but some Mk. IIBs (such as KF 558 illustrated) also entered naval service. The Harvard III was similar to the Mk. IIA, but had a 24-volt instead of a 12-volt electrical system. Serial numbers of the 564 allotted under Lend–Lease were EX 847 to 999, EZ 209 to EZ 258, EZ 459 to EZ 799 and FT 955 to FT 974. One 550-h.p. Pratt and Whitney Wasp engine. Loaded weight, 5,250 lb. Max. speed, 205 m.p.h. at 5,000 ft. Service ceiling, 21,500 ft. Span, 42 ft. Length, 29 ft.

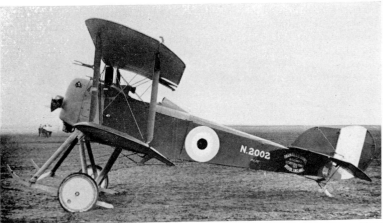

PARNALL HAMBLE BABY CONVERT

Seventy-four of these landplane converts of the Hamble Baby seaplane (see main text) were built by Parnall at their Bristol works, the serial numbers being N 1986 to N 2059. They were employed mainly for training purposes at various R.N.A.S. flying schools, including Cranwell.

PARNALL PETO

This small two-seat reconnaissance seaplane of the late 'twenties was unusual in that it was designed to operate from the Royal Navy's submarine *M. 2*, in which a special hangar was provided. The Peto was built of stainless steel and could be catapulted from the submarine's deck. Two prototypes were built: N 181 with a 135-h.p. Armstrong Siddeley Mongoose engine, and N 182 with a 135-h.p. Bristol Lucifer IV engine. The Peto illustrated, N 255, is one of the six production aircraft with Mongoose engine. The first two pilots to fly the Peto aboard a submarine were Lt. C. W. Byas and Lt. C. Keighley-Peach, and they were fortunate in that they received both flying pay and submarine pay. The Peto was not an unqualified success and lacked an adequate ceiling. It is believed that the loss of the *M. 2* off Weymouth was due to the misinterpretation of an order concerning the opening of the Peto's hangar doors. The Peto had a maximum speed of 113 m.p.h. at sea level and could climb to 5,000 ft. in 11 mins. Its endurance was 2 hrs. and its loaded weight 1,950 lb. Span, 28 ft. 5 in. (8 ft. folded). Length, 22 ft. 6¼ in.

(Photo from J. M. Bruce.)

PEMBERTON–BILLING P.B. 9

This little single-seat scout was designed and built in the surprisingly short time of eight days, and it made its first flight in August 1914. It was not produced in quantity, but the prototype was purchased by the Admiralty and served for a time as a trainer at the R.N.A.S. flying school at Hendon. One 50-h.p. Gnome rotary engine. Max. speed, 78 m.p.h. Climb, 500 ft./min. Endurance, 3 hrs. Span, 26 ft. Length, 20 ft.

(Photo from J. M. Bruce.)

PEMBERTON–BILLING P.B. 25

Twenty P.B. 25 single-seat scouts entered service with the R.N.A.S. at Eastchurch and Hendon during 1916. They had the serial numbers 9001 to 9020, and 9002 is illustrated. The P.B. 25 was developed from the P.B. 23 'Push-Proj' of 1915 and was armed with a single Lewis gun firing forward. One 100-h.p. Gnome or 110-h.p. Clerget engine. Max. speed, 99 m.p.h. Endurance, 3 hrs. Span, 33 ft. Length, 24 ft. 1 in.

PERCIVAL PROCTOR

Over 1,000 Proctors were built for the R.A.F. and Royal Navy during the Second World War for use as trainers and communications aircraft. Of this total, the F.A.A. received 100 Mk. IA and 50 Mk. IIA from the parent company at Luton and 100 Mk. IIA from Hills of Manchester. The Royal Navy's Proctors were mostly employed for the training of wireless telegraphists. The Proctor IIA BV 559 is illustrated. One 210-h.p. D.H. Gipsy Queen engine. Max. speed, 160 m.p.h. Climb, 1,020 ft./min. Range, 660 miles. Service ceiling, 17,000 ft. Span, 39 ft. 6 in. Length, 25 ft. 10 in.

PORTE BABY

This three-engined (two tractor and one pusher) flying-boat was built by May, Harden and May of Southampton to the designs of Sqd. Cdr. Porte, famed for his association with the Felixstowe flying-boats described in the main text. Eleven Porte Babies (Nos. 9800 to 9810) were built and saw service with the R.N.A.S. on North Sea patrols from Felixstowe and Killingholme. The Baby first entered service in November 1916, and some were still in action at the time of the Armistice. Two 250-h.p. Rolls-Royce and one 260-h.p. Green engine in early versions: later Babies had three 325-h.p. Rolls-Royce Eagle VII or 360-h.p. Eagle VIII engines. Crew of five. Loaded weight, 18,600 lb. Max. speed, 92 m.p.h. at sea level. Service ceiling, 8,000 ft. Span, 124 ft. Length, 63 ft.

(*Imp. War Museum Photo.*)

R.E. 5

The R.E. 5, the first aeroplane to be produced in quantity at the Royal
Aircraft Factory, Farnborough, made its appearance in 1914. It was used
mainly by the R.F.C., but one example reached the R.N.A.S. and was
flown to Dunkirk on 27 September 1914 by Sqn. Cdr. A. M. Longmore
(later Air Chief Marshal Sir Arthur Longmore). It was later used for a
bombing raid on Courtrai. One 120-h.p. Austro–Daimler engine. Max.
speed, 78 m.p.h.

(*Air Ministry Photo.*)

R.E. 7

The R.E. 7 was a development of the R.E. 5, and it first appeared in 1915.
It was used mainly by the R.F.C., but six examples were handed over for
the use of the R.N.A.S. It was fitted at various times with a great variety
of engines, ranging from the 120-h.p. Beardmore to the 280-h.p. Rolls-
Royce Eagle. Max. speed with the 120-h.p. Beardmore was 82 m.p.h.
Span, 57 ft. Length, 31 ft. $10\frac{1}{2}$ in.

(*Photo from G. Haddow*)

R.E.P. PARASOL

About 12 of these early monoplanes are believed to have served with the R.N.A.S. before the First World War. No detailed particulars of the type are available.

(*Short Photo.*)

SHORT TANDEM TWIN

This aeroplane, with the Triple Twin the first multi-engined aircraft ever built in Great Britain, was purchased by the Admiralty in 1911 and used at the Naval Flying School at Eastchurch. It had two 50-h.p. Gnome rotary engines, one driving a tractor and one a pusher airscrew, the pilot being seated between.

SHORT TRIPLE TWIN

This early Short, also used by the Naval Flying School at Eastchurch from 1911, was powered by two 50-h.p. Gnome engines. The front engine drove twin airscrews and the rear engine a single pusher.

SHORT S. 27

This box-kite biplane, fitted with an eight-cylinder E.N.V. engine, first appeared in 1910, and provided the basis for a series of Short biplanes, all of which were used in the earliest days of naval flying in Great Britain when Royal Naval officers were trained at the Royal Aero Club aerodrome at Eastchurch, at first on aeroplanes privately owned by Mr. Frank McClean and loaned to the Admiralty.

SHORT MODIFIED S. 27

This aeroplane was a development of the S. 27 from which it differed in having strut-braced extensions to the top wings. Later models were also to be seen with a small nacelle for the pilot and passenger. The most famous of the modified S. 27s was No. 38, which was fitted with three air-bags (attached to the undercarriage struts and beneath the tail) enabling it to alight on water. On 1 December 1911 this feat was achieved by Lt. A. M. Longmore (later Air Chief Marshal Sir Arthur Longmore), who flew No. 38 on to the River Medway. On 10 January 1912 Lt. Samson used the same aeroplane to make the first take-off from the deck of a British warship (H.M.S. *Africa*) whilst it was at anchor off Sheerness. On 9 May 1912 this performance was repeated by Lt. Gregory, R.N. from the deck of H.M.S. *Hibernia* as it was steaming in Weymouth Bay at 15 knots. The modified S. 27 was fitted with a single 50-h.p. Gnome rotary engine.

(*Imp. War Museum Photo.*)

SHORT T. 5

The T. 5 was the first tractor biplane built by Short Brothers, and it first appeared early in 1912. The original model, with uncovered rear fuselage, was owned by Mr. Frank McClean. The type was quickly adopted by the Admiralty, and served with the Naval Wing of the R.F.C. both as a landplane and as a seaplane, the latter with a single centre float and two smaller floats below the wings. 70-h.p. Gnome rotary engine.

(*Photo from J. M. Bruce*)

SHORT S. 38

The S. 38 was developed from the S. 27, and the original aircraft, which flew at the end of 1912, was in fact a rebuilt S. 27. It was of greater overall dimensions and offered much improved accommodation for the crew of two. S. 38s were built by Pemberton–Billing Ltd. and White and Thompson Ltd. as well as by the parent company. The type entered service with the Naval Wing in 1913, and a few remained in action with the R.N.A.S. after the outbreak of war. They were used for coastal patrol from Great Yarmouth (the observer in the rear seat being armed with a rifle), and later saw service as training aircraft at the R.N.A.S. flying schools at Chingford and Eastchurch. One 80-h.p. Gnome engine. Max. speed, 58 m.p.h. Span, 52 ft. Length, 35 ft. 6 in.

(Photo from Sir Murray Sueter)

SHORT S. 41

The prototype S. 41 first appeared early in 1912 as a landplane: later it was fitted with floats and was flown in the Review of the Fleet at Weymouth on 8 May 1912. An improved version (No. 20, illustrated) entered service at Great Yarmouth in July 1913 and took part in the Naval Review of that year. No 20 remained in service on North Sea patrols until June 1915. One 100-h.p. Gnome engine. Max. speed, 60 m.p.h. Span, 50 ft. Length, 39 ft.

(Imp. War Museum Photo.)

SHORT (ADMIRALTY No. 42)

This type first appeared at the 1913 Olympia Exhibition as a seaplane. It bore a considerable resemblance to the S. 41, from which it was developed. Purchased for the Naval Wing, it was allotted the official number 42 and participated in the 1913 Fleet manœuvres. Afterwards it was given a land undercarriage and was one of the aeroplanes taken to Ostend with Cdr. Samson's Eastchurch Squadron of the R.N.A.S. on 27 August 1914. One 80-h.p. Gnome engine. Max. speed, 65 m.p.h. Span, 48 ft. Length, 35 ft.

(*Photo from J. M. Bruce*)

SHORT (ADMIRALTY No. 3)

This two-seat pusher biplane, the only example of its kind, was acquired by the Naval Wing in 1913 and used for training at Eastchurch. In August 1914 it was taken overseas with Cdr. Samson's Eastchurch Squadron, but is not believed to have seen any serious operational duty. The engine of No. 3 was an 80-h.p. Gnome.

(*Photo from J. M. Bruce*)

SHORT ADMIRALTY TYPE 74 SEAPLANE

Also known as the Improved S. 41, this seaplane entered service with the R.N.A.S. in 1914 and took part in the Naval Review of July. Serial numbers allotted were Nos. 74 to 80, 180, 182, 183 and 811 to 818. Three Type 74 seaplanes (Nos. 811, 814 and 815) joined four other seaplanes in the historic raid on Cuxhaven from the carriers *Arthusa*, *Engadine* and *Riviera* on Christmas Day, 1914. The Type 74 had a 100-h.p. Gnome engine.

(*Imp. War Museum Photo.*)

SHORT FOLDER SEAPLANE

This was one of the earliest aeroplanes to incorporate folding wings. The first two Folders (Nos. 81 and 82) had two-bay wings and were closely related to the S. 41. Later Folders (including No. 119 shown on the photograph) had three-bay wings. The original Folder, No. 81 took part in the Naval manœuvres of July 1913 and carried an early type of wireless transmitter. On 28 July 1914 a Short three-bay Folder from Calshot flown by Sqn. Ldr. A. M. Longmore (later Air Chief Marshal Sir Arthur Longmore) made the first successful air-torpedo drop in Great Britain. The weapon used on this historic occasion was a 14-in. torpedo which weighed 810 lb. Two Short Folders (Nos. 119 and 120) were among the seven R.N.A.S. seaplanes which raided Cuxhaven on Christmas Day, 1914. One 160-h.p. Gnome engine. Max. speed, 78 m.p.h. Span (three-bay version), 67 ft. Length, 39 ft.

(Imp. War Museum Photo.)

SHORT S. 81 SEAPLANE

This special seaplane, No. 126, was supplied to the Naval Wing in 1913 for a series of experiments with 1½-pounder Vickers semi-automatic guns, one of which is seen in the photograph. The S. 81 was known as the Gun-carrier; it served at Great Yarmouth, and in 1915 was carrying an even heavier gun, the 6-pounder Davis. The employment of such guns in aircraft did not prove a practical proposition and there were no operational applications of the weapon. The S. 81 was fitted with a 160-h.p. Gnome engine.

(Photo from J. M. Bruce)

SHORT ADMIRALTY TYPE 135 SEAPLANE

The Type 135 was a development of the Short Folder, and it also had folding wings. Only two were built: No. 135, with a 135-h.p. Salmson, and No. 136 (illustrated), with a 200-h.p. Salmson engine.

The Short 135 seaplanes were both used in the celebrated R.N.A.S. raid on Cuxhaven on Christmas Day, 1914, and No. 136 later served in the Dardanelles with the seaplane-carrier *Ark Royal*. Max. speed, 65 m.p.h. Span, 54 ft. 6 in. Length, 39 ft.

SHORT ADMIRALTY TYPE 166 SEAPLANE

Developed from the Short 135, the Type 166 was designed to carry an 810-lb. 14-in. torpedo, though there is no record of this weapon having been used operationally by the aircraft in service. The parent firm built six (Nos. 161 to 166) and the Westland Aircraft Works 20 (Nos. 9751 to 9770); the photograph shows the first of the Westland-built Type 166 seaplanes on the Hamble River in 1916. The Type 166 was used by the R.N.A.S. at Calshot and Thasos and in the seaplane-carrier *Ark Royal*. One 200-h.p. Salmson engine. Loaded weight, 4,580 lb. Max. speed, 65 m.p.h. Span, 57 ft. 3 in. Length, 40 ft. 7 in.

(Short Photo.)

SHORT (140-h.p. SALMSON) SEAPLANE

Ten seaplanes of this type were built, Nos. 9781 to 9790, and No. 9790 is illustrated. They served with the R.N.A.S. seaplane station at Calshot from 1916 onwards. The engine was a 140-h.p. Salmson radial.

SIKORSKY HOVERFLY I

The Hoverfly I was the British version of the Sikorsky VS-316, designated R-4 in the U.S.A.A.F. Fifty-two were supplied to Britain under Lend–Lease arrangements and the photograph shows KK 984 of the batch KK 969 to KL 113, most of which served with the Royal Navy. The Hoverfly I was the first type of helicopter to be used by the R.A.F. and F.A.A. and provided invaluable experience in service flying of this type of aircraft. One 180-h.p. Warner engine. Loaded weight, 2,530 lb. Max. speed, 82 m.p.h. Main rotor diameter, 38 ft. Length, 35 ft. 3 in.

SIKORSKY HOVERFLY II

This helicopter, the R-6A of the U.S.A.A.F., was also supplied to Great Britain under Lend–Lease and served both with the R.A.F. and the Royal Navy. Fifteen went to the F.A.A. for training and communications duties in 1946. One 245-h.p. Franklin engine. Loaded weight, 2,600 lb. Max. speed, 100 m.p.h. Service ceiling, 10,000 ft. Main rotor diameter, 38 ft. Length, 47 ft. 11 in.

SIKORSKY WHIRLWIND H.A.R. 21 and H.A.S. 22

These Whirlwinds, built by the parent company in the U.S.A. and supplied to Britain under M.D.A.P. arrangements, preceded the Westland-built Whirlwinds (see main text) in service with the F.A.A. About 25 were delivered, the H.A.R. 21 being the equivalent of the U.S. Marines' HRS-2 and the H.A.S. 22 of the U.S. Navy's HO4S-3. H.A.R. 21s equipped the Royal Navy's first operational helicopter squadron (No. 848) in November 1952 and on 20 March 1953 went into action for the first time in Malaya. No. 848 Squadron performed general utility and transport duties. A second naval squadron (No. 845) equipped with the H.A.S. 22 became the Royal Navy's first helicopter anti-submarine unit. No. 845's H.A.S. 22s were equipped with dipping sonar gear and began operational duties on 15 March 1954. One of the Whirlwind Mk. 22s (WV 222) was used extensively by H.R.H. the Duke of Edinburgh (including flights from the grounds of Buckingham Palace) for personal transport and designated V.V.I.P. 22. The H.A.R. 21 (illustrated) was powered by a single 600-h.p. Pratt and Whitney Wasp R-1340-40 and the H.A.S. 22 by a 700-h.p. Wright Cyclone R-1300-3. The H.A.R. 21s were numbered WV 189 to WV 198 and the H.A.S. 22s WV 199 to WV 205 and WV 218 to WV 225.

(*Imp. War Museum Photo.*)

SOPWITH BAT BOAT

The Bat Boat, which first appeared in 1913, was the first flying-boat to be built in Great Britain. It entered service with the Naval Wing (No. 118) and took part in the Royal Naval Review of July 1914. On the outbreak of war it was used on sea patrols from Scapa Flow until November 1914. One 100-h.p. Green engine. Loaded weight, 1,700 lb. Max. speed, 65 m.p.h. Span, 41 ft. Length, 32 ft.

(*'Flight' Photo.*)

SOPWITH THREE-SEATER TRACTOR BIPLANE

This biplane, which seated two passengers side by side in the front cockpit and the pilot behind in the rear cockpit, appeared at the same time as the Bat Boat in 1913. It was adopted by both the Naval and Military Wings of the R.F.C., and on the outbreak of war in 1914 the R.N.A.S. had six. Two went overseas with Cdr. C. R. Samson's Eastchurch Squadron and operated from Dunkirk: other did patrols from Great Yarmouth. One 80-h.p. Gnome engine. Loaded weight, 1,550 lb. Span, 40 ft. Length 29 ft.

SOPWITH SOCIABLE

Also known as the Tweenie, this two-seat side-by-side biplane was fitted with dual control and used for training by the Naval Wing of the R.F.C. in 1913–14 at Hendon and Eastchurch. It was fitted first with an 80-h.p. and later a 100-h.p. Gnome engine and had the official serial number 149. The photograph shows the Tweenie at Hendon, where it was flown extensively by Lt. Spenser Grey, R.N.

(Imp. War Museum Photo.)

SOPWITH SEAPLANE (ANZANI)

Three seaplanes of this type were delivered to the Naval Wing of the R.F.C., beginning with No. 58 in July 1913. The others were numbered 59 and 60. They were used at Cromarty and Great Yarmouth seaplane stations and one participated in the Naval Manœuvres of 1913. The engine was a 100-h.p. Anzani radial.

(*Imp. War Museum Photo.*)

SOPWITH GUN BUS

This two-seat pusher biplane first appeared in 1913 as a seaplane trainer for the Greek Naval Air Service. Six further Gun Buses ordered by Greece were taken over by the Admiralty in 1914 and fitted with landplane undercarriages. Serial numbers allotted were No. 801 to 806. These aircraft carried a machine-gun in the front cockpit and were fitted with a 100-h.p. Gnome Monosoupape engine. They were used mainly for training at Hendon. Later examples were also built, as illustrated, with a 150-h.p. Sunbeam engine and a modified nacelle. Max. speed, 80 m.p.h. Span, 50 ft. Length, 32 ft. 6 in.

(*Imp. War Museum Photo.*)

SOPWITH ADMIRALTY TYPE 807 SEAPLANE

The Type 807, based on the earlier 'Round Britain' Contest seaplane, was first supplied to the R.N.A.S. in July 1914 and it incorporated the folding wings first patented in the Short Folders. At least 12 Sopwith 807s entered service and operated both at home (at Calshot and Great Yarmouth) and overseas (in the Dardanelles and East Africa). Some were carried in the seaplane-carrier *Ark Royal*. One 100-h.p. Gnome Monosoupape engine. Max. speed, 80 m.p.h.

(*Imp. War Museum Photo.*)

SOPWITH ADMIRALTY TYPE 860 SEAPLANE

Used by the R.N.A.S. on patrols in home waters during 1915 and 1916, the Type 860 was designed to carry an 810-lb. 14-in. torpedo. Eighteen were delivered to the R.N.A.S. The engine was a 225-h.p. Sunbeam.

(*Imp. War Museum Photo.*)

SOPWITH SPINNING JENNY

Officially known as the Two-seater Scout, this aeroplane was more or less a landplane version of the Type 807 and at least 24 were delivered to the R.N.A.S., where they were employed on anti-Zeppelin patrols from Hendon, Great Yarmouth and Killingholme. Armament was rudimentary and usually consisted of grenades, pistols or rifles. They enjoyed little success and were mostly withdrawn by the end of 1915. Serial numbers allocated were Nos. 1051 to 1074 and No. 1064 is illustrated. One 100-h.p. Gnome Monosoupape engine. Max. speed, 69 m.p.h. Service ceiling, 3,000 ft. Span, 36 ft.

(Photo from H. H. Russell.)

SOPWITH B. 1

The B. 1, which bore a close relationship to the Cuckoo, was a single-seat bomber which first appeared early in 1917. Only one example was built, serialled B 1496, but it saw service with the Fifth Wing of the R.N.A.S. at Dunkirk, where it was used on bombing raids alongside D.H. 4s. One 200-h.p. Hispano–Suiza engine. Loaded weight, 2,945 lb. Max. speed, 118½ m.p.h. at 10,000 ft. Climb, 15½ mins. to 10,000 ft. Service ceiling, 19,000 ft. Span, 38 ft. 6 in. Length, 27 ft. The bomb-load was 560 lb.

Photo from J. M. Bruce.)

SPAD S. 7

This famous French fighting scout, which first flew in May 1916, was ordered for the R.N.A.S. by the Admiralty, and contracts for 120 placed with the firm of Mann, Egerton of Norwich. In December 1916 the Admiralty agreed to hand over 60 of their Spads to the R.F.C. in exchange for Sopwith Triplanes. The following February it was agreed to divert all R.N.A.S. Spads to the R.F.C. The photograph shows a Spad S. 7 with a R.N.A.S. serial number (N 3399). One 140-h.p. Hispano–Suiza engine. Loaded weight, 1,632 lb. Max. speed, 119 m.p.h. at 6,500 ft. Span, 25 ft. 8 in. Length, 20 ft. 3½ in.

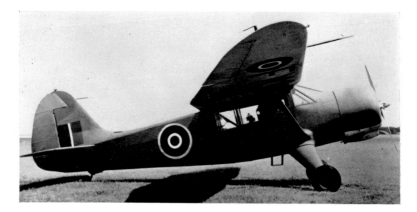

STINSON RELIANT

This American civil aircraft first appeared in 1933. Five hundred military versions were transferred to the Royal Navy under Lend–Lease arrangements, and employed for navigation training and communications. Nos. 722 and 733 Squadrons were equipped. The serial numbers allocated were FB 523 to FB 772 and FK 814 to FL 163. The Reliant illustrated is FK 818. Crew of four. One 290-h.p. Lycoming R-680 engine. Loaded weight, 4,000 lb. Max. speed, 135 m.p.h. Span, 41 ft. 11 in. Length, 29 ft. 6 in.

('*The Aeroplane*' *Photo.*)

SUPERMARINE SEAFANG

The Seafang (to Spec. N. 5/45) was the naval counterpart of the Spiteful and 150 were ordered for the F.A.A. in May 1945. Only eight aircraft were delivered from the original order, serialled VG 471 to VG 478 inclusive. The Seafang 31 had a Rolls-Royce Griffon 61 engine and fixed wings: the Seafang 32 a Griffon 89 engine, contra-rotating airscrews and folding wings. Max. speed, 475 m.p.h. at 21,000 ft. Climb, 4,630 ft./min. Range (maximum), 1,120 miles. Service ceiling, 42,000 ft. Span, 35 ft. (27 ft. folded). Length, 34 ft. 1 in. Production Seafang 32 illustrated.

398

TELLIER FLYING-BOAT

Two of these French-designed flying-boats were acquired for the R.N.A.S. They were allocated the serial numbers N 84 and N 85. The Tellier boat N 85 is illustrated in special camouflage whilst undergoing trials at the Isle of Grain.

THOMAS T. 2

This two-seat biplane was produced by the Thomas Bros. Aeroplane Company of the U.S.A. and designed by an Englishman, B. D. Thomas, who bore no relationship to the American proprietors. Twenty-four were ordered by the Admiralty for the R.N.A.S. in 1915: they were in two batches of 12 numbered 3809 to 3820 and 8269 to 8280. One 90-h.p. Curtiss OX-5 engine. Max. speed, 83 m.p.h. Climb, 10 mins. to 3,800 ft.

VICKERS GUNBUS

The F.B. 5 Gunbus, the first British two-seat fighter aeroplane, made its appearance in 1914. It was used mainly by the R.F.C., but about 15 were delivered to the R.N.A.S. beginning with No. 32. This resulted in the aeroplane being known as the Type 32 in the R.N.A.S. Subsequent serials were 861 to 864 and 3595 to 3606. Nos. 1 and 4 Squadrons of the R.N.A.S. used at least one Gunbus each in France in 1915, but there is no operational record of other naval Gunbuses. One 100-h.p. Gnome Monosoupape engine. Loaded weight, 2,050 lb. Max. speed, 70 m.p.h. at 5,000 ft. Service ceiling, 9,000 ft. Span, 36 ft. 6 in. Length, 27 ft. 2 in.

VOISIN PUSHER BIPLANE

This well-known French aeroplane of the First World War was used by both the R.F.C. and R.N.A.S. between 1915 and 1917. In the R.N.A.S. the Voisin served as a bomber with No. 1 Squadron (later No. 1 Wing) and with No. 2 Wing at Mudros. Four Voisins were also used by No. 8 (Naval) Squadron in East Africa from March 1916. One 140-h.p. Canton–Unne engine. Loaded weight, 2,959 lb. Max. speed, 62 m.p.h. at 6,500 ft. Service ceiling, 10,000 ft. Span, 48 ft. 5 in. Length, 31 ft. 3 in.

VULTEE VENGEANCE

The Vengeance two-seat dive-bomber was supplied to Great Britain from the U.S.A. under Lend–Lease and used mainly by the R.A.F. in Burma. Some of the later deliveries were converted for target-towing duties and saw service in this rôle both with the R.A.F. and the Royal Navy. Fleet Requirements Units with the Vengeance T.T. IV were Nos. 721 and 733 Squadrons. One 1,700-h.p. Wright Double Row Cyclone engine. Loaded weight, 12,480 lb. Max. speed, 279 m.p.h. Service ceiling, 24,300 ft. Span, 48 ft. Length, 40 ft.

WESTLAND WYVERN T.F. 1

The original Wyvern torpedo-strike fighter was designed to Spec. N. 11/44 and the prototype (TS 371) flew on 12 December 1946. Illustrated is the second prototype (TS 375): there were also three other prototypes and 10 pre-production aircraft. All these early Wyverns had the 2,690-h.p. Rolls-Royce Eagle 22 piston engine. Loaded weight, 21,879 lb. Max. speed, 456 m.p.h. at 23,000 ft. Range (maximum), 1,180 miles. Service ceiling, 32,100 ft. Span, 44 ft. Length, 39 ft. 3 in. A production Wyvern T.F. 1 (VR 133) was used for trials aboard H.M.S. *Eagle* in 1952.

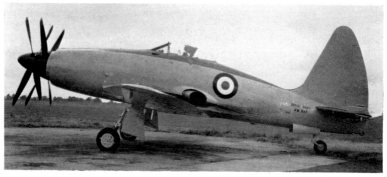

WESTLAND WYVERN T.F. 2

The Wyvern T.F. 2, the first variant with a turbo-prop power plant, was produced to Spec. N. 12/45. First flight was by VP 120 on 18 January 1949, powered by a Rolls-Royce Clyde of 4,030 e.h.p. On 22 March 1949 the first Armstrong Siddeley Python version (VP 109) made its first flight. A production batch of 20 T.F. 2s (beginning VW 867) was ordered: 13 were delivered as such and the remaining seven converted to T.F. 4 standard (see main text). The third production T.F. 2 (VW 869) is illustrated.

WESTLAND WIDGEON

The Widgeon is an improved version of the earlier S-51 Dragonfly and the first civil prototype flew on 23 August 1955. It features a redesigned nose and passenger cabin and incorporates an improved flying control system and an increased operating C.G. range. Most Dragonflies formerly used by the Royal Navy were returned to the makers for re-building to Widgeon standard. One 550-h.p. Alvis Leonides 521 engine. Loaded weight, 5,900 lb. Main rotor diameter, 48 ft. Length, 41 ft. 2$\frac{3}{4}$ in. Max. speed, 95$\frac{1}{2}$ m.p.h.

(Imp. War Museum Photo.)

WHITE AND THOMPSON FLYING-BOAT

Designed originally at the same time as a twin-engined flying-boat for the 'Round Britain' contest for seaplanes, cancelled on the outbreak of war, the type was adopted by the R.N.A.S. for anti-submarine patrol duties, and eight production aircraft (designated White and Thompson No. 3) were delivered with the serial numbers 1195 to 1200, 3807 and 3808. One 120-h.p. Beardmore engine. Loaded weight, 2,400 lb. Max. speed, 85 m.p.h. Crew of two, side-by-side. Span, 45 ft. Length, 27 ft. 6 in.

(Photo from J. M. Bruce.)

WHITE AND THOMPSON 'BOGNOR BLOATER'

This biplane, remarkable for its wooden monocoque fuselage, was first flown in March 1915. Ten were delivered to the R.N.A.S. with the serial numbers 1171 to 1182 and entered service at coastal air stations at Eastbourne, Great Yarmouth and Killingholme. One 70-h.p. Renault engine.

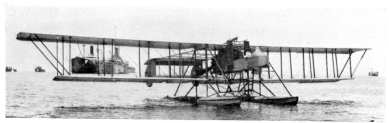

(*Imp. War Museum Photo.*)

WIGHT PUSHER SEAPLANE

This larger pusher seaplane was developed from a type first shown at
Olympia in February 1913. The five-bay wings, unusual in themselves,
were made to fold in production aircraft. Eleven examples were built for
the Admiralty with the serial numbers 155, 171 to 177 and 893 to 895.
No. 176, which appears in the photograph, was one of two Wight Pusher
Seaplanes sent to the Dardanelles aboard the seaplane-carrier *Ark Royal* in
February 1915. They were used for reconnaissance flights over the
Turkish lines. One 200-h.p. Salmson radial engine. Loaded weight
3,500 lb. Max. speed, 72 m.p.h. Span, 63 ft.

(*Photo from J. M. Bruce.*)

WIGHT ADMIRALTY TYPE 840 SEAPLANE

The Wight Type 840 was designed as a torpedo-carrying seaplane to the
same requirements as the more famous Short Type 184. It could carry a
single 810-lb. 14-in. torpedo, but there are no records of this weapon
having been used in action, It served with the R.N.A.S. at Felixstowe,
Scapa Flow and Gibraltar on anti-submarine patrol between 1915 and
1917. No. 835 (illustrated) was one of the batch 831 to 840 built by the
parent company, which also produced Nos. 1300 to 1319 and 1351 to 1354.
About 70 White 840 seaplanes were delivered to the R.N.A.S., including
sub-contracted aircraft by Beardmore of Dalmuir and Portholme of
Huntingdon. A landplane version also existed. One 225-h.p. Sunbeam
engine. Loaded weight, 4,453 lb. Max. speed, 81 m.p.h. Span, 61 ft.
Length, 41 ft.

Non-rigid, semi-rigid and rigid Airships supplied to British naval requirements 1914–19

The construction of rigid airships began in Great Britain in 1908 with the commissioning from Vickers Ltd. at Barrow-in-Furness of R. 1 (unofficially named 'Mayfly') by the Admiralty. Launched on 22 May 1911, 'Mayfly' was wrecked beyond repair whilst being taken from its shed on 24 September 1911, and naval airship development received a setback until in July 1913 the building of two further rigid and six non-rigid airships was authorised.

Meanwhile, the use of airships by the British Army continued, but from November 1913 they were all handed over to the Naval Wing of the R.F.C., which became the R.N.A.S. in July 1914. Airships then remained under naval control until December 1919, when all air units were transferred to the R.A.F., Coastal Area.

By the outbreak of war, the former Army airships *Beta*, *Gamma*, *Delta* and *Eta* had been augmented by *Astra Torres* (a non-rigid bought from France in 1913) and Naval Airship No. 4, a semi-rigid based on the German Parseval design. The latter two airships were the only ones to be used operationally by the R.N.A.S. (though three more Parsevals were later added) until from March 1915 onwards the construction of small non-rigid airships was begun. These non-rigids served throughout the war on anti-submarine patrol, convoy escort and coastal reconnaissance and were developed through the Sea Scout, Coastal, Coastal Star and North Sea series.

Rigid airships made their appearance again from 27 November 1916, when R. 9 (built by Vickers) made its maiden flight. Rigid airship sheds for the R.N.A.S. were completed at Howden in December 1916, at Pulham in February 1917, at Longside in March 1917, at East Fortune in April 1917 and at Cranwell in June 1917. Nine rigid naval airships were completed. The last of these, the celebrated R. 34, was launched in March 1919.

ASTRA-TORRES (NAVAL AIRSHIP No. 3)

This non-rigid airship was used by the R.N.A.S. for patrols (each of about 12 hrs. duration) over the English Channel from 10 August 1914. It was the only British airship of its period to be armed, carrying a single Hotchkiss machine-gun.

PARSEVAL (NAVAL AIRSHIP No. 4)

A rigid design of German origin, the Parseval No. 4 was used on Channel patrols in company with Naval Airship No. 3 from 10 August 1914. It was based at Kingsnorth, the first R.N.A.S. airship station. It was later joined by other Parsevals (built by Vickers under licence), which were numbered 5, 6 and 7: all were used for training purposes.

S.S. (SEA SCOUT) NON-RIGID AIRSHIPS

Construction of these small airships, used chiefly for searching narrow channels such as Dover Straits and the Irish Narrows, began in March 1915, and 36 were supplied to the R.N.A.S. The first Sea Scout base was established at Capel (Folkestone) on 8 May 1915 and the second at Polegate (Eastbourne) on 6 July 1915. By the end of 1915 there were five S.S. airships at Capel and three at Polegate. The airships S.S. 1, 2, 3, 7, 8, 9, 10, 10A, 12 to 20, 23, 24 and 25 were fitted with a B.E. 2C type car. S.S. 28 to 39A had a Maurice Farman type car and S.S. 27, 40, 41 and 42 an Armstrong Whitworth type car. The Sea Scout illustrated has a B.E. 2C car.

S.S.Z. (SEA SCOUT ZERO) NON-RIGID AIRSHIPS

This improved version of the S.S. airships, known as the Zero, was first built at Capel in June 1916 and the first S.S,Z. was flown to St. Pol (Dunkirk) on 21 September 1916. It was originally intended for towing by ships of the Belgian Coast Patrol and by Monitors so as to assist gunnery spotting. Sixteen S.S. Zeros had been delivered by July 1917, and altogether the R.N.A.S. received 66, numbered S.S.Z. 1 to 20 and S.S.Z. 25 to 70 inclusive. The S.S. Zeros were preceded by six S.S.P. airships, numbered S.S.P. 1 to S.S.P. 6. Two S.S. Twin airships (with two 75-h.p. Rolls-Royce Hawk engines) were also used experimentally and numbered S.S.T. 1 and S.S.T. 2.

C. (COASTAL) NON-RIGID AIRSHIPS

Twenty-seven of these airships, numbered C. 1 to C. 26, entered service with the R.N.A.S. The last of the line, C. 26, is illustrated. The Coastal airships had a trefoil section envelope of 170,000 cu. ft. capacity and had an endurance of 11 hrs. at 45 m.p.h. The Coastal type was first ordered in June 1915 and the first airship assembled at Kingsnorth in September 1915. The first R.N.A.S. airship station with Coastals was Pembroke, commissioned in January 1916, from whence the first Coastal flight took place on 9 June 1916. Other Coastal airship stations were commissioned at Pulham (February 1916), Howden (March 1916), Longside (March 1916), Mullion (June 1916) and East Fortune (August 1916). On 6 September 1916 experiments were conducted in the refuelling of an airship from a ship, using C. 1 and the light cruiser *Canterbury*. Coastal airships were used for patrols off Land's End, the mouths of the Humber and the Forth, north of Aberdeen and off the Norfolk coast. It is on record that one of these airships served continually for over two years, in that time flying a distance of over 66,000 miles. Power was provided by two engines of 220 and 100 h.p. respectively and a crew of five was carried. Maximum speed was about 50 m.p.h. and the cruising endurance 24 hrs.

C STAR (COASTAL STAR) NON-RIGID AIRSHIPS

This designation was used to signify the Coastal airships which had been improved and modified. Airships so modified were identified by the star on the envelope, as in C Star 1 illustrated.

N.S. (NORTH SEA) NON-RIGID AIRSHIPS

Twelve of these airships, the last non-rigids to be made in Great Britain, were built for the R.N.A.S. They were numbered N.S. 1 to N.S. 12 and had a trefoil section envelope of 360,000 cu. ft. capacity. First ordered in January 1916, the North Sea type was ready in February 1917 and N.S. 1 was delivered to Pulham, where in June 1917 it flew 1,500 miles during a 49½-hr. flight. The North Sea airships were from July 1917 concentrated at East Fortune, but there were numerous difficulties with the power transmission gear, and they could not be used with the Fleet in the manner originally intended. In 1919 N.S. 11 set up an endurance record for non-rigid airships by remaining airborne for 101 hrs. during a non-stop cruise of 4,000 miles. The normal duration of the North Sea airship was about 24 hrs. and the maximum cruising speed about 58 m.p.h. Power was provided by two 240-h.p. Fiat or two 250-h.p. Rolls-Royce engines.

RIGID AIRSHIP R. 9

Built by Vickers Ltd. at Barrow-in-Furness, the R. 9 made its first flight on 27 November 1916 and was delivered to Howden on 4 April 1917. It was used chiefly for training purposes by the R.N.A.S. Two 180-h.p. Wolseley Maybach and one 250-h.p. Rolls-Royce engine.

RIGID AIRSHIP R. 23

Built by Vickers Ltd. at Barrow-in-Furness, the R. 23 was delivered to Pulham on 15 September 1917. It had four 250-h.p. Rolls-Royce engines (one in each of the forward and aft cars and two in the centre car) and attained a speed of 55 m.p.h. In 1918 the R. 23 was used for a series of experiments in carrying its own defensive fighter aeroplane for launching in flight. Two Sopwith 2F. 1 Camels (N 6622 and N 6814) of No. 212 Squadron were used and one of them can be seen in the photograph.

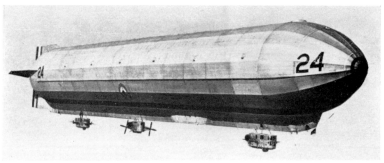

(*Imp. War Museum Photo.*)

RIGID AIRSHIP R. 24

This airship, generally similar to the R. 23, was built by Beardmores at Inchinnan, Renfrew, and was delivered to East Fortune on 28 October 1917. It was used for training purposes by the R.N.A.S.

(*Imp. War Museum Photo.*)

RIGID AIRSHIP R. 25

Another airship in the '23' class, the R. 25 was built by Armstrong Whitworth at Barlow, Selby, Yorkshire, and was delivered to the R.N.A.S. station at Howden on 15 October 1917.

(*Imp. War Museum Photo.*)

RIGID AIRSHIP R. 26

R. 26 was the first of five more '23' class airships ordered for the R.N.A.S. in January 1916 and was built by Vickers at Barrow-in-Furness.

411

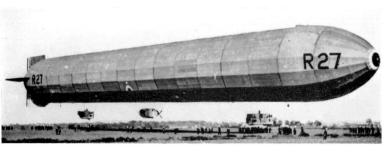

RIGID AIRSHIP R. 27

One of the two airships of the '23X' class to be completed, the R. 27 was built by Beardmores at Inchinnan, Renfrew. The other two '23X' air-ships (R. 28 by Beardmore and R. 30 by Armstrong Whitworth) were cancelled after the capture of the German Zeppelin *L. 33* in September 1916.

RIGID AIRSHIP R. 29

Sister-ship of the R. 27 in the '23X' class, the R. 29 was built by Armstrong Whitworth.

RIGID AIRSHIP R. 31

The R. 31 and R. 32 were built by Short Bros. at Cardington on the principles of the wooden Schutte–Lanz airship of German origin. They had five 250-h.p. Rolls-Royce engines and 1,500,000 cu. ft. capacity.

RIGID AIRSHIP R. 33

R. 33's design was based on that of the German airship *L. 33* which came down at Little Wigborough in Essex on 24 September 1916 after being damaged by gunfire. It was built by Armstrong Whitworth and was powered by five 250-h.p. Sunbeam engines. The capacity of the envelope was 2,000,000 cu. ft. It served with the R.N.A.S. at East Fortune and Howden and went on to serve with the R.A.F. until 1927. In 1925 and 1926 it was used for air launching experiments with the D.H. 53 Humming Bird lightplane and the Gloster Grebe fighter.

(*Imp. War Museum Photo.*)

RIGID AIRSHIP R. 34

R. 34 was the last rigid airship to be used before airships were abandoned by the Admiralty at the end of 1919. It was a sister-ship of the R. 33 and was built by Beardmores. In July 1919, R. 34 made the first airship crossing of the Atlantic, flying from East Fortune, Scotland, to Long Island, U.S.A., a distance of 3,130 miles in 108 hrs. 12 mins. The return flight, helped by favourable winds, occupied only 75 hrs. 3 mins. This historic flight was the first return crossing of the Atlantic by aircraft of any kind. The R. 34 was commanded by Major G. H. Scott, A.F.C.

APPENDIX C

A list of aircraft-carriers and seaplane-carriers of the Royal Navy 1913–58

This list does not include warships which have carried small numbers of aircraft for launching from a turret-platform, or from a catapult. In November 1918 over 100 aircraft were being carried in ships of the Grand Fleet other than aircraft-carriers. Twenty-two light cruisers had been fitted with aircraft launching platforms and all battleships and battle cruisers carried a two-seater aircraft on the forward turret platform and a single-seat fighter on the aft turret platform.

At the outbreak of war in September 1939, the F.A.A. had 115 catapult aircraft in warships as well as 225 aircraft in aircraft-carriers.

NAME	DESCRIPTION	COMMISSIONED	REMARKS
Activity (ex *Empire Activity*)	Escort Carrier 14,250 tons 15 aircraft	May 1942	British-built
Albatross	Seaplane Carrier 9 aircraft		Originally built for Royal Australian Navy. Operated F. A. A. Walrus squadron, W. Africa and Madagascar, 1939–1943
Albion	Carrier 26,000 tons 45 aircraft	May 1954	First with mirror landing aid, autumn 1954
Ameer (ex *Baffin's*)	Escort Carrier 11,420 tons 20 aircraft	Oct. 1942	*Smiter* class (lease-lend)
Anne	Seaplane Carrier 2 aircraft	1915	Former French steamer
Arbiter (ex *St. Simon*)	Escort Carrier 11,420 tons 20 aircraft	Sept. 1943	*Smiter* class (lease-lend)
Archer (ex *Mormacland*)	Escort Carrier 12,000 tons 20 aircraft	—	*Archer* class (U.S.-built)
Argus	Fleet Carrier 15,750 tons	Sept. 1918	First with flush-deck. Formerly *Conte Rosso*. Embarked first air torpedo squadron (Cuckoos) 19 Oct. 1918. Queen Bee tender, 1937
Ark Royal	Seaplane Carrier 6,900 tons 10 aircraft	1915	First to be fitted exclusively for seaplane carrier work. Later named *Pegasus*
Ark Royal	Fleet Carrier 22,000 tons 70 aircraft	1938	Sunk 14 Nov. 1941
Ark Royal	Fleet Carrier 46,000 tons 80–100 aircraft	Feb. 1955	First with deck-edge lift and operational steam catapult
Atheling (ex *Glacier*	Escort Carrier 11,420 tons 20 aircraft	Sept. 1942	*Smiter* class (lease-lend)

NAME	DESCRIPTION	COMMISSIONED	REMARKS
Attacker	Escort Carrier 11,000 tons 15–20 aircraft	Sept. 1941	*Attacker* class (U.S.-built)
Audacity	Merchant Aircraft Carrier	1941	Originally *Empire Audacity*, converted from German merchant ship *Hanover* to be first MACship in July 1941
Avenger	Escort Carrier 12,000 tons 20 aircraft	—	*Archer* class (U.S.-built)
Battler (*Mormacmail*)	Escort Carrier 11,000 tons 15–20 aircraft	April 1942	*Attacker* class (U.S.-built)
Begum (ex *Balinas*	Escort Carrier 11,420 tons 20 aircraft	Nov. 1942	*Smiter* class (lease-lend)
Ben-My-Chree	Seaplane Carrier 4 aircraft	1915	Formerly Isle of Man packet. Launched first air torpedo attack in Aegean 12 Aug. 1915
Biter	Escort Carrier 12,000 tons 20 aircraft	—	*Archer* class (U.S.-built). Became French *Dixmude*
Bulwark	Carrier 26,000 tons 45 aircraft	Nov. 1954	Angled deck
Campania	Seaplane Carrier 20,000 tons 10 aircraft	April 1915	Ex-Cunard liner; 200 ft. flying-off deck for 10 trolleyed seaplanes
Campania	Escort Carrier 12,450 tons	June 1943	British-built. Loaned as travelling exhibition ship to the Festival of Britain in 1951 before return to merchant service
Centaur	Carrier 26,000 tons 45 aircraft	Sept. 1953	First with operational angled deck
Chaser (ex *Mormacgull*)	Escort Carrier 11,000 tons 15–20 aircraft	June 1942	*Attacker* class (U.S.-built)

417

NAME	DESCRIPTION	COMMISSIONED	REMARKS
Colossus	Light Fleet Carrier 14,000 tons 39–44 aircraft	Sept. 1943	To French Navy as *Arromanches* in 1951
Courageous	Fleet Carrier 26,500 tons 48 aircraft	1928	Sunk 18 Sept. 1939
Dasher	Escort Carrier 12,000 tons 20 aircraft	—	*Archer* class (U.S.-built)
Eagle	Fleet Carrier 26,400 tons 21 aircraft	1922	First with off-set super-structure. Formerly *Almirante Latorre*. Sunk Aug. 1942
Eagle	Fleet Carrier 46,000 tons 80–110 aircraft	Oct. 1951	Modernised March 1955
Emperor (ex *Pybus*)	Escort Carrier 11,420 tons 20 aircraft	Oct. 1942	*Smiter* class (lease-lend)
Empress	Seaplane Carrier 4 aircraft	Aug. 1914	Converted Channel packet
Empress (ex *Carnegie*)	Escort Carrier 11,420 tons 20 aircraft	Dec. 1942	*Smiter* class (lease-lend)
Engadine	Seaplane Carrier 4 aircraft	Aug. 1914	Converted Channel packet. Launched seaplane at Battle of Jutland
Fencer	Escort Carrier 11,000 tons 15–20 aircraft	April 1942	*Attacker* class (U.S.-built)
Formidable	Fleet Carrier 29,240 tons Over 60 aircraft	Nov. 1940	Scrapped in 1953
Furious	Fleet Carrier 22,450 tons 33 aircraft (originally 8 aircraft)	1916	First landing on ship under way—Dunning's Pup, Aug. 1917. Modernised in 1918 and again in 1925. Scrapped in 1945
Glorious	Fleet Carrier 26,500 tons 48 aircraft	1928	Sunk 8 June 1940

NAME	DESCRIPTION	COMMISSIONED	REMARKS
Glory	Light Fleet Carrier 18,000 tons 39–44 aircraft	April 1945	Served in Korean War, 1951–53 *Colossus* class
Hermes	Seaplane Carrier 3 aircraft	May 1913	Parent ship of Naval Wing, R.F.C. Sunk Nov. 1914
Hermes	Carrier 12,900 tons 15 aircraft	1923	World's first aircraft-carrier built as such. Sunk April 1942
Hermes (ex *Elephant*)	Fleet Carrier	Now building	To have fully angled deck of 8 degrees
Hunter (ex *Trailer*)	Escort Carrier 11,000 tons 15–20 aircraft	May 1942	*Attacker* class (U.S.-built)
Illustrious	Fleet Carrier 31,790 tons Over 60 aircraft	May 1940	Modernised in 1948 and 1951
Implacable	Fleet Carrier 32,110 tons 72 aircraft	May 1944	Modernised in 1948 and 1951
Indefatigable	Fleet Carrier 32,110 tons 72 aircraft	Aug. 1944	Modernised in 1950
Indomitable	Fleet Carrier 29,730 tons 65 aircraft	Oct. 1941	Modernised 1948–50
Khedive (ex *Gordova*)	Escort Carrier 11,420 tons 20 aircraft	Jan. 1943	*Smiter* class (lease-lend)
Magnificent	Light Fleet Carrier 14,000 tons 34 aircraft	—	To Royal Canadian Navy
Manxman	Seaplane Carrier	1916	Formerly Isle of Man packet
Nabob (ex *Edisto*	Escort Carrier 11,420 tons 20 aircraft	—	*Smiter* class (lease-lend)
Nairana	Light Carrier 3,000 tons 8 aircraft	Sept. 1917	Formerly Australian mail steamer *Nairana*
Nairana	Escort Carrier 13,455 tons	—	Same class as *Campania* and *Vindex*. To Royal Netherlands Navy, February 1946

NAME	DESCRIPTION	COMMISSIONED	REMARKS
Ocean	Light Fleet Carrier 17,720 tons 39–44 aircraft	June 1945	First jet carrier landing —Vampire, 3 Dec. 1945. Served at Suez 1956. *Colossus* class
Patroller (ex *Keeweenaw*)	Escort Carrier 11,420 tons 20 aircraft	May 1943	*Smiter* class (lease-lend)
Pegasus	Light Carrier 3,000 tons 9 aircraft	Aug. 1917	Formerly Great Eastern steamer *Stockholm*
Pegasus	Depot Ship	—	Re-named from *Ark Royal* in 1935
Perseus (ex *Edgar*)	Ferry Carrier 16,500 tons	Completed March 1944	Intended as *Colossus* class but completed as aircraft mainten- ance ships
Pioneer (ex *Mars*)	Ferry Carrier 16,500 tons	Completed May 1944	
Premier (ex *Estero*)	Escort Carrier 11,420 tons 20 aircraft	March 1943	*Smiter* class (lease-lend)
Puncher (ex *Willapa*)	Escort Carrier 11,420 tons 20 aircraft	Nov. 1943	*Smiter* class (lease-lend)
Pursuer (ex *Mormaclaud*)	Escort Carrier 11,000 15–20 aircraft	July 1942	*Attacker* class (U.S.- built)
Queen (ex *St. Andrew's*)	Escort Carrier 11,420 tons 20 aircraft	Aug. 1943	*Smiter* class (lease-lend)
Rajah (ex *Prince*)	Escort Carrier 11,420 tons 20 aircraft	May 1943	*Smiter* class (lease-lend)
Ranee (ex *Niantic*)	Escort Carrier 11,420 tons 20 aircraft	June 1943	*Smiter* class (lease-lend)
Ravager (ex *Charger*)	Escort Carrier 11,000 tons 15–20 aircraft	July 1942	*Attacker* class (U.S.- built)
Raven II	Seaplane Carrier 2 aircraft	1916	Former French steamer
Reaper (ex *Winjah*)	Escort Carrier 11,420 tons 20 aircraft	Nov. 1943	*Smiter* class (lease-lend)

NAME	DESCRIPTION	COMMISSIONED	REMARKS
Riviera	Seaplane Carrier 4 aircraft	Aug. 1914	Converted Channel packet
Ruler (ex *St. Joseph*)	Escort Carrier 11,420 tons 20 aircraft	Aug. 1943	*Smiter* class (lease-lend)
Searcher	Escort Carrier 11,000 tons 15–20 aircraft	1943	*Attacker* class (U.S.-built)
Shah (ex *Jamaica*)	Escort Carrier 11,420 tons 20 aircraft	April 1943	*Smiter* class (lease-lend)
Slinger (ex *Chatham*)	Escort Carrier 11,420 tons 20 aircraft	Sept. 1942	*Smiter* class (lease-lend)
Smiter (ex *Vermilion*)	Escort Carrier 11,420 tons 20 aircraft	Sept. 1943	*Smiter* class (lease-lend)
Speaker (ex *Delgada*)	Escort Carrier 11,420 tons 20 aircraft	Feb. 1953	*Smiter* class (lease-lend)
Stalker	Escort Carrier 11,000 tons 15–20 aircraft	March 1942	*Attacker* class (U.S.-built)
Striker	Escort Carrier 11,000 tons 15–20 aircraft	May 1942	*Attacker* class (U.S.-built)
Thane (ex *Sunset*)	Escort Carrier 11,420 tons 20 aircraft	—	*Smiter* class (lease-lend)
Theseus	Light Fleet Carrier 18,000 tons 35 aircraft	Jan. 1946	Served in Korean War 1950–51 and at Suez 1956. *Colossus* class
Tracker	Escort Carrier 11,000 tons 15–20 aircraft	March 1942	*Attacker* class (U.S.-built)
Triumph	Light Fleet Carrier 18,000 tons 35 aircraft	April 1946	Served in Korean War 1950. Became officer cadet training ship 1953 *Colossus* class
Trouncer (ex *Perdito*)	Escort Carrier 11,420 tons 20 aircraft	June 1943	*Smiter* class (lease-lend)

NAME	DESCRIPTION	COMMISSIONED	REMARKS
Trumpeter (ex *Lucifer*)	Escort Carrier 11,420 tons 20 aircraft	Dec. 1942	*Smiter* class (lease-lend)
Unicorn	Maintenance Carrier 14,750 tons	Mar. 1943	Re-designated ferry carrier June 1953
Venerable	Light Fleet Carrier 18,000 tons 35 aircraft	Completed Dec. 1943	To Royal Netherlands Navy as *Karel Doorman* in 1948. *Colossus* class
Vengeance	Light Fleet Carrier 18,000 tons 35 aircraft	Completed Feb. 1944	Sold to Brazilian Navy. *Colossus* class
Victorious	Fleet Carrier 30,000 tons Over 60 aircraft	May 1941	Re-built with angled deck 1957
Vindex	Seaplane Carrier 7 aircraft	Sept. 1915	Formerly Isle of Man packet. First landplane take-off by Bristol Scout Nov. 1915
Vindex	Escort Carrier 13,455 tons	Completed May 1943	British-built
Vindictive	Carrier (later Seaplane Carrier) 9,996 tons	Oct. 1918	Formerly light cruiser *Cavendish*. First operational catapult take-offs in 1925 after reconversion to cruiser
Warrior	Light Fleet Carrier 18,000 tons 35 aircraft	Jan. 1946	Experiments with flexible deck 1948–49

INDEX

Aircraft are listed below under their type name and not the manufacturer's name, except where no type name has been allotted. An index under manufacturers will be found on page 5. Airships (both British and German) are listed under their numbers. Under the section *Squadron Aircraft Illustrated* will be found a list of R.N.A.S. and Fleet Air Arm squadrons whose aircraft appear in pictures.